SOCIALISM IN A CRIPPLED WORLD

Christopher Hampton was born in London in 1929, is married and has one daughter. After training at the Guildhall School of Music and Drama, he worked for a time as pianist and conductor before giving up music for writing. His translation of a René Guillot book (Methuen, 1961) was followed by a children's story, *Island of the Southern Sun* (Chatto & Windus, 1962). From 1962 to 1966 he lived in Italy, teaching English in Rome and other cities. He now teaches at the Polytechnic of Central London, which he joined in 1968, and has been lecturing at the City Literary Institute since 1973. His poems and articles have appeared regularly in print since 1960, and he has organized many readings and programmes of poetry and music. Publications include *The Etruscans and the Survival of Etruria* (London, 1969; New York, 1970), two volumes of poems – *An Exile's Italy* (1972) and *A Cornered Freedom* (1980) – and (as editor) *Poems for Shakespeare* (1972 and 1978). *The Etruscans* was the first of a series of books dealing with the cultural, political and historical conditions underlying European civilization – the others being *Rome: The Authoritarian City* (1972), *Awareness and Apathy* (1974) (both as yet unpublished), and the present volume, *Socialism in a Crippled World*. He is now at work on a novel set in the England of 1918–26.

Socialism
in a Crippled World

CHRISTOPHER HAMPTON

Penguin Books

Penguin Books Ltd, Harmondsworth, Middlesex, England
Penguin Books, 625 Madison Avenue, New York, New York 10022, U.S.A.
Penguin Books Australia Ltd, Ringwood, Victoria, Australia
Penguin Books Canada Ltd, 2801 John Street, Markham, Ontario, Canada L3R 1B4
Penguin Books (N.Z.) Ltd, 182–190 Wairau Road, Auckland 10, New Zealand

First published 1981

Filmset, printed and bound in Great Britain by
Hazell Watson & Viney Ltd, Aylesbury, Bucks
Set in VIP Plantin

CONTENTS

Acknowledgements 7

Part One
1 Theory and Practice: A Divided World 11
2 Marx: The Critical Challenge and Its Consequences 38
3 Mass Manipulation and the Survival of Dissent 67

Part Two
4 Dislocation and Despair: Eliot's View of History 99
5 Dickens: The Intuitive Radical 117
6 Literature: The Dialectics of Actuality 133
7 Shakespeare: The Revolution of the Times 143

Part Three
8 Actuality and the Abstract: The Alienating Process 175
9 The Necessity of Dissent 188
10 Blake's Dialectic: The Prolongation of Mental War 205
11 Progress and Reaction in the Age of Revolution:
Wordsworth, Shelley and Burke 221

Part Four
12 The Quest for a Qualitative Social Order 247
13 The Derangement of European Civilization 257
14 Democratic Freedom: Rhetoric and Actuality 272
15 Means and Ends: The Closing of the Circle 293
16 Socialism: The Struggle for the Future 304
Bibliography 322
Notes 326
Index 347

ACKNOWLEDGEMENTS

Permission to use extracts from the following copyright works is gratefully acknowledged:

WOLFGANG ABENDROTH, extract from 'The Absolutism of the Hohenzollern State and the Rise of the Social Democratic Party', in *Upheaval and Continuity*, ed. E. J. Feuchtwanger, published by Oswald Wolff (Publishers) Ltd, 1977.

W. H. AUDEN, lines from *New Year Letter*, from his *Collected Poems*, and lines from *September 1, 1939*, from *The English Auden*, reprinted by permission of Faber and Faber Ltd.

BERTOLT BRECHT, lines from 'Not What Was Meant' in *Brecht: Poems – Part Three 1939–1956*, reprinted by permission of Eyre Methuen Ltd.

J. BRONOWSKI, extracts from *William Blake and the Age of Revolution* (1972), reprinted by permission of Routledge and Kegan Paul Ltd.

T. S. ELIOT, lines from *Ash-Wednesday*, *Four Quartets*, *The Hollow Men*, *The Love Song of J. Alfred Prufrock*, and Chorus from *The Rock*, from his *Collected Poems 1909–1962*, and extracts from *The Cocktail Party* and *The Idea of a Christian Society* reprinted by permission of Faber and Faber Ltd.

FREDERIC JAMESON, extracts from *Marxism and Form: Twentieth-Century Dialectical Theories of Literature* (copyright © 1971 by Princeton University Press), pp. xvii–xviii. Reprinted by permission of Princeton University Press.

WALTER JENS, extract from 'The Classical Tradition in Germany – Grandeur and Decay', in *Upheaval and Continuity*, ed. E. J. Feuchtwanger, published by Oswald Wolff (Publishers) Ltd, 1977.

LESZEK KOLAKOWSKI, extracts from *Marxism and Beyond* (1971), reprinted by permission of Rosita Colin.

GEORG LUKÁCS, extracts from *The Meaning of Contemporary Realism* and *Essay on Thomas Mann*, reprinted by permission of Merlin Press Ltd.

HUGH MACDIARMID, lines from *Third Hymn to Lenin*, reprinted with permission of Macmillan Publishing Co., Inc. from his *Collected Poems* (revised edition), © Christopher Murray Grieve 1948, 1962, 1976. Copyright © 1967 by Macmillan Publishing Co., Inc.

LOUIS MACNEICE, lines from *Autumn Journal*, reproduced by permission of Faber and Faber from *The Collected Poems of Louis MacNeice*.

THOMAS MANN, extract from *The Magic Mountain*, translated by H. T. Lowe-Porter, reproduced by permission of Secker and Warburg Ltd; and extracts from *Order of the Day: Culture and Politics*, published by permission of Alfred A. Knopf Inc., copyright 1942 by Alfred A. Knopf.

HERBERT MARCUSE, extracts from *One-Dimensional Man* (1964), reproduced by permission of Routledge and Kegan Paul Ltd.

VICTOR SERGE, extracts from *Memoirs of 'a Revolutionary 1901–1941*, translated and edited by Peter Sedgwick, © Oxford University Press 1963. Reprinted by permission of Oxford University Press.

R. H. TAWNEY, extracts from *The Acquisitive Society*, reprinted by permission of Bell and Hyman.

EDMUND WILSON, extracts from *To the Finland Station*. Copyright 1940, 1972 by Edmund Wilson. Renewed © 1968 by Edmund Wilson. Reprinted by permission of Farrar, Straus and Giroux, Inc.

Part One

'Action without theory is blind. Theory without action is barren.'

Lenin

1

THEORY AND PRACTICE:
A DIVIDED WORLD

Most of the issues that dominate the world in the late twentieth century have their roots in the revolutionary upheavals which erupted with such explosive force in the last decades of the eighteenth – that turbulent age heralded by the American War of Independence and determined by the French Revolution, together with the parallel developments of the Industrial Revolution and the twenty-two years of total war that followed. For these upheavals, culminating in the triumph after 1848 of bourgeois capitalism, radically transformed man's conception of his world and his conception of himself, and set in motion new revolutionary energies, new forces for social change which, born out of the ruthlessness of capitalist exploitation, were to bring into being the socialist revolutions of the twentieth century.

When Tom Paine, writing in 1792 in *The Rights of Man*, predicted that 'the present generation will appear to the future as the Adam of a new world',[1] he was giving voice to a psychological response that strikingly registers the momentous nature of the events he had been privileged to witness and to take part in. As he clearly understood, the Revolution represented a giant step forward. But his prediction began to take on a peculiar irony in the light of the ways in which the Revolution was to develop; for he was in no position to see 'the change beyond the change', to anticipate the hidden contradictions inherent in these great events – the fact that, in dialectic terms, they represented but the beginning of a new stage in the contradictory struggle for progress. The Adam that made his re-appearance in 1789 as a challenge to the authority of the God-ordained hierarchies of the *ancien régime* came not to lead the dispossessed to their inheritance, but only to assert the rights of a revolutionary liberal bourgeoisie. In other words, Paine's Adam was to find this new world of his, so recently freed from one class tyranny, taken over by another; to have his claim to inheritance betrayed into the hands of the middle classes; and thus to be denied afresh his right to a place in the world. Eden still belonged, it seemed, to the privileged few; the rest were to remain among the dispossessed, in the spirit of God's *original* verdict upon Adam, as banished tillers of the soil, mere instruments for the wealth of others.

Nevertheless, new possibilities, new horizons, new concepts of relationship, new and hitherto unthinkable prospects for mankind were initiated during that period of ferment which – however fiercely resisted, suppressed, by the new forces of conservative authority – could not any longer be dismissed or nullified. The rights and interests of the anonymous masses, that is, had become a force to be reckoned with almost for the first time, even by the very manner in which they were exploited; and today we are still engaged in the struggle for these rights and interests, in the process of what may be loosely called (against the confusion of ideologies) the struggle for democracy.

Indeed, it was the logic of middle-class capitalism, its rampant self-interest, its exploitation of industry and labour, its thirst for new markets, its incitement to an increasingly aggressive rivalry between the nations and its ruthless imperialism, that created the antagonistic conditions of this struggle for democracy and the violent impact it has had – in Europe, in Russia, in South America, in China, in Africa – upon the history of the twentieth century. And though it seems that now, in the last quarter of the century, the struggle itself has become more confused and problematical – undermined and threatened by the various contradictory forms it has taken, and by the revolutionary technologies which, in their subtlety and sophistication, are so rapidly transforming the world – the great human issues remain as imperative as ever. In fact, in the essential sense, there is almost everything still to be fought for; and it has to be fought for in terms of the inbuilt historical contradictions and perversities that everywhere persist as obstacles to freedom, among which none have proved more threatening or more difficult to reconcile than the 'domination over men of all the forces and powers they themselves have created'.[2]

There is a great deal then at stake. And, in a world divided against its common interests – not only on the level of ideology and economic power, but also in terms of nationalistic aspiration, the antagonism of state and people or of class and class – no simple straightforward ways are to be found of ensuring the triumph of these common interests. But they exist nevertheless, as incentives to be fought for. And since the struggle for them is, at root, a struggle for the fundamental issues of community, the ends and aims of life as communal co-operative process, what matters here is what these issues, ends and aims may come to signify in the context of the constantly changing, developing patterns of human activity. Whether or not we can make our world an Eden, it must be continually stressed that these issues have their true significance not as abstractions, as abstruse generalities, but as energies, interests and influences firmly rooted in the sensuous particular realities of people's lives.

Confronted by the often paradoxical distinctions between these realities and the abstract systems of order devised to control them, it is the task of those who care what happens to people in the future to do what they can, by ruthless critical examination, to clarify the conditions under which the fundamental human issues and aims can be freed to function in genuinely communal terms as nourishing conditions for sanity and equilibrium. But we have to be equipped for such a task. And in order even to be capable of undertaking it, we must put ourselves in a position of vigilant and sceptical opposition to all concepts and systems of order that stand in the way of emancipation and human progress. We must set ourselves against the lip-service of the literalists, the interests of the status-conscious, the makers of hierarchies, the fence-builders who would seek to maintain the acquiescence of the people by sealing them off into separate categories and compartments. We must make ourselves alert to the ways in which 'the false light of the systematizing spirit' continues to operate not only through the political and social structures of a nation's life, but also by means of the dominating sleight-of-hand of the technological process. And we must be aware too of the extent to which societies (whatever their claims) continue to be manipulated by those who have always in the past made sure they commanded the techniques of control – those, that is, who are closed to the questions that postulate real distinctions, real freedoms and real respect for the non-conformist complexities of the human condition. But above all we must not allow ourselves to be deceived into believing that the world is not, as it has always been up till now, a world that prospers on suppressed majorities.

No one has set a more rigorous or a more challenging standard for this task than Karl Marx, pursuing through four decades of a disastrous and fateful century his uncompromising analysis of the capitalist structure of European society. For what Marx made the basis of his revolutionary philosophy was the unarguable existence of man as a sensuous particular human being in opposition to the abstract forces and powers – nature, God, capital, property, money, the state – under the domination of which he had for so long been forced to serve as a machine-like cipher of the will of the few. Man, he contended in his early *Critique of Hegel*, is the basis of society, 'its true ground . . . not merely implicitly and in essence, but in existence and in reality'; and in this sense 'the individual *is* the social being', the source of all social vitality and of all thinking about society, and therefore all the *forms* of society; because the 'essence of *man* is the *true community* of men', and 'men, not as abstractions, but as real, living, particular individuals *are* this community. *As* they are, so it is too.'[3]

Not, it should be stressed, that Marx is here advocating a version of the laissez-faire concept of man's place in society by which the 'enlightened' individual should be left free, 'unfettered by state control', to act as he thinks fit.[4] In his concept of society, the emphasis lies upon the individual as a *social* being, whose essence is the 'aggregate of social relations'. From which it follows that the individual who, in pursuing his own interests, however enlightened, is detached from or opposed to, rather than the focus of, the community, alienates himself from his essence and thus betrays the community. Or, to put it in other words, if man is estranged from himself by being cut off from the potential community he belongs to, then 'the society of this estranged man is the caricature of a true community', and 'his activity is a torment to him, his own creation confronts him as an alien power, his wealth . . . as poverty'.[5] And what Marx sought to re-establish with his criticism of the existing order and the abstract economic and political forces that governed it was the primacy of man as the essence, the maker, of community, the creative source of all social reality.

It was the object of criticism, as a weapon directed against the enemies of mankind, in Marx's view, to pluck 'the imaginary flowers of the chain [that enslaves him] not in order that [he] shall continue to bear that chain without fantasy or consolation, but so that he shall throw off the chain and pluck the living flower'. Hence, as Marx defines it, setting down the terms of his method, 'the criticism of religion disillusions man, so that he will think, act and fashion his reality like a man who has discarded his illusions and regained his senses, so that he will move around himself as his own true sun'. And hence, as 'it is . . . the task of history, once this other-world of truth has vanished, to establish the truth of this world', so 'it is the immediate task of philosophy, which is in the service of history, to unmask self-estrangement in its unholy form once the holy form has been unmasked. Thus the criticism of heaven turns into the criticism of earth, the criticism of religion into the criticism of law and the criticism of theology into the criticism of politics.'[6]

This was the basis on which Marx began to build his monu mental indictment of the capitalist world, of man exploited and of man alienated; of the political, social and economic mechanisms that determine the character of men and mould their consciousness. He saw it as his task to expose for what they were the mystifying alien powers that controlled men's lives and to delineate the actual conditions these powers masked, in order to lay foundations which would enable man to re-organize his world as a community, as 'the perfected unity in essence of man with nature'.[7] This, of course, was the way he saw it at the start; for, as he was later to argue, it is 'the modes of production', the economic structures of society, that determine man's capacity to create a community, or that dictate the *kind* of community he creates, and it is therefore these modes of production that have to be re-organized. Nevertheless, the generating source of the dialectic that produced *Das Kapital* remains this qualitative concept of man in the setting of a rational human order. And in the beginning, moved by indignation, his moral purpose sharpened and directed by a rigorous application of the dialectic process, he set himself 'to depict the stifling pressure which all the different spheres of society exercised on one another'. It was the task of criticism, as he says, to engage in 'a hand-to-hand fight' with the enemy – against 'a society infinitely divided into the most diverse races, which confront one another with their petty antipathies, their bad consciences and their brutal mediocrity, and which, precisely because of their ambivalent and suspicious attitude towards one another, are dealt with by their masters without distinction . . . as if their *existence* had been granted to them by *licence*', forcing them 'to recognize and to acknowledge the fact that they are *dominated, ruled* and *possessed*'.[8]

Today, that task remains to be completed. For still we are faced with social systems everywhere as deeply divided and fractured as ever by the alienating abstracts and irrational interests of economic and political power, which have assumed, if anything, even more lethal control over the fate of men since the emergence of totalitarian bureaucracy and the staggering advances of technology. Indeed, it ought by now to be as plain to us as it was to Marx that the issues of the present and therefore the shape of the future depend crucially upon the manner in which we complete the thought of the past;[9] for it is a fact that the issues of the past cannot become lessons on which to build for community unless or until we have been able to resolve them satisfactorily. And those who shut their eyes to the evidence of the past and the actualities of inheritance are likely to live in a diminished present. Having built our institutions up by stealth and circumnavigation or by perverted application of the principles of humanizing order, we can have no right to assume that we have built for permanence. In the struggle for the future, what we have to remember is that whatever liberties and rights we may have won – and there are many millions who have still not won them – are built on history's wrongs – the wrongs of a Pitt, a Palmerston, a Bismarck, a Thiers, of a thin minority protected from the ugliness by civilized and sensitizing standards in their assumption of the wealth provided by the broken health of millions; or the wrongs of perverted dogmatists like Napoleon, Hitler or Stalin, building grandiose mausolea for the enslavement of the masses. We cannot repay the debt we owe to those who have been starved of their rights and basic needs unless we can make ourselves the consciences of history, and learn to concentrate the powers we have to vindicate the sufferings of the deprived and the betrayed in building for a *genuinely* rational human order in the world. But how can we do this? Certainly not by assuming the issues of the past are dead. For new injustices proliferate from the old, and if we ignore them they will go on breeding around us out of sight.

No one, wherever they live, can afford to be complacent about the superior protection of the laws and institutions that define their lives and safeguard their supposed liberties. Complacency breeds myopia, and myopia prevents us from recognizing the seemingly stable structures built to protect us as instruments that stifle liberty, that produce a Northern Ireland, a Watergate, a Vietnam, a Hungary, a shut Russia. Our betrayals may be rooted into what we do not see around us walking home, the very structures of democracy we in the West build upon, subsiding, fractured and against all sense left unattended. How was it possible, for instance, for fascism to triumph so completely in Germany and in Italy between the wars, if not as a consequence of continual failure to act against the economic and social aberrations that existed or to recognize the real nature of the threats they offered? The Nazi vision of society was a manifestation of irrationality and of rabid perversion rooted in the substance of democracy itself, or emerging from the forms it took in Germany, France and England, where the ruling classes thrived (with callous indifference to the needs of their subject peoples) upon the exploitation of industrial resources and an increasingly aggressive competition for the markets of the world. The arrogant imperialism of the Great Powers, or of the blinded minorities that ruled them, could have led nowhere else than to confrontation and catastrophe. Not that one could have imagined this taking the form it actually did take. But all the same there is no denying the unspeakable obscenities of the First World War, that lurid twilight of the gods created by the monstrous hypocrisies and inhumanities of European rule; and it was these that made the Third Reich possible, even as they brought about the ferment of unrest and violent upheaval that led to revolution in Russia.

As for the historic *achievement* of the Russian Revolution, it could not have occurred at all except as a consequence of the repressive violence and inhumanity that characterized the development of Western capitalism in the nineteenth century. That much is clear. But what of the appalling aftermath of the achievement, its great appeal so quickly degenerating into nightmare? What of the murderous facts that Victor Serge and Trotsky and thousands of committed communists had to face up to in the period of Stalin's triumph – of a Russia plunged into a Reign of Terror comparable in its savagery to that of France in 1793–4? The Stalinist system seemed to have betrayed the very essence of the emancipatory spirit of the Revolution and to have become yet another tyranny of intolerant power – a rigid monolithic structure shut to criticism embodying a cynical inversion of the struggle. Could such a structure become a society fit to satisfy 'man's self-esteem, his sense of freedom', what Marx envisaged as a 'community of men that can fulfil their highest needs'?[10] Can any form of genuine community be created on the basis of universal terrorism and repression and mass murder?

'What is terrible when you seek the truth,' wrote Victor Serge in his *Memoirs of a Revolutionary*,

is that you find it. You find it, and you are then no longer free to follow the biases of your personal interests, or to accept fashionable clichés. I immediately discerned within the Russian Revolution the seeds of such serious evils as intolerance and the drive towards the persecution of dissent. These evils originated in an absolute sense of the possession of truth grafted upon doctrinal rigidity. What followed was contempt for the man who was different, for his arguments and his way of life. Undoubtedly, one of the greatest problems each of us has to solve in the realm of practice is that of accepting the necessity to maintain, in the midst of the intransigence which comes from steadfast beliefs, a critical spirit towards these same beliefs and a respect for the belief that differs. In the struggle, it is the problem of combining the greatest practical efficiency with respect for the man in the enemy; in a word, of war without hate. The Russian Revolution, although led by men who were upright and intelligent, did not resolve this problem; the character of the masses had received, from the experience of despotism, a fatal stamp whose effects were imprinted in the leaders themselves.[11]

Faced with this reality, Serge many times found himself 'on the brink of a pessimistic conclusion as to the function of thinking, of intelligence, in society', as a consequence of encountering, everywhere he went in Russia, 'fear of thought, repression of thought, an almost universal desire to escape or else to stifle this ferment of restlessness'. But he did not surrender his right to think, to continue questioning. Having been a political exile since his birth, and having known 'both the real benefits and the oppressive hardships of an uprooted man', his convictions had not been formed in the academic institutes, but from the harshness of experience.[12] 'Early on,' he says in the *Memoirs*,

I learnt from the Russian intelligentsia that the only meaning of life lies in conscious participation in the making of history . . . It follows that one must range oneself actively against everything that diminishes man, and involve oneself in all the struggles which tend to liberate and to enlarge him. This categorical imperative is in no way lessened by the fact that such an involvement is inevitably soiled by error: it is a worse error merely to live for oneself, caught within traditions soiled by inhumanity.[13]

Serge wrote this as a man who had lived through tragedy and dispossession, having been reviled, branded as an enemy, hunted down and imprisoned, for his right to think and to question, to doubt, to be different, to live his respect for the belief that differs. He did not write in order to curry favour or to justify himself to others, but only to try to be a witness to the truth as he had learnt it. And his conviction, the tone of fearless honesty that runs through his book, is the more impressive because of the terrifying record of adversity it had to pit itself against. There are those who might point out, of course, that Serge was one of the more fortunate among the men who dedicated themselves to the revolutionary challenge, in that he survived. But this is a fact which he would be the last to deny. He survives as a witness, and he writes as a man with a responsibility towards the truth. For the book is more than a record of his own experiences; it is a tribute to the courage and the determination of the countless people who died miserably and anonymously for the kind of beliefs he stood for. 'I have,' he says,

outlived three generations of brave men, mistaken as they may have been, to whom I was deeply attached, and whose memory remains dear to me. And here again, I have discovered that it is almost impossible to live a life wholly devoted to a cause which one believes to be just; *a life, that is, where one refuses to separate thought from daily action.* The young French and Belgian rebels of my twenties have all perished; my syndicalist comrades of Barcelona in 1917 were nearly all massacred; my comrades, friends of the Russian Revolution, are probably all dead – any exceptions are only by a miracle. All were brave, all sought a principle of life nobler and juster than that of surrender to the bourgeois order; except perhaps for certain young men, disillusioned and crushed before their consciousness had crystallized, all were engaged in movements for progress. I must confess that the feeling of having so many dead men at my back, many of them my betters in energy, talent and historical character, has often overwhelmed me; and that this feeling has been for me also the source of a certain courage, if that is the right word for it.[14]

What special quality was it in him that enabled Serge to survive humiliation, vilification, death and defeat not only undiminished but deeply strengthened in his conviction that the higher aims of man were worth fighting for? Was it some sort of deep-seated moral consciousness of the issues involved – his vision of community? Was it his sense of the example offered by so many of his dead comrades, inspiring him to rise above himself and speak for others? Or was it the fact that he had a clearly worked-out intellectual system of beliefs to build upon and make war with against despair and breakdown and surrender?

Similar questions might be asked about Marx himself, whose life is sharply divided into two periods by the failure of the 1848 Revolution, which deprived him of immmediate hopefulness and turned him into an impoverished exile. As Bertrand Russell points out,[15] perhaps Marx's tenacity and industry, his sheer capacity to keep going and to triumph over defeat and despair, even in face of the most appalling conditions, are explicable only in terms of the strength and stability of his moral and intellectual convictions.

Not that this could ever explain the nature of the achievement. Seeking to define such a man as Marx, and to discover what it was that held him concentrated to his monumental task – what gave him courage and incentive to continue in that deadly city of his exile – one would have to ask oneself how any such phenomenon can *ever* be defined or explained. There is the face, of course, the great maned head, from which, through faded photos, comes a sense of giant will and challenge. And the eyes seem the eyes of a man who sees beyond the dark horizons that are proof *against* the dark. But these, and the words that blaze and sear, contending with the nightmare *rule* of the dark, are the signals and proofs of the engine's power, not what fuelled it, lay behind it. We have to ask what kind of impulse it is that produces such abundance, such exhaustlessness. For it seems – as with the great rivers, eddying and swirling down their courses, that begin from tiny trickling well-springs – inexplicable, a force that drives the mind inexorably along its chosen paths. Can we profitably call it indignation, anger, a sense of injustice? The Jew's desire for vengeance against the killers of community? Is it something of this sort that brings the juices out and sets them on course against the assembled powers, the respected vampire forces, of the earth? Or is it what he calls 'this incubus', this 'hideous and evil dream' tormenting him, that drives through figures, dates, events and all the mutilated histories of man to forge his unappeasable and rigorous vision of a healed world?

Whatever it is, it is not a negative or a passive energy. For Marx did not spare himself. His was 'a life's work in the agony and sweat of the human spirit, not for glory and least of all for profit, but to create out of the materials of the human spirit something which did not exist before'.[16] And in this great task he was as much sustained by the vigour and the strength of the intellectual foundations he laid for himself as by any of the more obscure and radical qualities he possessed. Indeed, without these intellectual foundations he could hardly have persisted, as he did, in the laborious preparation of a mammoth work; for he had much pain and suffering to put up with and little enough encouragement, except from a few friends and disciples, to give him incentive to keep going, especially in the first ten years of his exile in London.

The importance of such foundations, and their value for us as primary sources for incentive and replenishment, for the exploration of reality, is the strength of the basis they provide, the cogency and logic and coherence of their application to the problems that confront us in the struggle for understanding and awareness against those forces in the modern world, those killers of community, that threaten to disarm and to destroy. They were not conceived in order to 'confront the world with new doctrinaire principles and proclaim: Here is the truth, on your knees before it!'; but to 'develop for the world new principles from the existing principles of the world' for the purpose of creating a genuinely rational human order in place of the corrupt perverted structures that existed.[17]

Marx is at once firm and precise in laying his foundations. Fascinating though it may be to try to explain exactly what combination of motive and of psychological need it was that drove him to find other foundations than those already available, or to subject the Hegelian model to quite such elemental and searching analysis, the fact that he did so, and that, in postulating for philosophy a new and challenging set of problems, he was postulating for himself possible means of answering certain basic questions that had formed in his mind concerning the relation between philosophy and reality, and so of initiating the struggle between the old world and the new, is what matters. Of course, it is necessary to recognize – especially in the light of the ways in which Marx built *upon* the foundations he laid with his critique of 'the fried doves of absolute science' – that the psychological conditions that determine the direction of a man's thinking are an incalculable force that has to be contended with and vigilantly controlled. But this in itself is the strongest possible reason for the necessity of *laying* firm foundations. For they provide the indispensable basis upon which to build a stable, rational structure – a structure at once constructive and inclusive that will hold firm against attack without perverting the laws of reason by turning itself into a fortress for the defence of untenable ideas. Thus Marx lays his cornerstone for a philosophy that will have the actual power, by shaping its dialectic terms into weapons of denunciation, to play some sort of direct part in the world of human action. 'The question whether objective truth belongs to human thinking,' he asks, 'is not a question of theory but a *practical* question.' That is, 'the truth – i.e. the reality and power of thought – must be demonstrated in practice. The dispute over the reality or non-reality of thinking that is isolated from practice is a purely *scholastic* question.'[18]

In making this declaration, the second of his *Theses on Feuerbach*, Marx puts his finger upon an essential and insistent problem characteristic of the peculiarly abstract nature of so much intellectual activity in the Western world. And at the same time he defines in these Theses the grounds which led him later to give up philosophy and devote himself instead to the analysis of capitalist society. For him, both Hegel's concept of the 'contemplative, knowing subject' and Feuerbach's materialism were abstract and one-sided interpretations of the world – Hegel because he reduced history to an emanation of the spirit, and Feuerbach because, though 'not satisfied with abstract thinking', he disregarded the active element, the practical activity that fashions the object, 'sensuousness as *practical*, human-sensuous activity'.[19]

The dilemma for philosophers was the isolation of thought from action, of theory from practice, which itself was symptomatic of the dichotomies – in the thinking of Church and State, in the separation of class from class, in the hypocrisies enshrined in political and social institutions – that everywhere declared the irrationality and divisiveness of the very structure of society and the ethical principles that governed the behaviour of man towards man. And this is a dilemma which has still not been resolved, for the very fact that it is bound up with so many of the intricate psychological and intellectual assumptions of Western man. It is not a question only of the instincts of self-interest, self-assertion and fear, or of the will to power, the need for security gained at the expense of others; but of the intellectual attitudes Western man has been indoctrinated with for two thousand years, rooted in the various manifestations of Platonism and the divisive influence of Christian concepts of reality, which encouraged and deepened the separation of the functions, even to the point at which politicians, statesmen, leaders of the churches, writers and thinkers – most of those, in fact, who have had any influence in the world – had ceased to be aware of the dichotomy, or to be capable of thinking their way out of it.

Hence the phenomenon of nineteenth-century leaders of society, nineteenth-century critics of society, nineteenth-century politicians, nineteenth-century critics of literature, developing arguments (intended as relevant) that have often only the most tenuous connection with the actualities that are their substance and their ultimate justification. And hence – however high-minded, however dignified and seemingly humane – the falsity, the hypocrisy or the inadequacy of their response to the world they supposed themselves to be making sense of and offering wise prescriptions for. Reading them – reading Mill and Ruskin and Carlyle and Arnold and Trollope and Gladstone and Disraeli and so many of the inheritors of minority affluence – one is conscious of a disturbing inability to respond to certain intolerable conditions in the life of their time, an almost schizophrenic failure to connect one activity with another. And in the light of Marx's insistence that thought as a purely scholastic contest is utterly unrelated to the human realities which ought to be the source and the aim of thinking, one comes to appreciate that no intellectual activity can be pursued meaningfully if it is pursued in abstraction from other activities related to it. But that is precisely the way in which, for example, Matthew Arnold, as a representative figure of his time (and there are many others), developed his concept of culture, considering himself at once a literary critic and a self-confessed critic of social and political issues. In other words, the truth of thought, of theory, whatever the subject, is registered, determined and confirmed not by its detachment from the actualities of the world it is part of but by its application to them; and if the acid test of application demonstrates fundamental discrepancies and inadequacies in the theoretical process, then the theory must be modified, altered, expanded or thought through again till it has been made conversant with the rigorous and inclusive demands of actuality.

The root of the problem, as Russell points out, writing of Marx, is the manner in which 'philosophy has taken over from the Greeks a conception of passive contemplation, and has supposed that knowledge is obtained by means of contemplation',[20] even though the psychology of Western man has defined itself, in so many basic senses, as voraciously active and predatory. And this has been the mainstream assumption, no doubt to a great extent through the pervading influence of the peculiarly passive bias of Christian thinking, of most European thinkers and critics. It is the essential *principle* for such critics as Arnold, with his plea for inaction, aided by 'right reason and the will of God', in the pursuit of harmonious perfection; or with his definition of the critical function as the 'disinterested love of a free play of the mind on all subjects, for its own sake'; and with his description of the way this free play of the mind operates – as 'an instinct prompting it to try to know the best that is known and thought in the world, *irrespectively of practice, politics, and everything of the kind*'. For him, what is important is 'to value knowledge and thought as they approach this best, *without the intrusion of any other consideration whatever*'.[21] One notes, particularly, the final emphasis, which is that knowledge is to be valued for itself alone, as some sort of aesthetic absolute and in total abstraction from all considerations that might tend to challenge its supremacy. But that is to make nonsense of what knowledge is related to and what it functions in terms of; for quite obviously it cannot function in terms of itself. Its justification is the human context it emerges from and is determined by – if, that is, it is anything more than purely abstract. And if it is not determined by or related to any human context, then (as knowledge – knowledge in the sense implied by Arnold) it must in consequence be strictly meaningless, and should be left to the mercies of those 'docile echoes of the infinite will' who (according to Arnold) are to be envisaged as the true workers of the future, the true interpreters of the 'essential movement of the world'.[22]

Marx was quick to recognize how deeply characteristic such conceptions were of the divisive and dislocating process of capitalism, and to expose the vitiating fallacy of pure disinterested contemplation – that concept of thinking which, by resolutely following the law of its own nature, keeps 'aloof from what is called the practical view of things'. As he argues in his early demonstration of the aims of communism: 'It can be seen how the resolution of *theoretical* antitheses . . . is possible *only* in a *practical* way, only through the practical energy of man, and how their resolution is for that reason by no means only a problem of knowledge. It is also a *real* problem, a problem which *philosophy* was unable to solve precisely because it treated it as a *purely* theoretical problem.'[23]

This defines a fundamental principle: that all genuine (that is, more than purely theoretical) problems of the thinking mind are determined by the active nature of man's response to reality. Indeed, it is Marx's view that 'we are always active, even when we come nearest to "pure" sensation: we are never merely apprehending our environment, but always at the same time altering it'. And this, as Russell observes, *'necessarily makes the older conception of knowledge* inapplicable to our actual relations with the outer world. In place of knowing an object in the sense of passively receiving an impression of it, we can only know it in the sense of being able to act upon it successfully. That is why the test of all truth is practical. And *since we change the object when we act upon it, truth ceases to be static, and becomes something which is continually changing and developing.'*[24]

Thus we see that what Marx is concerned philosophically (and actually) to expose in his concept of knowledge is the very manner in which we conceive and respond to society as a human reality. He refutes, that is, the contemplative, static concept of society that has its roots in the conservative 'master–servant' concept that Plato set forth in *The Republic*: an unchanging, closed, authoritarian system, a structure built upon 'arrested change', or forced stability, in terms of which the masters remain masters and the servants servants for ever.

Such a conception of society has its reflection today in the monolithic structure of the Soviet state, as in most other totalitarian systems, whether of the right or the left. Based upon certain absolutes that are not to be questioned, it is ironic that not a few of these 'theistic' states should have developed from Marxian roots, to demonstrate once again the perverseness and the blind dogma of human thinking, its wilful refusal to connect the abstract with the concrete, and the manner in which the pseudo-light of theory must, when dislocated from the actual needs of living people and set up against them, in practice betray, deprive and alienate. This one can only regard with astonishment; for it is a phenomenon that pertains, not to the error-stricken past, but to the process of history that is actually in the course of being made, here and now, in the late twentieth century. It is of course easier to accept, in the wisdom of hindsight, that people should have found it difficult to relate their theories to the needs of their time. But to be incapable of applying the lessons of the past to the needs of the present, to persist in that dangerous, alarming separation of the faculties which has wrought such havoc upon the human race, seems symptomatic of a congenital incapacity to understand or to read the evidence spelt out by history or with such cogency and precision by Marx himself. Strangest of all is the process by which, in the application of Marxism, what Marx refuted and condemned should itself become enshrined in the structure of socialist societies.

This process is not, however, new. The authoritarian concept of society has been clearly defined for us, and with imperious rhetoric – a rhetoric that survives today, among his conservative inheritors – in the kind of structure envisaged by Edmund Burke in his *Reflections on the Revolution in France*, and its violent opposition to the beginnings of the revolutionary struggles of the modern world. For here the sources of intolerant, arbitrary power are evident. A mysterious divine law rules and ordains the contracts of society, a law that human beings have no right to question, that denies man both his natural and his social rights except according to its own superior disposition. According to Burke, reacting violently to the alarming events in France, every society is 'but a clause in the great primeval contract of eternal society, linking', as he phrases it, 'the lower with the higher natures, connecting the visible and invisible world, *according to a fixed compact sanctioned by the inviolable oath which holds all physical and all moral natures, each in their appointed place'*.[25]

In such terms, the contract of society is *unalterably* fixed, an absolute decreed by the 'manuscript-assumed authority of the dead', as Tom Paine scornfully comments, and therefore in fact no contract at all.[26] The masters have their appointed place and the servants have their appointed place – presumably fixed for them by some sort of all-embracing Divine Justice embodied in the rights of Kings and ruled by some sort of Abstract-Noun-Group invested with divine right which goes by the name of Authority. And not one of us has any choice but to accept and to submit, since apparently we are bound to do so by 'inviolable' oath – by an oath we swore, that is, before we were born. As the 1688 declaration of parliament to William and Mary declares: 'We do humbly and faithfully *submit* ourselves, our heirs and posterities, for ever.'[27] But what this actually means when reduced to comprehensible human terms is that the 'lower natures' are bound by inviolable oath, and 'by consent of force', to obey the 'higher natures'; and that if these lower natures should dare to go against their oath, 'the law is broken, nature is disobeyed, and the rebellious are outlawed, cast forth from this world of reason, and order, and peace, and virtue, and fruitful penitence, into the antagonistic world of madness, discord, vice, confusion, and unavailing sorrow'.[28]

Thus do protest and resistance – the kind of protest and resistance Burke himself had witnessed with such shocked outrage in the upheavals of the French Revolution – threaten to destroy the absolute, God-ordained balance of the hierarchic order of the masters, and to replace it with a disorder and a chaos that sound suspiciously like a Burkeian definition of hell. Similarly, Adam's claim to rational participation in the resources of God's Eden had brought forth the outraged response: 'Behold, the man is become as one of us, to know good and evil,'[29] followed by the command that he be driven out and kept from tasting further of the delight of the knowledge of paradise.

It was just such a concept of social order – authoritarian, rigid, fixed, appealing in the classic Platonic–conservative manner to divinely appointed absolutes which are ultimately contemptuous of the rights and sufferings of all who are relegated to the lower levels – that Marx set out to attack in his exposure of the 'crass materialism' underlying Hegel's doctrine of the State. For, though in Burke's scheme the higher natures were a different breed, with different, higher and more sensitive needs, they were also the manipulators of repressive laws to maintain their supremacy and the tyranny of wealth, and to keep the masses cowed, 'that they might spend the days of wisdom', as Blake was to write in *Jerusalem*, 'In sorrowful drudgery to obtain a scanty pittance of bread,/In ignorance to view a small portion & think that All.'[30]

They were, however, the masters, the indispensable leaders, without whom (according to Burke) society would be unable to function – the 'necessity that is not chosen, but chooses', 'that admits no discussion and demands no evidence'. As for the lower orders, one can only assume that such creatures – their station fixed by the inviolable pre-natal oath of their contract – were incapable of being anything other than what they were, a sort of servant-race, an insect-species. Or rather, in the words of Davies Giddy, patron of science, later president of the Royal Society, it was firmly believed that to educate such people 'would in effect be found to be prejudicial to their morals and happiness; it would teach them to despise their lot in life . . . render them factious and refractory . . . enable them to read seditious pamphlets, vicious books, and publications against Christianity; it would render them insolent to their superiors; and in a few years the result would be that the legislature would find it necessary to direct the strong arm of power towards them, and to furnish the executive magistrate with much more vigorous laws than were now in force'.[31] But, as Shylock put it: 'Hath not a Jew eyes? Hath not a Jew limbs, organs, dimensions, senses, affections, passions?' However obvious this may seem to anyone who has any genuine feeling for the human race, in Burke's time it required a revolution to point it out, because of the apparent inability of the privileged few to comprehend the fact that the anonymous many were actually human beings like them. 'If you prick us, do we not bleed? If you tickle us, do we not laugh? If you poison us, do we not die? and if you wrong us, do we not revenge?'

In terms of the social philosophy set forth by Burke– the reactionary conservatism which, with its 'assumed, usurped dominion over posterity',[32] was to dominate the politics of Britain till at least 1832 – such sensitivity, such human responsiveness, had no place. The hierarchic structure of society required the lower natures to remain anonymous, humble, passive, a neutral and obedient work-force, bound to their appointed place (poverty producing plenty) by the fixed laws of the great primeval contract of eternal society. It did not require them to feel, to display emotion, to have ideas; their natural role was to obey. Thus, Burke and his peers were particularly shocked that these lesser creatures should believe they had the right to question the order of things or to harbour resentment against their masters. They considered such liberties irresponsible and destructive. And as for the revolutionary activity of the French people, and what Burke calls their 'paltry and blurred sheets of paper about the rights of man', this was a blasphemy against the very essence of the civilizing process, the 'moral and physical disposition of things', the fundamental laws of nature, 'to which man must be obedient by consent of force'.[33]

The palpable irrationality of this dogma has its context of course in the violent upheavals of a revolutionary age which, with its ruthless European wars, put intolerable pressures equally upon the struggles of the radical humanists. But it was also to have a powerful influence upon the politics of the nineteenth century, and to cast its shadow forward into the twentieth, as one aspect of a struggle that is still going on. In the light of the emergence in our midst of the fascist concept of the master-race, and the appalling manifestations of superiority by which the Nazis degraded, vilified and exterminated the Jews of Europe, reducing them to the level of the very lowest forms of insect-life, Burke and his political church are to be seen as symptomatic of certain attitudes the human psyche seems fatally attracted and impelled to adopt. For what is most striking about the Burkeian view of society is its appeal to a mystical unapproachable authority, a governing set of laws claimed to be beyond man's reach, but actually manipulated by the few to command the unquestioning service of the ignorant many. Though cast in the language of the eighteenth century, not only does it enshrine and extend theories stemming from the tyranny of the absolutist monarchs and the mysticism of Christianity; it is one of the sources of, and has much in common with, those anti-democratic authoritarian political systems which have played so disastrous a part in the shaping of twentieth-century politics. Naturally, Burke's *Reflections* have their own specific frame of reference, and this in its detail is not transferable. It is the underlying assumptions of Burke's thinking that are so depressingly familiar: his defence of despotic power against 'the tremendous breaking forth of a whole people . . . from the destruction meditated against them'[34]; his acceptance that it is natural for the vast mass of mankind to be in a state of repressed servitude to 'the puppet-show of state and aristocracy' and government by terror; the terms of argument he uses, by which concern for 'society' detaches itself from concern for people, and by which theory itself is pursued in total

separation from the actualities which involve the sensuous particular *needs* of people – people as organic, suffering, human
beings. And we find such assumptions familiar because such are
the assumptions and terms of argument – basically contemptuous
of and indifferent to people as people – that have made it possible
in this century to mutilate and maim and dislocate and kill with
such unspeakable callousness in the name of human betterment
and social justice.

Thus we arrive at the essential dilemma, the essential paradox: of
theories supposedly directed to the creation of a rational and creative
social structure that become instruments of irrational and destructive power. And the essential problem is how to reconcile such
theories with the irreducible and complex realities from which they
are often so blatantly divorced; or to demonstrate their inherent
falsity. In short it is imperative to subject *all* theory to the most
rigorous criticism of the grounds on which it is based in the spirit of
the Marxian principle that the test for it is practice. But this,
unfortunately, is where the deepest confusions lie; for where his
basic interests are at stake, man builds his theories on irrational
foundations that side-step or disregard the tests of practice, and is
driven by economic and social forces to impose upon the intractable
substance of reality his distorted vision of it. The aim, for instance,
of the political visionary who would make the world conform to *his*
idea and force it to modify its structure to accommodate his vision of
it, becomes a destructive and twisted aim if he has to kill half the
world to achieve it.

The problem has been eloquently stated by Lord Acton in his
essay 'The History of Freedom in Antiquity':

If you will bear in mind that Socrates, the best of the pagans, knew of no
higher criterion for man, of no better guide of conduct, than the laws of each
country; that Plato, whose sublime doctrine was so near an anticipation of
Christianity that celebrated theologians wished his works to be forbidden
lest men should be content with them, and indifferent to any higher dogma
– to whom was granted that prophetic vision of the Just Man, accused,
condemned and scourged, and dying on the Cross – nevertheless employed
the most splendid intellect ever bestowed on man to advocate the abolition
of the family and the exposure of infants; that Aristotle, the ablest moralist
of antiquity, saw no harm in making raids upon a neighbouring people, for
the sake of reducing them to slavery – still more, if you will consider that,
among the moderns, men of genius equal to these have held political

doctrines not less criminal or absurd – it will be apparent to you how stubborn a phalanx of error blocks the paths of truth.[35]

What is most astonishing and disheartening about all this, assuming Acton's implications to be valid, is that it is as much the great thinkers of our civilization who have been responsible for blocking the paths of truth as anyone; and perhaps they more culpably than others because they had a greater responsibility towards the truth, particularly in face of all those morally binding decisions that have to be taken in total ignorance of their consequences. Indeed, ignorance of the consequences may not be sufficient to absolve men of responsibility for the ways in which their theoretical systems lend themselves to distortion and the service of intolerant and even absurdly irrational ends. The one persistent constant *cause* of error in the whole sorry history of the influence upon the world of the doctrines and prescriptions of philosophical, political and social thinkers – so it seems to me – has been the fatal tendency to disconnect, to isolate, to insulate, theory from practice; to separate the thinking process and what it conceives with its abstract propositions from the sensate, felt realities of the merely human world. And this separation of the faculties is the result of a failure of imagination which reduces human beings to counters, to ciphers, to manoeuvrable, alterable, dispensable elements of argument and of power. One recalls Blake's devastating insight:

> The Spectre is the Reasoning Power in Man, & when separated
> From Imagination and closing itself as in steel in a Ratio
> Of the Things of Memory, It thence frames Laws & Moralities
> To destroy Imagination, the Divine Body, by Martyrdoms
>   & Wars.[36]

And then there is Tolstoy's warning: 'If we once admit – be it only for an hour or in some exceptional case – that anything can be more important than a feeling of love for our fellows, then there is no crime we may not commit with easy minds, free from feelings of guilt.'[37]

The Tolstoyan conditional is, of course, far too simple and far too naïve to stand its ground against the challenge of the complex conditions of reality. But it stands as a sign, a signal, of the kind of reality which is embodied in *War and Peace* – 'that peculiar and characteristic reconciliation between the subjective intention and the novel's objective social material which we associate with the name of Tolstoy and in which both social and individual experience issue from the novelist's hand as though equally his own creation'.[38] For *War and Peace* itself stands as a monumental affirmation of the sort of 'concrete totality, completely present at every instant of its unfolding', which defines the connectedness of the sensate particularities of being with the objective circumstances that are their context – not the separation of the faculties, the alienation of parts, but their organic interaction. And it stands in rooted opposition to all forms of purely abstract theorizing, all systematic structures of the insulated thinking mind, which quickly lose touch with the indispensable rhythms and requirements of the human substance which are their source. There ought to be no philosophical or political doctrine that does not constantly refer back to the concrete primary sources for adjustment and modification of the separate, abstract parts. By making of a theory a thing superior to these sources we betray or falsify them – as in fact we may do at the opposite extreme, by yielding to journalistic methods that simplify, glossing over the fact that 'real thought demands a descent into the materiality of language and a consent to time itself in the form of the sentence'.[39] All writing must keep in touch, or it becomes meaningless or dangerously distortive, an instrument of betrayal. This I take to be the force of Marx's *Theses*, however later extended, on Feuerbach: that 'man must prove the truth . . . the this-sidedness of his thinking in practice'.[40] Because, as he says, 'the chief defect of all hitherto existing materialism,' and of most other systems of thought, 'is that fact, reality, sensuousness, is conceived only in the form of the *object of contemplation*, but not as *sensuous* human activity, practice, not subjectively. Hence, in contradistinction to materialism, the *active* side was developed abstractly by idealism – which, of course does not know real, sensuous activity as such . . .'[41]

He who wishes to break through the phalanx of error that blocks the paths of truth must therefore find a voice and a language and a form for all the contradictory psychological conditions of being that hover on the verge of speech, of embodiment, of distanced form; and all that defines and determines these conditions in the process of the interaction and the conflict between sensuous human activity and its objective social contexts. This is a formidable, and perhaps impossible, task; but it is a task that is necessary if we are to be able to do anything to resolve the actual dilemmas that exist for people in a world of alienating abstracts so deeply unconducive to their needs. In the fullest possible sense, that is, we must be able to say: 'Look, look! This, this!' – even in face of all the impersonal, mechanical structures that surround us, the containing framework, the 'other world' of abstract forces we are subject to. And thus we must be able to demonstrate what it *is* that people have to share, in the recognition that they are at once unarguably individual and inherently social, and that in the concept of the human community lies the secret of the ultimate fulfilment of the individual, since the individual alone or against his fellows is a divided being, a man estranged or alienated from the common interests of his world.

Marx's criticism of Feuerbach is among other things a criticism of his compulsion 'to abstract from the historical process and to fix the religious sentiment as something by itself and to presuppose an abstract, *isolated*, human individual'.[42] This was a necessary preliminary step for Marx towards bridging the gap between theory and practice. And the rigour of his methods demonstrates the necessity of *maintaining* a critical position wherever the dislocation of theory from practice is to be detected; for the record of history is rife with the disastrous effects of abstract thinkers upon the course of human events. Looked at from the darkness of 1940, surrounded by the blatant imperatives of war, to W. H. Auden it seems

> The flood of tyranny and force
> Arises at a double source;
> In Plato's lie of intellect
> That all are weak but the Elect
> Philosophers, who must be strong,
> For, knowing Good, they will no Wrong,
> United in the abstract Word
> Above the low anarchic Herd;
> Or Rousseau's falsehood of the flesh
> That stimulates our pride afresh
> To think all men identical
> And strong in the irrational.[43]

Registering the mystical, abstruse theories adopted by the idealist philosophers in Germany and the kind of thinking they nourished, the later development of the Germanic consciousness comes as no surprise. What are we to make, for instance, of the impact of Fichte, who constructed his theory of moral law and moral reason upon the concept of the 'absolute ego'; who, in maintaining that 'the world is nothing but the material of our duties', attempted to expound philosophically the religious mystery of creation? What are we to make of his concept of the absolute ego? As an abstract idea, an undemonstrable assumption, beyond all proof, it cannot be defined or even envisaged except in terms of God. 'Knowledge is not mere knowledge of itself,' he states, 'but of being, and of the one being that truly is, namely God.'[44] In other words, it is essentially and ultimately intangible, and the whole edifice of Fichte's thinking a grandiose justification for the transcendental fiction of the absolute, ideal being – that being who was later to become, in Nietzsche's terms, the superman, embodying the heroic morality of the German psyche. This stretching to extremes of idealist principles, a peculiarly Germanic manifestation of the romantic neurosis, on one level takes the form of Schopenhauer's pessimism, passivity and gloom, and on another the Dionysiac frenzy of the Nietzschean will to power. And out of such metaphysics came the irrational assumptions of Fichte's *Addresses to the German People* and the manner in which like views were applauded, encouraged and echoed throughout the nineteenth century by the ruthless builders of German nationalism, and above all by the arrogant Chauvinism of Bismarck who, in managing to transform all that was liberal, humanitarian and democratic in German society into a conservative, militaristic and monarchical nationalism, laid those foundations of power that were to lead inexorably to 1914 and 1933. 'Only the German, the original man, who has not become dead in an arbitrary organization,' Fichte declared, voicing the curiously backward formulation of the social and economic structure of the German world, 'really has a people and is entitled to count on one, and he alone is capable of real and rational love of his nation.'[45] Such assertions ought to have been laughed to scorn by all men of reason who heard them; but instead they were made respectable, and Fichte, as the recognized leader of the transcendental metaphysicians, rewarded in 1810 by being made Rector of the new Berlin University. Thus was confirmed that fatal derangement, that spirit of fervour, which was to become the driving force of Germanic nationalism – in 1810 no more perhaps than a mild symptom of reaction to the disorders of European war, but palpable enough, even then, to serve as a warning signal to civilized opinion. Except that civilized opinion had itself been undermined by war, and was to prove impotent (however radical) to deflect the German nation – or what was to be made of it once bourgeois stability and *Realpolitik* had been achieved – from the course it had set out upon – defined, as Fichte cries, by 'the devouring flame of higher patriotism, which embraces the nation as the vesture of the eternal, for which the noble-minded man joyfully sacrifices himself, and the ignoble man, who only exists for the sake of the other, must likewise sacrifice himself'.[45] This is the language of intoxication, the kind of language that lends itself to the intolerant nationalist, the fanatical reactionary, the Nietzschean prophet of race. 'You lonely ones of today, you who stand apart,' as Zarathustra proclaimed, 'you shall one day be a people; from you who have chosen yourselves, a chosen people shall arise; and from it the superman.'[46] For it is, in all essentials, the kind of language that made Hitler and shaped his vision of the German Reich.

It is possible to see this now, in the hindsight of the destructiveness of European history. What is important, however, is to see it as an example and a warning, rather than as just another absurd phenomenon of history. For it was determined not only by the abstract balance of the social and economic forces that were at work upon it, but also by the actions and reactions of men. Such men as Fichte may have been the products of their age, but their ideas sank into people's minds; and we should be under no illusions that the modern world has rid itself of their like. They inhabit high places, and influence the economic and social policies of great nations. And they are adept at deceiving both themselves and others into believing that they have unarguable prescriptions to offer, imposing upon reality, as Fichte did with such success, the straitjacket systems of dogmatic principle.

There is no infallible way of resisting the call of these intoxicants, because the nature of their influence depends upon so much more than any rational or concrete evidence that might be marshalled against them. Whether or not they succeed is unfortunately more a matter of the surrounding economic and social conditions, and the general uninspectable psychological atmosphere of the society they launch themselves upon. Fichte himself was appealing to a people divided into many separate states, large and small, and to the unexamined longing among these people for a united Germany. And he was appealing to them on grounds not of humanitarian reason and justice, but of national pride and of those obscure inflammatory emotions that cluster around such vaguely tumescent ideas as the patriotism for which a man will suffer 'all'. And there is no doubt that his influence and the influence of those who came after him, was determined – in spite of the effort to create a rational structure for German society – by the very disbalance, the divisiveness and disunity of a Germany split up into many states governed according to the archaic laws of their feudal monarchs or dukedoms. It is significant, for instance, that the failure of the revolutions of 1848 was a failure on the part of a bourgeoisie too weak to dominate the absolutist feudal structures it had challenged, and persuaded to give up its political and social objectives for the pursuit of a united Germany and the rewards of property. As Thomas Mann pointed out, looking back from 1939: 'The unhappy course of German history, which has issued in the cultural catastrophe of National-Socialism, is in truth very much bound up with that unpolitical cast of the bourgeois mind, and with its anti-democratic habit of looking down with contempt from its intellectual and cultural height upon the sphere of political and social action.'[47] The consequence, for Mann, of the attitude taken by a man like Schopenhauer towards the 1848 revolution, and of the 'political passivity' of the intellectual German bourgeois, 'his contemptuous dismissal of democracy, his scorn of freedom', was 'nothing less than the enslavement of the citizen to the State and to power-politics'.[48]

Thus, after 1848, with the real power centred upon the militaristic disciplines of the Prussian Junker class, and the call to nationalism, to the pride of Germanic roots, accentuated in the spirit of Fichte and Hegel, the scene was set for the emergence of Bismarck in the fifties and the establishment of his anti-democratic anti-liberal policy of blood and iron, for the construction of a Germanic empire founded upon industry and finance and political hegemony. Under these conditions the growth of a rational democratic alternative became more and more impossible, and the creation of the oppressive and abstract machinery of state power more and more a threat to the stability of Europe. The great social and political issues were being controlled in Germany, France and England by a minority of powerful, remote, intolerant men, the architects and agents of a ruthless exploitation of economic wealth, including the appropriation of the resources of other continents and of course the labour of the oppressed millions. The capitalistic tyranny of these men, the élite classes of Europe, extending their commercial war to the markets of the world, pushing the logic of their anti-social policies to the ultimate limits in an aggressive contempt for the needs and rights of subject peoples everywhere – at home, in Africa, in India, in the Far East – rapidly brought the civilization of the West to the very edge of disaster.

Faced with the appalling record of the history of destructiveness they did so much to create, and with the conflicting ideas and issues that have emerged since 1945 from its tangled pattern of events, no one is likely to find it easy to keep the paths of truth clear, or even to know which among them to take through the continually changing post-industrial landscapes of his world. Outraged, deceived or confused by the contradictory evidence we pick up as we go along, misled by the seeming proofs of the past, and by our own subconscious conditioned assumptions, we become – often without knowing it – rigid, closed, burdened with opinions that gradually blind us to perception till incapable of responding at all to the challenge of those potentialities that point forward and turning *from* the struggle to seek comfort in a wearied conservatism. ('History,' as Eliot puts it, defining the trap, 'has many cunning passages, contrived corridors/And issues, deceives with whispering ambitions,/Guides us by vanities.')[49] And so, by degrees, imperceptibly weakened by the traps we tread – like Schopenhauer, with his 'melancholy and his critical spirit, his reverence for suffering and his hatred alike of "indecent optimism" and progress'[50] – we sink back into disillusionment and privacy. Or we turn in longing for some *other* kind of resolution than that which the phenomenon of history seems capable of offering, neutralized by the alienating pressures of a world rife with contradictions that no man can protect himself against. Or so it may seem to some.

2

MARX: THE CRITICAL CHALLENGE
AND ITS CONSEQUENCES

It was exactly such alienating pressures and aberrations that Marx set out to challenge in his exposure of the sources of social conflict and his treatment of cultural and political history as a complex dialectic phenomenon involving the oppressed classes as a major force. By demonstrating the significance of the underlying forces at work upon the structures of society, his methods and terms of reference transformed our thinking about politics. And 'as a constant stimulus to the social intelligence and social memory of mankind' these methods have enabled us, in the words of Leszek Kolakowski,

to see, on the one hand, how man in society is formed by the struggle against nature and, on the other hand, the simultaneous process by which man's work humanizes nature; to consider thinking as a product of practical activity; to unmask myths of consciousness as resulting from ever recurring alienations in social existence and to trace them back to their real sources.[1]

In his immediate response to the events in Europe (and particularly in Germany) throughout 1848 and 1849, Marx set to work to apply his thesis that the truth – the reality and power of thought – must be demonstrated in practice, by embarking upon a profound and scathing analysis of the nature of the revolutionary movements of his time. With his far-seeing grasp of the essences of political struggle, and his unwavering perception of the problems of power, he was not to be seduced by the euphoria of class triumph into becoming an apologist for any of the forces that dominated. In the context of the principles worked out and lucidly defined – first in the *Critique of Hegel's Doctrine of the State* and other early works and then with his *German Ideology* of 1845 (unpublished at the time) and the Communist Manifesto of 1847 – he had laid the strongest foundations for attack. Thus he was able to adopt a clear, detached and ruthlessly critical position when it came to the test. His commentaries on Germany in the *Neue Rheinische Zeitung* remain as penetrating and as hard-hitting today as they must have seemed to the readers of the paper in 1848 and 1849, especially when he had launched his brilliantly sustained attack upon the Camphausen ministry and the Hansemann 'Ministry of the Deed' which took over from it.[2] The argument seems an irrefutable and devastating indictment of betrayal, the betrayal of the Revolution – which Marx was too perspicuous and too realistic to be deluded into thinking could succeed, except in terms of the triumph of those capitalistic forces which were unleashed by it. His command of polemic and his firm historical analysis of the classes active upon German politics at the time were too deeply rooted in his knowledge of the actualities of power to lead him to misunderstand the situation. The Revolution had erupted in the German cities at the instigation of the bourgeois classes in alliance with an ill-defined and almost non-existent proletariat upon a body-politic feudal in its structure and fragmented into many conflicting parts, the heterogeneous duchies, princedoms and kingdoms that made up the German nation. It was inevitable, therefore, that this revolution would be doomed. How could it be otherwise if such had been the fate of the February revolution in Paris, which in the June Days was to have its shameful climax in the brutal betrayal and massacre of the workers? The logic of such revolution was the triumphant assertion of middle-class power; and, in Marx's own words, 'the real birthplace of the bourgeois republic was not the *February victory*, but the *June defeat*',[3] a situation ripe for the machinations of men like Louis Napoleon. No revolution, as Marx had already argued convincingly, could hope to be consolidated except through a sequence of transformations, with each new stage of it prepared for and equipped in awareness and the need for action – first by an overthrow of the long-established feudal system by a strong and confidently radical bourgeoisie, and then, as a natural consequence to this, by the overthrow of the bourgeoisie by a strong and united proletariat – a class capable of taking power and equipped to rule.

What happened in the crucial months after the Berlin and Prussian revolutions was, in Marx's analysis of the situation, first an apparent overthrow of the reigning feudal monarchies, etc., by an equivocal bourgeoisie led by Camphausen, and then by the

Hansemann ministry, 'which was to change passive resistance against the people into an active attack on the people, the Ministry of the Deed' – and thirdly, as Hansemann began to overplay his hand, by a re-assertion of the very powers of feudal absolutism which had in March been overthrown and replaced by Camphausen. As Marx puts it in December 1848:

After the March deluge – a deluge in miniature – had subsided, it left behind no monsters on the surface of the Berlin earth, no revolutionary colossi, but rather creatures of the old style, thickset bourgeois shapes: the liberals of the United Diet, the representatives of the class-conscious Prussian bourgeoisie.[4]

And this Prussian bourgeoisie

was thrown to the highest position in the state, not as it would have liked, through a *peaceful transaction with the Crown*, but through a *revolution*. Against the Crown it had to represent not its own interests but the people's interests, i.e. it had to act against itself, for a *popular movement* had cleared the way for it. However, in the eyes of the bourgeoisie, the Crown was not only the divine umbrella behind which its own profane interests were concealed. The inviolability of its own interests and the corresponding political forms had the following meaning when translated into constitutional language: the inviolability of the Crown.[5]

For the feature of the Prussian March revolution was its provincial and strictly sectional nature; it was neither national nor German. Its bourgeoisie, unlike the French – which, in alliance with the people against the monarchy, the nobility and the established church, had forcefully engineered the French Revolution – represented not the genuine forces of modern society but the old order. It was 'inclined from the start to treachery against the people and compromise with the crowned representatives of the old society'. It found itself 'at the steering wheel of the revolution, not because the people stood behind it, but because the people pushed it forward'. It was little more than

a stratum of the old state which had not been able to break through to the earth's surface but had been thrown up by an earthquake; without faith in itself, without faith in the people, grumbling at those above, trembling before those below, egoistic in both directions and conscious of its egoism, revolutionary in relation to the conservatives and conservative in relation to the revolutionaries, mistrustful of its own slogans, which were phrases instead of ideas, intimidated by the storm of world revolution yet exploiting it . . .[6]

And it was on such insecure foundations, on such irrational and dangerously equivocal principles, that Germany was forced to build in the years to come, when the increasingly ruthless expansion of commerce began to take on a more and more aggressive nationalistic form. One cannot wonder at the growing distortion of the development of German nationalism or at the fanatical militarism round which its leaders welded the concept of Teutonic unity. The derangement that was to lead, as we now see, to the violent extremism of the Nazis was already there in embryo in the impotence of the liberal middle classes to assert a new order for the unleashed forces of the modern world over the old. What Marx was to hope for and to work towards in his response to German affairs – 'it is our interest and our task to make the revolution permanent until all the more or less propertied classes have been driven from their ruling positions,' he was to write in March 1850[7] – was to be continually thwarted by the power of the reactionary, counter-revolutionary forces of the Germanic world, both in Germany herself and in the ominous manoeuvrings and conflicts of Germany and Austria, in the complex interactions of the ruling forces of European politics and the bid for economic supremacy.

All the same, the measure of his grasp of the conditions of the time is the manner in which, against these obstacles, the radical opposition was encouraged to grow and to adjust itself to each new barrier that emerged. And from the scope and range of his analysis in the *Neue Rheinische Zeitung* and the *Neue Rheinische Zeitung Revue*, to take these alone, Marx proves himself the indispensable analyst of the great events of 1848 and 1849. This is not *simply* a matter of his sure command of the facts; but, far more important, his determination to unmask the pretensions and hypocrisies of power and what lay behind the new façades that were being erected throughout Europe as a consequence of the upheavals. Indeed, in defining the conflicting forces that were at work in this period of explosive change, he defined for himself and for us the causes of the failure of the various revolutionary movements and the consequences for the future, thus confirming the veracity of his own political convictions as laid out in the Communist

Manifesto. Above all, he was a pitiless critic of good intentions, for he knew that in terms of the ruthless nature of the class struggle, the struggle for supremacy, good intentions are never enough. As Engels has it, writing of the political romanticism of the Slavs: 'Since the positive world, the real situation of their country, offered no points of contact [by which to focus their democratic convictions with their nationalistic feelings], there was nothing left to them but the otherworldly "kingdom of the dream", the realm of pious wishes, the politics of delirium';[8] so Marx defines the "Lamartinian rhetoric of brotherhood", set forth by the European Central Committee led by Mazzini and Ledru-Rollin. 'For them,' he writes with scathing contempt,

the whole revolution consists merely in the overthrow of the existing governments; once this aim has been achieved, 'victory' will have been won. The movement, the development, the struggle, then comes to an end, and under the aegis of the then ruling European Central Committee the golden age of the European Republic and the permanent rule of the nightcap can begin. Just as they hate development and struggle, these gentlemen hate thought, callous thought – as if any thinker, including Hegel and Ricardo, would ever have achieved that degree of callousness with which this mealy-mouthed swill is poured over the heads of the public. The people are not to worry about the morrow, they must empty their heads of ideas. When the great day of decision comes, they will be electrified by mere physical contact, and the riddle of the future will be solved for the people by a miracle. This summons to empty-headedness is a direct attempt to swindle precisely those classes who are most oppressed.[9]

The essential strength of Marx's view is that he sees the steps ahead, the 'change beyond the change'. He is *primarily* concerned with the 'riddle of the future', and with the political forces that will be the keys to that future. Not for him the miracles, by which progress is based upon belief in 'a social condition which has God and His law as its apex, and the people as its base', as in the Mazzinian Manifesto of August 1850.[10] Not 'Here is the truth, on your knees before it!'[11] But the development of new principles for the world from the existing principles of the world; a new politics from the old, according to the peculiar phenomenon of the class struggle and the ways in which it will develop, both in the terms of capitalist expansion and the strength of the working class. For these are the real issues, not the mystifications imposed upon them by authority; and they have to be seized upon, distinguished and set in their proper context, even in order to have any hope of creating the conditions of progress.

Marx had too acute a sense of the cruelties and miseries that men were forced to suffer as a consequence of the mystifications of inverted thinking, and too deep an awareness of the process by which man in society had allowed himself to be deceived and estranged by the abstract alien powers that are the source of his enslavement, to have a soft view of the options open to society. He himself had been brought up, of course, like all men of his time, on the culture of bourgeois democracy and *its* revolutionary demands. But, armed by this culture with critical weapons of great force, he made it his business to break through the façades of its power and identify the antagonistic social forces they concealed, which he knew would have to be faced up to and worked out according to the logic of their interaction – the struggles and collisions of the oppressed against the oppressors. Nor did he flinch from the necessity of facing up to the fact that the outcome of the conflict between these antagonistic forces would depend ultimately on the relative intensity of the will to triumph of one class over another. In other words, in his recognition of the inevitability of the class struggle, the rise of a militant proletariat, he accepted the necessity of a violent confrontation – not reconciliation, not peaceable absorption, but a kind of war, such as that which had after all determined the rise to power of the middle class, who now (in the twentieth century) throw up their hands in horror at the thought that their civilization should be challenged by the same ruthless methods.

This is of course a view based upon the actualities, the view of a man who examines the complex interactions of the social context to find out what is happening, and who deduces *from* what is happening (or as deeply as possible what he sees happening) what can (or what will or what could) happen in the future. But it is not the view of a *detached realist*, an observer. Marx is committed – committed to what, in terms of the struggles of the peoples for justice and emancipation, he sees emerging. His commitment, that is, has its source not in any abstract dogma *imposed upon* the world, but in the potentialities of the existent social structure and its inherent antagonisms. But his commitment does inevitably have in it *elements* of idealism, even in its very concept of 'the change beyond the change', its vision of a society of the future which, fully developed, will produce 'man in all the richness of his being, the rich man who is profoundly and abundantly endowed with all the senses',[12] and a world in which theory and practice have been reconciled, and all alienating abstract powers eliminated. Which is to say that Marx *believes* in the capacity of man to rise above the constricting limitations that have up till now narrowed his vision and cramped his human powers, and is convinced that once he has freed himself from the destructive antagonisms of class interest – the class interest determined by bourgeois capitalism – and exchanged the abstract oppressiveness of commercial competition for the free and open associations of the human community, the creative activity of the masses, humanity will at last have achieved a truly rational social world with man as its essence and its maker. There is no doubting the generosity, the large-mindedness, the creative confidence, of such belief and such conviction, or the manner in which its advocacy puts the carping reservations and suspicions of all kinds of critics to shame. But it nevertheless implicitly *assumes* that the workers of the future will have the strength and the sagacity to create a new kind of world; that when they have at last overthrown the bourgeois system and made themselves the new ruling class, they will resist the temptation to set themselves (or their representatives) up as the new oppressors; that they will seek the means to eliminate the very principle of divisive rule and bring the war of the classes to an end. The questions implicit in the assumption are not of the kind that Marx had any real opportunity (apart from the evidence provided by the Paris Commune) to test. His task was to prepare the way, to define the necessary terms and conditions – to awaken and to educate the working classes of the world to the urgent problems that faced them, of seeking by all the means at their command to fit themselves for the task of objective government in order to fulfil the great aims of communism.

For Marx the acute observer, Marx the economist, Marx the theorist of class struggle, and Marx the committed leader of the working classes in their revolutionary role, was also Marx the utopian at the very least in this: that he saw in the coming proletarian triumph the beginning of the promise of the end of class struggle and the institution of a classless society. And in terms of his vision, there could be no justification for a dictatorship of the proletariat other than that it should make itself the instrument of classlessness. But the implication that it would do so precisely *because* it represented a majority of the people and would for that reason sweep away the conditions for the existence of class antagonisms must of necessity remain an assumption. Does such a concept make sufficient allowance, for instance, for the fact that all men in society, including the workers, are divided into classes or parties or groups of one kind or another? True, there was widespread evidence in Marx's own lifetime of solidarity and co-operation and the recognition of common interests among the working classes of Europe; but the division of labour also kept them very much divided and separate and therefore confused in their aims. True, the experience of the International Working Men's Association held out prospects for the future 'unparalleled in the history of the past'; and for Marx this was the proof that 'in contrast to the old society, with its economic miseries and its political delirium, a new society is springing up'.[13] But still it remains an assumption founded on belief that the new society will not be of such a kind as to re-establish systems of privilege and of rank which place people in positions of power and so in a depressingly familiar manner expose the unborn millions to new exploitation and oppression. The evidence offered by history since Marx's death of the struggle for a new and classless society gives little cause for confidence that such a radical transformation is in fact possible. It could be argued, in fact, that the Russian Revolution – or rather the manner in which Lenin and then Stalin applied the principles of Marxism – has proved as great an obstacle to the achievement of Marxian aims as the resilient forces of capitalism. For the institution of 'socialism in one country' and its consequent effect upon the concept of the International was a devastating blow to the progress of socialism in Europe. And the development in Russia and Eastern Europe of the party itself into a new and oppressive bureaucracy that has usurped the rule of the working class as a parasitic growth upon it, controlling and containing the needs of the people, and holding them in a vice-like grip which forbids all dissent and all attempts at reform as heretical and treacherous, constitutes a fundamental betrayal of the aims of revolutionary Marxism.

But that is beside the point. The Marxian argument builds its confidence and its expectations not upon the sorry proofs of man's inability to resist the traps of the past, but upon what he is capable of and has proved himself to be capable of when given the encouragement and the confidence to believe in himself and to develop to the full his powers as a man and as a citizen. This indeed is the essence of its strength. Marx was concerned not with the failures of the past or the present, with the fact that one attempt or another to create a socialist society should fall short of its aims, but with the necessity of building for success out of the antagonistic *conditions* that are the causes of failure. For him, the concept of an ultimate social aim, an envisaged goal, a creative synthesis derived from these conditions, was what provided his argument with the indispensable incentive, the essential driving force, the energy and thrust of commitment without which it would have been unthinkable. Of course, it has to be recognized that, implicit in this concept, is the possibility that such a synthesis, the bringing to a final end of class war by means of the rule of the proletariat, might be no more than the beginning of yet another thesis in the dialectical process – a new beginning of the class struggle, and thus renewed misery for the mass of the people. Which would mean too that the Marxian struggle for social justice leads only to the establishment of new *forms* of unjustice, as it always has done in the past.

But if this is so, the risk has to be taken. As Trotsky was to write thirty-seven years after Marx's death, the Revolution 'carries on the struggle with the old world, falling and rising until its final victorious moment in the name of a new ideal to enrich man and to form a new man'.[14] He did not assume that the Revolution had been *won* in 1917; 1917 was only the beginning, along the 'general line of its historic action'.[14] And Marx, before him, was confident that the time was coming when – with mankind at a higher stage in his development, having at last come of age and begun to show signs of shaking off his infantilist prejudices – there would be no falling back into the mire of confusion that had so consistently deceived him in the past, but that we had reached the point at which we could begin to understand how much more deeply it is to our benefit to live in mutual collaboration for the common ends of all than in continual enmity. That is the aim – the creation of a social system in which the Lenins and the Marxes, having done their work, will have become unnecessary! Not that it can be achieved without a great deal of work, for the key to such an aim lies still 'in the difficult struggle of the working-class, in its growth, in its persistence, in its defeats, in its repeated efforts, . . . in the growing will and intensity of the struggle'.[15] And we have only to look around us at the world as it is today, at the apathy, irrationality and discord that infect it, to note how far we still seem to be from getting close enough to that aim to think of it in other terms than those of the nightcap.

For many, in Edmund Wilson's opinion, the ultimate problem of the justification of the Marxian system was that Marx had always failed to explain how the old society would be 'replaced by an association in which the free development of each will lead to the free development of all';[16] how 'this condition was to be arrived at after the dictatorship he contemplated had been clamped down'. In Wilson's words:

He never did really explain it; but he threw out, in the *Critique of the Gotha Programme*, some intimations as to how socialist society was to be constituted in its initial stages. The exalted vision of release which swims beyond the range of his early writings here gives way to a prolongation of something like the world we know. The new order, which has been moulded in the womb of the old, will inevitably be born with its likeness. The classes will have been abolished; but inequalities will still exist. There will not yet be any such thing as an equal right to pay and what it purchases. Such phrases as 'equal right' and 'equitable distribution', which occur in the Gotha Programme, though they once had a certain significance, are today obsolete rubbish. 'No higher system of right can be recognized than is permitted by the configuration of the economic level and the phase of cultural development determined by this configuration.' Since there will still persist differences in ability, physical and intellectual, produced by the society of the past, so that there will be differences in the extent or intensity of the work that different men will be able to perform, and since value is created by labour, the workers of the socialist society will have unequal, not equal, rights. (The whole question of whether the work of a stronger or more intelligent man *does* necessarily exceed in 'extent or intensity' – from the point of view of effort expended – the work of a weaker or duller is always ignored by Marx; as is also the question of the incentive provided by higher pay for more or more exacting work, which has contributed in the Soviet Union to creating a new class inequality.)

It will be only 'in a higher phase of communist society, after the enslaving subordination of individuals subjected to the division of labour shall have been done away with, and thereby also the antithesis between physical and intellectual work, after labour has ceased to be merely a means to live but has become itself the prime necessity of life, after the forces of production have also increased with the all-round development of the individual and all the springs of co-operative wealth are more abundantly flowing', that 'the narrow horizon of bourgeois rights' can finally 'be quite overpassed and society inscribe on its banners: "From each according to his ability, to each according to his needs!" '

It will be seen that, though Marx had pointed out the naivete of the utopias of his socialist predecessors, the prospect of the future he invoked, with its more abundant flowings of the springs of co-operative wealth, was still itself rather utopian. He had simply thrust the happy consummation a little farther off into the future.[17]

Today, Marx's vision of the future seems as far off as ever. But there is no denying its validity. It has been the dominating incentive to rational political thinking in the twentieth century, in spite of the fact that it has lent itself to such lamentable developments as that of Stalinist Russia and suffered such apparent eclipse in the West. For its principles stand as a challenge to humanity to reconstruct society; and millions have responded by adopting its revolutionary methods in the struggle for an equitable world.

The point is that as Marx conceives it this struggle and the process by which the oppressed are to overthrow their enemies are inevitable. Violence is the only way to rid societies of their unjust systems, since no ruling force will ever voluntarily or even by gradual progression relinquish power. But, according to Edmund Wilson, a violent overthrow seemed inevitable to Marx only because he

was incapable of imagining democracy. He had been bred in an authoritarian country . . . Furthermore, he was himself, with his sharp consciousness of superiority, instinctively undemocratic in his actual relations with his fellows . . . finally – what is doubtless fundamental – it is exceedingly difficult for one whose deepest internal existence is all a wounding and being wounded, a crushing and being crushed, to conceive, however much he may long for, a world ruled by peace and fraternity, external relations between men based on friendliness, confidence and reason.[18]

This is not the kind of argument that can be seriously defended, though it might just serve to explain something of the driving force and energy that lie behind the work. For to reduce the objective intellectual achievement to the merely subjective and the psychological, to suggest that Marx's devastating analysis of European capitalism in action and his call to the working class to organize against it can be defined in terms of emotional hurt and the chemistry of temperament, is to trivialize not only the *significance* of the achievement but also the actual conditions it reflects. Or does Wilson really believe that the ruthless exploitation and oppression of the working masses was somehow exaggerated and distorted by inflamed neurosis, a diseased psyche? If it was difficult for Marx to conceive a world ruled by peace and fraternity, friendliness, confidence and reason, this was not because of his private internal condition, but rather because the world he knew was so palpably ruled by war (economic and commercial war) and fratricide (the deprivation and estrangement of millions of human beings), and by contempt, indifference, mistrust, greed, egotism and irrational will! Incapable of imagining democracy? In a world in which the concept of democracy was little more than a hypocritical mask for the justification of the enslavement of the mass of the people; in which, during an 'intoxicating epoch of economic progress . . . death by starvation rose almost to the rank of an institution . . . in the metropolis of the British empire',[19] he concentrated all his energies and all his 'sharp consciousness of superiority' upon creating the conditions for a democracy that did not exist, a democracy founded on equal rights and duties and emancipation for all from 'social misery, mental degradation, and political dependence'.[20] This, clearly, is not Edmund Wilson's concept of democracy. But again and again through his work, and particularly in his leadership of the International Working Men's Association, Marx proved himself eminently capable of imagining *his* concept of democracy. In his inaugural speech to the International in 1864, for instance, and his instructions to the Delegates of the Geneva Congress in 1866, his reports to the Brussels Congress in 1868 and that of Basle in 1869, he defines it with unequivocal concern for his 'fellow working men'. And if his reaction to others sometimes appeared to be undemocratic and even intolerant, this was no doubt because he demanded the same standards and sense of purpose from others as he demanded from himself – his task being to create among the mass of working men a full consciousness of their great aims, their 'protection, advancement, and complete emancipation', 'without regard to colour, creed, or nationality',[21] in a spirit of 'fraternal co-operation'. And he knew that *this* concept of democracy could not be achieved without facing up to, and unmasking, the massive obstacles that stood in its way, which did not exclude the equivocal assumptions of middle-class laissez-faire democrats.

Of course, in certain parts of the world, conditions have improved dramatically since the foundation of the International Working Men's Association. But the contradictory circumstances of the struggle for emancipation remain unresolved, both in the so-called communist world and in the capitalist West, because new forms of economic and social tyranny have accompanied the technological revolution to hold people in subjection. Therefore, though events may have invalidated certain *aspects* of Marx's diagnosis of the economic and social evils of his time, his methods of criticism apply with equal cogency and relevance to the underlying problems of the twentieth century. This is not to say that the Marxian system has to be accepted as an infallible guide to the future to the exclusion of all others. It is to say that it remains an indispensable weapon of criticism and of struggle, to be measured against each changing situation and used as a text for the continuing debate that must go on as to 'what is to be done'; as the basis for evaluation of the terms of the struggle for the future and the eventual implementation of social policies.

This is indeed the way that Lenin himself used it – by adjustment and by adaptation to the particular needs of the situation in Russia, and his own unwavering adherence to the principles of revolutionary action, in the spirit of the *Communist Manifesto*. But Lenin had to deal not with an advanced industrialized country with established bourgeois traditions emerging from its own revolutionary process, but with an autocratic medieval despotism. How he might have acted in the context of the situation in England, for instance, is another matter. Would the same appalling fratricide have been the consequence of revolution here, as William Morris implies in *News From Nowhere?* Would the Russia that he led through the civil war have had to go through what it had to go through if she had not had so many implacable enemies to contend with? How would she have developed if the revolutions in Hungary and above all Germany had managed to survive against the opposition of the Western powers? There are so *many* questionmarks. At any rate, the Russian Revolution succeeded, whatever the cost; and Lenin cannot justly be condemned for the harsh application that he made of Marxist theory. He was acting as the instrument of history, having long prepared the ground, according to the declaration of the *Manifesto*, 'that the first step in the revolution by the working class is to raise the proletariat to the position of ruling class, to win the battle of democracy'.[22] And he went into action, he and his colleagues, with open eyes, organizing the upheaval *as* its instrument, recognizing the nature of the obstacles that had to be overcome, the magnitude of the effort that would be required to overcome them, and the intolerable strain this effort would place upon the people who were the substance of the Revolution. He knew, in other words, that the building of socialism in Russia could be achieved only at great cost and at great risk and in an unflinching acceptance of the moral consequences.

That it went so badly wrong was no doubt built into the situation that took over, substituting for the momentum, the excitement and diversity of revolutionary activity an inflexible machinery of totalitarian control already fit for the *dherzymorda* and attuned to his own perverted needs. But in the thick of civil war not even Lenin could have foreseen the outcome. After all, he did not see himself as dead or Trotsky as eliminated. He saw himself leading Russia forward according to his own clear concept of the new society he had done so much to bring through the fire. It is inconceivable that he would ever have permitted the Soviet Union to become what Stalin made of it, dragging it into deeper misery than ever its people had suffered under the cruellest of the Tsars and acting ruthlessly against the principle of internationalism that was of the very essence of Marxist thinking. That would have been to betray the whole of his life's work and all its patient planning for the spread of communism – that integrated policy of interaction which Trotsky later took it upon himself (almost alone) to advocate and to defend in his monumental struggle against Stalinism.

Lenin may have miscalculated the difficulties – for it seems clear from *The State and the Revolution*, written in the period between March and October 1917, that he failed to anticipate the kind of troubles the Bolsheviks were to find themselves actually confronted with. If so, he was at once to have any illusions he may have held on this count cruelly shattered by the appalling nightmare dilemmas of the New Russia. An 'insignificant minority consisting of the modern slave-owners – the landlords and the capitalists'[23] – seemed to him to stand in the way. But in actual fact, with the whole of the rest of Europe – of capitalist Europe anyway – mobilizing its forces against Russia, hundreds of thousands were to gather behind the banners of the landlords and capitalists, who were organizing the White Russian armies to destroy the nascent threat of the communist challenge. And even after the civil war had been won at such terrible cost in resources and energy, Lenin on his death-bed had to recognize the presence of a monstrous threat from within the party leadership itself, in its embryonic form at least – the horror of the degradation, no more than glimpsed as yet, into which (without him) the Revolution might be betrayed. For it is clear that he was aware of such a threat – the warnings he gave to Trotsky were clamorous enough and unequivocal enough. The trouble is they came too late – Lenin had provided no safeguards against the abuse and perversion of power already being enacted by Stalin. It must have been his sense of this that led him in his testamentary postscript to make a blunt statement on the subject:

> Stalin is too rude, and this fault . . . becomes unbearable in the office of General Secretary. Therefore, I propose to the comrades to find a way to remove Stalin from his position and appoint it to another man . . . more patient, more loyal, more polite and more attentive to comrades, less capricious, etc. This circumstance may seem an insignificant trifle, but I think that from the point of view of preventing a split and from the point of view of the relations between Stalin and Trotsky which I discussed above, it is not a trifle, or it is such a trifle as may acquire a decisive significance.[24]

His words certainly suggest alarm at the prospect of a man like Stalin, described in the testament itself as having 'concentrated enormous power in his hands', taking over the leadership, and it is as unequivocal in its advice as it is prophetic of what eventually happened. But Lenin did not stop here. He delivered a veiled but devastating attack upon Stalin in an article in *Pravda*, delayed for four weeks but published on 4 March, the next day broke off all personal relations with him, sent a message to those in Georgia who had been so brutally treated by Stalin and his agents, expressing 'outrage', and (with Trotsky) prepared for a final attack, to be delivered at the Twelfth Party Congress, due in April.

The tragedy was that, on 9 March, he suffered a third attack of the illness that had struck him down, and was never again to recover.[25] And at the Congress Trotsky himself, deceived by Stalin's manoeuvres and his mildness, refrained from launching the prepared attack, and instead decided fatally to wait for the opportunity of a joint action, in the hope that Lenin would get better. Thus, with the connivance of a triumvirate secretly formed by Stalin, the General Secretary achieved his first triumph, and from that moment on Trotsky was to be cast as the heretic, and to find himself continually out-manoeuvred. So that by the time Lenin's condemnatory statement came to be read – sixteen months after it had been written and four months after his death in January 1924 – Stalin had already had a chance to tighten his control of the machinery; for the indictment came in the wake of his cunning obeisance at the shrine of the dead leader, that preparation of the foundations of the Cult of Lenin which Stalin played so conspicuous a part in organizing, to become a central figure in the elaborate public death ceremonies, from which Trotsky was very conveniently absent. The testament was produced at a plenary session of the Central Committee in May, but in spite of its uncompromising nature, Zinoviev's motion that the testament should not be published was passed by forty votes to ten. Now, as Deutscher comments, Stalin 'could wipe the cold sweat from his brow. He was back in the saddle, firmly and for good.'[26]

Of course, Lenin could not have conceived what was to become of the system or the party he had done so much to create. His strictures on Stalin were made of a man whose unscrupulousness had hardly yet declared itself. But he saw the danger, and his judgement of character was acute enough, on the evidence of Stalin's ruthlessness over Georgia alone, to make him speak out, not only in the postscript but also in his urgent notes to Trotsky. And in these last-minute warnings are to be recognized an essence of the tragedy of the New Russia – that the party hierarchy had left itself dangerously exposed to manipulation in the hands of the wrong kind of leader. If Lenin had lived, Stalin would not have dared to act as he did. But Lenin died, and it was the cruellest possible blow to the progress of the Revolution that just at its most difficult and most testing period, with all those terrifying inheld energies gathering beneath the surface, in a situation of national exhaustion and political apathy, his death should have opened up such a vacuum at the top. For with Trotsky momentarily shattered, unwell, and off guard, unable to respond adequately to the need for leadership, the opportunity was unerringly seized by the one man who didn't hesitate to respond. The irony is that Lenin should have begun to worry about the succession only when he no longer had the energy or the time to formulate the nature of the threat convincingly enough to bring the message home to the party at large. It was left to Stalin to bring it home to them with overwhelming force in his own good time when, during the great purges, almost all of those who had backed him in 1924 were annihilated, not to mention the myriads of ordinary people slaughtered to make way for Stalinist socialism. This was the price that Lenin had to pay for being too late in voicing his fears!

As Trotsky was to write in his *Autobiography*, written from Prinkipo in 1929, of the immediate aftermath of Lenin's death:

The attitude towards Lenin as a revolutionary leader gave way to an attitude like that towards the head of an ecclesiastical hierarchy. Against my protests a mausoleum was built on the Red Square, a monument unbecoming and offensive to the revolutionary consciousness. The official books about Lenin evolved into similar mausoleums. His ideas were cut up into quotations for hypocritical sermons. His embalmed corpse was used as a weapon against the living Lenin – and against Trotsky. The masses were stunned, puzzled, and overawed. Thanks to its sheer bulk, the campaign of ignorant lies took on political potency. It overwhelmed, depressed, and demoralized the masses. The party found itself condemned to silence. A regime was established that was nothing less than a dictatorship of the apparatus over the party. In other words the party was ceasing to be a party.[27]

How *far* Lenin can be held responsible for such consequences it is difficult to say. It is clear that he did not build sufficient checks into the structure of the party to withstand them, and he might even have laid the very foundations which helped Stalin to succeed. And he certainly made too few allowances for the possibility of his own early death. But his was not a Tsarist's temperament. Ruthless and unwavering though he was against the enemies of Russia, he would never have allowed himself to degenerate into unlicensed butchery, the mad irrational fanaticism that defines the Stalin era and has so deeply stained and compromised the record of the Marxist concept of society.

Or would he? We shall never know. But the story that used to be told in Moscow about Lenin brought back to life by a breakthrough in medical science suggests not. As Daniel Counihan tells it,

Lenin walked a little unsteadily out of his mausoleum in the Red Square, shrugged off the congratulations of the Politbureau, and demanded to be left alone and undisturbed in his old office, with the complete files of *Pravda* from the day of his death. When, after some weeks, it was noticed that food left for the great man outside his door was no longer being taken in, the doctors began to fear that perhaps their success had been only temporary, and with some trepidation, they broke into the office. They found no one there; but everywhere, in disordered heaps, lay crumpled and torn copies of the newspaper, and on the desk was a note. It said: 'Gone to Geneva. We have to start again from the beginning.'[28]

As a commentary upon Lenin's conception of the nature of the Soviet state, this wistful little story makes its point sharply enough. For Lenin, as a man of action, retained his objective Marxist vision of socialism as a system based on people and their struggle for possession of the springs of co-operative wealth. The evidence of the civil war cannot be used against him, merciless as that proved him to be against White Russian prisoners. And who knows how the situation might have developed, as it was beginning to, *had* he recovered and moved ahead with Trotsky? At any rate, as things turned out, it could hardly have been more disastrous, creating a totalitarian machinery with a licence for repression and for mass murder which kept the Russian working classes (urban and peasant) in the grip of a stultifying life-denying vice for twenty-five years.

This, it could be argued, was not so much the fault of the system itself as the direct result of Stalin's opportunist manipulation of Marxism, his assumption of dictatorial powers in the context of the economic and social backwardness of a country which had only just been freed from a semi-feudal despotism and the psychology of a people (the peasant masses in particular) unaccustomed to the rights, responsibilities and freedoms they had won. But there was no denying that in the methods by which the Bolshevik party had sought to embody the principles of

Marxism and to lay the foundations of its power as a dictatorship of the proletariat it exposed the system to just such aberrations and flaws as Stalin was to take such complete and catastrophic advantage of. Thus came into existence a ruthless totalitarian state which, in the name of a process Marx himself had spent all his powers of argument to keep rooted in the actualities of the real world and the living potentialities of real people, created forces and powers as alienating and as oppressive and as inhumanly inverted as the system it was supposed to be replacing. For it is in its failure to enact and to embody the fundamental principles – man as the subject of society, freed from the alienating forces of abstract power into full and communal participation in the making of his world – on which Marx built, that this totalitarian concept of social good remains irreconcilable with the needs of the peoples of the world as it is today.

Not, one would hasten to add, that the appeal of Marxism has diminished; for it continues to fire the imagination of millions throughout the world in their longing for justice and freedom and release from oppression, even in face of the fact that in its Stalinist application it embodies (or seems to embody) forms of injustice and unfreedom and oppression inimical to the aims of Marxism.

One of the clichés of the Cold War, and of the post-industrial conditions that have succeeded the Cold War, is that the West is the 'free' world while in Russia and the communist countries behind the Iron Curtain there is no freedom. This is obviously an integral part of the propaganda of the Western world in its attempt to ward off the challenge of communism and to win over those who are uncommitted; and it is one of the myths of ideology that keeps the world divided. But the repressive nature of the Stalinist system itself has done a great deal to strengthen this myth and at the same time to retard the advance of socialism, adding plausibility and force to the individualist appeal of the capitalist argument.

In this sense, distorted and divided by incompatible ideologies, the world seems today as far as ever from resolving the conflict of the classes and acting in any spirit conducive to the creative interests of mankind. Indeed, in spite of a vast increase in the methods of communication which ought to have brought people closer, the situation is confused and threatened by alignments of power based upon incomprehensible and dehumanizing abstractions that are continually falsifying and betraying the contexts in which people live their lives. How is anyone to answer the conclusions of the abstract theorists of Right, the realist fanatics of the Abstract Good, founded as they are on technological superstructures which reduce people to the status of computerized digits? They cannot, at least where the abstracts and the absolutes *control*, because people are not ciphers but human beings. But if we ask what these absolutes emerge from, it is a different matter. For their sources are the deep and passionate impulses that create the driving energies of human action – hatred, indignation, fear, love, compassion, greed, selfishness and selflessness. And they are nourished and intensified by injustice, oppression, cruelty, arrogance, superiority, class divisions, and the deep traumas and diseases brought into being by political systems that ignore, humiliate and degrade the human being. As Marx warned in his early study of communism: 'It is above all necessary to avoid once more establishing "society" as an abstraction over against the individual.'[29] For it is this abstraction and the alien powers it sets up which distort and betray 'the reality of man's essential powers',[30] and which it is thus the task of communism to emancipate man *from*.

But how to accomplish this task *without* once more establishing society as an abstraction? How to make society safe against the brutalizers and fanatics whose singleminded aim is domination, power? How to ensure the survival of the principles of both freedom *and* equality? For to take one's stand with those who, in the struggle for these indispensable conditions, have had to set their faces against the kind of compromise that stops short of violence, may be to risk them. That is the problem, for violence is a breeding-ground of irrationality and fanaticism. But it is a fact, which history persistently underlines, that the persuasive powers of reason (however compelling) are never enough to convince the enemies of reason of the destructive nature of their actions and beliefs. It is too much to expect of a Stalin, a Hitler, a Batista, an Amin, a Vorster. You cannot reason with the enemies of reason. You either institute restrictive laws to safeguard society against them and their ruthless will to power, or take the consequences. And when the democratic process backed by economic power puts them where it put a man like Batista, then the only course for those who have any respect for liberty and human dignity is the kind of course Fidel Castro chose, in the knowledge that the democratic process had been perverted, turned against the community, made to serve the interests of unscrupulous men. That is the logic of it. That is what the humanist who is more than a lip-service advocate of human rights and freedoms has to come to terms with in the end – the kind of logic that Marx and Lenin were intent on spelling out and would not falsify or let themselves be deflected from pursuing, and that Lenin rigorously applied.

We should not allow the unforeseeable consequences of this application to blind us to the nature of the attempt embodied in the Russian Revolution or the nature of the achievement, any more than we should allow ourselves to be blinded to the differences between Leninism and Stalinism. What Lenin had worked with such unwavering dedication and commitment to prepare the ground for – often without any prospect of success and in the worst possible conditions – had become a reality. At last, in spite of all the obstacles, against the enmity and hatred of the forces of minority privilege and capital, the first great steps had been taken for the organization of socialism, and a new voice, a new promise, a new spirit, had emerged to challenge the old and to assert its moral *right*, even by its actions, to challenge the old. Dissociating itself from the corrupt and egocentric rulers of Europe, it broke upon a world sunk deep in the lethal chaos of war as a great call to peace, a proclamation, a rallying cry to the peoples of the continent to rid themselves of the incubus of the past, speaking up for the oppressed and enslaved many everywhere. Against the odds, of course; but magnificently. 'Brothers,' wrote the poet Osip Mandelstam, later to become one of the countless victims of the Stalin terror, but in 1919 acknowledging the heroic necessity of the Soviet ordeal, 'let's try. A vast, clumsy and creaking turn of the helm. The earth is afloat. Cleaving the ocean as with a plough, we shall remember even in Lethe's cold that for us the earth has been worth a dozen heavens.'[31] Or, as Lenin himself put it in a *Letter to the Workers of America* in August 1918:

For every hundred mistakes of ours, there are ten thousand great and heroic acts. But if the situation were reversed, if there were ten thousand mistakes to every hundred fine acts, all the same our revolution would be and will be great and unconquerable, because for the first time not only a minority, not only the rich, not only the educated, but the real mass of workers themselves begin to build up a new life.[32]

Naturally, Lenin could not have expected such a statement to be greeted with anything but a sense of outrage and horror by the leaders of the Western world. The Revolution was a threat to 'civilization', the inalienable rights of the rich, the laws and institutions of the capitalist world as a whole, and therefore had to be destroyed, if possible. It was a threat because it was just, because what it stood for could not be denied, because it exposed the pretensions of the civilized by drawing attention to the humiliating fact that 'the greatest and most necessary part of a very rich nation', as Gerard Manley Hopkins had written of England long before, were forced 'to live a hard life without dignity, knowledge, comforts, delight, or hopes in the midst of plenty'.[33] The ensuing reaction was unequivocal. Churchill, voicing the disgust and shock of the privileged few, spoke of this 'foul buffoonery of Bolshevism', and made himself the grand co-ordinator for the anti-Bolshevik crusade; and the prodigious machinery of Western power was deployed around the boundaries of Russia with the avowed intention of crushing the Leninist state. It was futile for a mere individual like Arthur Ransome to ask people to 'look through the fog of libel that surrounds them and see that the ideal for which they are struggling is among those lights which every man of young and honest heart sees before him somewhere on the road'.[34] Though he might claim that the Bolsheviks were writing a page of history 'more daring than any other which I remember in the history of the human race', they were 'writing it amid showers of mud from all the meaner spirits in their country and in America and Britain'.[34] For Ransome's was not the voice of authority, of power; it was the voice of private conscience responding to a great event, and recognizing (perhaps merely instinctively) the unique historical significance of that event. The voice of authority and power was the voice of a morally discredited system – a system which, from behind its hypocritical façade of civility and rectitude, had long engaged the powers of Europe in an aggressive and murderous rivalry, 'a desperate struggle for the markets of the world', as William Morris declared. But not for the sake of the *peoples* of the world or their advancement. Far from advancing any such cause, or the cause of any civilization worth anything at all in moral or in communal terms, 'its whole energy, its whole organized precision', as Morris further puts it, was 'employed in one thing, the wrenching of the means of living from others' – not only at home, but in its imperialistic assertion of the right to exploit and to appropriate for commercial gain the territories of foreign states, 'prepared to ruin them without war if possible, with it if necessary, let alone meantime the disgraceful exploiting of savage tribes and barbarous peoples on whom we force at once our shoddy wares and our hypocrisy at the cannon's mouth'.[35]

But though this system had acted against every principle of civilized behaviour it had claimed to be the champion of, at the end of the total war its policies had brought about its power and authority still remained massive. The working men of Britain may have cried out 'Hands off Russia' in a gesture of comradely support for this first major step towards the creation of a new socialist world and the break-up of a 'rotten sham society'.[36] But they could not have hoped to prevail against the fury of hatred and of fear that had been aroused among the possessing classes, or against the economic and social institutions these people controlled in the interests of the ten thousand who, between them, owned half the area of the United Kingdom. The working people had no more power to dictate the policies of Britain in 1917 than they were to have in the years leading up to 1939, in spite of the evidence of mass sympathy for Russia and the potential strike-weapon of the trade unions. The psychology of democratic consensus – support, that is, for the system and an ultimate deference to those who were in control of the institutions constructed to inculcate respect and submission – had become so deeply ingrained as to persuade all but the most radical socialists among the working class to accept (or at least to tolerate) the slow and biased methods of parliamentary reform. Not that they had much choice when it came to confrontation. What happened to working-class opposition to the 1914 war and to Keir Hardie's great campaign? What happened to the miners in 1919 and again in 1926? Why was it the General Strike ended in such abysmal submission to the rule of middle-class law and order against such clear support for a just cause? Was it some sort of innate respect for authority, for King and Country? At any rate, even the misery of unemployment and persistent poverty and abundant proofs of the inequalities of class left the status quo intact. So that by the mid-thirties, with the Conservatives confirmed in office, it seemed all will to change had been controlled, leaving the natural rulers to pursue their natural policies without interference, to the edge of disaster and beyond.

In 1918 the Western allies emerged from their war unregenerate if weakened to assert once again the arrogance and the privilege of minority rights and the kind of competitive exploitation that had led them to the war. In other words, the war had taught them almost nothing; for between Versailles and Munich, they pursued policies which, consistent with the growth of fascism, and its uncompromising hatred of socialism, were to lead inevitably to 1939, in an unpalatable record of hypocrisy, fraud and deceit, of ineptitude and equivocation. It was this, indeed, that the Russian Revolution had stood out against and emerged as a challenge to – this tyranny of privilege and property, this devious pursuit of class interest and class security, with its cynical indifference (masked by the *civilities* of class authority) to the needs of the working masses. Who among us that has any genuine feeling for people or for the injustices they were forced continually to endure can look on such evidence as the profits made by the coal-owners during the war, which amounted to something like £25 million more than the total pre-war capital of the industry – while men worked underground for a miserable grudging wage and others were dying at the Front – with anything but a shudder of disgust and dismay? Or upon the grotesque comings and goings of European politicians and businessmen between the wars, during the financial crises of 1923 and 1929 or any of the critical events that led up to 1939 – events dominated by the rise of fascism and the British government's pusillanimous retreats before the threat of violence? Manchuria, Abyssinia, the Rhineland, the scuttling of the League of Nations, Spain, Austria, Munich – the very names are an indictment. By 1938, it had become only too obvious that the governing forces of both Britain and France lacked sufficient will and firmness of purpose to stand up against the irrationalists; that they seemed even to be encouraging fascism. The policy of non-intervention in Spain had been bad enough, since it virtually ensured the triumph of Franco. But the blatant betrayal of Czechoslovakia in September 1938 was the last miserable straw that broke the back of a policy at once bankrupt and morally indefensible in its abject sell-out to Hitler. One has to look hard to find any flicker of generosity or of genuine democratic responsibility – support for or defence of the rights and freedoms and legitimate demands of the common people – which almost everywhere confronted the veiled opposition of the power of institutionalized authority. As Thomas Mann wrote in 1938 of Munich and the thirties:

> There prevailed in the capitalist democracies of the west a sentiment stronger than any antipathy for Nazi Germany's mob rule and gangsterdom, for its debasement of moral standards, its shattering effect on cultural values; a sentiment stronger even than its fear of the anarchistic theory of nationalism, so perilous to the security of all established states. I mean the nightmare of bolshevism, the dread of socialism and of Russia. This it was that brought about the capitulation of democracy as a political and intellectual concept, and drove it to affirm the Hitler thesis, the division of the world into two camps, fascist and communist. This it was that made conservative Europe take refuge behind the fascist bulwark. Nobody would have deemed it possible that what had happened in Germany would repeat itself with such exactness and detail in the rest of Europe. It is uncanny to see how the wretched figure of von Papen, the conservative who delivered up Germany to Hitler, recurs again in the English Chamberlain. Everything is the same: the treachery, the underlying motives, above all the fundamental self-deception – since anyone can see that the forces there invoked to serve the end of any sort of conservatism were themselves a form of bolshevism, on a lower moral plane and without the humanitarian element.[37]

And this is the world that set itself to judge the world of Lenin's Russia! It is not with the gloating triumph of superior democrats secure in the justice of their system that we should look upon the sequence of events that led from Lenin to the murderous paranoia of Stalin, but as a tragedy, a catastrophic misfortune that has diminished us all. To have had to suffer as the Russian people had to suffer under Stalin or as Germany from the monstrous presence of the Nazi party we owe as much to the myopic selfishness, greed, hypocrisy and panic of the ruling few of Europe in their anti-social defence of minority interests at the expense of the community as to the systems that produced these violent aberrations. Perhaps more so, because the aberrations were to an incalculable extent encouraged by the reactionary policies and actions of the so-called Great Powers of the Western world – both before the 1914 war, in the development of their cut-throat imperialism which brought about the holocaust itself, and after, in the ruthless manner in which they sought the overthrow of the Soviet state, or in the crippling terms they imposed upon Germany at Versailles – not to mention the brutality of the Allied blockade of 1918–19, maintained in face of mass starvation and famine throughout Eastern Europe, and the later equivocal support given to Stalin and Hitler.

It is possible to go so far as to state that the policies of the Allied commission pursued at the end of the war, in seeking to stifle and crush the shortlived heroic revolutionary movements in Germany and in Hungary, were a direct incitement to the forces of right-wing fanaticism which eventually brought Nazism to power. You cannot repress the innate explosive energies of revolutionary feeling in a people without perverting them; and everywhere the institutions of organized authority were using all their resources, official and unofficial, to prevent the spread of the 'disease of socialism' and to encourage the setting-up of more acceptable alternatives, such as the substitution of Admiral Horthy for Bela Kun in Hungary.

Of course, it was not to be expected that the men who ruled the West would for one moment have tolerated the spread of socialism to Germany or to Hungary; and the blockade was one of the weapons they used to prevent it. But in putting all their out-dated unimaginative zeal into stamping out the 'foul buffoonery of Bolshevism', they not only created a scourge of hunger and death, but softened Europe to the schizophrenic irrationalities of the right, having nothing to offer themselves as an alternative apart from their own corrupt and hypocritical concept of democracy. For the pretentious façade of civility concealed a set of abstract legal principles and restrictions devised to perpetuate the rights and privileges of the propertied or monied few at the expense of the propertyless millions, according to market laws 'rigged by the miserable inequalities produced by the robbery of the system of Capital and Wages',[38] and backed up to the hilt by the instituted forces of law and order. What, for instance, was the significance of the gigantic charity food service of Herbert Hoover, which his organization (in collusion with America's European partners) first of all withheld, and then (once communism had been smashed) set moving – 15,000,000 tons of food shipped across the Atlantic for the 'salvation and stabilization of Europe'? When the Allied Blockade Council, which used the food as a blatant weapon to defeat socialism, vetoed the service, it must have been perfectly clear that they were condemning thousands to death by starvation. But for the Council, people were not the issue. 'I regard the blockade,' wrote Cecil Harmsworth, acting Minister of Blockade, 'as the easiest and cheapest method of applying pressure to Germany if pressure should be required.' Hoover himself was to describe such an attitude as 'absolutely immoral'.[39] Nevertheless he too submitted to the cynical logic of the manipulators, and by the end of 1919 he had become 'the darling of the frightened capitalists and aristocrats of Europe. All his brilliant professionalism went to defend the indefensible, and to make certain the rise of National Socialism – that travesty of the people's revolutions of 1919.'[40]

In other words, it was with a zeal born of panic and outrage at all they stood to lose that the ruling classes and their military strategists set themselves to defend what they conceived as the 'civilized world', the 'freedoms of democracy'. But what, with the unspeakable methods they used to subdue the *peoples* of Europe, did they achieve? A revolutionary fervour ruthlessly starved into defeat, almost everywhere except in Russia. And in Russia itself, an embattled people, a Bolshevism tragically besieged, forced into deeper and deeper convulsions of deprivation. A Lenin faced with internal enemies who were given maximum support from all the so-called champions of liberty and self-determination in the West and left with no alternative than to close his ranks until the very groundwork of intolerance and dogmatism which became the ultimate trap for the betrayal of all he had worked for had been laid. What had started as a 'superb and courageous social experiment', and might, had it been given half a chance to take root in Germany and Hungary and Italy, have helped to create a very different kind of future for the masses of the Continent, had now been sealed off, isolated, its outlets and complements throttled or driven underground. With Europe's revolutionary upsurge effectively contained by the combined efforts of the Western Allies, with mutilated nations humbled into submission, a huge gaping abyss was left as a festering legacy of imperialistic war and democratic peace. As Lenin declared in 1920, the world was going to have to fight a slow and painful battle to create socialism from 'the mass of human material twisted by centuries of slavery, serfdom, capitalism, petty nationalist economies, and the war of all against all'.[41] In Russia famine, disease, cold, civil war and blockade had, in 1919 and 1920, caused the deaths of something like eight million people. It was appalling, and made worse by the ruthless opposition of the West. Is it any wonder, under such conditions, that the Bolshevik leaders should have begun to form themselves into a rigid Inquisition of the Righteous? By 1921 even Lenin had no choice, in his desperate need to enforce discipline, but to make it his business to crush all internal opposition. At the Tenth Party Congress he had a bleak answer for those delegates who put forward an urgent plea for freedom of speech and the right to criticize. 'Comrades,' he retorted, 'do not let us talk only about words, but about their content . . . It is a great deal better to discuss with rifles than with the theses of the opposition! We need no opposition! Either on this side or on that.'[42] There was no room for criticism or for compromise. Conditions had dictated the assertion of extremist action. To survive there had to be unquestioning acceptance of the party's authority. 'The whole history of Bolshevism,' Lenin had pointed out in 1920 in *The Infantile Disease of Leftism*, 'both before and after the October Revolution, is full of cases of manoeuvring, of conciliation, of compromises with other parties, including bourgeois parties',[43] but now, with enemies on every side, within and without, everything depended upon the uncompromising leadership of the party. Thus was voiced and enshrined as official party policy what was later to be carried to its ultimate totalitarian conclusion in the embodiment of Stalinism – the 'compete abolition of all fractionalism', which was to mean in due course the elimination of every single voice, however unarguable, that would not obey the absolute dogmas of the Master.

And in the perverted logic of this cornered dogmatism is echoed the inherent violence, the callousness and hypocrisy, of the Allied powers, the manoeuvrings and double-dealings of pseudo-representative democracy. If the great struggles of the Soviet peoples were being reduced to 'a glib and narrow philosophy' that had already, according to Bertrand Russell, commenting on a visit he made to Russia in 1920, killed off the Revolution, what else could he have expected? The horrors of Bolshevism reflected the horrors of the world. Russell's dream of men who would be 'erect, fearless and generous'[44] in the making of a creative human society had after all to take account of the four-year horror of a European war in which millions of erect, fearless and generous men had been sacrificed to the arrogant rivalries of democratic nationalism. Why should he have assumed, as he must have done, that Russia would be somehow different, surrounded by the malice and hatred of the imperialists and burdened with a heritage that had exacted superhuman efforts from a people taxed beyond endurance? Perhaps the men of his dreams had already died in Russia; and there is little doubt that many of them were slaughtered on the battlefields of France. Europe had done its best, deliberately or otherwise, to stamp out such men in the interests of abstract policies of capitalist aggrandizement. There is an inexorable logic to David Mitchell's observation about Churchill's aggressive anti-Bolshevism in 1919. 'As the chief impresario of counter-revolution, he did more than any single person (with the possible exception of Hoover) to make the Iron Curtain possible.'[45] Because the logic of Churchill's crusade was the logic of a capitalist imperialism turning from the bloodbath of war to re-assert its authority, and thus (with its continuing appeal to inequality) to pursue the creation of conditions conducive to the growth of fascism and Hitlerism, which were themselves but the nightmare extension of that logic and openly solicited (for all their innate violence and contempt for human values) as a check to the menace of the communists. True, by the thirties, Churchill had changed his tune and turned his invective against the cowardly submission of the men of appeasement and the dangers of Nazi power. But by then the damage had been done, and the course of the European future had been set toward the murderous imbecilities of war, according to the logic of the inhumanity of the leaders of Europe in their retreat from progress.

3

MASS MANIPULATION AND THE
SURVIVAL OF DISSENT

The antagonistic ideologies that define the balance of power in the world today appear to be more firmly under control and more rationally organized against disaster than they were in the first half of the twentieth century. But, since these ideologies have their roots in the irrational history of that pre-1945 past, there can be little cause for confidence that the foundations on which they are based are any the more secure, or that they hold out any greater promise for the freedoms of mankind in the future. If anything, the great advances that have been made since 1945 in science and technology have created a situation more potentially dangerous than ever, because more abstract, more sophisticated, more insidious, more enveloping, more total, and as such far less easy to combat or even to recognize as dangerous. For the technological procedures that have so deeply extended, transformed and invaded the environments of people's lives are being accepted and utilized exactly as if they were the indispensable instruments of social progress. Indeed, what they appear to be capable of offering in terms of the easing of conditions and the raising of living standards for the underprivileged and the dispossessed as aids to comfort and to satisfaction, has already to a great extent conditioned people into believing that they are at last being provided with the means and the power to fulfil their innate human needs. And it is precisely at this level, in the sheer pervasiveness, the ubiquitous presence of these technological resources, that the dangers and the threats to human freedom are to be identified. Because, whatever their potentiality as instruments of human advancement and a rational means of answering the problems of the world, such resources are peculiarly suited to the hidden aims of those who control the institutions of society, and thus to being utilized as weapons of totalitarian power to deceive and subjugate.

In other words, in the post-war world, a new kind of tyranny has emerged – a tyranny based upon the revolutionary technologies developed out of war which substitutes spuriously factual quantitative concepts of reality for the qualitative historical complexities of the human world, and in its pervasive intrusion into the privacy of the home disrupts the organic continuity and rootedness of people's lives, their sense of time and place and history, their grasp of what and who they are. As Herbert Marcuse has pointed out, referring directly to the manner in which technology is being manipulated to maintain the passive servitude of man:

The suppression of the dimension of thought and of action [in society], is a suppression of history, and this is not an academic but a political affair. It is a suppression of society's own past – and of its future, insofar as the future invokes qualitative change, the negation of the present.

A universe of discourse in which the categories of freedom have become interchangeable and even identical with their opposites is not only putting into practice Orwellian or Aesopian language but is also repulsing and ignoring historical reality – the horror of fascism; the idea of socialism; the pre-conditions of democracy; the content of freedom. If it is possible for a bureaucratic dictatorship to define communist society, for Fascist regimes to function as partners of the Free World, for the welfare programme of enlightened capitalism to be successfully defeated by labelling it 'socialism', and the foundations of democracy to be harmoniously abrogated in democracy, then the old historical concepts have been invalidated by . . . re-definitions . . . which, imposed by the powers that be and the powers of fact, serve to transform truth into falsehood[1] –

that is, to substitute falsehoods for truths as if they *were* truths or as if such opposites were interchangeable.

It is becoming increasingly difficult to counteract these falsifying substitutes, which tend to ignore the contradictions of reality and to dismiss them as myths. In terms of the re-definitions that have already been made, the great mass of the labouring classes in industrial societies are even being persuaded to believe that the Marxian proletariat is nothing but 'a mythological concept'; for in fact 'the reality of present-day socialism makes the Marxian idea a dream'.[2] Which is to say that the dialectical idea of struggle and of opposition, defined by Marx and by Lenin as a historical necessity, has itself been undermined and sidetracked. Not that the economic and social evils against which the struggle was urged have been resolved; but that the qualitative aims that determined the struggle in the past – conceived as essentially a historical struggle – are being obscured behind the masks of technological efficiency, which offers comfort and satisfaction in place of the struggle or even as the *ends* for which the struggle itself has throughout history been fought. Therefore the real problem is how to keep the distinctions clear between means and ends, and how to fight the manipulators (social, political, commercial) who would seek to fob off means as ends to keep people quiet. What makes it so difficult is that in the modern world 'the technological controls appear to be the very embodiment of Reason for the benefit of all social groups and interests – to such an extent that all contradiction seems irrational and all counteraction impossible'.[3] In this respect 'the established universe of discourse bears throughout the marks of the specific modes of domination, organization and manipulation to which the members of society are subjected'; and such restrictions are not to be evaded. 'People depend for their living on bosses and politicians and jobs and neighbours, who make them speak and behave as they do; they are compelled, by societal necessity, to identify their own personal lives with the things they function in terms of. How do we know? Because we watch television, listen to the radio, read the magazines and newspapers, talk to people.'[4]

What this tends to suggest is that, in terms of the technological developments and triumphs of the post-atomic world, history is being radically falsified, and man's historical struggle for awareness and emancipation and the tragic human scale neutralized and undermined. Indeed, the question continually asks itself, as Marcuse has asked it: 'How can the administered individuals – who have made their mutilation into their own liberties and satisfactions, and thus reproduced it on an enlarged scale – liberate themselves from themselves as well as from their masters? How is it even thinkable that the vicious circle be broken?'[5]

Looking back to the strikingly different world of 1917, one looks back with astonishment at that extraordinary upsurge of will and courage and audacity when (in the midst of war) the Russian people changed history; and one wonders even how it ever came about. The people – or at least an emancipated section of the people – were asserting their determination to be free from the oppression that had held them down for centuries, and asserting it in however terrible a manner with a profound and irrepressible sense of the qualitative ends they were fighting for.

The ferment was intense and infectious. In St Petersburg people were in spate, exhilarated, intoxicated, rich with an immoderate utopian sense of promise and of release, aware that something unique and historic was happening. Men and women met in the streets and talked and argued and disputed with passion, as if their lives depended on it. For suddenly, from being the mere passive instruments of an incomprehensible process, they were being asked to play their part in the making of history, entrusted with responsibilities and expected to put them into practice. Which is what, for a period at least, they did. The Revolution was made not by Lenin and Trotsky and the Bolsheviks alone, but by the formation of the Soviets of the proletariat faced with the task of creating order out of the chaos and building a new world from it. In the process no doubt there was disunity and strife and fear and cowardice and failure; no doubt the opposition stood silent or kept to their houses or watched. For it was inevitable that with such an upheaval there should be violent reaction and resistance; and no doubt this was already gathering momentum for the post-October struggle, strengthened and incited by the enemies of the Revolution throughout Europe. But between March and October, and in the months immediately succeeding the Bolshevik triumph – and even in the terrible debilitating conflicts of the civil war – the Revolution held its own and countless people fought for it with total commitment and intensity. They may not have known what their sacrifices were laying the foundations of. But at the time they were living through a ferment of history, an upheaval of expectation and of hope in which they *themselves* were the protagonists, the makers.

What they had to face up to was the monumental, daunting challenge of the Revolution – years of struggle, chaos, hatred, killing; bringing with it 'immense new tasks and immeasurable difficulties', as Trotsky emphasized in 1924;[6] and in the exhaustion and the apathy of the aftermath, a gradual tightening and clamping-down of chains; and with the party organization penetrating 'into the thick of the people', the defeat and usurpation of the working class, and Stalin's triumph. So that now, sixty years on, with the situation radically transformed, the ferment has long been stilled or checked, and the Revolution has become an Orthodoxy with its own line of saints and heretics. Now, the monolithic structure of the Soviet state, organized as a bureaucratic dictatorship, imposes its repressive authority upon the people, demanding from them uncritical allegiance and obedience in return for the rewards of the technological process – even as the very different (or seemingly different) systems of the West, those 'freer', more formally democratic and less interventionist systems, are doing in their own ways. A framework of abstract machinery is being universally imposed upon the peoples of the advanced industrialized countries, instilling acceptance and conformity, not only by coercive means (the various powers of authority) but also by means of all manner of satisfactions, aids and comforts made possible by technological developments. And this framework is continually being strengthened by the awe-inspiring advances of science to which the super-powers dedicate vast resources in their race for supremacy and control. It is a process which has proved irresistible and relentlessly effective in its power to manipulate the institutions of society, to distract people from recognizing what is being done to them, and to neutralize the creative dialectics of dissent without which they cannot assert their rights. Which means that the struggle for emancipation, for the freeing of consciousness, for human fulfilment, for the kind of independence and awareness that is conducive to unstunted being, to trust and confidence and a sharing delight in life, is going to have to be fought with much subtler weapons than in the past. It cannot openly challenge its enemies, because they have in their hands all the organs of power. It will have to proceed rather by infiltration, by cunning, by mockery, by unrelenting investigation of the methods that prevail, and by constant critical attack in the effort to break the stranglehold of those who would seek to reduce human beings to the manageable dimensions of the cipher.

Leszek Kolakowski, for instance, has conceived the philosopher as jester – 'he who moves in good society without belonging to it, and treats it with impertinence; he who doubts all that appears self-evident'.[7] And this kind of dissident is 'motivated not by a desire to be perverse but by distrust of a stabilized system. In a world where apparently everything has already happened, he represents a movement of imagination and thus defines himself also by the resistance he must overcome.' And if, in this sense, 'philosophy undermines the absolute, if it rejects *the uniform principles to which all reality can be reduced*, if it confirms the pluralism of the world and the mutual non-reducibility of things, and hence confirms human individuality', it does so not in the name of self-sufficiency or of egotism, but in pursuit of genuine social fulfilment – that is, 'in its relations to the world – relations of dependence, responsibility, and resistance'.[8]

And as he puts it with cogency and wit: 'There are more priests than jesters at a king's court, just as there are more policemen than artists in his realm. Apparently it cannot be otherwise. The preponderance of believers in mythology over its critics şeems inevitable and natural; it is the preponderance of a single world over the multiplicity of possible worlds.'[9]

But how, the philosopher as Jester might have asked (as Kolakowski the Jester-philosopher asks), 'can the conviction that historical necessity exists and that it must be implemented by brutal and terrifying means be reconciled with the recognition of absolute values – with the belief that certain kinds of behaviour are prescribed and others forbidden under all circumstances?'[10] The priests might answer this, as the Soviet Stalinists have answered it, with the dogmatic view that historical necessity and morality are inseparably connected and bound up with the system they preach, against which there can be no argument because the priests fervently believe it to be the repository of all possible and potential moral values. Today, these priests and their sycophants are manipulating the universe of discourse to control and to force their various peoples into conformity with all the powerful weapons they have at their command – from moon-probes to television, from secret missile systems to newspapers, from bureaucratic intimidation and officialdom to the propagandist impact of Olympic-winning squads. And this is true whether they happen to be the devotees of a religion which goes by the name of 'free democracy' (as in America) or of one that (like Stalinism) operates by bureaucratic indoctrination from the party machine. In Russia, the situation of 1917 no longer exists, for the Jesters were then still recognizably Jesters, and had not turned themselves into priests to obscure the terms of the struggle and degrade 'socialist morality' into a hypocritical myth to protect an establishment. But now the hypocrisy has become a rigid façade, an infallible mystique, behind which to manipulate people and to frustrate all attempts to permit anything but a perverted echo of the socialist moral code from getting through to them. Now there is a gulf between precept and practice that is as wide as an ocean, and as deep; though the fear of the priests is that this ocean could be crossed in a moment or narrowed at a stroke – since, though it is metaphorically there, it is of course not an ocean at all but merely a wall raised by will and by indoctrination to maintain the status quo and to keep the truth from breaking through.

The manner in which such hypocrisies of power echo the structures of similar hypocrisies in the past is all too depressingly apparent. To the Western observer, with his prejudices and his distant outsider's view, the façades of Soviet hypocrisy often seem as palpable and as deadly as the façades put up by the Church in the seventeenth century to protect its own power structure; though because of his position he is unlikely to see the façades of his own system quite so sharply outlined. Not that he can argue he is in any position to judge with any certainty, even though in looking at the distanced system as an outsider he may find 'the heap of disorderly impressions' which make up his ordinarily individual perception of the way life functions 'suddenly transformed into a paradise of neat universals'.[11] For the reality is too complex. But if he has a firm enough grasp of moral rules as they emerge from the historical process, and is detached enough to be able to separate these rules or to distinguish them from the expediencies that so often dictate the policies of political systems, he will know that 'between submissiveness to the world encountered and obedience to moral imperatives yawns an abyss on whose brinks the great tragedies of history have been enacted; tragedies of conspiracies and uprisings foredoomed to failure, and, across the chasm, those of collaboration with crime because of belief in its inevitability'.[12] But he will also need to know that 'no one can be absolved of moral responsibility for supporting crime on the grounds that he was intellectually convinced of its inevitable victory'; that 'no one is relieved of the moral obligation to oppose a system of government, a doctrine or a social order that he regards as base and inhuman by pleading that he considers it historically necessary'.[13]

It may not seem difficult sometimes to decide, especially when the issues do not involve one personally. But caught up in the thrusts of change, driven along by the violent fervour of the 1917 Revolution, say, as Dr Zhivago was, it might not be so easy to make up one's mind. (Zhivago found himself condemning the Revolution for its callous indifference to and its brutality against the lives of ordinary people.) One may even find oneself, in spite of one's intentions, on the wrong side. As Kolakowski puts it: 'the whole tragedy lies in the fact that we are compelled to make morally binding decisions in total ignorance of their consequences'. Or, to put it even more bluntly, 'ignorance does not absolve [us] of responsibility, because there are situations in which it is our moral duty to *know*'.[14]

Therefore those who act, or who give their support to action, must accept that, taking the risk that their judgement will turn out to be wrong, the responsibility for the consequences is theirs. But that is not the way things work. Many of us fail to *recognize* that we are wrong; indeed, though we may be trapped in the abyss between intention and achievement, we are very often able to delude ourselves into believing that we are right, and that we have actually achieved what we set out to achieve. But, as Kolakowski observes:

> The values we have espoused can never justify a lack of knowledge of the actual results of the social action we have undertaken. We are not absolved of neglect, laziness, or sleepy indolence in respect to the need for ceaseless verification of our choice; our ignorance is not to be condoned if it leads us to conform to crime. The borderline between innocent ignorance and deliberate blindness cannot be drawn; in the last analysis we are responsible for both . . . This being so, we are obliged to know everything that argues against us. Each of our choices contains a risk, and none can pretend to be final and irrevocable simply on the grounds that it is being fulfilled.[15]

In the real world, the distance between intention and achievement, idea and actuality, theory and practice, often seems unbridgeable as ever – made greater even by the confusions and deceits of those who either cannot or will not see things straight. It was Marx's deep awareness of the manner in which ideas and theories, the abstractions of the mind, had usurped man's place as the real subject of his world, that led him from the first to embark upon his ruthless criticism of the existing order of things. He was the man, in Kolakowski's words, 'who sought to build a bridge between the two cliffs, and on this bridge utopian socialism was essentially to be overcome' in the interests of a creative combination of duty ('*Sollen*') and existence ('*Sein*').

He summed up his view in the words: 'We must force ossified attitudes to dance by humming their own tune to them,' which is to say that people create their own history – not arbitrarily, but by yielding to the pressure of conditions. Marx devoted the greater part of his life to discovering the natural melody of history, and yet those who carried on his theoretical work were constantly obliged to re-consider this problem, to compose over and over again a posthumous opera based on the unfinished manuscript of *Capital* and in the light of new experience to answer the same question: 'What is to be done?'[16]

Lenin's question, reflecting the endless confrontation of current experience with a purely imaginary ideal, echoes back at us today, and we have as little chance of discovering a solution that will not have unforeseeable and unpalatable consequences. It is perhaps even more difficult to answer today, because the dialectic struggle for truth has solidified and stabilized into false and falsifying polarities of power between East and West; but also because, with the triumph of technology, the great conflicting issues are no longer so clear-cut. When the enemies of promise make themselves the spokesmen of social community, when cynical exploitation cannot be distinguished from a policy of emancipation, when what seems release imprisons, what indeed *is* to be done? 'Here,' the Jester confirms, 'we face a question which can never be fully resolved in a manner applicable to all the accidents of history, but must be tackled anew for every actual historical situation that occurs – for each is new, each is non-recurrent, and none are susceptible of analysis merely by invoking analogies from the past.'[17]

What we are to make, for instance, of the worsening economic situation that is striking at the foundations of the European social structure and beginning to expose new and dangerous antinomies ripe for exploitation from the forces of reaction depends of course upon our ability to read the issues deeply enough, the underlying historical issues, the problems and conflicts that are at work. But this demands not only a Marxian perspective, but also a new application (in the light of all the transformations that have taken place over the last hundred years) of the Marxian method. For today, with what Kolakowski describes as 'the sclerotic religiosity' of Stalinism[18] perverting the principles and methods of Marxist thinking out of all recognition, and turning Marxism into 'a concept of institutional, rather than intellectual, content',[19] the situation is utterly changed. It can be no light matter for anyone to profess the theories of Marx in the context of the incessant mutilation they have been subjected to from those who speak as the authentic inheritors on the one side and by the leaders of the anti-communist world on the other, let alone from students and demagogues who spout their Marxist clichés everywhere in between. He who would wish to keep his balance and his faculties must make himself a master-dialectician and an incessant questioner. Or if that proves too rigorous a task for most of us, there is the steadying example of a man like Victor Serge to reassure. For Serge – continually threatened, hounded and besieged by Stalinist intolerance – was faced with the bluntest possible assaults upon his belief in 'the scientific spirit of Marxism' without surrendering it or going under. His example demonstrates not only the moral integrity of the man himself, but also the vital part that his Marxist principles played in keeping him actively engaged in the struggle for truth. Under the circumstances, it is hardly surprising that such a man should have considered it 'a positive disaster . . . that a Marxist orthodoxy should, in a great country in the throes of social transformation, have taken over the apparatus of power'. Because 'whatever may be the scientific value of a doctrine, from the moment it becomes governmental, interests of state will cease to allow it the possibility of impartial inquiry; and its scientific certitude will even lead it, first to intrude into education, and then, by the methods of guided thought, which is the same as suppressed thought, to exempt itself from criticism'. And as he puts it, with a precision learnt in the hardest school:

The relationships between error and true understanding are in any case too abstruse for anyone to presume to regulate them by authority; men have no choice but to make long detours through hypotheses, mistakes and imaginative guesses, if they are to succeed in extricating assessments which are exact . . . for there are few cases of complete exactness. This means that freedom of thought seems to me, of all values, the most essential.[20]

The struggle for truth, that is to say, became for Serge (as for countless others) a struggle for the freedom to think, to differ, to be different, against a totalitarian concept of the state (euphemistically described as the 'dictatorship of the proletariat') that refused to tolerate any challenge to its abstract doctrines, and proceeded to implement its rule (first in Russia and then in Eastern Europe) by a ruthless suppression of criticism, which spared neither the arguments nor the lives of even its greatest revolutionaries, let alone the energies of the working masses.

Under these conditions, the position of the intellectuals of Eastern Europe after the Second World War could not have been easy; and for writers like Brecht, Arnold Zweig and Theodor Plevier, who had *chosen* to return to East Germany from exile abroad, the contradictions must have seemed particularly acute. Their rejection of the capitalist system and their commitment to the principles of communist reorganization made it difficult for them to protest too loudly over the repressive measures adopted by the Grotewohl–Ulbricht regime in the fifties, for they knew that to do so would have been to antagonize the authorities, diminish any power they might have had to influence the people themselves, and even to risk their own freedom, as well as to give gratuitous propaganda to the opponents of socialism in the West. Not that they did *not* speak out when they felt the necessity called for it, if not always publicly. Brecht, for instance, supported by Zweig and others, made a number of protests against 'dictatorial proposals' concerning the arts, and wrote poems (such as 'Listen While You Speak' and 'The Office of Literature') which were clearly critical of the policies of the regime. But often their only course, short of putting themselves in the impossible position of condemning the system they had accepted, seemed that which Arnold Zweig later adopted to protect his vision of socialism: what he called 'the art of mental reservation'. Faced with the icy chill of Stalinist conformity under the harshness of the Ulbricht regime, what else could they have done, other than defect to the West?

Many dissident intellectuals have since been exposed to intolerable pressures, particularly in the Soviet Union, and some of them have been driven to accept the only alternative to silence or to prison, however reluctantly, much to the delight of the Western press and the publicists of capitalism. But in the Germany of the 1950s the dilemma was a painful one for the genuine Marxist as much as for the creative artist who was committed to socialism. Was he to turn his back upon the struggle for betterment defined by the land reforms and the socialist reorganization of resources that was being attempted in the G.D.R. and find himself sliding into an alignment with the enemies of socialism? Or was he to hold his ground for the sake of what had been gained and what might in the future be achieved, in spite of the evidence that surrounded him of contempt for human truth and of the falsifying absolutism that was being imposed upon the people? Brecht puts the dilemma trenchantly enough in 'Not What Was Meant':

When the Academy of Arts demanded freedom
Of artistic expression from narrow-minded bureaucrats
There was a howl and a clamour in its immediate vicinity
But roaring above everything
Came a deafening thunder of applause
From beyond the Sector boundary.

Freedom! it roared. Freedom for the artists!
Freedom all round! Freedom for all!
Freedom for the exploiters! Freedom for the warmongers!
Freedom for the Ruhr cartels! Freedom for Hitler's generals!
Softly, my dear fellows . . .

The Judas kiss for the artists follows
Close upon the Judas kiss for the workers.
The arsonist with his petrol bomb
Sneaks up grinning
To the Academy of Arts.

We didn't ask for elbow room
To invite him in, but only
To snatch the bomb from his soiled hand.
Even the narrowest minds
That are intent on peace
Are more welcome to the arts than the art lover
Who is also a lover of the art of war.[21]

It is easy for the Western observer, secure in the assumptions of his democratic liberties, to criticize, and only *too* easy for him to throw up his hands in horror when he sees what he considers an essential freedom being threatened. But, as Sartre has pointed out, the kind of criticism that really matters is that which comes from inside, because, based upon the actual conditions of the struggle for socialism, it is the only kind of criticism that is morally and ideologically authentic. 'One must, as it were, be a Marxist,' George Steiner comments, 'in order to have the right to know and to say why such a position is either tragic or utopian.

There is, according to Sartre, no alternative condition of honesty – only, he would say, a more or less tawdry muddle of outworn, ignorant or frankly reactionary postures.'[22] In other words, the real challenge of the struggle taking place within the people's democracies is only to be registered by such men as Serge, Kolakowski, Brecht, Bloch and Zweig, who know what that struggle signifies and what is at stake, who are personally and directly confronted with the forces that Marxism is up against and are thus under constant pressure from these forces. Take the bitter irony of Brecht's 'The Solution'; his response to the worker's revolt of 17 June 1953:

> After the uprising of the 17th June
> The Secretary of the Writers' Union
> Had leaflets distributed in the Stalinallee
> Stating that the people
> Had forfeited the confidence of the government
> And could win it back only
> By redoubled efforts. Would it not be easier
> In that case for the government
> To dissolve the people
> And elect another?[23]

Or take his accusatory *Counter Song to 'The Friendliness of the World'*, which strikes at the oppressive puritanism of authority:

> So does that mean we've got to rest contented
> And say 'That's how it is and always must be'
> And spurn the brimming glass for what's been emptied
> Because we've heard it's better to go thirsty?
>
> So does that mean we've got to sit here shivering
> Since uninvited guests are not admitted
> And wait while those on top go on considering
> What pains and joys we are to be permitted?
>
> Better, we think, would be to rise in anger
> And never go without the slightest pleasure
> And, warding off those who bring pain and hunger,
> Fix up the world to live in at our leisure.[24]

Nothing that the outsider can have to say about the nature of the struggle against totalitarian oppression can possibly match the statements of those who are actively involved in it. Brecht speaks with the moral right and authority that comes from a lifetime's commitment to socialism, and the position he chose for himself after the war affirms that right unequivocally. His is not the voice of the libertarian democrat criticizing from a safe distance. It is that of a man who has experienced the contradictions of the struggle, concretely, from within; who has faced up to the difficult problems arising from the challenge of these contradictions.

Likewise the philosopher Ernst Bloch, who had defined his own commitment to socialism in the thirties and chosen to stay in East Germany after the war. When in 1946 Bloch affirmed that 'the working man is the root of history', he was voicing the hopes of many people confronted at the time with the daunting task of shaping a socialist future out of the ruins of war. He firmly believed that once the working man 'has understood himself and, beyond alienation, taken root in a true democracy, something will then come into being in the world which no one has so far ever known: a true home'.[25] But he knew that this belief would have to be fought for, against the contradictions of reality, with defiance and with hope. For he did not delude himself that the East German Communist Party had the answers. He understood just how difficult the task was likely to be, recognizing that such aims as he stood for would have to be pitted against the brutal challenge of the struggle for the material pre-conditions without which a socialist society (so it seemed) would have to remain a mere fantasy. And so it was. The next few years – from 1946 onward – were to offer the severest tests to the principles he and others were most deeply concerned to promote. Faced with the increasing rigidity of totalitarian practice dictated by the policies of the Soviet Union, intellectuals like Bloch had no choice but to accept the directives and limitations imposed upon them, while at the same time continuing to write for the future, even sometimes without the prospect of immediate publication. It was the bureaucratic 'office for literature', as Brecht puts it, which determined whether or not their work was ideologically acceptable. But though differences inevitably arose between the functionaries of the party and the individual, these differences did not in the early years lead to the kind of harsh repressiveness that was later to be the fate of a number of East German writers and thinkers. Brecht, for instance, never considered himself restricted or threatened by official doctrine, because in his view official doctrine (however unpalatable) was part of the necessary interplay of the struggle for socialism, within the context and the framework of which he had chosen to work. Therefore, he stood up to what he believed to be narrow-minded and uncreative in the policy towards art, but at the same time, in his relish for the dialectical encounter, himself remained open to discussion and criticism. When, to take a case which was at once seized upon in the West as evidence of the worst kind of bureaucratic censorship and interference, the authorities decided, for 'ideological and artistic reasons', to withdraw the Brecht–Dessau opera *The Trial of Lucullus* after its March 1951 première, both Brecht and Dessau responded positively, engaging in the discussions that were held with characteristic ebullience and even agreeing to certain minor changes in the text, which led to the production of a new version of the opera in October 1951.

Brecht's psychology was not, in other words, that of a Western liberal. He was a socialist, and as such (in the words of Ernst Bornemann, writing in the *Kenyon Review* in 1959) he felt

that it was not only the right but the *duty* of the Party to correct him. And he felt that he was constantly improving the political effectiveness and the artistic clarity of his work in the process of correcting it under party guidance. But of course, the more changes he made, the more Brechtian became his prose, his logic, his dramatic technique . . . Brecht took to the discussions like a duck to water . . . He made his changes, publishing a new version, and had the old one printed side by side, explaining exactly why he had made the change.[26]

In the West, there was shock and pity for Brecht in his ordeal. The sacrosanct principle of artistic autonomy was being attacked, and the inalienable right of the individual to act or to write as he thought fit. But then, in all its essentials, Brecht's concept of art was itself incompatible with the laws of the market democracy, of commercial laissez-faire, that ruled in the West. He believed the artist had a duty – 'to be intelligible to the broad masses of the people, taking up their forms of expression and enriching them – adopting and strengthening their point of view – representing the most progressive section of the people in such a way that it can take over the leadership.'[27] And it was this concept that determined his opposition to, or his acceptance of, the party's edicts and regulations. He knew that socialism could not be achieved by the individual on his own. His dialectical awareness and sense of history made it clear to him that 'there is no more difficult advance than back to reason', and that the artist could only make himself an instrument in the cause of that advance by recognizing the contradictory conditions that involved him in the struggle for an authentic socialism. Thus he had earned the right not only to speak out but also to submit; and in doing so he did not need the righteous support of the Western press.

As for Bloch, professor of philosophy at Leipzig's Karl Marx University, his position was less public and (for a time) less controversial, as one would expect of an academic. Accepted for his distinguished reputation and his pre-war record of opposition to the fascist threat, he was at first quietly confirmed by the party as 'a worker on the philosophical front', though at the same time his interpretation of socialism – humanist, critical, analytical – was treated with a certain degree of reserve that kept him from reaching any wider public than that provided by the esoteric circles of the universities themselves. As Otto Gropp was to pronounce in 1957, in an official party judgement following the Thaw, on his 'revisionist' ideas: 'In his view of the world Ernst Bloch proceeds from man. It is this that lends his philosophy its basic character and differentiates it a priori from dialectical materialism.'[28]

It was the sudden dramatic change of attitudes brought about by the Thaw that were to lead to such judgements. From the quiet obscurity of university life, Bloch was to find himself abruptly and perhaps unaccountably exposed to the stir and the dazzle of public controversy. In 1954 and 1955 the first and second volumes of *The Principle of Hope* were published throughout Germany in large editions and talked about; in 1955 the philosopher was awarded the Silver Order of Merit, and on top of that, the National Prize; and in 1956 he delivered three major lectures at Leipzig University on the renewal of Marxism to a hall packed to overflowing. For a short time at least he was everywhere spoken of as a force to be reckoned with, his ideas quickening and encouraging the young intellectuals of East Germany to an extraordinary outburst of militant thinking, which had its impact upon every part of the communist world, though he remained almost unknown in the West. Bloch had made it the thesis of his lectures to question and to criticize, and in this sense to attack, the pervasive mythologies of absolutism, and the manner in which (in his view) the party's literalist application of theory had perverted the very nature of the Marxist dialectic. 'When there is no freedom of choice', he proclaimed, 'there can be no progress.'[29] This echoes the question Brecht had asked in 1953 in his protest against the administrative control of art: 'How can an intimidated art move the masses to great and bold deeds?' Bloch was uttering what in the West was nothing but a tired commonplace of democratic method, but in Eastern Europe had become a fresh and burning issue, an issue of explosive significance. And this is one fundamental difference between criticism delivered from within the communist world and any such criticism launched against it from outside. It touches an exposed and sensitive nerve. And whereas a Bloch or a Brecht speaks with the urgency and authenticity of men who are centrally involved in the struggle for change, no outsider has even the moral right, let alone the power, to do so.

This is not to say that criticism from outside is irrelevant or worthless, but that it lacks the psychological intensity and cogency, the force and pressure actually experienced by those who find themselves confronted by the challenge and the threat of an intolerant orthodoxy. The embattled socialist intellectual faces an entirely different situation in his attempt to awaken a dialogue for freedom that will re-assert (as he thinks) the principles and methods of Marxism against the rigid claims of bureaucratic doctrine. As Bloch has pointed out, it is not only fulfilment, but also its opposite – failure, emptiness, the defeat of utopia – that beckons on the horizon. But, on the other hand, how is the thirst for freedom to be controlled so that it will not degenerate into those forms of freedom that betray the working masses and play into the hands of Western capitalism? The problem is to find the kind of balance that can avoid the stifling inertia of the extremes.

In a very different atmosphere from that which left Brecht free – though it is questionable even so whether Brecht, with his subtle grasp of irony and contradiction, would have chosen quite such open confrontation – the price Bloch had to pay for coming out into the open rather than continuing to work on behind the scenes was perhaps a milder one than many intellectuals in the people's democracies had to pay in the aftermath of the Thaw. An official decree, authorized by Ulbricht, accused him of having 'seduced the youth', and he was therefore simply 'retired', withdrawn from circulation, forced to submit in silence to ideological denigration from the party specialists. 'What kind of philosophy is this,' Kurt Hager was to write in 1957, 'which bears these political fruits and which so contaminates the children of workers and peasants and our young comrades?' His crime had been to stir the minds of other, younger, philosophers – Gunther Zehm and Wolfgang Harich in particular – to cogent theses attacking and denouncing Stalinist theory and practice. Zehm, of the University of Jena, had produced a 300-page manuscript dealing in classical Marxist terms with 'the problem of cosmic homelessness and the alienation fostered by Stalinism', and calling upon all intellectuals to form an 'international of the mind'. His book was at once confiscated, and Zehm himself sentenced to four years' hard labour. And Harich's Sixteen Theses on the future of Marxism, outlining a re-appraisal of all modern socialist theory, cost him a harsh ten-year sentence. As for Bloch, he suffered his sentence of enforced retirement for four years, till at last, with the raising of the Berlin Wall, the vilified revisionist broke with the communists and defected to the West.[30] This action in effect defines Bloch's melancholy recognition of defeat. The bureaucratic ruling class, with its rigid application of dogma perverting the necessarily critical process without which socialism, in his concept of it, could not advance, had asserted its supremacy. Against the mechanism of enforced obedience to a body of regulations and untouchable truths determined by the party, there was nothing further he could usefully do as a philosopher to influence the development of communism in East Germany. It must have seemed as evident to him then as it was later to Kolakowski that 'theoretical knowledge of society continues to be a condition for the successful struggle of the communist movement'; and that 'if this movement is not to stagnate, it must still be nourished by advances in theory, created and nurtured by communist intellectuals',[31] whose 'theoretical work cannot be useful to the revolutionary movement if it is controlled by anything besides scientific stringency and the striving for true knowledge'.[32] Bloch had spoken out not as an opponent of communism or as an opportunist seeking the lime-light, but as a philosopher, concerned, in the *interests* of communism, that thought should be free, and that it was the *duty* of the intellectual to speak out for such freedom against the pseudo-

Marxist bigotry and jargon of official party policy, which (as he had seen) was determined by the struggle for power of narrow-minded literalists.

In the light of all the perversions of the Marxist argument that have arisen from the matrix of Stalinism, it has become increasingly and harshly apparent that the great struggle for sanity and rationality and for the release of the deprived masses from their shackles is today no longer simply a struggle between capitalism and socialism. If the capitalist system still remains more or less intact – a formidable barrier to be overcome, an enemy yet to be defeated – other enemies exist, spawned from the ideologies that have opposed the capitalist world, enemies ruthlessly dedicated to the building of systems at once rigidly and cynically resistant to the dialectic pressures of reality and the needs of people. For now we *know* that the distinguishing line dividing Hitlerism from Stalinism is little more than the mythology by which such systems of mass-manipulation were given their licence to function. Now we know that the difference between social responsibility and social irresponsibility is defined not only by the creed we profess but also (and more basically) by the stance we take towards *all* reactionary thinking. Now we know that no revolutionary left politics can remain a politics for people, or can resist the fascist temptations of power, without continuing to permit the fullest freedom of thought to its people. Now we know that the transformation from committed critic into fanatical priest, from inveterate opponent of injustice and inhumanity to instrument of inquisitional power, is but a single step; that all absolutists are potential betrayers in so far as they permit the abstracts of the system they profess to override consideration of the complex human interests that are their primary justification.

So it is that the struggle for a genuinely human and humanizing order in the world remains a struggle against the inherently destructive process by which man, the real subject of human society, is deceived into believing that the abstract concepts invented by the human mind (the minds of men either bent on deceiving others or deluded by their own perverted thinking into enshrining or deifying what they have invented) are themselves the essence, the subject, the starting-point of social reality and the life of the species. 'My universal concern,' Marx wrote in 1844, 'is only the *theoretical* form of that whose *living* form is the *real* community, society, whereas at present *universal* consciousness is an *abstraction from* real life and as such in hostile opposition to it.'[33] Further, since it is a fact that man is conditioned by the world he lives in, that it is society – 'the general character of the social, political and spiritual processes of life' – that determines his consciousness, the problem of creating a community is therefore a problem of making his society the servant of his organic human needs. It is, in other words, at *root*, a struggle against abstraction, against mystification, aggrandizement, mythology, the tyranny of omniscient authority – those awe-inspiring objects (such as God, Nature, Property, Money, the State) that man has invested with superior powers, and which have tended throughout history to usurp his place in the world and to turn him into an object, a servant, a slave, an instrument, a cipher of unarguable and unseen forces, or of (in fact) the will of those who have had the audacity and the cunning to elect themselves the advocates, the deputies, the priests of such forces. And so it is a struggle for the re-assertion of the particular, the concrete, the real – since (in Blake's words) 'General Forms have their vitality in Particulars, and every Particular is a Man.'[34] But at the same time, in the Brechtian sense, it has to be a struggle

to uncover the causal complex in society – to unmask the dominant viewpoint as the viewpoint of the rulers – to write from the standpoint of the class which already holds the broadest solutions for the most pressing problems humanity has ever faced, emphasizing the dynamics of development – concretely – but making abstractions possible. These are gigantic assignments . . . and we will allow the artist to apply all his imagination, all his originality, all his humour, all his inventiveness, towards its fulfilment.[35]

And this in itself demands a continual application of the weapon of criticism – a criticism directed against all political, social and economic mechanisms that exploit and alienate, no matter what their provenance.

Which is to say that, if any form of genuine socialism is ever to prevail, it must be unwavering in its pursuit of the principles of community and of freedom it builds upon, and not allow itself to be seduced or deceived by the abstracts of power that all too easily take their place. It must continue, that is, to be an oppositional force (even as Trotsky made himself an oppositional force) committed to the liberation, the emancipation, of people from the oppression of the alienating forces (of whatever kind, capitalist or communist) that threaten them. And at the same time it must commit itself to the balancing – the continual balancing – of the positive and negative energies in the social structure, in the knowledge that these energies are constantly exposed to new and unpredictable influences in the endless dialectic process of reality. It will not allow itself to be seduced from this vigilant critical stance because it knows to what depravities, what monolithic travesties of the living substance, such congealed thinking leads. It will remain sharply, even suspiciously, aware that 'man's decadence begins whenever the . . . rational understanding becomes depraved in the service of mythologies, blind emotions, and national hatreds', as Kolakowski puts it.[36] Indeed, the very position of the Left as a creative force must depend upon the clarity and constancy with which it maintains its basic principles, which Kolakowski defines as:

Radical rationalization in thinking; steadfast resistance to any invasion of myth into science; an entirely secular view of the world; criticism pushed to its utmost limits; distrust of all closed systems and doctrines; striving for open-mindedness, that is, readiness to revise accepted theses, theories and methods; esteem for scientific innovation; tolerance towards differing scientific standpoints, together with a simultaneous preparedness for war – even one of aggression – against every manifestation of irrationalism; and above all, a belief in the cognitive values of science and in the possibility of social progress.[37]

Such thoroughgoing scepticism, such intellectual preparedness, rigorously applied, would seem to be as indispensable today as the call for a ruthless criticism of the existing order seemed to Marx in 1843. For the cynical opportunism and the doctrinaire hypocrisy that have so disfigured the ideologies of both capitalism and communism since 1914 are not to be modified, let alone dislodged, without a constant and equally ruthless criticism. How, otherwise, we might ask, with Kolakowski, are we to 'free the morality of everyday life from the nightmare of historiosophy? How can we liberate it from that pseudo-dialectic which makes morality a tool of history and then makes history a pretext for villainy?'[38] The task of the genuine socialist – the kind of man, that is, who by the consistency, integrity and objectivity of his principles has earned the right to speak up for the real needs of people in society – is to find an answer to these daunting questions and with every weapon he has at his command to set himself to free man from the nightmare depravities that have overtaken him. This is a task that is fraught with dangers, of course. To wage battles of such harshness is to risk being hardened and insensitized and morally blinded. He who would seek to resolve it constructively, as Fidel Castro has stressed, cannot ever allow himself to fall into the trap of believing that he is the exclusive guardian of truth, or that he and his kind have any special right to the fruits of victory, when or if they should come. Part of the essential difficulty of the task is to keep oneself open to criticism and to the awareness of one's own partial grasp of reality, in the knowledge that no one *possesses* truth, since it is always changing, and being changed, by history, by time, by events, by all the complex interactive elements that are at work upon reality. Which means that there *is* no final resolution to the task of building a society; that the struggle for creative equilibrium and fulfilment that we aim towards (defined as it is by the conflicts of man within himself and within society) can never be complete; and that all absolutist systems of social order, seeking to impose inflexible laws, the domination over men of all the forces and powers they themselves have created, set up barriers destructive to the non-conformist actualities of the human process, and therefore have to be actively and critically resisted. The nature and the magnitude, for instance, of Stalin's betrayal of the Revolution demonstrate unequivocally enough the dangers of absolutism, and no more convincing proof of this is to be found in the record of twentieth-century history than the spectacle of the Moscow trials of the mid-thirties – a spectacle 'so hallucinatory in its masochism and sadism that it seemed to surpass human imagination'.[39] It was indeed in the midst of these trials (May 1937) that Trotsky published his classical indictment of Stalinist bureaucracy, *The Revolution Betrayed*, with Radek, Pyatakov, Sokolnikov, Zinoviev and Kamenev already sentenced, and the execution of Tukhachevsky and the other generals, together with a great many officers of the Red Army, about to be carried out. The terrifying evidence of what can happen to man if he puts his faith in an abstract ideology and bows before its dogma was there for all to draw conclusions from; and none drew conclusions with more penetrating bitterness than Trotsky, one of the two greatest architects of the Revolution, in the objective but impotent protest of his book. For it was total, and it was unanswerable, in its contempt not only for human life but also for all concern for truth or for principle. How, Trotsky asked, could *any* concept of communism be built out of such an abominable tide of lies?

The process of extermination took place in all ideological spheres, and it took place the more decisively because it was more than half unconscious. The present ruling stratum considers itself called upon not only to control spiritual creation politically, but also to prescribe its roads of development. The method of command-without-appeal extends in like measure to the concentration camps, to scientific agriculture, and to music. The central organ of the Party prints anonymous directive editorials having the character of military orders, in architecture, literature, dramatic art and the ballet, to say nothing of philosophy, natural science and history. The bureaucracy superstitiously fears whatever does not serve it directly, as well as whatever it does not understand.

All of which is 'the most disgusting inheritance from the old world. It will have to be broken into pieces and burned at a public bonfire before we can speak of socialism without a blush of shame'.[40]

The enormity of the inhumanity of this betrayal is cruelly reflected in the words that echo back at us from a pamphlet Trotsky wrote in 1904, when he was still in the process of thinking his way through the great theoretical and practical issues that confronted the revolutionary leaders at the time. Referring to the 'foredoomed Utopia' of Jacobinism, he says: 'The counterpart to their absolute faith in a metaphysical idea was their absolute distrust of living people.' And that, it seems, is the difference between the revolutionary socialist and the Jacobin. 'They were Utopians; we aspire to express the objective trend. They were idealists . . . we are materialists . . . They were rationalists, we are dialecticians . . . *They chopped off heads, we enlighten them with class consciousness*'! And, defining his grounds for the running dispute he was engaged in at the time with Lenin's rigorous and uncompromising authority over the question of the policies and aims of the Russian Social-Democratic Workers' Party, which led to the split between the Bolsheviks and the Mensheviks, he had these ominous remarks to make: 'Lenin's methods lead to this: the party organization at first substitutes itself for the party as a whole; the central committee substitutes itself for the organization;

and finally a single "dictator" substitutes himself for the central committee." '[41] It was a devastating prognosis, though no one then was in any position to appreciate the tragic stress it was later to take, with Trotsky himself as an impotent witness, and Lenin mercifully dead. The man who wrote these words, ruthlessly isolated and deprived of power by the actions of the man who made himself the Lord of All the Russias, found himself 'reduced to interpreting events and trying to foresee their future course', as he puts it in his diary. Not that he was 'for a moment free to withdraw from his ceaseless and ferocious duel with Stalin. His past drove him to action as pitilessly as it cut him off from the prospect of action.'[42] In Trotsky's fate – and continually in the heroic losing battle he waged for the future of Russia – as in the terrible fate of so many of his revolutionary colleagues, are focused the tragedy of the Revolution, the triumph of Stalinism and Nazism, the stultification of reason, the defeat of sanity. What had happened, Trotsky asked, to 'the political conscience and understanding of the great mass of communists? . . . Was there no spark of intelligence, of international solidarity and of responsibility left' among the communist parties of the world? After Hitler's triumph in Germany, the answer was starkly apparent. Not only had Stalinism 'irretrievably debased the entire communist movement';[43] the world itself had surrendered its will to the rule of barbarism and madness, the rampant absolutism of the diseased mind, the spell of the monster in the blood. For this was the era of the monolithic lie, the dog returning to its vomit, schizophrenia incarnate in the very concept of the state, the hypnosis of the tribe. And there was nothing that could halt its nightmare domination of the psychic powers of man but carnage and catastrophe. What Trotsky saw inexorably emerging out of the struggle for the future was what he himself (as he knew) had helped unleash. Not that such knowledge, or even the invidiousness of his position as a hunted exile, in any sense discouraged him. Trotsky's will to fight, his courage, his energy, the revolutionary intensity of his thinking, had been forged and sharpened in the great years with Lenin. He was a Marxist, after all. As he writes in his diary on the eve of 1937: 'This was Cain's year' – the year of the murdered brothers. But Trotsky wrote this on his way to Mexico. *He* had escaped; and (history having spared him) he was not to be stopped from speaking out for what had been betrayed, even in the atmosphere of panic and terror that had seized the world. In fact nothing could stop him short of what actually did – butchered into silence in a manner entirely appropriate to the methods of his enemy. This, as Victor Serge observes in melancholy acknowledgement, was 'just the hour for the Old Man to die', this 'blackest hour for the working classes'.[44]

It would be tempting to compare the position of Trotsky the exile, the Marxist critic of his world, with that of Marx himself; for both stood out as inveterate opponents of the irrational systems that prevailed in their time, and both were forced by the nature of their activities to leave their countries and continue their work abroad. Whether Trotsky was the equal of Marx as an intellectual, as a thinker, one might well have cause to doubt – for Trotsky wrote no *Capital* to set beside the original. But then he did not need to. His task, as a Marxist, was different – to extend and to clarify, to spell out; and above all to act, to embody. And from the moment Stalin declared himself, Trotsky became the great defender of the spirit of the Revolution, even as he had proved himself one of its great makers. One wonders how Marx would have coped had *he* had to face the immensely more difficult tasks that Trotsky, embodying the Marxist process, had to face; or how he would have reacted as an observer – whether he would have criticized Trotsky for his volatile temperament, as Lenin did, and what he would have said about Trotsky's failure to command the situation after Lenin's death. It is difficult, at any rate, to think of him as an apologist for the bureaucratic dictatorship of Soviet Russia, and inconceivable that he would have accepted any such concept as Stalin's 'socialism in one country'. On this last crucial point, as on many of the most basic issues of theory and practice, he would surely have confirmed, in Trotsky's reponse and in the uncompromising nature of his opposition to Stalin, that this was what had to be done. He would certainly have subjected Stalinism to an analysis as devastating and as condemnatory as that with which he startled capitalist Europe from 1847 onward, and have countered Stalin's cynical and terrorist destruction of the International by re-grouping it afresh, as Trotsky did, in order to regenerate and revitalize the European parties in their struggle against the enemies that surrounded them on every side. One cannot see Marx tolerating for one moment the stultifying and murderous tyranny of Stalin's policies towards the communist

parties in Germany in 1932 and 1933 and the Spain of the Civil
War, which helped to assure the victory of fascism. One sees him
acting, in fact, as Trotsky acted – directing his unrivalled dialectic
skills with unremitting energy and intensity to the task of agitating
and awakening people to the terrible threats that faced them from
these hypnotic killers of the will who had seized control of things.
He would have struck unerringly (if perhaps with as little success
as Trotsky) at the cynicism and hypocrisy of these perverted
dogmas founded on his name wherever such dogmas had assumed
jurisdiction over the destinies of human lives. It is even conceivable
that he would have radically re-examined (in the spirit of his 1872
preface to the Communist Manifesto, written in the wake of the
Paris Commune) his own intellectual premisses in the light of such
perversions. As a builder of bridges in a fractured world, seeking
the unifying conditions that would create 'a community of men
that can fulfil their highest needs',[45] he would have been as
disgusted by the depravities of Stalin as by those of Hitler and the
culpable pusillanimity of the West; and condemned them unequivocally. Those forms of state capitalism, of bureaucratic tyranny,
of 'social fascism', that emerged in Russia in the thirties to trample
contemptuously underfoot the legitimate aspirations of the Russian people, would have seemed to him an abhorrent nightmare
degradation of his aims. For, in his view, 'communism deprives
no man of the power to appropriate the products of society; all it
does is to deprive him of *the power to subjugate the labour of others
by means of such appropriation*'.[46] And if, for him, 'the proletarians
have nothing to lose but their chains', and a world to win,[47] the
question is whether they have won, or are winning, that world in
Russia; whether in losing the chains that bound them to Tsarist
despotism, they did not find themselves as cruelly bound to
others. The question is whether you can *ever* win a world of
'freedom' for the people if you have to suppress and kill great
numbers of the people to do so. Is the subjugation of millions and
the murderous repression of millions in *any* sense the kind of price
that could possibly win such a world? Can the power to subjugate
the labour of others become a blatant general tool to be used to
deprive man of the power to subjugate the labour of others?

Marx had never considered it possible for Russia to become the
first builder of a communist state. It was economically too
backward. The despotism of the Tsars had retarded the develop-

ment of those conditions which, in Western Europe, had brought into being a powerful middle class ready to exploit the potentialities of the Industrial Revolution, and as a consequence a growing and strengthening proletariat which could organize itself for power. There was a great vacuum in the middle, between the autocratic rulers and the peasantry. Thus, for Marx, the fundamental contradictions conducive to the growth of communism were lacking. It is hardly surprising, then, that in Marxian terms, the Revolution should have gone so disastrously wrong; that the Russian people should have had to suffer such intolerable convulsions, such outbursts of genocidal fury, or should have had imposed upon them a machinery of such monolithic power, dictating with the force and inflexibility of a steamroller the 'union and agreement of the democratic parties of all countries'.[48] The monstrous superstructure of Stalinist rule, imposed from above in the spirit of Tsarist despotism, seemed to be intent upon crushing beneath it everything that questioned it in a 'universal exploitation of communal human nature',[49] thus transforming the Marxian aim – that association in which 'the free development of each is the condition for the free development of all' – into a nightmare travesty of what it is supposed to signify.

Of course, the blunt facts of twentieth-century history have gone against Marx's theory that the grounds for communism and for the triumph of the proletariat would be created from the contradictions of capitalist development in the advanced industrialized countries. As Wilhem Reich pointed out, as early as 1933:

The political events in the various countries of the world during the past thirty years have clearly shown that revolutionary revolts take place more readily in industrially undeveloped countries, such as China, Mexico and India, than in countries such as England, America and Germany. And this is the case, notwithstanding the existence of disciplined, well-organized workers' movements rooted in old traditions in the latter countries. If bureaucratization, which is itself a pathological symptom, is abstracted from the workers' movement, the question arises as to the exceptional entrenchment of conservatism in Social Democracy and in the trade unions in Western countries. From the standpoint of the psychology of the masses, Social Democracy is based on the conservative structures of its followers . . . [And] the strength of the Social Democracies during the crisis years shows just how completely the workers had been infected with this conservatism.[50]

For Reich, the phenomenon of the triumph of fascism in the Western democracies was connected with the failure of the revolutionary Left to recognize the psychological issues that dominated the social environment of the working classes. The struggle for social progress could not, that is, be resolved by simply appealing to people in economic or political terms. And in his view this failure to get at the roots of things, to grasp their contradictory operation, and thus to overcome political reaction, was characteristic not only of the Western democracies, with their ingrained conservatism so closely allied to fascism, but also of Soviet Russia, where Marxism had 'degenerated to hollow formulas and lost its scientific revolutionary potency in the hands of Marxist politicians', to create 'a rigid state capitalism in the strict Marxian sense of the word'.[51] A socialist society was a society of which one could speak in *real* terms of 'the socialization of the means of production'. But 'in Soviet Russia the social industries are certainly not managed by the people who work in them, but by groups of state functionaries'; and there can be no prospect of this situation being changed 'until the masses of working humanity have become structurally mature, i.e. conscious of their responsibility to manage them'.[52]

But Stalin had forged a weapon of dictatorship in the name of communism that, far from encouraging responsibility among the masses, made them into the helpless subservient instruments of a terrorist policy of state tyranny more absolutist and more stultifying and far more culpable because of what it preached – in *spite* of its success – than what it had swept away. This Trotsky made super-human but unavailing efforts to check, calling upon the communist world at large to stir itself from its paralysis and organize against such strangulation. He did so unflinchingly, in face of a constant stream of abuse, vilified as an enemy, as the accomplice of Hitler and ringleader of a gang of terrorists, by a man who was slaughtering his opponents wholesale both inside and outside Russia. And Marx would certainly have done the same. It was a hopeless task, of course, in the short run; for by 1936 Stalin was in complete control, and Trotsky an outlaw, unable even to defend himself. But it was a task that had to be fulfilled and pursued to the bitterest end, for the sake of the future, even though it should end in personal defeat and oblivion.

It is in this context, against the knowledge of the monstrous aberrations, the inhuman cynicism and hypocrisy issuing from the application of ideological principles aimed at eradicating all such cankers, that the radical socialist must think his way forward. He cannot afford to ignore the terrible proofs he has been given of what intolerant theory can do to people. Stalin put paid for good to the myth that villainy, corruption and inhumanity are all on one side; that the only imperialist enemy is the quixotic villain of the bourgeois West created by the rule of property and money. For the revolutionary creed pledged to the overthrow of capitalism and the creation in its place of a new and rational society shaped for people has proved in its embodiment equally villainous, corrupt and inhuman, and equally imperialistic. It has become, in the articulation of the Stalinist state, a new enemy, a new conservatism, an orthodoxy, a Church for the faith, a retrogressive power. Not that this need discourage those who seek the creation of a genuinely rational community, a social order fit for people to live in terms of; but only that they must always beware of the lure of mythologies and false illusions, the mystifying vision of that class of men who see themselves as the priests of the political order. As Kolakowski has pointed out: 'The priest is the guardian of the absolute; he sustains the cult of the final and the obvious as acknowledged by and contained in tradition.'[53] He is the authoritarian minister dispensing abstruse dogma to lesser beings, backed up by a 'dictatorship of doctrinaire schemes in intellectual life, the dictatorship of the police in public life, and military dictatorship in economic life'.[54] The socialist, on the contrary, works critically and democratically to build a community of shared responsibilities and shared pleasures, the duties and delights of equals. His dilemma may be defined by the problem of how far one can 'push the demand for tolerance without turning against the idea of tolerance itself', of how to 'guarantee that tolerance will not lead to the victory of forces that will strangle the principle of tolerance'.[55] And in this spirit he will need to be vigilant against all absolutes, 'for a vision of the world that offers us the burden of reconciling in our social behaviour those opposites that are the most difficult to combine: goodness without universal indulgence, courage without fanaticism, intelligence without discouragement, and hope without blindness'.[56]

What he will need, in other words, is conviction with scepticism, reason and imagination, a passionate questing view of reality, a refusal to be taken in by the fervour of the visionary, and above all a clear understanding, always, of the Marxian principle that *man* is the basis of society – even in the context of the fact that Marx went far beyond this in determining that it was the economic conditions that determined 'the general character of the social, political and spiritual processes of life',[57] and therefore man's capacity to create community. For it is man who remains (potentially at least) the motivator and the essence behind the political, social and economic mechanisms that determine the character and the shape of his life; and thus the agent of transformation, the source of energy that breaks the conditioning husk, the chains that bind. And here the all-important question, for the individual as for the community at large, is how to create the kind of social order that can achieve this transformation – that will serve the needs and aspirations of ordinary people (often so ill-equipped) both as a quickening incentive to emancipation and as a protection against those who, for their own irrational ends, would seek to keep people ignorant and in thrall. To this end, Marxian methods are indispensable; not part of 'a doctrine that must be accepted or rejected as a whole', a set of dogmatic principles for the worshipper; but as

a vital philosophical inspiration affecting our whole outlook on the world, a constant stimulus to the social intelligence and social memory of mankind. It owes its permanent validity to the new and invaluable points of view it opened before our eyes, enabling us to look at human affairs through the prism of universal history; to see, on the one hand, how man in society is formed by the struggle against nature and, on the other hand, the simultaneous process by which man's work humanizes nature; to consider thinking as a product of practical activity; to unmask myths of consciousness as resulting from ever-recurring alienations in social existence and to trace them back to their real sources. These perspectives enable us, furthermore, to analyse social life in its incessant conflicts and struggles which, through countless multitudes of individual goals and desires, individual sufferings and disappointments, individual defeats and victories, together compose a picture of uniform evolution that – we have every right to believe – signifies on the grand stage of history, not retrogression but progress.[58]

Part Two

'Only through the objective unfolded wealth of human nature can the wealth of subjective human sensitivity – a musical ear, an eye for the beauty of form, in short, senses capable of human gratification – be either cultivated or created.'

Karl Marx,
Economic and Philosophical Manuscripts

4

DISLOCATION AND DESPAIR:
ELIOT'S VIEW OF HISTORY

After such knowledge, what forgiveness? Think now
History has many cunning passages, contrived corridors
And issues, deceives with whispering ambitions,
Guides us by vanities. Think now
She gives when our attention is distracted
And what she gives, gives with such supple confusions
That the giving famishes the craving. Gives too late
What's not believed in, or if still believed,
In memory only, reconsidered passion. Gives too soon
Into weak hands, what's thought can be dispensed with
Till the refusal propagates a fear. Think
Neither fear nor courage saves us. Unnatural vices
Are fathered by our heroism. Virtues
Are forced upon us by our impudent crimes.[1]

The view of history defined by T. S. Eliot in these fourteen
lines from his dramatic monologue *Gerontion* is not to be judged
by the objective rational standards of the historian. It reflects a
psychological, subjective, emotional response to a deranged world,
the despair of a man – 'an old man in a dry month' incapacitated
by some sort of psychic disaster – whose belief in the very *concept*
of history as a record of the civilizing human process has been
shattered. For of course, on one level, the poem is a response to
the trauma of war. 'After such knowledge, what forgiveness?'
Gerontion cries – to which there can be no rational answer. Set
apart, an alienated and impotent spectator, by-passed by the
positives of life, this man waits without hope, or almost without
hope, for release from the torment of nothingness he feels. In his
crippled view of things, the future is no more than an empty
dream and the struggle for the great aims and ends of life a derisive
echo of the past, because for him the real world of people's lived

and living histories has receded to a shadowy vaporous abstract. Lost in the 'dark wood' of the psyche in the aftermath of a private catastrophe – 'I that was near your heart was removed there-from/To lose beauty in terror, terror in inquisition' – he is unable to find any answering affirmative in his contact with the outer world that will give him the confidence or the will to stir himself from apathy and seek the way out.

> I have lost my passion: why should I need to keep it
> Since what is kept must be adulterated?
> I have lost my sight, smell, hearing, taste and touch:
> How should I use them for your closer contact?[1]

Nothing is left to such a man, it seems – possessed, like the Gerontius of Cardinal Newman's poem, by a sense of 'ruin which is worse than pain . . . a masterful negation and collapse'[2] – but withdrawal, resignation, surrender, renunciation, the death of the body –

> An old man driven by the Trades
> To a sleepy corner.

Whether he is ever to experience the mystical transformation that is the theme of Newman's poem, he is at any rate too far gone ever to be part again of the world where histories are made and the struggle for life continues, as it does and as it must, in both the subjective and the objective sense, beyond ruin, beyond loss, beyond adulteration. He has sunk too deep into the labyrinth of disabled being, 'drunk among whispers', to be of any use to others. All he can hope for, as Eliot implies, is some form of salvation from the world beyond this world: but here, while he lives, he is doomed to endure a lingering sense of the nothingness of being, of emotional death.

This nightmare glimpse of catastrophe, of a man trapped with the wreckage of his life in a limbo of vacancy, of desiccated feeling, has its own strange fascination as a case-history of breakdown. It is symbolic in the general sense of the breakdown of European civilization in the aftermath of the 1914 war, and in particular terms of what can only be described as a condition of violent primary shock. But since the voice that speaks is the voice of a sensibility crippled by disaster, of a man who has no ghosts, it can have little to say to those who live beyond disaster in the world of human events and actions, of history in the making, where people are engaged (with other people and their living needs) in the necessary struggle for solvency and survival and community. It might serve perhaps as a warning against surrendering to the aberrations and neuroses of subjective being. But what can these 'thoughts of a dry brain in a dry season', this 'chilled delirium', have to offer as an incentive to the living? That way leads, however imperceptibly, to dislocation, breakdown, subsidence, apathy, oblivion, a living death. And the living are concerned with the living, and the continuity of history as a record of the aspirations and the aberrations of man.

In which sense, however deceptive and confusing, history becomes a means by which to replenish and to renew; and as embodied memory it gives perspective and context to the world we live in and to our understanding of the nature of our *place* in that world. For even by the ways in which it extends and sharpens our awareness of the actualities of the past, so it extends and sharpens our awareness of ourselves and of our futured present. Indeed, in the strict sense, 'all history,' as John Berger writers in *G*,

is contemporary history: not in the ordinary sense of the word, where contemporary history means the history of the comparatively recent past, but in the strict sense: the consciousness of one's own activity as one actually performs it. History is thus the self-knowledge of the living mind. For even when the events which the historian studies are events that happened in the distant past, the condition of their being historically known is that they should vibrate in the historian's mind.[3]

This is what one may define as a constructive, exploratory view of history – history as discovery, as the living moment rediscovered or the lived moment recovered in the present, re-enacted in the historian's mind.[4] It is at the opposite pole to the view defined in *Gerontion*: history as a form of derangement, as knowledge dislocated. But then in *Gerontion* Eliot is already on his way to shaping for himself 'that negating path to God which is one of the classic forms of religious mysticism . . . to seek the absolute through guilt, sin, and despair'.[5] And this is not the path that history takes. History is a process whose function is to penetrate the opaque disordering surface of the world in action, its bewildering complexities, the hard skins that form upon that surface by an accumulation of undifferentiated facts, in an attempt to grasp the relevance, the logic, the underlying pattern and the actuality of events. And one thing is certain: that we cannot get at the pattern by abstracting ourselves from the historical process, or (as Eliot has done) by attempting to 'fix the religious sentiment as something by itself and to presuppose an abstract, isolated human individual'; which is what his renunciatory view of reality postulates – an individual who, in search of God, is thus essentially isolated not only from the historical process but also from the conditions and complexities of the world he actually inhabits.

But how do we keep ourselves open to the influence of this process and the things it has to teach us? How do we defend ourselves against confusions that deceive and alienate? No doubt first of all by adopting, if we can, a cool and rational attitude towards the outer world; by constructing for ourselves an intellectual framework which will permit us freely to observe and to record the complex interplay of the forces and impulses at work around us; by keeping a sceptical and distanced eye upon the unfolding pattern as it changes and develops; by refusing to make facile judgements upon the continuing questions and dilemmas that confront us, and resisting the temptation to build around our fundamental predilections a fortress of dogmatic opinion. But most of all by never losing sight of the fact that it is people who make history – people not as abstractions but as real, living, particular individuals, and the impersonal forces of action and reaction they generate; that history is a record of the contradictory proofs of man's struggle for equilibrium and sanity. All the higher aims of civilization, one must be continually stressing, have their origin not in ideas or in abstract principles but in the existence of the individual himself, of which even the most elevated institution is but a sophisticated manifestation.

Thus, to abstract from the historical process is to abstract from its essence, and by doing so to betray that essence. When, for a man like Eliot, the world is made to seem devoid of meaning; when, as his despair defines it, differences are eroded, polarities dissolve, and the 'supernal life', ineffable and outside time, becomes the one sure refuge for the self, one might well sympathize with the dilemma of the man as a perplexed individual fighting for survival, but one has to recognize that his attempt to resolve for himself the problems of living in the world are unlikely to be of much benefit to those who are trying to face up to the threat and the challenge of reality and to come to terms with the conditions that determine their existence. And when, in the same spirit, and as a man of influence and authority, Eliot takes it upon himself to conclude 'that whatever reform or revolution we carry out, the result will always be a sordid travesty of what human society should be',[6] one is no more encouraged to believe that he has any solutions to offer the oppressed peoples of the world that might serve to answer their urgent social needs. For *his* solution is to exhort us all to 'become Christians' and to revert to the questionable standards defined by the Christianity of Europe, thus inviting us to continue to submit to the oppressive institutions of the past. One wonders indeed whether he has anything to say to his world and its needs that is not coloured by the bitterness and the ache of his own sense of alienation and disillusionment. 'We are the hollow men,' he writes in the anguish of shocked dismay at the horror and the hypocrisy of the Western democracies in action. 'We are the stuffed men . . .':

> Shape without form, shade without colour,
> Paralysed force, gesture without motion.[7]

It is an indictment, this vision of the 'dead land', the 'cactus land', where

> Lips that would kiss
> Form prayers to broken stone.

It is a vision of a bankrupt world, which holds out no hope except for that of 'death's twilight kingdom'. As Eliot sees it in the despair of his yearning for a smashed past, it is an indictment of the world of post-war Europe, collapsed, subsiding; of the bankrupt irrationalities of the imperialist West, whose institutions and élitist orders had dragged humanity into the obscene mockery of the war. But registering its horror – 'In this valley of dying stars /In this hollow valley /This broken jaw of our lost kingdom' – is this all life has to offer? The epigraph to *The Hollow Men*, from Conrad's novel *Heart of Darkness*,[8] refers to the white man's murderous exploitation of the Congo, the expansion of a capitalist Christian culture in its most degrading form. In other words, the poem seems a bleak refutation of the civilization that permitted and condoned such enormities. But to what end? Is there any

escape from the trap of that civilization and its bankrupt hypocrisies? Not apparently by seeking answers in the historical struggle,
the human struggle for renewal. For if the poem refutes the
literalist materialism attacked in *The Wastle Land*, it makes its
implicit appeal to what Eliot later (in *Ash-Wednesday* and elsewhere) prescribes as his answer to the evils of his time: a return to
the discipline and the authority of a static and absolute order,
submission to a state of being in which 'the lost heart stiffens and
rejoices', where, in 'the Garden/Where all love ends', we shall
'have our inheritance'.[9] But this submission, in concrete social
terms, is a submission to the institution of the Church, which, as
the embodiment of spiritual power, was inseparable from the
hypocritical system that had imposed its imperialist policies upon
Africa, and by specious methods remote from the ethics of
Christianity, justified and stood behind those who had betrayed
into war the peoples of Europe.

Of course, the significance of Eliot's poetry is its embodiment
of the bankruptcy, the inhuman abstractness, the impotence and
dislocation of the civilization of his world – the world, that is, of
the cultivated élites who, controlling all the institutions and organs
of the state, legislated and manipulated the issues of his age. And
Eliot is a representative figure of his time – in the sense in which,
as he says, the great writer writes his time – to this extent at least:
that it forced him to write the way he did, or that its bankruptcy,
impotence and dislocation so deeply affected and disabled him
that it inevitably *became* his theme and his dilemma, and in the
end the trap from which he could only escape by some sort of
regressive retreat from life and the hurt it had caused him into the
fortress of Christian orthodoxy that was to colour and to determine
the drift of all his subsequent work.

But it is debatable whether he was a writer representative of the
larger, wider historical currents of his time. Against the context of
the revolutionary changes, the massive upheavals and contortions,
the complex record of the struggles of human beings in this
century – not only in resistance to evil but also in the selfless
pursuit of liberation and dignity, the emancipation of the
oppressed and the defenceless – he takes his place as the
representative of a restricted and disdainful élite. For Eliot is
among the cultivated few speaking to the cultivated few, lamenting
the past and prescribing a return to the values of the past, in spite

of the fact that history had exposed these values as destructive and thus unacceptable because utilized to the detriment of the health of the very structure of society itself.

The problem here – at least for those who have a grasp of historical perspective and of the potentialities of the present, and the struggle for the future – is not with Eliot's formal, innovatory, linguistic techniques, which are the manifest sign of his distinction as an artist, but with his attitudes, the content of his work, its regressive, renunciatory themes. Though Pound (and others) praised the work 'for its fine tone, its humanity, and its realism',[10] it is precisely on this level that it is most ambiguous, most open to criticism. Fine the tone may be in rhythmic, musical, aesthetic terms – and it is often very moving in the transparency and spareness of its verbal patterns and in its representation of religious despair and hope; but in terms of the vision of *humanity* it registers – its attitude towards people – and the realism it reflects, it is at once negative, disdainful and reactionary. For what it registers is the stages of the poet's personal retreat, his withdrawal, from participation in the crucial political and social issues of his time – even a refutation of the *validity* of these issues ('not here the darkness, in this twittering world');[11] and *with* that refutation an assertion of the essential isolation of the individual in 'the world of perpetual solitude', as a man 'alone with God'. It registers, in fact, a rejection of the struggle for community in the world of men as a sordid travesty. For him:

There is no help in parties, none in interests,
There is no help in those whose souls are choked and
     swaddled
In the old winding-sheets of place and power
Or the new winding-sheets of mass-made thought.

The only help, it seems, though it cannot be so in fact, is in God. Hence, the reality it reflects it turns against the world to reject and condemn reality, the objective reality of the external social order – envisaged as 'devising the perfect refrigerator', or 'working out a rational morality', or 'printing as many books as possible', or 'plotting happiness and flinging empty bottles', or turning from 'vacancy to fevered enthusiasm for nation or race or what you call humanity'.[12] The fine tone, that is, has a derisive edge to it that denies the achievements of humanity, presumably because (as Eliot clearly designates in *The Rock*) humanity appears to have denied God; and it is therefore both ungenerous and inhumane. It represents, moreover, a wildly irrational attack upon the social and historical concerns of humanity, even in the associations it sets up, by linking such things as refrigerators and rational morality, happiness and empty bottles, as if they were inherently connected, and thus implying the utter futility of all social activity. It may *be* that a fevered enthusiasm for 'what you call humanity' is deplorable, but the ungenerous assumption that people turn from *vacancy* to enthusiasm as if these were their only habitual states is even more to be deplored.

Views of this sort, rooted in distaste and mistrust of the mass of the people, reflect the assumptions of many Western intellectuals in the twenties and thirties – that 'the people, the mass, represented the principle of irrationality, of the merely instinctive, as opposed to the superior powers of reason'. With such a conception, the Western democracies undermined their strongest defence against the spread of fascist power, which was built upon a ruthless appeal to the irrational, the psychology of mass hysteria.[13] If the leaders of Britain and France had really wanted to unmask the hostility of fascism towards the people, they would have needed to concentrate on the fallaciousness and mendacity of this appeal, and used their power to protect and strengthen the creative energies of the people from its slanders. But by treating the common people with ill-disguised condescension and putting their trust in divisive and persistently devious policies, they only succeeded in weakening resistance to the irrational appeal of Nazism. According to Lewis Namier, it would appear that 'intellectuals who had seen themselves as the rational leaders of mankind . . . were to find that the disintegration of spiritual values . . . had released demonic forces beyond control by reason'.[14] But if this was so, the blame was not to be laid upon those who had spent their lives fighting for a world in which the rights and needs of the millions might be answered. It was so because too many of the so-called rational leaders of Europe – the Baldwins, the Chamberlains, the Hoares, the Lavals, the Daladiers – belonged to a hypocritical élite whose muddled thinking and fear of the Left gave support to specious and inhumane spiritual values – values that paid little more than lip service to the needs and rights of the millions. It was so, that is, because, whatever the intentions of these men, their policies at best failed to oppose and at worst condoned (and even secretly admired) the arrogant assertiveness of fascist power.

In such a context as this, the writer has a very special part to play, both intellectually and artistically, as a witness to the underlying human values of his time. Thus, in seeking to define the character of Eliot's work and the nature of its response to the objective historical concerns of the world it is part of, it is important for us to know where it stands and what it represents, who it speaks for, and why; because, in terms of the struggle for clarity and rationality against the forces of mystical irrationality that threatened Europe in the thirties, this matters crucially. As Georg Lukács has written: 'Talent and character may be innate; but the manner in which they develop, or fail to develop, depends on the writer's interaction with his environment, on his relationships with other human beings.'[15] And the manner in which Eliot's talent and character developed was clearly determined by, among other things, his consistent personal opposition to socialism, liberalism, democracy, and all the implications of 'the threat which mass society poses to the ruling élite'.[16] What one is concerned with here, as Lukács points out in his essay *Franz Kafka or Thomas Mann*, is not the 'directly political attitudes, but rather with the ideology underlying [the writer's] presentation of reality. The practical political conclusions drawn by the individual writer are of secondary interest. What matters is whether his view of the world, as expressed in his writings, connives at that modern nihilism from which both Fascism and Cold War ideology draw their strength.'[17]

On these terms at least, I do not think it can be denied that Eliot's view of the world – in its constant appeal to a regressive Christian orthodoxy, its metaphysical pursuit of a timeless condition of being which advocates escape from the determining condition of time, its rejection of the struggle for democracy and the aspirations of the masses, its refutation of the logic and justice of such a struggle in favour of the intangible mystical laws of God's logic and justice – does in fact encourage such connivance, even as it led him in the 1930s to fraternize in print, however ambiguously and diffidently, with the ideas (if not the politics) of fascism.

The point is that Eliot, having early suffered some kind of

profound psychological disorientation, of personal disablement –
brought about perhaps by the alienating inhibiting pressures of
the world he grew up in – writes from the very beginning in terms
of damage and of loss and deepening despair, as a man for whom
the things of this world seem increasingly futile and meaningless.
Even in *Prufrock*, for instance, a deep sense of weariness and of
negation prevails. 'I should,' Prufrock says, 'have been a pair of
ragged claws /Scuttling across the floors of silent seas.'[18] And
with the shock of the War, this condition is at its most extreme:
'I can connect /Nothing with nothing. /The broken fingernails of
dirty hands';[19] for *The Waste Land* creates that vision of disaster
and of breakdown from which no escape seems possible except
perhaps into the remote promise of the words from the Upanishads
at the end, and the fragments from Isaiah, Dante, Arnaut Daniel,
the anonymous Latin, and de Nerval, which – suggesting the
disciplines of a lost order – point forward to a mystical 'other'
world beyond this world's perplexing waste.[20]

It is hardly surprising, therefore, that Eliot should have rejected
the influence of anything that hinted at a secular social ethic as a
solution to the problems of survival and of solvency. He had set
his course (or had had it set for him) in an opposite direction,
mystical, religious, which – finally crystallizing in his acceptance
of an institutional right-wing Christian orthodoxy – was to
determine the nature of his reaction to the fundamental issues of
social and ideological crisis. For him the future is 'a faded song',
'the way up is the way down, the way forward is the way back';[21]
and, sickened by the actual present, he turns away from it to a
contemplation of its metaphysical equivalent, the timeless moment
of death, the moment *between* time, 'at the still point of the
turning world'.[22] In the end, neither reason nor faith can reconcile
him to the rooted actualities of the human world. Here is a place
of disaffection . . . Tumid apathy with no concentration /Men and
bits of paper', the 'eructation of unhealthy souls /Into the faded
air, the torpid /Driven on the wind . . . in this twittering world'.[23]
Trapped in the seemingly insoluble contradictions posed for him
by his innate predilections, he sees everything reduced to a
condition of futility, distorted and distorting, for which the only
salvation appears to be his conception of a resolutely Christian
society. Or, to put it in other terms, salvation lies in the
metaphysical quest for God:

We must be still and still moving
Into another intensity
For a further union, a deeper communion
Through the dark cold and the empty desolation,
The wave cry, the wind cry, the vast waters
Of the petrel and the porpoise. In my end is my beginning.[24]

As a personal attempt to resolve a subjective dilemma, this is a moving and impressive utterance. And up to a point one can appreciate the force and drift of Eliot's argument for a Christian community. But the fact that he could have thought it even credible that a *merely* Christian society – least of all one organized on the hierarchic lines he prescribed – could answer the complex conflicting needs of the great mass of the peoples of the modern world, is a measure of his remoteness from and his inability to cope with, or even to envisage, the nature of the problems that are there to be dealt with.

It may be that for Eliot, writing about Baudelaire, 'the recognition of the reality of Sin is a New Life; and the possibility of damnation is so immense a relief in a world of electoral reform, plebiscites, sex reform and dress reform, that damnation itself is an immediate form of salvation – of salvation from the ennui of modern life, because it at last gives some significance to living'.[25] But what possible incentive or consolation could this give to anyone seeking positive conditions on which to build his life, and faced with the massive social injustices of the modern world, that condemn so many to a life of poverty and deprivation? Sin, it seems to me, is not the issue. The very perversity of the conjunction – of damnation as salvation, of damnation as release from the boredoms of reality – suggests a view of humanity similar to that which juxtaposes the 'plotting of happiness' with the 'throwing of empty bottles'. It expresses an ill-disguised contempt for the concerns and interests of ordinary people, and has nothing to contribute to the crucial issues of the human (that is, the extra-Christian) community but a gesture of weary dismissal. Indeed, on the subject of people's beliefs, Eliot is not inclined to flatter. In his Commentary to *Criterion* No. 12 (in April 1933) he turns his attention to communism and its appeal to 'those young people who would like to grow up and believe in something'. 'Stupidity,' he writes, 'is no doubt the best solution of the difficulty of thinking.' And, as if this were not condescending enough, he cannot resist adding that 'it is far better to be stupid in a faith, even in a stupid faith, than to be stupid and believe nothing . . . I would even say that, as it is the faith of the day, [!] there are only a small number of people living who have achieved the right not to be communists.'[26]

The tone is unmistakably contemptuous, the attitude austerely superior, the mood one of impotent irritation, 'paralysed force'. The despicable majority seems, at any rate, to belong to an order of being incapable of intelligence, and if capable of faith (even of a stupid faith) more likely to commit some kind of unspeakable vulgarity. What is one to make of such an unpalatable and ungenerous view of humanity, so devoid of compassion or of common human feeling? Nothing *can* be made of it, for it offers no way forward towards any position – Christian or otherwise – that involves caring for people. It is too insensitive; and, in relegating people to some nether region one has no intention whatsoever of visiting, it deserves to be dismissed with indignation. Better on any count, however 'soiled by error', the unrepentant humanism of a Victor Serge. 'It is worse,' one recalls, 'to live for oneself, caught within traditions soiled by inhumanity.'[27] But Eliot's own answer, in *After Strange Gods*, is that 'in a society like ours, wormeaten with liberalism, the only thing possible for a man with strong convictions is to state his point of view and leave it at that'.[28]

The trouble is that people are rarely content to state their point of view and leave it at that. Nor will the dynamic changing structure of the human world and the essentially inquisitive nature of human responsiveness permit a point of view to be left at that. Life leaves nothing *at that*; and no man of responsibility can possibly proceed on the basis that the effect of what he says or does is not (partly at least) his responsibility. To 'leave it at that' is to abdicate responsibility, just as to profess to be 'interested in political ideas, but not in politics',[29] is to indicate some sort of congenital failure to see the connection (and the significance) between theory and practice. But such equivocation is deeply symptomatic of Eliot's habitual attitude towards the outer world. It is all of a piece with his plea for a contemplative, static, Christian concept of the social process – which, like Burke's, is anti-liberal, authoritarian, closed; and with his equivocal attraction towards fascism in the late twenties and early thirties. It represents a wilful reluctance to take a responsible position or to think ideas through to some constructive and positive conclusion, however unpopular. One may not find it palatable to hear him state: 'I confess to a preference for fascism in practice, which I dare say most of my readers share';[30] but such a confession seems at least to sound a note of conviction, even if it does presume too much from his readers. But what are we to make of it against his dismissal the year before (*Criterion* 8, 1928) of both fascism and communism, because they 'seem to me to have died as political ideas, in becoming political facts'?[31] Apparently, his preference for fascism in practice is a preference for dead political ideas; and there is little to be made of that sort of equation. It simply confirms the equivocal stance of the alienated conservative intelligentsia of Western democracy towards those barbaric defenders of privilege and power who were so soon to be dictating the rules and bullying Europe into pusillanimous retreat.

These enemies of reason built their triumphs upon the equivocal and the confused, in Abyssinia, Spain, the Rhineland, Austria, and at Munich. They knew what they wanted, and set out to achieve it. In face of *their* convictions it could never have been enough to state a point of view and leave it at that. But then few of Eliot's political and social views suggest that he was a man of strong conviction. Rather, they give the impression that he was possessed by a sense of weariness and distaste for the concerns of society. 'The world,' he writes in *Thoughts After Lambeth* in 1931, 'is trying the experiment of attempting to form a civilized but non-Christian mentality.' And at once comes the response, delivered with abrupt Olympian disdain, to a world no more than a quarter Christian: 'The experiment will fail.'[32] There is no equivocation, it seems, about this. It will fail, full stop. Eliot is clear. His mind is made up. It will be 'a sordid travesty of what a human society should be'.[33]

This last statement comes from Eliot's essay *The Idea of a Christian Society*, which, written eight years on from *Thoughts After Lambeth*, puts forward a more considered view of the place of Christianity in a non-Christian world. But still it is assumed that the only alternative to the 'regimentation and conformity' of a totalitarian democracy 'is a religious control and balance, that the only hopeful course for a society which would thrive and continue its creative activity in the arts of civilization, is to become Christian'. And this is the context in which he defines what he sees as 'the fundamental objection to fascist doctrine, the one which we conceal from ourselves because it might condemn ourselves as well . . . that it is pagan'. All other objections, whether 'in the political and economic sphere' or 'to the oppression and violence and cruelty' by which fascism had prospered, are apparently of secondary importance. The crucial fact for Eliot is that fascism rejects Christianity. But then he levels the same charge against the Western democracies. Having deceived ourselves, as he says, 'that *we* have a Christian civilization', we merely 'disguise the fact that our aims, like Germany's, are materialistic'. Which is as much as to say that there is no *fundamental* distinction to be made between fascist and non-fascist societies, and that the only hope for civilization from either (irrespective of their politics, since politics remains a subsidiary issue) is to become Christian – though this is a hope that Eliot seems to have little faith in, since he himself sets against it the perverse fact that 'in all civilized countries the masses of the people have become increasingly alienated from Christianity'.[34]

Not everyone, fortunately, thinks in such vague (and vaguely dislocated) terms. Fortunately, there are many who consider it necessary and desirable to attempt the experiment of forming 'a civilized but non-Christian mentality', and to do what they can to help it to succeed, whatever the odds, rather than dogmatically (or gloomily) to assume its failure. But then Eliot, by his own 'transcendent lassitude' as William Chace has written, 'is absorbed into a class of people that wills no change, sees all progess as hostile, and would return to a state of affairs (usually imaginary) in which the restless motion of men and of their minds towards greater awareness and liberation would be stilled. Thus the reactionary impulse, whether or not he so desires, everywhere guides his arguments to their final forbidding implications.'[35]

Of course, there is much more to Eliot than his negativity, disdain and gloom. With his innovatory skill as a poet (stylistically the most revolutionary poet of his time) he involved himself in the struggle as he knew it for solvency and equilibrium, and pursued it through public crisis and psychic disability with scrupulous concern for what he most believed in, even though his firmest convictions ran counter to the creative ideas and needs of his age.

One can only accept that he sincerely believed that to put himself on the side of the authoritarian institutions in the struggle against liberalism (let alone *socialism!*) was to plead for the ideas and needs his age required for its sanity and health. And if history has proved him wrong and his prescriptions misplaced, it may be that we have as much to learn from his example, and from the anguish of his attempt to understand the world he suffered, as from anyone.

It is pointless, at any rate, to wish that Eliot had been another *kind* of writer. He *was* what he was. He acted as he felt himself able to act. He wrote what he felt he had to write. And if we are aware of the inadequacies and defects of his response to the complex issues of the living world, we are at the same time poignantly aware of his dilemmas as a man who had had his path chosen for him – and nowhere more intensely than in the lucid embodiment of the quest for being and place, for reconciliation and redemption, for the 'impossible union' of love – itself unmoving – at the 'point of intersection of the timeless /With time', that marks the achievement of *The Four Quartets*.[36]

But ultimately the nature of one's response to a writer of Eliot's distinction depends upon the nature of one's response to the world, and the nature of one's convictions and beliefs concerning the functions of literature and the part it plays in the life of its time, the ways it reflects and registers the conditions and complexities of that life and the people – those 'older creatures and more real' – who are its essence. And it seems to me that, though Eliot's distinctive contribution to the life of his time – the contribution he makes with *The Four Quartets* and *The Waste Land* and certain of his critical writings – is not invalidated by the illiberal stance he took towards the outer world, it is lessened by this and by the psychic disaffection that colours it, his inability to respond to so much that is central to the continuing challenge of the present and the future, to the needs of the oppressed millions, and to each one of those millions as a delicately organized, particular human being.

His contribution is lessened, one would stress, not invalidated. For of course Eliot is too important a poet to be ignored. As Leavis has observed:

The defeated genius *is* a genius, and the creative power is inseparable from the significance of the defeat. Eliot was a victim of our civilization.

We all suffer from the malady that afflicts it, and the power with which he makes us recognize the malady and feel it ('Cry what shall I cry?') for what it is, establishes him as a great poet of our time, one whose work has the closest relevance to our basic problems. This is not to say that his diagnosis, in so far as he offers one, is acceptable. But it is not to be dismissed as merely unacceptable.[37]

Indeed, it would be absurd and reactionary to do so; for the work compels attention, and has been given it in abundance. Nevertheless, Eliot's 'recoil from human responsibility', his negative concept of time and change, his denial of history as a rational process, and of the struggle for creative continuity and community, the social actualities that surround him, and his substitution of religious idealism for the proofs of historical progress, represent a divisive and distorted vision of reality, a dislocation between personal subjective truth and the social contexts in which truth is rooted, or between the individual and his world, and thus an alienation from the concerns of human history and human relationship.

Eliot's work may be defined as the record of an attempt to work out his own salvation with diligence, to free himself from

> the final desolation
> Of solitude in the phantasmal world
> Of imagination, shuffling memories and desires,

as Sir Henry Harcourt-Reilly says in *The Cocktail Party*.[38] And in his quest for a pattern of values, a reconciliatory order that could make sense of a devastated world, it is hopelessness and despair, the sense of the nothingness to which he is reduced, paradoxically, that enable him to rejoice 'that things are as they are', 'having to construct something / Upon which to rejoice'. Thus, as he puts it in *Ash-Wednesday*, taking the step that is already implicit in *The Waste Land* and *The Hollow Men*:

> Because I do not hope to turn again
> Because I do not hope
> Because I do not hope to turn
> Desiring this man's gift and that man's scope
> I no longer strive to strive towards such things
> (Why should the agèd eagle stretch its wings?)
> Why should I mourn
> The vanished power of the usual reign?[39]

In this way he chooses, or seems to choose – dismissing (or seeming to dismiss) the vital proofs and the rooted conditions of the actual world of human aspirations ('the infirm glory of the positive hour') in favour of a mystical (and metaphysical) alternative, beyond hope. But in making that choice, or in having it made for him, Eliot's crippling experience (the air become 'thoroughly small and dry') places him (the alienated victim) on the side of the illiberal institutions above the world of common human interests and common human needs. And it is in this respect that his work has its gravest limitations. It speaks, that is, a language of disaffection, and holds too narrow a view of the richly varied patterns of human life to stand comparison with the work of the greatest writers – of writers such as Shakespeare, Tolstoy or Dickens, whose art stays close to, and draws its strength and resilience direct as it were from, the vital creative energies of the living world, and is not to be lured by dogmatic absolutes and abstracts into a betrayal of these life-enhancing actualities.

The distinctions one is here concerned to make are not with the purely aesthetic or the purely literary qualities of a man's work – for to deal with the purely aesthetic or the purely literary is to deal with falsifying abstracts – but, taking these as an integral part of the artistic process, with what that work has to say about the human situation, and the struggle of living people to achieve a tolerable life for themselves in a world which has for most of the history of the human race ignored the claims of all but the privileged. What is most important in a work of literature is its power to celebrate, to embody and to make us share, the pleasures and sufferings of men and women in the complex world that subsists around them. And the greater the work, the deeper its insight and its sensitivity, the less likely it is to lose touch with the primary sources or to betray them by making of an idea or a concept a thing superior to them.

This would seem an obvious point to make. But unfortunately the divorce of theory from practice, of form from content, of culture from its roots, of the aesthetic experience from what gives it substance, the machinery from what it is supposed to serve, society from people, the idea from the actuality, continues to infect, to damage and to endanger not only the organic integrity, the quality and coherence of the work of art, but also (and more destructively) the coherence and integrity of the structure of reality itself, the rational framework within which people live their lives. And therefore, obvious or not, it needs to be continually stressed. For the dislocating pressures of the modern world – of a world which has become increasingly abstract, uniform, technological – are such that, if we do not keep a constant and watchful eye upon the dangers that threaten us, we shall find ourselves effectively isolated, estranged (as Eliot was) from the objective driving forces of society. In fact, 'we are obliged,' as Kolakowski puts it in his essay *History and Hope*, 'to know everything that argues against us,'[40] and to adopt a rigorous scepticism as much to the bigotry of fact as to that of the dogmatist. But not only this. In a world that, for the artist, seems often to reduce itself to a hostile, inhuman chaos, distorted and distorting, it is essential, as a moral duty even, to be always seeking those links and connections, those rational binding principles, which encourage perspective and community, and which will enable a man, as an artist, in the words of Georg Lukács, 'to portray the present age truthfully without giving way to despair'.[41]

5

DICKENS:
THE INTUITIVE RADICAL

The work of Charles Dickens defines a view of mid-Victorian society which stands in the sharpest contrast to the prevailing values of the time, marked by the ruthless commercialism of the middle classes, their divisive manipulation of the institutions of society, their pretentiousness and hypocrisy in the pursuit of wealth. It thus differs fundamentally, both in its literary aims and its social implications, from the kind of view defined by Matthew Arnold in *Culture and Anarchy*, which argues the superiority of art and culture over the claims of political action – the 'rough and coarse actions going on around us'[1] – in the struggle for social justice, and urges undivided support for the 'sacred' framework of the established order against the needs of the common people. Dickens looks at his world not from the point of view of the ruling class or of some sort of intellectual élite, but as the people see it; and for him the tangible material realities of their lives and their intangible spiritual values are to be regarded not as opposites but as complements. He *begins* from the people and, with his richly imaginative powers of characterization, his intuitive and unarguable humanity, his feeling for the sufferings and pleasures of ordinary people under an oppressive system, he celebrates their particularity, their complex democratic presence in all its diversity. Arnold, on the contrary, begins with culture, and sets the spiritual *against* the material, thus reflecting the abstract divisive mentality of the ruling class itself. He sees the common people, the 'raw and uncultivated many', as anarchic and irresponsible, and a *threat* to 'culture', the 'singleminded pursuit of perfection'; and he looks upon the appalling problems of the time from a position at once aloof and abstract, even to the extent of separating culture from politics, and advocating the 'unflinching' repression of what he calls the anarchic masses in order to make society safe for the privileged in their pursuit of 'sweetness and light' and 'harmonious

perfection'.[2] His position is defined in terms of the idealist 'refusal
to recognize that spiritual values have a material basis', which, as
Arnold Kettle puts it, 'is in its various forms the mental sustenance
of class division'.[3]

Though Dickens is not entirely free of the alienating negatives
of class that disfigured his world, his awareness of the uglier
aspects of the capitalist system, sharpened by indignation and an
irrepressible sense of occasion, provides him with an endless
source of material for the ridicule and caricature on which his art
thrives and feeds so abundantly. Deeper than this, however, are
the joyousness and exuberance, the vitality and tenderness of his
art, springing from innate sympathy for the common people of
England – the poor, the propertyless, the downtrodden, the
unimportant, the raw and uncultivated – who are considered not
from the standpoint of superior middle-class virtue or in any spirit
of condescension, but from their own very real and essential sense
of place in a social system their humanity puts to shame. Dickens
is not to be described as a writer of the working class, or (in any
definable sense) even as a socialist writer, for he consistently
affirms his lower-middle-class origins; but he is very definitely a
radical – a writer who works from within, from below, from the
roots, rather than (in the Arnoldian sense) from above. Like the
ordinary working people who form the living substance of his
books, he has a great respect for material reality, and an ability,
as Kettle observes, 'to face, absorb and cope with a remarkably
wide area of reality', his art being 'deep because it is broad and
tough and balanced'.[4] He instinctively assumes 'man to be man,
and his relation to the world to be a human one', as Marx has it in
a commentary on Timon's great tirade against the power of
money; and on this assumption he knows that 'love can be
exchanged only for love, trust for trust, and so on'.[5] For Dickens,
as for Marx, this is a fundamental principle, and to break faith
with it by exalting anything above it is to break faith with life
itself. But Dickens is deeply conscious that his society *has* broken
faith with life by exalting the alien powers of property and of
wealth above the health and well-being and happiness of its
people, and thus betrayed humanity. As Shakespeare's Timon
confirms in his savage diatribe, cursing money as the principle
that has betrayed *him*: 'This yellow slave /Will knit and break
religions; bless th'accurst; /Make the hoar leprosy adored; place

thieves, /And give them title, knee, and approbation, /With senators on the bench', as 'the visible god /That solder'st close impossibilities, /And mak'st them kiss'.[6] So it becomes for Marx 'the universal means of separation and betrayal', creating those distinctions which divide people from each other, asserting the superiority of those who have it over those who do not, corrupting the very nature of the individual and communal life of man.[7] And so it is for Dickens, writing (in works like *Oliver Twist, Bleak House, Little Dorrit* and *Hard Times*) his indictment of a divisive social order that enshrines money and property and what the privileged few prefer to call enlightened self-interest as its central values. These books (and nowhere more profoundly than in *Bleak House*) make him a telling witness for the defence of the oppressed and a bearer of true consciousness and humane conscience against the rule of the 'whores of reason'.[8]

All his work, indeed, carries the seal of such a witness. He is acutely aware of the callousness, the brutality and injustice, the alienating disunity of his world. This does not prevent him from affirming the quality and the comic actuality of the lives of his characters; but it angers and saddens him. And though he cannot bring himself to take the ultimate step that leads to radical social *action*, he is often profoundly indignant and appalled at the barbarous inhumanity that surrounds him on every side, which he sees little hope of changing through parliamentary reform. And it is a fact that his feelings bring him very *close* to taking such a step, as *Hard Times* clearly demonstrates, though this novel also registers the manner in which he shies away from it.

In *Hard Times*, let us therefore affirm, his instinctive sympathy for the oppressed working class comes closest to being realized as an overt commitment to radical political change. For here the situation is at once uniquely and harshly an embodiment of the exploitation of the capitalist against the labourer, and all the elements of confrontation are present. Here Dickens is even prepared to risk the fictional structure of the book, reducing it to the furthest point conversant with the exploration of character for the sake of his political theme and the unequivocal indignation of its moral statement. It is pared down almost to its elements. It has little of the scope and range and richness of *Bleak House*, for instance – which, with its pervasive and devastating metaphorical power, attacks the very structure of society itself as a system of inexorable blind force in the fog and dust and confusion of which men and women (and children) are worn down, broken, crushed. But then it is a different *kind* of book; an attempt to resolve different kinds of problems. And though, for what he was after, density is here ruthlessly sacrificed, though Dickens denies himself the potentialities for psychological development contained in, say, the story of Louisa Bounderby's dilemma, his acute eye for detail remains undiminished, bringing into sharp relief the struggle between Bounderby and Blackpool, and providing a merciless picture of the life-negating ugliness of the town that blights Blackpool's life with the woman he loves and destroys him. True, Dickens makes Slackbridge, the strike leader, a mere grotesque, and maintains in the book the stand he took in the 1840s against the Chartists and gave embodiment to by writing of the Gordon riots in *Barnaby Rudge*. Clearly, too, the way he treats Blackpool as a mere victim of the system rather than a fighter indicates that he rejects the logic of organized action from the working class in defence of their rights. In other words, for all his sympathy, for all his instinctual understanding of the plight of the oppressed, Dickens never goes so far as to commit himself to their cause. His fear of the beast unleashed, his sense of the shock of Chartist agitation at Birmingham and Newport, and 'the atrocious designs to which these [Physical Force Chartists], beyond all question, willingly and easily subscribed', as he put it in 1848, remain with him. And it is this middle-class fear of upheaval, the manner in which he is ultimately conditioned to accept the settled order of his world, even in spite of his contempt for its oppressive institutions, which keeps him from identifying himself with the struggles of the working class. He is not prepared to risk 'the cause of rational liberty and freedom' to the unknown consequences of mass action; and to him not only Slackbridge but all agitators are, it seems, to be regarded 'as enemies of the common weal, and the worst foes of the common people'.[9]

Nevertheless – though *Hard Times* confirms this attitude – the story of the hounding of Stephen and the contrast between him and his enemies leaves us in no doubt whatever whose side he is on and how deeply his feelings are engaged. Not for him the abstract aestheticism of an Arnold, relegating the common people to the sidelines as 'irresponsible roughs' and wreckers indulging in their right to 'do as they liked'. He may have been contractictory in his attitudes and intellectually ill-equipped in the sense in which, as Chesterton writes, he was 'very largely what is called a self-made man; which means that he was taught, not by himself, but by other people; and by other people acting as they really act in the real world, not as they pose before pupils they are paid to teach'.[10] But these weaknesses are also one of the sources of his great strength. If he did not always see very clearly, in Angus Wilson's words, 'he saw very deeply into the world he lived in; perhaps indeed not clearly because so deeply';[11] and it is this depth of vision and of feeling that is the source of his unwavering respect for the common working people. Not that he despised intellect or reason – far from it. They were an indispensable complement to and an ultimate means of confirming his respect and his trust. But he did believe, and with overwhelming justification, that the theories and solutions of so-called intellectuals and acknowledged experts on matters concerning human beings were too often distorted or absurdly inapt because too clear, too abstract, too dismissive, too little concerned with the *actual* problems of *real* people – like Jo, Gridley, Little Nell and Blackpool, dispossessed in their inhuman world.

'I have great faith in the Poor,' he writes in 1844; 'to the best of my ability I always try to present them in a favourable light to the Rich; and I shall never cease to advocate their being made as happy and wise as the circus tamers of their condition in its utmost improvement, will admit of their becoming.'[12] This, we do not need to stress, is fundamental; and from it we recognize in Dickens a lover of humanity – a lover who also became a fighter after his own fashion, and a fighter for a creed. His creed was never revolutionary, never more than firmly reformist; but it was never abstract and never superior. It was the creed of a man who believed in the common people – convinced that they had the wisdom, energy and intelligence to better the community they belonged to. But this is a truth which the 'Indifferents and Incapables' of the governing classes either refused to accept or were incapable of rising to, and which Arnold and many other intellectuals and artists of the time, misled by their elevated conservative sentiments and fearful for their minority privileges, did their best to minimize. Arnold, indeed, saw the common people as crude, insensitive and violently anarchic, though on the whole they were nothing of the kind. He urged conscription and repression as the best methods of keeping them in their place and ensuring the safety of the state. To him it seemed no crime that they should be sent to the Crimea to learn a sense of public duty and discipline; whereas to Dickens the war itself was to come to seem an insult to the very *idea* of public duty and discipline, not only for the culpable inefficiency and muddle with which it was waged, but above all for the cruel indifference displayed by the authorities towards the sufferings of the soldiers. 'I have never doubted Lord Palmerston,' he wrote of one of its chief instigators, who was made Prime Minister in 1855 to ensure victory, 'to be the emptiest impostor and the most dangerous delusion ever known.'[13] It was a time of gloom and despondency, for Dickens believed that such leaders 'will never be wiser until they and the table and the lights and the money' – defining the nature of the parliamentary game they have been playing – 'are all overturned together'.[14]

He could put no faith in a system that had so mismanaged the affairs of the nation as to alienate and undermine the morale of the mass of its people. The manipulators of that system, the Circumnavigation Offices by which it was operated, were to become the target of his fiercest mockery in *Little Dorrit*. No, all his sympathy and depth of feeling were reserved for the victims, to whom he dedicated the resources of his art in an exposure of the unacceptable conditions of their crippled world. To him it was an outrage that their sufferings and their capacities should be so cruelly discounted and reduced to mere quantitative terms, as the dispensable machinery of profit and loss. To him

not all the calculations of the National Debt can tell me the capacity for good or evil, for love or hatred, for patriotism or discontent, for the decomposition of virtue into vice, or the reverse, at any single moment in the soul of one of these its quiet servants, with the composed faces and the regulated actions. There is no mystery in the [engine]; there is an unfathomable mystery in the meanest of [these people], for ever. Supposing we were to reverse our arithmetic for material objects, and to govern these our awful unknown quantities by other means?[15]

What Dickens had in mind with his 'other means' was not government by 'the best that has been thought and known in the world',[16] the exclusive theories of a few people with sufficient wealth and sufficient leisure and sufficient culture to ignore the less palatable conditions of their world, but the pursuit of equality and fraternity; not liberty on its own, which permitted a hundred thousand families the unlicensed right to command large incomes and the crippling labour of the millions, but a liberty based upon respect and social justice, and a full awareness of the rights of others. For him the ugliness and squalor, the intolerable suffering and the destitution, seemed a crime of unspeakable magnitude that struck at the very heart of the social order. And for him, it was the selfishness, ineptitude, greed and insensitivity, the hypocritical concept of virtue and probity, the contempt and indifference of the ruling classes, that had brought this criminal situation into being – thus creating a social order dangerously divided against itself, in which the market laws of wealth and property ensured the degradation and the impoverishment of whole classes of people.

There was no justifying such degradation. It was a crime against society, and above all against the innate potentialities of human beings. For there was an 'unfathomable mystery in the meanest of them', a richness and resource, an intelligence and a dignity, that even their poverty could not stifle, destructive and humiliating though it was. These working people were, in other words, as capable of the finer feelings as their delicately cultivated masters with their delicately cultivated superiority. Thus, even confronted by the crude incitements of the agitator Slackbridge:

That every man felt his condition to be, somehow or other, worse than it might be; that every man considered it incumbent on him to join the rest, towards the making of it better; that every man felt his only hope to be in allying himself to the comrades by whom he was surrounded; and that in this belief, right or wrong (unhappily wrong then), the whole of that crowd were gravely, deeply, faithfully in earnest; must have been as plain to anyone who chose to see what was there as the bare beams of the roof and the whitened brick walls. Nor could any such spectator fail to know in his own breast, that these men, through their very delusions, shared great qualities, susceptible of being turned to the happiest and best account; and that to pretend (on the strength of sweeping axioms, however cut and dried) that they went astray wholly without cause, and of their own irrational wills, was to pretend that there could be no smoke without fire, death without birth, harvest without seed, anything or everything produced from nothing.[17]

Dickens will not betray these people, will not let the arguments of their oppressors, or of those who would justify such arguments, take him in. He may compromise by painting Slackbridge black to allay the possible fears of his predominantly middle-class readers, but he will not leave them in the complacent illusion that their comforts are the just rewards of a Christian community. He will show them bleakly what they would prefer to forget, and have the courage to do so whether they like it or not. For he cannot put literature and morality into watertight compartments. Since literature is primarily concerned with people and the contexts of the social order that defines their lives, it has no choice but to concern itself with the crucial moral issues of that social order. And if it is to have any significance at all, it has to be prepared to take its stand in defence of the dignity and quality of human life and to be inveterately critical of all in the social life of its time that tends to threaten or to diminish man.

What so distinguishes the work of the later Dickens especially is that it does not hesitate to take its stand, and that it speaks with such inherent concern and compassion of the sufferings and aspirations of the common people. One is constantly aware, in this work, of 'a deeply felt need to go beyond the mere affirmation of existing conditions', as Georg Lukács writes of his great contemporaries Balzac and Tolstoy, 'to explore values not to be found in present society – values which come to be thought of, necessarily, as hidden in the future'.[18] Not that Dickens finds it possible in the end to affirm 'the utopian perspective' – for if he goes deep and ranges wide in his portrayal of the contradictions of his age, his last great works are darkened by a sense of the oppressive weight of the massive superstructures of society. But he does nevertheless build his world upon values that are essential to the survival of community – the intangible values of human relationship and human feeling, of love and friendship and sympathy, the 'holiness of the heart's affections'. And in spite of the squalid, demeaning conditions so many of his characters find themselves having to cope with, his innate humanity, his sense of the comic and the ludicrous, and his instinctive trust in the capacity of man to endure even the worst calamities, keep him from surrendering to that deadly pessimism which is the blight of the alienated middle-class intellectual.

Macaulay described *Hard Times* as the embodiment of a 'sullen socialism'.[19] But such a description is bound to sound strange to those who read the book with any sympathy or with an ear for its underlying tone and rhythm. It is a stark, unyielding book, perhaps; and there is little in it one could define in any systematic sense as socialism, which in fact had yet to become an articulate and organized movement among the people. But Dickens could not have been the novelist he was if it had not been for the influence upon him of the pressures of the working-class struggle and the Chartist movement that affirms its most revolutionary position; and in the 1850s and 1860s his novels clearly carry forward the spirit (if not the letter) of Chartism, 'and in some ways even deepen it and bring it nearer the spirit of socialism'.[20] For what Dickens affirms most deeply in *Hard Times* is his radical sense of the wisdom and the generosity, the openness and the 'safe solid sense' of the working man, and of the outrage committed against him by his so-called betters. He knew, as Stephen Blackpool knew, what needed to be done, even though he could not bring himself to spell it out in terms of necessary action; and in his dramatization of the pathos of Blackpool's case, he demonstrates the inadequacy of the things that were actually done; and nowhere in his work shall we find a more direct or more appealing declaration of what was wrong than Blackpool's naïve statement to Bounderby in Chapter Five of Part Two:

'Sir, I canna, wi' my little learning, an' my common way, tell the gennelmen what will better aw this . . . but I can tell him, what I know will never do't. The strong hand will never do't. Victory and triumph will never do't. Agreeing for to make one side unnat'rally awlus and for ever right, and t'oother side awlus and for ever wrong, will never do't. Nor yet lettin alone will never do't. Let thousands upon thousands alone, aw leading the like lives and aw faw'en into the like muddle, and they will be as one, and you will be as anoother, wi' a black impassable world betwixt yo, just as long or short a time as sitch-like misery can last. Not drawin nigh to fok wi' kindness and patience and cheery ways, that so draws nigh to one another in their money troubles, and so cherishes one another in their distresses wi' what they need themseln . . . will never do't till the sun turns t'ice. Most of aw, rating em as so much power, and reg'laten 'em as if they was figures in a soom, or machines: wi'out loves and likes, wi'out memories and inclinations, wi'out souls to weary and souls to hope – when aw goes quiet, draggen on wi' 'em as if they'd nowt of the kind, and when aw goes onquiet, reproaching 'em for their want of sitch humanly feelings in their dealings wi' yo – this will never do't, sir, till God's work is onmade.'[21]

This (for all its passive acceptance of the status quo) is a critical statement impassioned by the intensity of concrete feeling. It has the ring of authenticity about it because it seems to have been spoken from the depths of a man's lived experience. Blackpool's words, that is, are not a theoretical argument, the wisdom of a man detached from or superior to the misery they appeal on behalf of; but of a man stultified by that misery. They come unforced and confused out of the organic context of his world and are made vivid by his despair – the despair of a man who knows what suffering is and knows in his blood the wrongs are deep and real and shaming. 'Look,' he says, 'how we live, an' wheer we live, an' in what numbers, an' by what chances, and wi' what sameness; and look how the mills is awlus a goin, and how they never works us no nigher to onny dis'ant object – ceptin awlus, Death.' Stephen sees himself as a victim of this situation; and he appeals to Bounderby, as one of 'them as is put ower me, and ower aw the rest of us', to set it right.[22] But Bounderby is not interested in setting it right; he sees in Stephen nothing more than a trouble-maker. All he is interested in is utilizing his machinery (both people and machines) to produce its profits for the enrichment and the cultivation of the few. Thus this 'machinery' – which Arnold talks about as a threat to Culture in its encouragement of working-class unrest – is for Dickens a threat to *people*; and that defines the fundamental difference between two such opposite views. For Bounderby (and Arnold, strange as it may seem) are on the side of the institutionalizing establishment, and Dickens is on the side of the institutionalized (and dispossessed) working people – who are shut off on one side of 'a black impassable world', and regulated by the system just as if 'they was figures in a soom, or machines'.

Hard Times takes Dickens further and deeper in his confrontation with the harsh realities of his time than he had ever before been prepared to go, even to the point of sacrificing, as never before, his incomparable gift for the comic and the absurd. It is as if he had got so close as to expose the bony structures of his world, as if in fact he had got too close to see much else than its harshness and its ugliness. But the bony starkness of the book is powerful, primary. It brings sharply into focus the overriding issues Dickens himself found it necessary as a matter of common humanity and moral duty to wrestle with. For what it makes clear is that there are *no* issues – not even the issue of artistic autonomy – more important than the issues of social and political justice. In so far as these political and social issues crucially affect the quality of people's lives, they are *more* important than art, for indeed they are the conditioning context out of which art is shaped and upon which the health and quality of culture and civilization depend. It is, at any rate, clear that no novelist whose work is not centrally concerned with and constructed in the awareness of such issues is likely to have much that is significant to say about his world or the ways people live in it.

This is not to say that the writer has to make himself a propagandist or a didactic moralist. He may become both in the course of his attempt to understand the enigmas of reality. But whether he does or not – and the greater his creative gifts the more completely will he leave didacticism behind, as Dickens does in his greatest works and pre-eminently in *Bleak House* – he will always owe the perplexed and struggling world that is the material he draws upon his moral concern and responsibility. Indeed, the writer who ignores this concern and responsibility, or who confuses it, who isn't continually testing himself against it, is unlikely to be much more than a purveyor of ephemeral entertainment. And lacking such concern he must even find himself betraying the concreteness, the intimacy and potentiality of human feeling, and either becoming an instrument of the manipulative system, the machinery of delusion, or turning his back on it.

No serious artist can afford to turn his back on the great central issues of his world. For it is the manner of his response to these issues that will determine the quality of his work as a human statement. Formal and technical achievement cannot in themselves do this. It is what he has to say about the nature of the world he lives in and how he sees this world that matters. It may be that he will see this world and its organization as irrational, inhibiting, hypocritical, oppressive and stunting. And if he does so, he can have no choice but to resist the forms it takes and, in shaping his work, make it his concern to represent the struggle for another *kind* of world rather than take a neutral view of what he sees or withdraw into a crippled subjectivity which evades the issues, thus condoning the irrationality and the oppressiveness. It is to Goethe, Tolstoy, Balzac, Stendhal, Belli, Beethoven, Dickens, George Eliot, Thomas Mann, one looks for the affirmation of unstunted vision, for they see the world as it is and as it can be, in the universal and ultimately objective terms which define and give perspective to the deadly conflicts and collapses of the social struggle. They do not give in or turn aside in contempt or disgust or indifference. They do not separate art and reality. They confront, they stand up to, penetrate, attack, respond. They demonstrate, enact and absorb, what confronts them. And in looking closely at the characters they have created and the world they live in, they define the nature and the extent of their concern for these creatures, for the dilemmas they face and for the social forces that shape their lives.

As for those writers who postulate renunciation, personal withdrawal, the autonomy of privacy, an irrational subjectivity, a severance of the ties that link personal vision to the objective realities of society; who cry out for a non-existent unattainable reality which, because it is not there, contaminates and distorts the reality that is; and who in so doing set themselves above the struggles of real people in the real world – such writers are either themselves victims or supporters of the systems that enslave. 'The greatest poverty,' one might say, 'is not to live in a physical world'; to allow oneself to be seduced from attending to the problems of this physical world into pursuing a non-existent perfect other world which leads one to renunciation, mysticism or despair, or simply to a life separated from reality, spent in a vacuum of comfortable illusions.

There is of course another sense in which, for the writer, what does not *yet* exist is to be set against the actualities of the world as it is, and conceived as an essential creative counterpoint, an aim and a purpose to be fought for. There is, in other words, another *kind* of vision than that of either the realist or the escapist; that, seeing 'what lies beyond the immediate objective', 'demands a terminology which is not confined to the world of concrete actuality'.[23] This is not to be confused with the sort of vision that rejects or negates reality in favour of some dislocated fantasy world that makes up its own laws. The kind of vision I am thinking of here is that which has its highest manifestation perhaps in the last plays of Shakespeare, and particularly *The Tempest* – rooted in the actualities of time and history and change. It functions 'not in order to escape the exigencies of the depressing actuality, but in order to insist on a whole structure of values and perspectives that must emerge in the conscious mind in order to assert the inner truth of that actuality, and give man the knowledge of his own participation in the historical process which dissolves the actuality'.[24]

This kind of vision is not a negation of but an essential complement to the realist vision of a Dickens, for it adds depth and perspective and a context of expectation to the veracity, the concreteness and concern for quality so characteristic of Dickens. And it is in the work of William Morris, writing in the last decades of the nineteenth century, that it has its most committed and creative expression. For Morris was at once a realist and a socialist – an artist with a dialectic socialist view of history, who was able to grasp the necessary logic of connection between the actual situations of the life around him and the unrealized possibilities of social experience implicit in the concept of socialism. He took that logical step forward into active participation which Dickens was unable to take. For him, it was not enough to be a realist; realism on its own, in the world as he knew it, could lead *only* to despair. One had to look beyond the present, to 'the change beyond the change'.[25] And Morris saw it as his task to create a vision of reality that would take into account the disastrous alienation of man from the social and political conditions of his world and the contradictory nature of these conditions. As the old man Hammond puts it, looking back from the resolution of the twenty-first century in the dream world of *News From Nowhere*:

When the hope of realizing a communal condition of life for all men arose, quite late in the nineteenth century, the power of the middle classes, the then tyrants of society, was so enormous and crushing, that to almost all men, even those who had, you may say despite themselves, despite their reason and judgement, conceived such hopes, it seemed a dream. So much was this the case that some of those more enlightened men who were then called Socialists, although they well knew, and even stated in public, that the only reasonable condition of Society was that of pure Communism (such as you now see around you), yet shrunk from what seemed to them the barren task of preaching the realization of a happy dream. Looking back now, we can see that the great motive-power of the change was a longing for freedom and equality, akin if you please to the unreasonable passion of the lover; a sickness of heart that rejected with loathing the aimless solitary life of the well-to-do educated men of that time.[26]

A longing for freedom and equality; a sickness at heart – these are the contradictory, quickening sources of Morris's socialist aesthetics and his unequivocal commitment to the cause of the people, as of Dickens's realism. Or, to put it another way, it could be said that the starting-point of Morris's vision of reality is his awareness of alienation, his 'sense of the radical dislocation of consciousness from historical reality (with its potential for change)'. And it is from this complex dialectic view of things that he conceives the tasks of art. Art has 'to create a new consciousness that moves away from the immediate towards the possible'. And in order to give art the power to see 'the future in the present . . . realism has to be transcended'. Which is not to say that art can ever escape the alienating conditions that determine the life of the citizen. What it has to do is to transform these alienating conditions 'into revolutionary consciousness by the recognition of the collective possibilities of the mind's curve away from actuality'. In other words, 'for Morris, in dreams begins responsibility'.[27]

It is the insistence of responsibility and of a whole structure of values concerning the place of literature in a world in which the survival of people matters at least as much as the survival of literature that gives such cogency and force to Ellen's attack in *News From Nowhere* upon the social attitudes of nineteenth-century novelists:

'As for your books, they were well enough for times when intelligent people had but little else in which they could take pleasure, and when they must needs supplement the sordid miseries of their own lives with imaginations of the lives of other people. But I say flatly that in spite of all their cleverness and vigour, and capacity for story-telling, there is something loathsome about them. Some of them, indeed, do here and there show some feeling for those whom the history-books call "poor", and of the misery of whose lives we have some inkling; but presently they give it up, and towards the end of the story we must be contented to see the hero and heroine living happily in an island of bliss on other people's troubles; and that after a long series of sham troubles (or mostly sham) of their making, illustrated by dreary introspective nonsense about their feelings and aspirations, and all the rest of it; while the world must even then have gone on its way, and dug and sewed and baked and built and carpentered round about these useless animals.'[28]

As for Dickens, he was never one of this breed of supernumerary story-teller. His work takes its vitality and vividness from the ground-rhythms and the everyday routines of the world he lived in and the energies and aspirations of the ordinary people who kept it going. It celebrates, at once actively and with passionate wholeheartedness, the actualities of the lives of these people – the makers and producers of social wealth, among whom were the diggers, the sewers, the bakers, the builders and carpenters. And since his art is broad-based and deep and balanced in its vision of society, it also includes among its characters the useless animals who, with their sham troubles and their hypocrisies, are part of the social process. However, Dickens never allows his heroes and heroines the luxury of living 'happily in an island of bliss' on other people's troubles. He may sentimentalize them, but they are often, like Little Dorrit, deeply scarred by the sorrow and unhappiness and degradation of others; or, like Jo, Richard or Nell, they become the victims of an inhuman system created for the benefit of others. Stephen himself – having (literally at the end and symbolically from the beginning) fallen into the pit that has cost him his life, even as it has 'cost wi'in the knowledge o' old folk now livin, hundreds and hundreds o' men's lives' who have pleaded vainly with 'the lawmakers for Christ's sake not to let their work be murder to 'em' – dies hoping 'that aw the world may on'y coom together more, an' get a better unnerstann'in o' one another, than when I were in't my own weak seln'.[29] For indeed there seemed to Dickens no other way to make that world better. Thus, his major characters learn to appreciate that the true delights and satisfactions of life are to be found in the rewards and recognitions of community – affirmed by the manner in which, through their own sufferings, they learn to understand how closely their lives are bound up with the lives of other people and thus with the troubles of other people. And if Dickens was not able to go far enough in demonstrating what active steps needed to be taken to combat the inhumanities of his oppressive civilization, he went a long way beyond most of his contemporaries in defining, with his marvellously sensitive and varied register of the interwoven patterns of life in England, the shame and disgrace of the actual conditions imposed upon the people in a class-divided world.

'In these days,' William Morris was to write in 1882, twelve years after Dickens's death, the issue between art, that is, the godlike part of man, and mere bestiality, is so momentous, and the surroundings of life are so stern and unplayful, that nothing can take serious hold of people, or should do so, but that which is rooted deepest in reality and is quite at first hand: there is not room for anything which is not forced out of a man's deep feeling because of its innate strength and vision.[30]

He might well have been writing about Dickens; for Dickens, with all his intense enjoyment of human activity, its absurdities, its pathos and comedy, its degradation, its cruelty, its triumphs and defeats, was just such an artist.

6

LITERATURE:
THE DIALECTICS OF ACTUALITY

We cannot hope to contribute very much to the struggle for a concept of reality in which people matter – least of all if we happen to be writers – by standing aloof from the struggle or withdrawing from it in disgust and despair because the real world refuses to conform to our subjective demand for the perfect solution. Our business is to fight for a world in which the dialectics of community and connectedness will be able to function – in which the separation of practice from theory, of politics from culture, the subjective and the objective, the internal and the external, the particular and the general, may be overcome, and the dislocations that have deepened the irrational divisiveness of man and the world he lives in diminished.

And to this task art has much to contribute. 'Utilitarian economists, skeletons of schoolmasters, commissioners of Fact, genteel and used-up infidels, gabblers of many little dog's-eared creeds,' Dickens cries, attacking the hypocrisies of people in authority, 'the poor you will have always with you.' And his exhortation to these representatives of society is unequivocal. 'Cultivate in them, while there is yet time, the utmost graces of the fancies and affections, to adorn their lives so much in need of adornment.' For we neglect this task – and with it the task of awakening the selfish and the hypocritical or the shoulder-shrugging to an awareness of their responsibility – at our peril. If we remain indifferent to the plight of the deprived, then, 'in the day of your triumph, when romance is utterly driven out of their souls, and they and a bare existence stand face to face, Reality will take a wolfish turn, and make an end of you.'[1]

Dickens delivered his warning at a time when many cultivated people preferred to say nothing, or to justify the situation as it stood. He delivered it at a time when, in William Morris's indignant words, 'the wonderful machines which in the hands of just and foreseeing men would have been used to minimize repulsive labour and to give pleasure – or in other words added life – to the human race', were being 'so used on the contrary that they have driven all men into mere frantic haste and hurry, thereby destroying pleasure, that is life, on all hands: they have instead of lightening the labour of the workmen, intensified it, and thereby added more wearisome yet to the burden which the poor have to carry'.[2] Today, none of us should be under any illusion that the consequences of the cruelty, the moral hypocrisy and indifference of that time are not still working away at the foundations of our world, or that its underlying issues have been satisfactorily resolved. For if today the situation no longer provides the dramatic and shaming contrasts that disfigured the Victorian world – with its 'terrible spectacle . . . of two peoples, living street by street, and door by door – people of the same blood, the same tongue, and at least nominally living under the same laws – but yet one civilized and the other uncivilized'[3] – still the mass of the people remain unemancipated. The class divisions and inequities persist, the material and cultural benefits of society continue to be enjoyed by a very small minority, and a huge proportion of the country's wealth (in terms of property and money) remains in the hands of little more than ten per cent of the population. In other words, the warnings of a Dickens or a Morris retain their urgency, and we are as much in need as ever of what they stood for and stood against; of men who know that art itself cannot evade the issues of responsibility; that it exists for (and on behalf of) people as a moral and ethical and social act and never for itself alone, aloof above the storm. And what of those artists who, rejecting this, feel 'they have no choice save to do their own personal individual work unhelped by the present, stimulated by the past, but shamed by it, and even in a way hampered by it'? Who feel that 'they must stand apart as possessors of some sacred mystery which, whatever happens, they must at least do their best to guard'? Morris provides his own answer to such a dilemma. 'It is not to be doubted,' he says, 'that both their own lives and their works are injured by this isolation. But the loss of the people; how are we to measure that? That they should have great men living and working amongst them, and be ignorant of the very existence of their work, and incapable of knowing what it means if they could see it!'[4]

Since 1789 the issues of social and political struggle have become too important to ignore, even for the artist. Though great works of art may be formally self-contained and complete, still it is *what* they say that must always be the ultimate justification for the forms they take, since they are *content* too, however inseparably the form determines the quality of the content and the work. Whether it is Giotto or Aeschylus or Sophocles or Shakespeare or Raphael or Michelangelo or Dante or Mozart or Beethoven or Balzac or Tolstoy, the content of the work is an embodiment in form of the struggle for a shared and sharing world, however ambiguous or seemingly self-contained. For in actual fact no work of art is self-contained or self-complete. As an essentially social act it participates in a living world, the world of people's responses, people's feelings, the conditions of their lives, the world they live in. And its voice is a voice that speaks *to* that world about order and harmony and conflict and equilibrium and paradox and reconciliation and intimacy and delight and longing and a thousand refractions of the civilizing human faculties – as a voice aspiring to, and celebrating, the creative community of man *in* his world.

Of course, it would be absurd to argue that the work of art should demonstrate a partisan political position; that as a social act it should also make itself an overtly political act. Though defined in scope by the logic of the historical and social conditions of its own time, it is concerned with many other levels of reality than the political; and to insist that it should *be* overtly political would be to deny it that autonomy that gives it its special general significance and to reduce it to the level of the tract. Great artists will not be pinned down, or permit their sensibilities to be blunted by the demands of the literalist, whatever their sympathies. The stand they take may well be on the side of the humanizing values which generate political actions for the betterment of the conditions under which people live; and it may be that their art will even clearly symbolize, as Goya's did, and Delacroix's, and Belli's, the struggle for political and social justice. But as artists they will be concerned with *more* than politics in the narrower sense – which is *not* to say that they should not be concerned with politics at all, because obviously politics affects their positions as artists. First of all, they are concerned with 'things as they are'; with looking at the world in terms of its ambiguous particulars, the obstinately concrete facts of people's lives; with all that, beyond the purely organizational conditions that define their circumstances, gives them their living place as individual particular beings distinguished from each other in the particular part of the world they inhabit – and this includes all that they are in themselves and all the obscure and uninspectable influences that have gone into shaping their existence.

It is the abstract theorizing faculties, and the dislocating systems that issue from them, that have commonly done most damage to humanity – the divorce of theory from practice, the insistence on imposing abstract principles upon the complex substances – the intricate organic patterns – of the human world, in wilful blindness to the actualities of that world. And one of the functions of art is to re-awaken us and keep us close to the subsistent continuity and connectedness of the world of living people. As Blake writes: 'General knowledge is Remote Knowledge; it is in Particulars that Wisdom consists and Happiness too. Both in Art and in Life, General Masses are as much Art as a Pasteboard Man is Human.'[5] Politics in isolation – even a politics that claims to seek to release people from oppression – is itself a species of Remote Knowledge, and in its refusal to take into account all the other interests people have, and its tendency to force issues upon them, often to the impoverishment of these interests, it is a dangerous perversion. As an isolated abstract machinery it is far more dangerous even than the reactionary individual or the man who abstracts himself from overt political action. For it turns men into bigots and fanatics, into blunted visionaries, who – driven by their theories – become deaf to all but their own dogmas and pursue their ends in total disregard for the basic human dignities, the right of others to be different. A politics that can deny its opposition is a politics that denies the primary differences of human intercourse and shuts its eyes to the nature of the human condition. It is a politics that proceeds *against* humanity, and for this reason alone to be condemned. Which is to say no more than what Marx had said in his Feuerbach theses about idealism: that it distorts and falsifies reality because it 'does not know real, sensuous activity as such', and thus degrades the particular organic human being into 'an abstract isolated individual'.[6]

Art, on the contrary, is essentially concerned with the particular, the actual, the human, and with the intricate contexts – physical, spatial, temporal, external, psychological, sensate – that involve us all. And in celebrating the immediacies, the fluctuating fortunes, the struggles, doubts and longings of its creatures in the psychological subtlety of their response to circumstance, to history and time and change, it reasserts the sanity of connection, continuity and interaction that determines the patterns of the lives of real people in the world of multiple and overlapping references which we call reality, and which cannot be reduced without betrayal or distortion. The point is that the work of art – or at least the significant work of art – seeks, not reduction, but intensification, the kind of illumination that transforms and penetrates the surfaces of things to enrich and deepen our experience of reality.

So it can be argued that even the purely aesthetic function of a work of art, as art – its power to charm, to divert, to weave its spell upon the senses, to work as pure 'calligraphy of pleasure',[7] has its special value. Art as 'nutriment of impulse', as replenishment, as a quickening and form-creating energy, transforming the merely fortuitous and the merely factual into poetry, is a sensitizing, life-enhancing force. But not in isolation, not divorced from all that is outside the work itself, all it draws upon and anchors in the sensate form; for it is the complex interactive process of reality – however indirect a part this plays in the actual work – that makes the experience of art significant. On its own, in isolation, it may be no more than a form of indulgent escapism to bolster up illusions and confirm indifference and complacency, an encouragement to quietist insularity, a sort of 'fiddling while Rome burns'. In this sense, and as nothing more than entertainment, art becomes a triviality, a titillating of the senses, an essentially frivolous pursuit that turns all ecstasy and all intensity, all it has to tell us of the urgency, the disturbance, the passion, the complexity and energy of life, to tameness and domestication. Then what is it but another instrument of servitude and of manipulation for the tranquillizing and the dulling of political and social and human awareness? Rather than the force it ought to be and is for creating in us a quickened awareness of what and who we are and thus encouraging an active and creative response to the challenge of actuality? If art is therapy, a source of healing magic for the wounded, and sustains us in defeat, it is so, or it becomes so, because it has the power to nourish in us renewed energy and desire for life. Art is not a wallpaper, a mere background pattern to the game of life. It is not a bubble-bath or a piece of technical expertise for the initiated. It is a human statement that discovers and illuminates the world through the passionate advocacy of its language; though it can only become this when it involves the active participation of those who are capable of responding to its language.

I take it as axiomatic that 'the aesthetic consciousness is a necessary step in man's struggle for self-awareness',[8] and that consequently the aesthetic qualities of a work of art are of primary importance in the experience of art. Nevertheless, the aesthetic consciousness is only *part* of the struggle, for the experience of art is not an end in itself, any more than the work of art is an end, but a process, by which the sensibility is expanded, sensitized, deepened. Indeed, for the artist himself, each work, however aesthetically and formally contained, is but a stage in a changing and developing process determined by his skill and perception, his particular psychological response to the conditions that surround him at the time, as by the very nature of the historical, social and political structure of his world. And in the significant works that he creates it is not simply the aesthetic sensibility – his sensate and imaginative faculties – that are involved. Somehow, in some profound and profoundly comprehensive way, the fundamental powers of the mind are 'echoed in the concrete sensuous form',[9] and in the scope and cogency of the argument.

The work of art, that is to say, is constructed according to the logic of its argument and the logic of its form, the one supporting and giving life to the other. And though in lesser works it may be possible to distinguish some sort of imbalance or of incoherence between the two, in the masterpiece such division or separation does not occur; the rationalizing faculties and the imaginative sensate powers of the mind have by the special skill of the artist been reconciled – by means (partly at any rate) of what Hegel defines as 'the expression of a particular mode of consciousness that is tied to images'.[10] There is more to it than that, however; art is not *restricted* to that mode of consciousness tied to images, though it is clearly founded upon it. Thomas Mann, for instance, often employs an equivalent of the kind of intellectual argument one associates with the abstract thinker. It is only an equivalent, because Mann's purpose is not to present a fully worked-out system of thought but rather to convey a dramatic embodiment of the thinker in action, as an aspect of character or a symbolic representation of the abstract intellect at work as part of an ethical–artistic scheme. But this reflects far more than that form of consciousness that functions in terms of images.

As for such a vision of reality as Shakespeare creates for us in the work of his maturity, from *Julius Caesar* onward, it cannot adequately be defined in such terms. Rather one might describe it, in Hegel's grandest claim for art, as 'a synthesis of the spiritual (or mental) and the physical, of the universal and the particular'.[11] But this is not very satisfactory either, though it may not be a problem for metaphysics, or even for aesthetics. And what of the metaphysical assertion that the 'truth' of a work of art is something totally *of* that work, and inseparable *from* it? One can understand the intention, in the sense in which it may be said that the particular order and structure of the work, and all that is embodied in it as a form, *is* its truth. But what this truth is if it 'cannot be stated, cannot be detached from the work itself',[12] must forever remain incommunicable, untransferable. In which case it must also remain detached from us, locked within the work. How then are we ever to experience it or to share it? How are we to *use* it? How is it to serve the needs of people? To become an instrument of emancipation? To function as releasing and revealing 'truths' within the context of the social reality that art is at its best an intermediary *for*? If its truth cannot be detached from the work itself to become part of the larger context of the 'truths' that surround it, then it cannot play its part in the making of this larger context. It must remain an irreducible and unmodified phenomenon. But this is to make of the work of art an absolute, to place it above or apart from reality in an untouchable sphere of its own, where, in effect, it is most likely to confirm the divisive interests of the privileged and unscrupulous few against the needs of the community, and thus to become an expression of the alien powers that stand in the way of emancipation and social justice. And great art, however stigmatized by such association, is surely neither repressive nor callous nor divisive in its appeal. It is human and flexible and open to the influence of all it comes into contact with, even as we ourselves are influenced by its effect upon us. But it remains a mere potentiality, an abstract construction, until we have given it our living attention. Its truth emerges not from what it is in itself, that is, but from the conjunction, the identification, the interchange between the individual human being, who brings to it his own sensation and grasp of the truth, and the object.

If it were possible to argue that the work of art is a self-contained hermetic structure, untranslatable and untransferable, then it would follow that it has no connection with the empirical sensible world of human experience beyond it. But the fact is that, being the product of a human intelligence, it has its roots and sources in that world, and reflects its actualities, the historical and social conditions of people's lives. We do not talk of the truth of a human being as something that cannot be stated except in terms of himself, because we know that his 'truth' is a composite of many things, the influences and experiences he is shaped by, the ideas, thoughts and feelings he has absorbed from the empirical sensible world he is part of. His 'truth' (whatever this may be) is determined not by any kind of hermetic, self-contained entity *within* himself, but by the nature of the dialogue he is capable of holding with his world through the operation of language, and by all the links that exist between him and other people. It is not an absolute, single condition, identifiable as he is identifiable physically, though his physical presence is part of his 'truth'. It reflects from him through what happens to him at many levels, revealed as much by his changing relationships, the kind of life he leads, as by the coherence and force of personality. He may, that is, impose a certain image of himself upon the outer world, which may or may not correspond with what he is in essence, but even this is influenced, modified and changed by the constantly shifting, reordering patterns of reality. For in fact truth is not a static principle. Since, in terms of the Marxian thesis already established, 'we change the object when we act upon it', truth is 'something which is continually changing and developing'.[13]

In exactly similar ways, this active principle affects the work of art, in spite of its having achieved an *apparently* fixed, definitive form of its own, a form that is no more and no less than itself. An active intelligence, a living human context, gives it its life, determines its truth. In itself a static structure, a common potential source of pleasure and illumination, it is animated and realized only through the interaction between it and the person experiencing it, and therefore becomes a part of that person's way of seeing things, modified and made afresh in terms of his own sensibility, his own historically and socially determined grasp of reality.

According to Marx's fundamental criticism of it, Hegelian idealism appears to deny the empirical sensible world, and to acknowledge true reality only in abstraction, in the Idea. 'Hegel,' Marx writes in his *Critique of Hegel's Doctrine of the State*, 'everywhere makes the Idea into the subject, while the genuine, real subject . . . is turned into the predicate.'[14] In these terms, being is reduced to thinking, the finite to the infinite: empirical, real facts are transcended, and it is denied that they have genuine reality.[15] Man's real existence, his relation to himself, his mobility, his natural sensuous being, are superseded, masked, by the abstraction. All that is actual becomes mere formality 'because it is abstract and because human nature itself is seen only as *abstract thinking being*, as self-consciousness',[16] with the consequence that 'real man and real nature become mere predicates, symbols of this hidden, unreal man and this unreal nature'.[17] And thus the abstract universal which ought to be a quality or attribute of the concrete world becomes the subject; while the real subject, the concrete world, becomes a mere phenomenal aspect of the former.[18] And thus it is, as Marx puts it in *Capital*, that 'the products of the human brain appear as autonomous figures endowed with a life of their own'.[19]

Marx is here concerned with the fetishist value that commodities assume in the capitalist world when they are abstracted from the actualities they are rooted in – a value that conceals and perverts the concrete nature of the social interchange between people in their various relationships. This may seem very distant from the issues that concern the 'truth' of the work of art. But in fact the problem is closely analogous; for Hegel adopts the same kind of idealist deification of the Principle, the Idea, in his theory of aesthetics. He assumes the Universal, the autonomous Absolute – art becomes an abstract entity, and its true reality is to be determined only in abstraction, as a value that transcends reality in the marriage of the sensuous and the spiritual. And the 'aesthetic consciousness' responding to the work of art derives delight from contemplation of its intangible properties – though, if this is so, it is not the artist's way of proceeding. As Blake puts it: 'Singular and Particular Detail is the Foundation of the Sublime.'[20] There is no difficulty in accepting that what Hegel calls 'the necessity of art' arises from man's rational need to 'impress the seal of his own inner being' on the external world. But if this is so, then the truth of art is very *much* determined by the rational needs not only of the artist himself, but also of the person who responds to it. And there is more to it than impressing the seal of his inner being on the external world; the experience of art is part of a far more complex process, because the artist's 'inner being' has itself been moulded and conditioned by the pressures and energies and actualities of the external world.

What we have to acknowledge, finally, is that art as a specialized form of human achievement, as a phenomenon that exists for the initiated and as an absolute value, for its own sake, has dubious application to the complex needs of man, because it then exists only for the enrichment of the privileged few. But these are the negative, restrictive terms imposed upon art by the standards of a class-divided world. And beyond such restrictions, involved as a life-enhancing and life-renewing force in the world of human struggle, it has a very important part to play in encouraging sanity and balance and in helping people – directly or indirectly – to respond to the world they live in qualitatively and concretely. It urges not abstraction but return to the sources, the living roots of being. It puts the subject and the predicate of the order of things squarely and sanely where they ought to be – not, as in Hegel's philosophy, with thought as the subject and being as the object, but the contrary – since being and the substances it is contained and determined by are the sources of all intellectual and imaginative acts. This being so, it continually refers us back to the actual, the physical, the sensuous, the real, and to the intangible essences of being as linked to these phenomena and manifested through them. If energy, as Blake said, is eternal delight, recognition – the recognition that comes from the embodiment of intangible feelings in the familiar things of the world around us – is a sign of that delight. For by that sign, or its manifestation, we *discover* reality, place and being *in* the world we live in. We do not pervert it or falsify it by abstracting ourselves from it; we come closer to it by being brought into intimate contact with its 'minute particulars', which themselves become the syllables of recognition.

7

SHAKESPEARE:
THE REVOLUTION OF THE TIMES

The great writers are witnesses to the rooted actualities of people's lives. They are concerned with men and women not as abstractions but as real, living, particular human beings, their needs and aspirations, the conflicts and collisions that characterize the changing patterns of the human struggle. But the writer's power to create living characters depends upon much more than this. It depends upon his power to create an organic living context, a comprehensible social world which will give them identity, place and position, verisimilitude and credibility; and thus upon the depth and range of his understanding of the historical and social perspectives of the world he himself is part of. For people cannot exist in a vacuum; they are essentially social beings involved in a constant process of action and reaction, of conflict and interchange with others; and as such have to be defined and embodied in terms of the complex conditions of social existence that surround them and make them what they are.

'Without theory,' Lenin once remarked, 'action is blind; [and] without action, theory is barren.' But theory itself is indubitably founded upon practice, the observation of the concrete particular process of human life in action; and all abstractions that lose contact with the actualities they spring from represent a potential danger that goes far beyond mere barrenness. For in the end such abstractions have a peculiar power to falsify and pervert reality, as Marx fully demonstrated in his criticism of Hegel and the abstract thinkers – those who, seeking to transform reality into terms of general categories, assume these categories as the very sources of reality, thus confirming and strengthening the rule of the alien powers that continue to dominate mankind.

To turn from even the greatest of the contemplative philosophers to the work of Shakespeare is to turn from theories divorced or detached from practice to a vision of reality that is anchored to the actual sources, that unites theory and practice, the abstract and the concrete, and offers us a profoundly balanced, creative and life-enhancing view of the world of human action – a sanity that, in its recognition of the contradictory nature of the human struggle, affirms the rooted energies of life against the forces of negation, darkness, placelessness, the alien powers man persists in setting above himself. As Yeats has put it, writing of the great tragedies: 'It is only when the intellect has wrought the whole of life to drama, to crisis, that we may live for contemplation, and yet keep our intensity.'[1] With Shakespeare, in other words, the intensity is at a maximum, and in the great tragedies we are the witnesses of elemental human energies, of conflicting social forces coming into violent collision. And, as Yeats again comments, referring to the instinctual sources upon which great art is nourished and renewed:

Shakespeare's people make all things serve their passion, and that passion is for the moment the whole energy of their being – birds, beasts, men, women, landscape, society, are but symbols and metaphors, nothing is studied in itself, the mind is a dark well, no surface, depth only.[2]

This, however, is a level on which discussion becomes impossible, because it lies beyond the reach of rational critical debate, and appears to deny the presence in Shakespeare's work of those powers of intellectual and rational awareness which are the complement to its vitality and depth. But there is surely no denying the objective controlling power Shakespeare has of harnessing and forging his energy and intensity into a coherent work of art and hence of *making* his people serve their passion or whatever else it is they serve. The fact is that Shakespeare's art derives its organic strength, its sanity and coherence, its anchored precision and veracity not only from obscure subconscious forces of being in the personality, but more specifically from powers of imagination deeply rooted in and quickened by the actualities, the contradictory, explosive conditions, the physical and psychological energies, of the age in which he lived – an age (like our own) rife with crisis and conflict and violent historical upheaval. His vision, that is to say, is rooted in the objective process of history, and organized in terms of a conscious understanding of that process. Thus he is able to register, with a commanding and deeply penetrating objectivity, the collisions of his world; the triumphant humanist character of its rising new men, the thrust and aggressiveness of hitherto controlled energies emerging as a challenge to the old feudal orders of society. And of course in the Yeatsian sense his people are themselves the embodiment of the vital motive power of individual action, generating with the whole energy of their being that passionate thrusting sense of drama and conflict which is of the essence of Shakespeare's art. But these people are all involved and implicated in a pattern of action and reaction, a structure of reality, which conditions and limits their capacity for action and makes of them but finite partial instruments. They live and breathe and act with the superb edge and buoyancy of living beings; but they act according to the limitations, the constricting necessities imposed upon them by a world they can none of them command. Because for Shakespeare the order of reality – the social order itself, the order of family relationships, of kinship, of community, of antagonistic interchange, of nature ('great creating nature')[3] – is largely determined by the conditioning forces of history, and the concepts of society valid for him in the age in which he lived.

One of the central symbols of Shakespeare's art is that of kingship – kingship as representing the bond and seal of order and authority and equilibrium that ensures the continuity of human society. Kingship is the abstract general sign and seal of kinship, of stability, of rational social continuity; and its embodiment is the fluctuating struggle (celebrated in almost every play) of powerful individuals attempting to impose their own defective vision of authority and of order upon the world around them, even as this must have seemed a reality to a man living in the shadow of a Renaissance court. But by the same token, Shakespeare's work is a continual exploration of the manner in which this sign of feudal authority, and the very structure of the feudal system itself, was being threatened and challenged. For the age in which Shakespeare lived was an age of expansion and of violent transition from the stability of the feudal world, in all its 'democratic unfreedom', to the much more disturbing and free-ranging world of Renaissance inquiry. Indeed, with the feudal system cracking, breaking, being undermined by the continual pressures of a new concept of social order, spurred on and quickened by religious and political dissent, the consequent disturbances set up at all levels were not of the kind to encourage settled views, a sense of comfort and security, of ease and complacency; but were on the contrary an incentive to a ferment of experiment and of exploration by which the very nature of the social process and of the individual's place in his world were to be transformed – exposed to constant collisions between the forces of order and the forces of change that were so soon to culminate in the regicide and civil war of the mid-century.

This sense of break-up is particularly evident in the great tragedies, all of them written during the first decade of the seventeenth century; and in none of them more concentratedly than *King Lear*. The conflict between Lear and his daughters, Gloucester and his sons, provides a devastating representation of the collapse of feudal authority, brought about by the loosening of the bonds that hold people together in obedience to

> . . . degree, priority and place,
> Insisture, course, proportion, season, form,
> Office and custom, in all line of order.[4]

And it is Lear himself, having no conception of the possible consequences, who institutes the change, who opens up his world to the competitive instinct. What he unleashes upon himself and upon his world is the law of the free market, of unprincipled ambition, of appetite, greed and will, conditions that are already at work in his world – the crudest and most violent blasphemy against the very concept of community (kingship as kinship, kind and kind, brother and brother, father, husband and wife, the roots of 'the moral laws /Of nature and of nations',[5] as Hector puts it in *Troilus*), and thus the stability and survival of society itself. The position is stated with unequivocal clarity, again in *Troilus*, by Ulysses, analysing the disunity of the Greeks before Troy:

> O, when degree is shaked,
> Which is the ladder to all high designs,
> The enterprize is sick! How could communities,
> Degrees in schools and brotherhoods in cities,
> Peaceful commerce from dividable shores,
> The primogeniture and due of birth,
> Prerogative of age, crowns, sceptres, laurels,
> But by degree, stand in authentic place?

Take but degree away, untune that string,
And, hark, what discord follows! each thing meets
In mere oppugnancy: the bounded waters
Should lift their bosoms higher than the shores,
And make a sop of all this solid globe:
Strength should be lord of imbecility,
And the rude son should strike his father dead:
Force should be right; or rather, right and wrong,
Between whose endless jar justice resides,
Should lose their names, and so should justice too.
Then every thing includes itself in power,
Power into will, will into appetite;
And appetite, an universal wolf,
So doubly seconded with will and power,
Must make perforce an universal prey,
And last eat up himself.[6]

This is exactly what happens to the ordered world of degree and authority that is King Lear's Britain – 'each thing meets / In mere oppugnancy' and destructive appetite. And this Britain, concretely rooted in its own world, is at the same time Shakespeare's England and reflects the historical conditions of the period of primitive accumulation by which the foundations of capitalism were being laid. Lear stands as the concrete embodiment of the values of the old world. He is the head of a rigidly feudal hierarchy, its monolithic authority, its crumbling bastion – vain, irascible, overbearing, accustomed to unquestioning obedience, to hearing what he wants to hear, and unable to distinguish hypocrisy from truth. The world he has ruled so peremptorily is in a state of dangerous suppressed disorder, and this in itself is the harshest reflection of the nature of his rule, even as his disastrous misjudgement of what his world needs reflects his own incapacity to see things as they are. In choosing to divide up his kingdom among his daughters, and thus 'to shake all cares and business from our age',[7] he has no conception of what it means to be divested of office and thus unprotected by the instruments of power with which he has so harshly and uncompromisingly surrounded himself. The abstract isolating machinery of kingship and its remoteness from the people has long blinded him to the natural laws of community and love and fellowship which are the basis of a just society; and in his blind assumption of the autocratic pride and egotism of kingship, he invites from his subjects only flattery and deceit. But it is not simply his vanity, his irascibility, his capacity for self-deception, his misjudgement of character, that bring about the collision that shatters his world. He and his personal imperfections are but one factor in a situation inherent with conflict and disorder, smouldering with suspicion and poisonous ambition, hovering on the edge of breakdown. It is not to be supposed, after all, that Goneril and Regan and Edmund have suddenly become the evil self-seeking creatures they so soon show themselves to be. They have been encouraged by the very nature of the world they live in to be so, and have long been so. 'I should have been that I am,' says Edmund, 'had the maidenliest star in the firmament twinkled on my bastardizing.'[8] They are what their world has made them, sharpened in them; the products of a perverted environment, a social structure in which the natural laws have been warped and undermined by decades of repressive rule. And they only await the opportunity, the licence, to act, to move in, to take over. Give them this, and they will need no further prompting – as they proceed at once to demonstrate, in the spirit of ruthless unprincipled self-seeking that governs their view or reality. It is inevitable, for they are the inheritors; Goneril and Regan, unlike their sister (in whom natural human affection remains untouched by cynicism), have the measure of their father's vanity and rashness of mood. The 'glib and oily art'[9] with which they buy their power is no more than a calculated device to achieve what they think of as theirs by right. Invited to flatter, as obedient daughters they flatter, and Cordelia is dismissed with contempt for throwing away her fortune by refusing to comply with an old man's whim; because all that counts with them is the material consequence, the acquisition of property and of power. As the representatives of a new and very different kind of social order nourished on years of thwarted ambition and grudging subservience against the bonds of nature and of duty and of moral feeling, they have been waiting for this with ill-concealed impatience. Indeed, if Gloucester's gloomy predictions are to be taken seriously, there is good reason to believe that they have already been quietly at work inciting unrest among the people. 'In cities, mutinies; in countries, discord; in palaces, treason,' the old man mutters; 'and the bond crack'd twixt son and father . . . We have seen the best of our time; machinations, hollowness, treachery, and all ruinous disorders follow us unquietly to our graves.'[10] And Lear himself seems to suggest that his decision to divide up his kingdom has been made at least partly in the awareness of some such undercurrent of unrest – thus proving he is not entirely blind to what is going on – 'that future strife /May be prevented now'.[11] He sees that much, but his wilfulness and arrogance prevent him from seeing any further. We know that what his decision actually does is to let loose against the bonds of order and authority and natural feelings all the pent-up forces of frustrated appetite and will in a fury of destructiveness that consumes his world; and that there is nothing he can do to stop this happening, since he has left himself utterly exposed. As the Fool points out, with the blunt simplicity of the seer, unable to hold his tongue: 'Thou hast pared thy wit o' both sides, and left nothing i' th' middle.'[12] For he knows that Lear, by divesting himself of his property, 'the sway, revenue, execution'[13] of his office, has lost all claim to proper regard in the kind of world that has taken over, controlled by those who have respect only for the laws of ruthless competition and unbridled appetite and property. The king, he sees, is now but a shadow of himself. For, as a mere man, he is 'nothing'; and, in Lear's echoing of the Fool, who is echoing the King's shocked response to Cordelia's negative, 'nothing can be made out of nothing'.

Ironically, it is the fall of the king from his remote position at the apex of an ossified order breaking up around him that gives him back his power to understand himself, because only then is he stripped of all that had kept him ignorant, isolated, screened from contact, cut off from the experience of those common human ties which are the roots of social continuity. Then, driven to madness, he sees it all, and with the bitterest clarity: 'Through rough tatter'd clothes great vices do appear: robes and furr'd gowns hide all.'[14] But he has to be brought violently down to the level of the bare earth, the irreducible condition of nature in all its rawness, before he can understand that even 'the basest and most poorest shape'[15] is worthy of respect or come to recognize how little he had cared, as king, for those 'poor naked wretches'[16] whom he now shares common cause with. And on this journey through the storm of the elements and the storm of his madness towards the re-discovery of the proofs of love, he has to travel through a long hell of shame and guilt – 'burning, scalding, stench, consumption'[17] – 'bound /Upon a wheel of fire',[18] before he can find his way back to the indispensable sources of health and sanity which his own blindness, or the blindness of his position (as opposed to the seeing blindness of Gloucester), had robbed him of. And by then, though Lear is at last reunited with Cordelia – his child-changed spirit stilled by the healing powers of love – it is too late for anything but the final recognition and the final severance amid the wreckage of his world. 'Is this the promised end?'[19] Kent asks in bleak despair, looking upon Cordelia dead in Lear's arms.

It is a devastating conclusion. But even such pessimism as this is softened and dignified by the tenderness of Lear's reunion with his daughter and its affirmation, unassailable beyond all hurt, of community; and though for Kent everything is finished, Edgar and Albany remain, as witnesses to the future. In other words, this tragedy, however bleak, does not bring the world to an end. It represents a struggle for survival against the forces of negation, evil, darkness, terror, death, oblivion, and it moves towards catastrophe, obliteration, the defeat of the spirit. But the end, in spite of the finality of death, is not defeat, but a kind of triumph – a re-discovery, beyond defeat, of the enduring bonds of kinship, community and love. It is the objective human scale of Shakespeare's vision, his deep awareness of the subsistent continuity of things, that makes it possible for him to affirm even in the forces of destruction the underlying preconditions of renewal. Indeed, his work – at once public and social and collective in its response to reality – is everywhere rich with the quickening energies of the life-process. And in the contradictions, the clashes and collisions of motive and will by which the struggles of his characters are defined, it is inclusive, not divisive. It speaks for a whole world, and for the people who play their part in making it, for the social and historical issues that shape their lives. And it is the fact that it does so with such penetrating insight into the objective social forces that govern the movement of men's lives that gives it such direct and cogent meaning for us in the twentieth century. For the world we live in is a world, like his, in crisis, exposed to pressures of like intensity; and still the great issues, the opposition between promise and performance, policy and conscience, revenge and reconciliation, retribution and reward, ambition and appetite, reason and energy, remain an unresolved challenge to *all* who would wish to speak for a whole world. And in a deeply pertinent sense, as Christopher Caudwell observes, Shakespeare's work seems to comprehend, 'at the dawn of bourgeois development, the whole movement of the capitalist contradiction, from its tremendous achievement to its mean decline'. It does so joyously and vividly in the comedies, and with unparalleled intensity in the great tragedies, ranging from the 'dewy freshness of bourgeois love in Romeo' to 'its fatal empire-shattering drowsiness in Antony'.[20] And it nowhere anticipates with more savage and emphatic power the conditions of the late capitalism that was to assume such oppressive and degrading control over men than in *Timon of Athens*.

For the insistent theme of this play, and the source of Timon's outraged denunciation, is the manner in which money, 'the visible god . . . that speakst with every tongue, /To every purpose', corrupts and perverts human character, and sets man against man, 'that beasts /May have the world in empire'.[21] In this sense, *Timon* is by far the bitterest and bleakest of the tragedies – vituperative, polemical, more overtly a tirade, less contained within its characters, with more of the raw and unabsorbed shock of feeling left exposed in the form and the language than in any other play of the period, as if he had not fully distanced into art the impact upon him of his own appalled insight into the realities of his world. Thus in parts the play itself seems open, raw, exposed – Timon's disaffection is absolute, his hatred uncompromising, founded on a reaction of total disgust, and there is no healing of the wound in him. The oppressive consistency of the theme, its relentless invective, and above all the nature of the imagery that dominates throughout, define an extraordinary new stress, an unmistakable (and perhaps excessive) underlining of a single central idea. As Kenneth Burke has written:

Timon can round things out by translating any particular situation into its corresponding absolute. If he digs for roots to eat ('Earth, yield me roots'), they become universal roots. If in the course of thus digging in the 'common mother' he finds gold, it is an ironically Midas-like gold, fecal gold, gold as defined by the touch that turns everything into the idea of corruption . . . It is a foul form of gold that this play features, a quality of imagery in keeping with the fact that invective itself is a way of fighting by means of verbal filth, and Timon's absolute brand of it would besmear all mankind.[22]

In its historical–social setting, the play directly reflects, on one level, the atmosphere of the princely courts of the Rennaissance and their lavish patronage. But on another level it defines that spirit of expansion and of competitive rivalry which, breaking the bonds of a decaying feudalism, had given licence and incentive to the new men of Europe – the adventurers, the traders, the merchants, the businessmen, the controllers of the markets. These new men, making their wills 'the scope of justice'[23] in the ruthless acquisition of material wealth, were thus able to attain positions of authority and power in the state. Appetite, greed, the will to possession seem to have become the dominating impulse, sweeping aside or making subservient to its ends all higher considerations, all principles, all moral values – such as had characterized the structure of feudal society, with its emphasis upon the moral qualities of nobility, generosity, kinship, community, place and degree. And the confrontation between this new world, in which 'policy sits above conscience', and the old is violent and irreconcilable, signifying the break-up of the intricate ceremonial order of the medieval world and the assertion of an aggressive individualism based upon new sources of wealth in the period of Primitive Accumulation.

The influence of money dominates the play, a corroding, alienating force that transforms everything into its opposite. Here Shakespeare's basic preoccupation with conflicts of will, the collision of irreconcilable interests locked in a life-and-death struggle, as embodied in the tragedies preceding *Timon*, is itself transformed. For Timon sets himself not against the wills of other individuals, but against Athenian society as a whole and the naked self-interest which determines its values and priorities. And he does so not in any spirit of active opposition, but as an idealist reduced to a condition of enraged disgust, withdrawing in disillusionment from all contact with his world. Unlike any other major character in Shakespearian tragedy, he stands alone, in strange and giant isolation – a man without family and without close relationships of any kind, even without a definable past, 'as if a man were author of himself / And knew no other kin', as Coriolanus says of himself.[24] He is there like some natural physical element, massive and forbidding, not to be explained away, or evaded.

Faced by Timon we are forced to ask ourselves why Shakespeare should have found it necessary to create a character quite so daunting and so adamant in his hatred. And surely at least part of the answer has to be that he was driven to do so as a consequence of the devastating questions he *himself* had found it necessary to ask about the nature of his world and its concerns. Timon veers from one extreme – of lavish Renaissance hospitality, of unstinting generosity and trust – to the other; from 'I could deal kingdoms to my friends, /And ne'er be weary'[25] to 'Destruction fang mankind'.[26] His disillusionment is total because his illusions about the people who surround him and the convictions they profess are so disastrously wrong. He *believes* implicitly (and one must say blindly, since Apemantus warns him bluntly enough) that Athenian society is as generous and as free and as magnanimous as he is. Being, as he thinks, wealthy in his friends, he believes that 'we are born to do benefits'; and asks what 'better or properer can we call our own than the riches of our friends?' Indeed, he is visibly moved by what he calls the 'precious comfort' of having 'so many like brothers commanding one another's fortunes'.[27] But this naïve utopianism, being the irrational indulgence of a rich man addicted to giving and himself seduced by the bargaining power of money, leaves him totally exposed to manipulation. For what he fails to appreciate is that his Athens is not the Athens of Pericles or Plato, but a city dedicated to the accumulation of material riches – a mean city of commerce; and thus a city whose social order is determined by and built upon the ethics of the market-place. Its citizens are motivated, that is, not by humanistic magnanimity, but by thrift and calculation, a common-sense eye to profit; and to them it is simple foolishness to behave like Timon, to give away one's property 'upon bare friendship without security'.[28] They understand their world for what it is; and, since it has taught them to dispense with pity and conscience, they do not scruple to use Timon to get what they can from him. To them, money and the accumulation of riches are the priorities – money, not men. Men merely reflect their economic position. If they are rich they are powerful. But deprived of the power their property gives them they become worthless, as the Poet puts it at the start of the play. Man as man – man and his essentially human qualities – does not count.

It is the shock of the realization of this that turns Timon into a hater of mankind. For him there is no middle ground. He is an extremist; his disillusionment is as extreme and as extravagant as his illusions. In this sense, he is to be looked upon as a kind of innocent, an indulgent idealist caught uncomprehending in a world in which money rules and policy dominates conscience – a world he does not understand because he has misinterpreted it from the start, attributing to it virtues and values that are no part of the way it actually functions, but are mere shadowy survivals from another age.

Under such conditions, discovering such disease of fellowship, such 'base metal',[29] among those he had thought of as his friends, it is hardly surprising that such a man as Timon should have turned his back upon society and preferred – 'a dedicated beggar to the air, /With his disease of all-shunned poverty' – to walk 'like contempt alone'.[30] And it is significant that, apart from the praise given by the three strangers to Athens who appear briefly in Act Three, and the response of Alcibiades, recognition of his innate goodness and humanity should come only from the dependent poor, who play no part in the making of money. As Timon's loyal steward comments, after sharing out among his fellow servants the little that remains of his master's household money:

> Who would not wish to be from wealth exempt,
> Since riches point to misery and contempt?
> Who would be so mocked with glory, or to live
> But in a dream of friendship,
> To have his pomp, and all what state compounds,
> But only painted, like his varnished friends?[31]

It is the bitterness of Timon's feeling against these 'mouth-friends', these 'glass-eyed' flatterers, which lets loose the withering force of his invective. He is a man who has lived, and acted, on the mistaken assumption that the riches of friendship and community are the true wealth of society, and that one's personal material wealth is there to be shared without stint for the nourishment of the bonds of brotherhood; because with him 'promise and performance' are indivisible. He is therefore the more shattered to discover what his friends are really like – how these people, finding he has nothing more to offer them, 'slink all away', leaving only 'their false vows with him, /Like empty purses picked'.[32] Disgusted with Athens, and with human society at large, he retires to the woods, where he lives on roots and berries, refusing with vitriolic and searing scorn all inducements to return – choosing instead to die alone, off-stage, his last words bleak with negation, hinting that he is planning to bury himself alive in an act of ultimate protest:

> Come not to me again, but say to Athens,
> Timon hath made his everlasting mansion
> Upon the beachèd verge of the salt flood,
> Who once a day with his embossèd froth
> The turbulent surge shall cover; thither come,
> And let my gravestone be your oracle.
> Lips, let sour words go by, and language end.
> What is amiss, plague and infection mend.
> Graves only be men's works, and death their gain.
> Sun, hide thy beams. Timon hath done his reign.[33]

It is this utter bleakness of negation we have to contend with, this very excess which makes it difficult for us to come to terms with the play; for it is overbalancing and uncontainable, a message of unqualified harshness. Yet come to terms with it we must if we wish to understand Shakespeare, his psychology, the nature of his vision of reality, the intensity of his challenge, and the presence of the negating forces that he was himself having to contend with and to attempt to reconcile.

From this point of view at least it is almost of *more* interest that Timon is not a finished work of art and not completely contained or rounded out. We are faced with an issue of monumental impact, an issue perhaps too large and too abstractly pervasive for even Shakespeare to handle successfully or get into focus. But that he did handle it, that he did respond to the challenge, is the measure of how serious an issue he considered it, and how deeply he must have seen it as a threat to be faced up to and if possible resolved. One might put it like this: that he was testing himself and his own innate powers against the threat of this destructive power of naked self-interest, symbolized by the substance gold – and perhaps in the awareness that he *had* to do so, even at the risk of failure, in order to be able to affirm his *own* vision of reality. And the result of this forbidding task, we must remember, was the conception and the embodiment of another great tragedy, *Coriolanus* – in this case fully developed and fully worked out. Think how close in character Timon and Coriolanus are – rigid, extremist, blunt, uncompromising, deeply flawed in their inability to recognize the realities of their world or to modify their attitudes in conformity with its hypocrisies. And think how similarly hypocritical, self-seeking and unprincipled are the people they both react so violently against. Of course there are profound differences: the Plebeians of Rome are more sharply formed than the merchants of Athens, and Timon represents a noble humanism betrayed by meanness, whereas Coriolanus is cold, proud, contemptuous of the people, a superior Patrician who sneers at their rights and claims, and dismisses them as worthless.

Nevertheless, as one commentator has put it:

> The connections between *Timon* and *Coriolanus* are so close and so striking that it looks rather as though the one play may have grown out of the other. *Timon*, which seems to have been abandoned by its author before he had properly finished it, is, like *Coriolanus*, the story of a man who comes to hate his native city because it has treated him with gross ingratitude. This story is paralleled and reinforced by another, that of Alcibiades, the soldier and statesman who is banished from Athens because he opposes honour and the soldierly values to the usury of the Senate, and who returns heading an avenging army. Plutarch couples Alcibiades with Coriolanus and compares them with each other, showing a decided preference for the Greek, who was much the better politician of the two. What could be more likely, therefore, than that Shakespeare, dissatisfied with what he had made of the stories of Timon and Alcibiades, should have taken up the same basic themes again in the form of a story which lay so ready to his hand as that of Coriolanus?[34]

The answer to the question seems obvious. But Shakespeare's handling of the Coriolan theme does not invalidate what he actually *did* make of *Timon*. For *Timon* has a theme essentially different in its emphasis and in its nature, in the whole force and drift of the action, from that of *Coriolanus*. And for this reason it has an immense interest in its own right, failure or not. For what fascinates here is the nature of the attempt Shakespeare makes *upon* such a theme, the fact that he should have taken up the challenge of it. What he makes of it is a strange, starkly contrasted morality play whose hero stands deluded in 'a dream of friendship', with his court a charade he believes in (or refuses not to believe in) till shocked awake by economic ruin, to become at once a man stripped bare, a 'naked gull'[35] in a world of self-seekers, hypocrites, 'mouth-friends', where, in the wreckage of all he had built his life upon, he is driven to the opposite extreme, deranged by the horror and the baseness. For now he sees how deeply the power of money rules men's hearts and commands their virtues; and his appalled discovery seems to strike at the very roots of human interchange, contaminating every decency. To him, in his prophetic indictment, gold – 'sweet king-killer', cause of 'dear divorce /Twixt natural son and sire', this 'bright defiler /Of Hymen's purest bed', that 'solderst close impossibilities, /And mak'st them kiss'[36] – is man's disease. It turns everything into its opposite – makes 'black, white; foul, fair; /Wrong, right; base, noble; old, young; coward, valiant'.[37] Or, as Marx spells it out, commenting on these very words:

What I as a man cannot do, i.e. what all my individual powers cannot do, I can do with the help of *money*. Money therefore transforms each of these essential powers into something which it is not, into its opposite . . . [It] is the external, universal means and power – derived not from man as man and not from human society as society – to turn imagination into reality and reality into mere imagination . . . [It] appears as an inverting power in relation to the individual and to those social and other bonds which claim to be essences in themselves. It transforms loyalty into treason, love into hate, hate into love, virtue into vice, vice into virtue, servant into master, master into servant, nonsense into reason and reason into nonsense . . .[38]

Thus the creative intuition of Shakespeare probes the incipient roots of a new and ruthless order bred from the ruins of the old, and reaches beyond its growing forms to anticipate in the outrage of Timon's vision the social inhumanities of nineteenth-century capitalism and the deep-running force of Marxian indignation. But what is most astonishing about this is the sustained energy and vitality, the unremitting harshness and penetration of the language of Timon as he rages against the 'smiling, smooth, detested parasites, /Courteous destroyers, affable wolves, meek bears', these 'vapours and minute-jacks'[39] who have betrayed and broken him. For this is a language that registers the death-agonies of the medieval order, the break-up of a world in which (as Timon wills it in his impotent curse):

Piety and fear,
Religion to the gods, peace, justice, truth,
Domestic awe, night-rest, and neighbourhood,
Instruction, manners, mysteries, and trades,
Degrees, observances, customs, and laws[40]

seem to be collapsing against the thrust and force of 'confounding contraries'. It is the language of a Lear writ large, made absolute, pushed beyond the limit, beyond help or hope, launched against mankind in a general malediction.

Such an indictment is, however, not the end, though it may seem so. It is one man's end, the collapse of a particular world within the larger world of human action. Shakespeare moves beyond it to contain its devastating criticism within a far wider and deeper vision of reality. For what gives the great plays (even this, the most negative among them) their enduring, life-enhancing scope and range is the other qualities they possess – qualities one might have thought there would be no room for, qualities so characteristic of Shakespeare that we are almost inclined to take them for granted: the tenderness, the compassion, the humanism, the gravity, the warmth. Which is to affirm that, even in face of the most annihilating negatives, his innate life-making powers were never brutalized, defeated or submerged. Indeed, he came out of the crisis delineated by the tragedies with a deeper and more passionate sensitivity to the human condition – changed, naturally, but one might say purified, purged, no longer quite in the same world – 'on the other side of mankind', as Paul Celan writes.[41] It was the experience of that hazardous journey through a poisoned universe (the period from *Julius Caesar* to *Coriolanus*) which gave him the power to achieve the glowing aftermath of the last plays. His sensate knowledge of disaster and of elemental struggle confirmed him in acceptance of the delight of life as a manifestation of the creative order of things. For there, beyond the terror – having mastered it, having fought his way through the darkness – he was free to let his genius play upon the varieties of moral action, and to put the seal of maturity and completeness to a lifetime's work.

In these last plays, that is, with their recurrent themes of wrongs committed, and of retribution, repentance, reconciliation and renewal, Shakespeare makes his summing-up. He celebrates a world transformed, a world rich with dream-like forms and presences, a world in which reality is subjected to higher powers shaping the destinies of men and women to a moral end. And in his preoccupation with these higher powers, with magic and miracle, he makes much freer play than ever before with the unities of time and place and circumstance. This has been represented by some readers as a sign of weakened control, as a dismaying drift into the region of the fairy-tale, and even as a sort of character-change in Shakespeare himself. But the plays cannot seem other to those who have any intimate knowledge of the work as a whole than a natural and organic culmination of all that has gone before. As Georg Lukács points out, writing of Thomas Mann, but in words that apply with singular force to Shakespeare:

If there is a consistent curve in a person's development from possibility to fulfilment, then his life is seen to have a synthetic character from the outset. Novalis called this the unity of fortune and temperament, Goethe the deepest happiness of the personality – the bringing to ripeness of one's early tendencies. This phenomenon may sometimes receive a mystical or semi-mystical explanation. Yet it is an important fact of life, a very significant perception of the relationship between character and circumstances. It is also an extreme. In very many cases the core of personality is too weak to maintain a structural identity through a ceaseless continuity of change. Yet each person has a tendency in this direction, for good or ill, and most people would value the measure and depth of personality by this kind of constancy, this continuous development of inherent endowment; they would all desire it for themselves. Of course, the dialectical thesis of the unity of identity and non-identity holds good here. The constant (those who are deeply rooted in their own natures) often undergo far more radical changes and upheavals than the inconstant. The point here is that a 'permanence in change' is achieved: the core of personality keeps its balance through and by means of the most extreme metamorphoses.[42]

This permanence in change is nowhere in literature quite so convincingly demonstrated as in the works of Shakespeare – in the language, the ideas, themes, images, symbols and metaphors that the language quickens with from play to play. They are the product, that is, of 'one significant, consistent and developing personality',[43] as Eliot confirms – of a deeply searching mind and a sensibility capable of giving shape to many of the issues that are of central concern and significance to Western man. We read them, and respond to them, for their perceptiveness, their insight, their profound exploration of the conditioning forces that shape the nature of man, and for what they have to offer *us* as human beings in search of answers perhaps to some of the enigmas of reality. As Albert Einstein once said: 'Reality is not given to us, it is put to us, like a riddle'; and this demands that we involve ourselves in the complexities and puzzlements of what it means to be alive, as Shakespeare did to the end in terms of the underlying historical conditions of his time.

Take, for instance, the great final scene from *The Winter's Tale*, and the sensation we get from it of emotional authenticity and of imaginative truth – of a profound inclusive vision revealing and playing upon the essences of an organic human order; the way it celebrates and enacts the nature of creative awareness and recognition. 'Oh, she's warm,' Leontes cries, quickening to the presence, the actuality, of the woman his jealousy had deprived him of sixteen years before. And then: 'If this be magic, let it be an art / Lawful as eating.'[44]

It is the intensity of the conjunction that matters, the exactness of focus between the intangible, the almost miraculous essence of feeling, and the bodily substance, the sensuous, demonstrable, daily functions – magic and eating; for the recognition is both to Leontes. Shakespeare's metaphor is invested with an urgency and a value that are the consequence of the elemental nature of experienced truth. The urgency and the value, that is, are not abstract or theoretical, but deeply felt in the shock of sensuous recognition through which the presence of Hermione is registered.

This kind of truth, 'shadowed, or revealed', as G. Wilson Knight comments, gesturing towards the meaning, 'is only to be known, if at all, within the subjective personality, the "I" not easily linked into an objective argument'. And the essence of his meaning is perhaps that such truths can only be embodied (as Shakespeare embodies them) in symbolic terms, in terms of metaphors and images (and as so often at such moments, of music), direct, by sensation and by association; and that they are not to be explained, since they have no existence in the abstract. Yes: 'Hermione's restoration not only has nothing to do with black magic; it is not even transcendental. *It exists in warm human actuality.*'[45] And the recognition of this quickening, this re-birth, comes (for us as much as for Leontes) as a gradual awakening into the pain and wonder of new life, very much as it comes in that marvellous recognition-scene between Pericles and Marina, with its sea imagery and its music, in *Cymbeline*, and in the manner in which Shakespeare himself describes, in *The Winter's Tale*, the earlier reunion between Leontes and Camillo:

They seemed almost, with staring on one another, to tear the cases of their eyes; there was speech in their dumbness, language in their very gesture; they looked as they had heard of a world ransomed, or one destroyed: a notable passion of wonder appeared in them; but the wise beholder, that knew no more but seeing, could not say if the importance were joy or sorrow; but in the extremity of the one it must needs be.[46]

This defines a vision of the making of a new world, a new community, out of the ruins of the old: a wakening to new levels of reality, based upon the fullest recognition of the rooted essences of feeling, the proofs of love – what Lear denied and through the tempest of the consequences of that denial finally recovered and died for. Shakespeare is reaching out here for the foundations on which all concepts of community and of creative social interchange must be built and without which all societies must fail. Because without the living proofs of trust and confidence and mutual respect and recognition to bind them there can be no co-operation. He is here, it may be said, setting out his blueprints for utopia, those conditions of rediscovery and rebirth which reshape the sensibility and the moral consciousness in terms of the actualities of a new world. And that is the stress of Wilson Knight's identification in the scene between Leontes and Hermione; for the identification is essentially defined as a release and a rebirth. In this sense at once aesthetic and fundamentally social, it must be visceral, sensuous, felt – a quickening in the blood, exactly as we see this happening to Leontes. For we are there *with* Leontes. We *become* what is happening to him. We *share* his experience, and the social nature of that sharing enlarges our experience of the social nature of all shared experience. With Leontes 'opening his free arms, and weeping / His welcomes forth',[47] we see life come awake again, breaking through the deadness. We sense the astonishment, the disbelief, the breathless choked depth of feeling rising to the surface like sap from some shut level of the self. And in the adrenalin shock of that recognition, reality is transformed, illuminated. What had begun with the crime and the blasphemy of a warped mind ('I have drunk, and seen the spider')[48] has given way to the healing powers of 'great creating nature', even as in the play winter gives way to summer. That is the measure of the utopian perspective of *The Winter's Tale*. It affirms the sanity of the moral, human order in terms of the creative laws of the natural world, and celebrates through the love of Florizel and Perdita, the children of divided parents, the rediscovery of these laws, the renewal of the self, a return to the roots, such quickening of potentiality that it seems 'with every wink of the eye, some new grace will be born'.[49]

What is most remarkable about this is the complex psychological depth of response it registers, the sensitivity, the tenderness, the urgency and strength that lie behind it. Shakespeare, probing the darkness around him, seeking resolution and reassurance in a violent world, 'working out a morality', as L. C. Knights observes of the Sonnets, 'based on his own finest perceptions and deepest impulses',[50] has no facile, complacent answers to offer. The triumphant affirmatives of these last four plays emerge out of the contradictions of reality, the tragic struggles and collisions of human beings and Shakespeare's understanding of their fundamental needs in the context of the alien oppressive powers that threaten them.

This insistent process, this sense of a quest for the creative equation, is nowhere more profoundly embodied than in *The Tempest*, Shakespeare's valedictory summing-up, which is uniquely dedicated to 'the great globe itself' and its mysterious creative energies. *The Tempest*, moreover, is peculiarly relevant to the great general issues concerning the nature of man's place in his world, the role of literature, in relation to the struggle for the future, and the part the artist himself has to play as a witness to the creative powers of man in a world threatened with the falsifications and betrayals of abstract theory. For it acutely reflects and focuses the spirit of what Marx was attempting to demonstrate in defining what the essence of human nature – of man as a part of nature, man in conjunction with nature – might actually come to signify when the sensate being is free to realize its subjective potentialities in objective social terms. And the drama does so with the more cogency in that it features as its protagonist a man who is specifically a philosopher – a man long and sedulously engaged in a search for understanding of his world and of the springs of action; one who, in pursuit of these settled aims, had long neglected the social and political claims of the real world as defined by his position as Duke of Milan. And its theme determines Prospero's attempt to reconcile his abstract philosophical vision with the actualities of the world as it is.

The Tempest is a vision of the world of history and time and human capacity, of power and the limits of power, the scope of man and the scope of nature, of illusion and reality. It represents an attempt to reconcile the opposites and contradictions of existence, things as they are and things imagined; to enact utopia, to unite dream and reality. But Shakespeare's perspectives are not utopian. Dream, for all its marvellous inventiveness, its power to illuminate and to enhance the life of man, to enrich and to extend his consciousness, cannot rise above or conjure away the substance of things. Its potency is rooted in and (like the play itself) dependent upon the contexts of objective actuality, and must acknowledge what exists – what place and time and change, by transformation, by incessant interaction and conjunction, unpredictably 'increasing store with loss, and loss with store,' are masters of. Though the dream is in us and part of the process, it outstrips and is outstripped by the unforeseeable but inexorable conjunctions of reality. And Shakespeare's deep awareness of the actualities of time and history, the concreteness, the immediacy, the startlingly concrete nature of the process of life happening around him in a revolutionized world, checks dream and sets it in its masterful context, putting a limit to wisdom, forcing even the higher human powers in the end to yield. But if the author of *The Tempest* demonstrates, with Prospero's final dramatic resignation of power, that he is not a utopian, it would be equally mistaken to assume that he is purely a materialist. For he sees the world as a complex phenomenon in which dream and actuality are deeply interwoven. He registers the irreducible objective existence of the outer world – the collapsing feudal system and the new humanism of the Renaissance – in the context of the inner world of Prospero's vision, as a structure enacted in the mind. He shows us, in metaphor, what the intellect and the imagination at their fullest stretch, working together, can achieve, as a symbolic parallel to what the Renaissance itself achieved in its enlargement of the understanding of the universe. For Prospero's 'enchanted isle' reflects a deeply Renaissance view of humanity. On one level, that is, it functions as a creation of the reasoning senses and of the will, to serve the exploratory powers of the intellect and to place man at the centre of his world, as its maker. And as a complement to this, it is a manifestation of the powers and energies of nature, and of man as a part of nature. But including this and beyond this it is at the same time a dream world, a baseless fabric woven by the intellect and the imagination, created *in* the mind and acted out (as the play is acted out) as an internal vision of reality – a vision that (as such) will melt 'into air, into thin air'. For at this level, as Prospero's philosophical utopia, it has no substance; it is an endless dialectic process breeding from each proof its matched antithesis – a vision of transient perfections traced upon the atmosphere, perfections broken into by the crude realities of the world as it is, the world of the island's physical presences and the world beyond the island, fed by appetite, greed, will, blind ambition.

This Prospero clearly recognizes at the very moment of his triumph when, in the midst of celebrating the contract of love between Ferdinand and Miranda, his dream of reconciliation, he is suddenly shocked awake at the realization that he had forgotten the conspiracy of Caliban. Reality, grating against the dream, intervenes, and 'to a strange, hollow, and confused noise' the revellers he has conjured up 'heavily vanish', leaving him touched with anger and forcing from him the bitter acknowledgement that we are nothing more than such stuff as dreams are made of, and that all we build with such care and concern is fated to vanish like a dream:

> The cloud-capped towers, the gorgeous palaces,
> The solemn temples, the great globe itself,
> Yea, all which it inherit, shall dissolve,
> And, like this insubstantial pageant faded,
> Leave not a rack behind.[51]

For such is the action of history in time – of the histories of cities and cultures and civilizations. They are dictated to, as all man's aspirations, by 'time's injurious hand', noted incessantly at work even as we note

> the hungry ocean gain
> Advantage on the kingdom of the shore,
> And the firm soil win of the watery main,
> Increasing store with loss, and loss with store,

to bring an 'interchange of state, /Or state itself confounded to decay'.[52] And all organic life is part of that process – destroying and replenishing in ways that man himself, for all his visionary plans, whatever his powers, cannot arrest or deny.

All the same, what the Prospero vision provides, even in its partial failure, is a unique awareness of the tenacity and the arduousness of the struggle; of the richness and multiplicity that had gone into the struggle; and of the paradoxical nature of reality itself. Indeed, the splendour of Shakespeare's imagined universe is the evidence it offers of the depth and range of the imaginative intellect in its attempt to forge a reconciliation between the opposites, a creative equation.

But even as 'the isle is full of noises, /Sounds and sweet airs, that give delight and hurt not',[53] and as (in like sense) the play itself is full of images and symbols of creative delight and the free play of the nobler human faculties; so this delight is matched and countered by the grossness that goes with it, the weight and substance of material things. And if the triumph of Prospero in bringing Ferdinand and Miranda together represents the triumph of love and delight and community overriding divisive power, it is checked by the salutary knowledge that it has its limits. For this triumph is inseparably involved with the amorphous, the half-formed, the incomplete, the crude essences that constitute the organic whole. Caliban the moon-calf jars and drags at Prospero's vision; Trinculo and Stephano stand with the lovers and beside them as the uncomprehending confusion of the senses; Antonio and Sebastian (momentarily subdued at the end) remain a continuing threat to community, bred on hate and the will to power in darkness, sunk in the 'evilly compounded vital I',[54] and incapable of rising above its diseased appetite, even when commanded by the powers of intellect and imagination, because not in possession of such powers, and capable only of being what their bankrupt self-seeking literalism permits them to be.

The fact that Prospero himself should have chosen reconciliation rather than revenge in dealing with such enemies is to be explained in terms of the historical and social background that had nourished in him his deep sense of the principles of order, balance and degree, of kinship and community. Drawn, by nature of his rooted sense of place in what he assumed to be a stable world, towards a life of contemplation, he had spent his life seeking the intangible essences of things. For even as Duke of Milan he was, as he says,

>   so reputed
> In dignity, and for the liberal arts,
> Without a parallel: those being all my study,
> The government I cast upon my brother,
> And to my state grew stranger, being transported
> And rapt in secret studies . . . all dedicated
> To closeness and the bettering of my mind.

Such studies were, it seems, indispensable; and for him the library 'was dukedom large enough'.[55] But this sedentary inclination could only be pursued by neglecting his duties and responsibilities. The dreamer, the visionary, the thinker had made the mistake of trusting the actualities of power into the hands of the literalists, and had failed to notice that his world was changing around him, being undermined by a new and unscrupulous breed of men, with his brother among them. That is, in pursuit of his utopian ideas, the bettering of his mind, his theory of equilibrium, he had ceased to concern himself with the actualities that are the indispensable complement to theory, and thus had left himself exposed to manipulation and conspiracy.

But in spite of the usurpation, Prospero's position as an exile is in the deepest sense a twelve-year extension of his way of life in Milan. Transported to the island by 'providence divine', with his daughter as the embodiment and sign of love and indeed his preserver, and with 'volumes that I prize above my dukedom',[56] he continues with his studies, as at home, as if this place *were* his study, as if he had never left Milan at all. The fundamental difference is that now, acutely aware of all he had failed to take into account back in Milan and thus of his own position as an alienated intellectual, he knows exactly where he is and what he has to do, and has long been directing his energies towards a confrontation with the forces that had betrayed him. Now, after twelve years spent mastering the secrets of the hidden energies and elements of his island world in the closest contact with the creative Ariel-spirit that controls them, he is at last in the position to enact his plan and bring his powers to bear upon his enemies. But he is aware too that, having reached the zenith, he must act decisively and swiftly to make his 'high charms work', since he knows that if he does not everything must fail and his fortunes for ever after droop.

Prospero's task has involved much more than the abstruse problems of his utopian vision – the problems of the prescient Renaissance humanist contemplating the universe. It has involved grappling with the problems of the real world and its complex incessantly changing conditions. And to this end, he has had to control in *himself* confusion and perversity, the base desires of the self – the desire for revenge, the desire to kill, to destroy, the lusts of the amorphous world of the instincts, as personified in Caliban, who remains to taunt him with his past and will not go away or be other than he is – the living proof of what is still there, however suppressed, in Prospero. Most disquieting of all, this embodiment of unrefined instinct – this palpable crude element in the world that Prospero commands – who has threatened more than once to possess Miranda, to pollute her and to people the isle with Calibans – comes very close to overthrowing him. Like Ariel, he is part of the natural elemental order of things which Prospero has so long sought to master and to harness to his ends. But unlike Ariel he resents Prospero, not only because he thinks of the island as his by right, but also because he feels the injustice of being continually abused and beaten and treated like a slave, especially since he was once made so much of, taught to speak and given such loving encouragement. Not being equipped with sufficient moral awareness to recognize the enormity of his crime against Miranda, he cannot understand why Prospero should be so vindictive with him. And when Prospero calls him

> A devil, a born devil, on whose nature
> Nurture can never stick; on whom my pains,
> Humanely taken, all, all lost, quite lost,[57]

one begins oneself to wonder why, and to ask just how much trouble he has *ever* been willing to take with Caliban and whether after all his rebellious subject hasn't some cause to feel indignant and resentful. For in truth, in his slow-witted simple way, Caliban shows himself capable of much more than Prospero will ever admit. He is possessed by a tantalizing sense of the beauty of the island and the pain of the delight of its 'sounds and sweet airs', as wakened in him by Prospero. But the trouble is he has not been given the power to rationalize his longings or to find release for them, except in sleep. 'You, /You taught me language,' he cries in his frustration, accusing Prospero; 'and my profit on't /Is, I know how to curse.'[58] Only in dream does he have any hope, and then it is as if

> The clouds, methought, would open, and show riches
> Ready to drop upon me, that when I waked
> I cried to dream again.[59]

So he too stirs, though he cannot on his own break free. Trapped in his bestial creature-frame he has no choice but to submit, however grudgingly, to the will of his master. He is Prospero's failure, the flaw in his utopian scheme – a 'thing of darkness'[60] he cannot bring himself to reason with and seems able to control only by adopting the repressive methods of a tyrant.

It is otherwise with his enemies. As 'one of their kind, that relish all as sharply',[61] he is able to forgive them when he has them in his power rather than act the tyrant because he can appeal to them in terms of a common moral code and expect his magnanimity to have some impact. Though Antonio and Sebastian remain, like Caliban, trapped within the self, they are in fact human beings. Prospero knows he cannot do much to make them see beyond their condition, as prisoners of the blinded will. For he knows they lack imagination and respect for others, all those qualities that make it possible for men to rise above their own self-bent view of things. He knows that they are gifted only with cunning, and that behind them lie the stunted lives of creatures of appetite, which he cannot hope to change. But at least he can impose upon them the knowledge of his own superior moral vision and shame them into submission. Apart from that he can do nothing. It is enough that he has triumphed, that for the moment the nobler human faculties have prevailed, that love and magnanimity have determined the outcome, that Miranda and Ferdinand are there, confirming the promise of the future, and that Ariel himself, the spirit of the island, inhabiting the air, as quick as light, as water, as birdsong, as the sap of the earth, is still at Prospero's command. But the future is not his. Prospero knows he must set Ariel free and give the island back to Caliban, and thus divest himself of his power. His plan accomplished, the lovers must now (for good or ill) become their own protectors.

On this enchanted island, the reflective powers of a lifetime's study are brought to fruition. But to what end? With what consequences, now that Prospero's reign is over? What is to happen to the baser elements? Who is to safeguard Prospero's achievements after he has resigned his power, and lacks 'spirits to enforce, art to enchant'?[62] He cannot master history, time, the human condition. The promise that he has engineered is ambiguous and shadowed by the unknown future. True, the evils of the past have for the moment been resolved; Prospero has put the record straight and demonstrated the triumph of creative will and justice. But what follows is not utopia but the recognition that the real world, the world of Milan and Naples and the interaction of people on each other, is not constructed to permit the embodiment of utopia. This does not of course invalidate Prospero's attempt – for without such attempts the perspectives of humanity would remain narrow and constricted, bound by the bankrupt literalism of people like Antonio, devoid of vision. Prospero had risked and lost his dukedom for a higher concept of reality than that which is defined by the pursuit of wealth and political power. But when the ultimate moment of assessment comes he has to accept that this 'brave new world'[63] Miranda looks out upon with such astonishment is not much different from the old, and that in it conspiracy and deception, theft and murder will continue to operate. And this, he knows, is not the kind of world Miranda has been equipped to cope with. She is innocent, untested, on the threshold of experience; and she has everything to learn.

Of course, at another level it can be argued, even in Prospero's terms, that nothing is ever the same, and that the new balance that has come into being from the 'fair encounter /Of two most rare affections'[64] has its own rich promise. Because for Ferdinand and Miranda the world *is* at once brave and new, and at a new beginning. They have not yet been exposed to the daily struggle against habit or to the influence of those who have already been conditioned and hardened by the pressures of the world they live in. Their problem is to learn to see things as they are rather than as they see each other and to learn from what they see without (if possible) having their vision dulled and warped by the traffic of life.

Prospero's philosophical utopia is a particularly cogent instance of the vision of Renaissance humanism. It exists in the context of the Neoplatonic philosophies that influenced Copernicus and Bruno, and the vision of a rational universe so radiantly defined in Raphael's *School of Athens*. But *The Tempest* represents that vision (and the creative optimism that is its inspiration) in the sober knowledge of its limits – a vision bounded and commanded by history and by the laws of nature as determined by the structure of society at a particular point in history. Prospero makes his great effort almost as if he were willing the realization of his long-prepared long-meditated dream. It is an effort to conquer the physical world, to harness the forces of nature, to influence history, to reconcile the opposites, and to neutralize the dangers that threaten the moral order he conceives for his utopia. As he answers Ariel, as his project gathers to a head:

> Hast thou, which art but air, a touch, a feeling
> Of their afflictions, and shall not myself,
> One of their kind, that relish all as sharply,
> Passion as they, be kindlier moved than thou art?
> Though, with their high wrongs I am struck to the quick,
> Yet with my nobler reason, 'gainst my fury
> Do I take part. The rarer action is
> In virtue than in vengeance: they being penitent,
> The sole drift of my purpose doth extend
> Not a frown further.[65]

This is a far cry from Timon's misanthropy. Shakespeare has found the way out of the trap of negation to offer his findings to the world – not as resignation, but as positive choice, as moral action, in the triumph of self-conquest; as a blueprint for the future.

But in doing so he does not offer us a package for utopia, the romanticist's glittering and unattainable prize. 'Their senses I'll restore,' says Prospero, 'and they shall be themselves.'[65] And in the recognition that he has no choice *other* than to restore them, he knows that when they *are* themselves again, they will be what their past has made them. But what he has done is to give that world his vision, his perspective, his example, adding to it the dimension of creative insight. And at the end he knows that, having yielded up his power, he cannot escape, that he is in the hands of time, confronted by the uncontainable scope and complexity of the real world, a small part of its continuity, its subsistent order.

If it were to be asked what bearing such a view as this can have upon the issues that face us in the twentieth century (and there are no doubt many who think of Shakespeare as nothing more than an overrated institution), one might answer that the issues which face us, as they face all who are seriously concerned with the nature of reality and of the human struggle, are the same issues fundamentally that Shakespeare faced up to so unflinchingly in the great tragedies and made his final attempt to reconcile in *The Tempest*. And it seems to me that if we read him with any sort of attention, we must accept that he has got these issues deep and seen them true; and that with all his marvellous intuition and intensity, his unerring perceptiveness and delicacy, what he has to say is of crucial importance to us. Not that we can expect to find him providing any definitive answers, because he makes it clear enough that there are none except in the falsifying terms of the abstracts of thought; but that his work, in its deepening exploration of the conditions and dimensions of the human struggle, offers at its most percipient and concentrated a record of the subsistent order of the universe as a natural, human, social process, which Prospero's enchanted isle – 'as strange a maze as e'er men trod', 'all torment, trouble, wonder, and amazement'[66] – triumphantly celebrates.

Part Three

'Rouse up, O Young Men of the New Age! Set your foreheads against the ignorant hirelings! For we have hirelings in the Camp, the Court, and the University, who would, if they could, for ever depress Mental, and prolong Corporeal war.'

William Blake
Preface to Milton

8

ACTUALITY AND THE ABSTRACT:
THE ALIENATING PROCESS

The struggle for resolution and equilibrium and fulfilment, the struggle against negation and surrender, the struggle of man to break out of the trap of his conditioning, is a struggle against the alienating abstractions that define the terms of his unfreedom. It therefore presupposes a conscious understanding of the underlying conditions of his world, the laws which control nature and society. And as such, this struggle, this process of dialectical adjustment to the constantly changing conditions of reality, has to be continually renewed. As Milovan Djilas comments, reflecting on the 'nature and course of Communism during a period of more than fifteen years' of bitter but confirmed resistance to its absolutist dogma: 'Victory is only a continuation of the struggle, only a discovery of the possibilities for a further struggle.'[1] Shakespeare understood the truth of this, taking his leave (as Prospero in the aftermath of victory) at the end of his last play. For the question that asks itself in the aftermath of all achievement is: 'How can one reconcile what in the beating mind becomes irreconcilable, a tissue of hypotheses, an endless dialectic process, breeding from each proof its matched antithesis and in the moment's change, some new and unforeseen conjunction, as the cells divide and pair again, to undermine finality?'[2]

Today, the world is as thick with enemies and threats as it was for Prospero and Shakespeare in the sixteenth century and Marx in the nineteenth, and if we are to be able to take our stand against them, or even to know what *kind* of stand to take, we shall need to be properly equipped to understand the nature of the problems that face us and what it is we are fighting *for*; and this will demand from us the highest critical and moral standards – the kind of standards that served Shakespeare himself and kept him alert to his own 'finest perceptions and deepest impulses'.

Of course, the world we live in is very different in structure from the world that Shakespeare knew. As Marx has pointed out: 'The abstraction of the *state as such* was not created until modern times. The abstraction of the political state is a modern product.'[3] And what Marx is suggesting about this process, which has brought about the separation, the estrangement of man within society, is that 'the whole phenomenon of the detachment of state from society (as of politics from economics, of public life from private life) is itself modern.'[4] Though Shakespeare himself deeply anticipated the process by which this would come about, in the sixteenth century, as Marx defines it, 'the classes of civil society were identical with the Estates in the political sense, because civil society was political society; because the organic principle of civil society was the principle of the state'. In other words, 'the identity of the civil and political classes in the Middle Ages was the expression of the identity of civil and political society'.[5] But what Shakespeare witnessed and registered with such percipience in his art were the peculiarly dramatic and painful beginnings of a new age – the age of Renaissance humanism, vigorous and ruthless, quickening in the aftermath of the stabilized unfreedoms of feudalism. By the nineteenth century this process of development had been taken to its logical conclusion; because, with the medieval estates transformed into social classes, and this transformation completed by the French Revolution, the 'class *distinctions* in civil society became mere *social* differences in private life and had no significance in political life and civil society'.[6]

The situation today has been carried even further by the advances of technology and the development of bureaucratic systems of control. In modern civil society the individual is 'integrated neither into a citizen community, as in ancient times, nor into a particular corporate community (for example, a trade guild), as in medieval times. In civil society . . . individuals are divided from and independent of each other.' Or, to be more explicit, as Fredric Jameson is in his book *Marxism and Form*:

the development of post-industrial monopoly capitalism has brought with it an increasing occultation of the class structure through techniques of mystification practiced by the media and particularly by advertising in its enormous expansion since the onset of the Cold War. In existential terms, what this means is that *our experience is no longer whole*: we are no longer able to make any felt connection between the concerns of private life, as it follows its own course within the walls and confines of the affluent society, and the structural projections of the systems in the outside world, in the form of neocolonialism, oppression, and counter-insurgency warfare. In psychological terms, we may say that as a service-economy we are henceforth so far removed from the realities of production and work in the world that we inhabit a dream world of artificial stimuli and televised experience: never in any previous civilization have the great metaphysical preoccupations, the fundamental questions of being and the meaning of life, seemed so utterly remote and pointless.[7]

But this in fact brings us back to the primary issues as these are defined by the Shakespearian vision. Because in that vision is embodied the confrontation of man with the forces of the universe, man exposed to crisis and the threat of annihilation in his struggle to command and to comprehend what is beyond his power, which here too puts the fundamental questions of being and the meaning of life at risk. The very force and energy, the penetrating human concern of Shakespeare's vision of reality – that concern which insists always on placing man as a sensuous particular organic being at the source of all concerns – provides a trenchant criticism of, and an incentive to oppose, the drift of events in the modern world. It stands in total opposition to that process of estrangement and of abstraction which Marx went to such lengths, both in his political and his economic analysis, to challenge. For, as he notes at the start of the *Critique*, 'the family and civil society are the preconditions of the state; they are its true agents'. And the basis of his attack is that in 'speculative philosophy it is the reverse. When the idea is subjectivized the *real* subjects – civil society, the family, "circumstances, caprice, etc." – are all transformed into *unreal*, objective moments of the Idea referring to different things.'[8] In fact, Shakespeare also attacks such an inversion of the social order in *Timon*, even though it seems that society and the state have not yet become estranged. He is fully and shatteringly aware of the ways in which men estrange themselves from each other and distort the structure of the state to their own ends, or find themselves trapped within the abstract machinery of action and reaction which defines the ways in which the inexorable movements of time and history work upon them. One has only to refer to *Hamlet* as to *Coriolanus*, or to *Lear*, or to the dislocations that take place in *Macbeth*, to recognize the urgency of his explorations into the psychology of men in their battle for life, and of his insight into those potentialities (those pre-conditions of the capitalist system) which were to develop so disastrously throughout the course of the seventeenth century.

It is a salutary vision of the human situation that Shakespeare's work offers because it offers an inclusive image of reality. And his work has its special meaning for us today above all *because* it reaffirms the human context against the vicious abstractions that dominate our lives, the divisions that persist, setting literature apart from politics and the citizen from the society he lives in. For with Shakespeare the divisiveness, the dichotomy, the sense of anguish, the torment of need, the alienating forces of the external world, are represented as basic issues, the tests of man's courage and strength, in a peculiarly organic interplay of opposing elements. Can it be said of him that he had no experience of the alienating pressures of life as we have known them? Surely not. He was alienated within his social world by the very nature of his inferior position as an actor, as is clear from 'the outcast state' he refers to again and again in the Sonnets. Thus we find him cursing his fate and wishing he were

> . . . like to one more rich in hope,
> Featured like him, like him with friends possessed,
> Desiring this man's art, and that man's scope,
> With what I most enjoy contented least.[9]

And thus, though the divisions of his world were never such as to inhibit in him his organic wholeness of vision, we note the speech and the accent of a man who registers the kind of dilemma familiar to the writer of today – alienated within society, prevented as an individual from playing his full part in the social life of his time, thrust into false positions, set apart because society itself has been disordered, dislocated, irrationally transformed by the historical process of capitalism and the ruthless manner in which it has exploited the resources of the commonwealth and the mass of the people who are its lifeblood. Timon foresaw the process by which this would come about, the power of money to destroy the organic living bonds of human relationships, 'the cold cash nexus' that was to become 'the universal means of separation',[10] thus poisoning the very roots of community and creating those conditions for the enslavement and degradation of whole societies which defined the monstrous inhumanities of the nineteenth century. And what of the explosive reactions to the tyranny of capitalist democracy?

Was it to be expected in an atmosphere so deeply divisive and embittered that the Marxian alternative would find the right conditions to develop without perversion? At any rate, we are faced with the bleak fact that in the so-called people's democracies an equally dismaying derangement has occurred, transforming the principles of socialism into a rigid absolutist creed enforced by bureaucratic party rule.

A clear awareness of these issues is crucial to the future and to the prospects for society in the future, the continuity of the struggle for emancipation and of the will to resist the apathy induced by the forces of abstraction that have sold so many into new and subtler forms of enslavement. Thus even a criticism of literature that ignores the 'questions on class, status, violence . . . questions about justice, power, control' is a crippled and diminished criticism. For such questions cannot be ignored; and any literature that ignores them and concerns itself exclusively with the private conflicts of people, leaving out the implications of their commerce with the world they live in, is a literature that is likely to find itself inadvertently supporting 'blind routine, obedience, authority'.[11] And how is a criticism that limits itself to questions of aesthetic order to deal with or to explain, *except* by ignoring, the phenomenon of such major figures as Eliot, Pound and Yeats lending their authority to the peculiarly barbaric and inhuman appeal of fascism? It cannot. But the problem exists nonetheless, and we have to reconcile the political attitudes of a Yeats with his greatness as a poet; to register at once the impurities that went into his 'devious and sometimes sinister political theories and activities' and the 'purity and integrity' that in the poetry are 'concentrated in metaphors of such power that they thrust aside all calculated intent'.[12] It is vitally important, that is, for criticism to have a grasp of the wider contexts within which literature exists. As George Abbot White has written:

> To speak about literature ideologically . . . would simply be *to reintroduce the world*; to raise old questions about the nature and purpose of literature and literary criticism; to ask, among other things, for a criticism, in Leo Marx's words, 'alert to lapses of moral vision'.

For the task, in response to reality as to literature, is the fundamentally critical task that refuses to permit one aspect of life to thrive at the expense of another; that sees moral vision (and its application) as essential to the aesthetic (and purely cultural) concerns of the artist, and any process which separates them as an aberration and (at least potentially) a betrayal. The problem is: 'How to make judgements both within and without history; how to make meaningful connnections, join those things which are different yet necessary; how to achieve unity of being so that one *does* what one *says*, *is* what one *believes*.'[13]

This is a problem of central significance to the survival of human freedom and of a world fit for people to live in; and because it is *that* first, it is so also to the critic of literature, who, as a part of his world, can only reflect and influence it as it is. And such a problem is at the root of Marx's thinking about society, since he knew that it radically determines the nature of society – a fact which subsequent critics of his work, including Lenin, tended to ignore as too difficult to reconcile with the revolutionary dogma necessary to the building of a new state. The disastrous consequences for all of us, critics of literature included, of the dichotomy between doing what one says and being what one believes, between the theories we profess and what we put into practice, are most devastatingly apparent in the social systems that have been imposed upon people; and they are nowhere more deeply underlined than in Lenin's ruthless application of Marxism. For Lenin believed that he was enacting his utopian dogma, and that such a society as the Bolshevik Party was organizing 'on the basis of a free and equal association of the producers, will put the whole machinery of state where it will then belong: into the Museum of Antiquities, by the side of the spinning-wheel and the bronze axe'.[14] It was a fine ideal, truly utopian in its faith in the future; but it remained dangerously out of focus with the actual conditions, and represents a monumental instance of the extent of the dislocation between idea and actuality. And if, as Lenin writes in 1917, more than sixty years ago, 'the destruction of the bureaucratic–military state machine is *the preliminary condition for every real people's revolution*',[15] then there must be something very much amiss between theory and action that such a condition should have remained unfulfilled. For it is surely not possible to accept the massive organization of bureaucratic power that dominates the Soviet Union today as fulfilling such a pre-condition. More appropriate, rather, would be the terms by which Lenin defined the England and America of 1917, as sunk into a 'bloody morass of bureaucratic–military institutions which subordinate every-thing to themselves and trample everything underfoot'.[16]

Lenin was adamant: 'the bureaucracy and the standing army are a "parasite" on the body of bourgeois society – a parasite created by the internal antagonisms which rend that society, but a parasite which chokes all its vital pores.'[17] But how else are the bureaucracy and the standing army and the labour camps and psychiatric hospitals of present-day Russia to be described? The indictment seems unanswerable. And the irony that echoes back from Lenin's words has a harsh and bluntly obvious implication: that all theory which ignores the basis on which it rests, the essential principle that the real people are the pre-conditions of any 'real people's revolution', is bound to end up by transforming these real people 'into *un*real objective moments of the Idea',[18] thus betraying the human substance which is the only justification for theory. In Soviet Russia, theory dominates and crushes and frustrates not only the people but also the very essence of socialist revolution, which is after all intended to *serve* the people; it has become divorced from, by imposing itself upon and forcing into sub-mission and conformity, the contradictory non-conformist chang-ing substance of reality. But this is only another way of saying that theory has become ideology, in the pejorative sense attached to it in Karl Mannheim's definition, as a system adopted by ruling groups who 'in their thinking become so intensively interest-bound to a situation that they are simply no longer able to see certain facts which would undermine their sense of domination'.[19] To put it more bluntly, what happens is that these ruling groups, in attempting to impose their systematic theories upon society, tend imperceptibly and disastrously to harden in face of the struggle for domination and to invest theory with a sort of absolute infallibility, till in the end the leaders become incapable of modifying and adjusting theory to the demands of reality. And it is then that ideology begins rigidly to oppose and to contort the nature of the human process it is dealing with and to make itself an enemy of progress and development and of all creative experiment. As soon as a revolutionary party ceases to be a party of opposition, and makes itself the ruling power, it ceases to be a revolutionary party, and becomes instead a new conservatism. From his position as the undisputed leader of the revolutionary party in 1917, Lenin takes the trouble to point out that 'there can be no thought of abolishing the bureaucracy at once, everywhere and completely. To believe that this can be done is to be a utopian,' he says. 'But to *smash* the old bureaucratic machine at once and to begin immediately to construct a new one that will permit us to abolish gradually all bureaucracy – this,' Lenin declares, 'is *not* utopian, this is the experience of the Commune.'[20]

Here one cannot help but notice the manner in which Lenin allows himself to be deluded into assuming that the second belief is not a utopian belief, even though it replaces one bureaucratic machine with another, because, firstly, the Commune seems to have proved it isn't and, secondly, he has dogmatically assumed that the revolutionary proletariat, unlike the bourgeoisie, has the superior will to abolish its own machine. But it is surely deeply utopian to suggest that any ruling group will wish to abolish the foundations of its power as soon as it has laid them. This may have seemed to be the achievement of the Paris Commune, but the Paris Commune was a limited event and lasted no longer than a few weeks. It was a very different matter when Lenin came to establish the foundations of the Soviet state. The Bolshevik party, as soon as it had smashed the Kerensky regime, at once set to work to consolidate its position; and over the years the idea of 'abolishing gradually all bureaucracy' has become an increasingly plaintive utopianism, receding further into the mythical distance with every brick that was added to the bureaucratic superstructure, and every person abolished to maintain it. 'What sort of government is it,' the heretic Djilas asks with a long experience of power behind him,

that finds its strength, and its justification before its own people, in falsehoods? What is the destination of a society that maintains and restores itself with injustice? What remains of ideas and ideals once they become means of terror and intimidation among their own adherents?[21]

The manner in which, and the rapidity with which, the Bolshevik leaders began to set up their bureaucratic–military institutions and their organs of repression demonstrates beyond all argument the dislocation of theory and practice, the triumph of dogma over logic, the substitution of an 'abstract-universal' for the actualities of the concrete world. Whatever its aims, in real terms this machinery of controls represented in a greatly intensified form all that Lenin had condemned so forcefully as the evil and inhuman attributes of bourgeois power. Is this the inevitable dilemma of revolution? Is this what Marx had spent his lifetime working for? Does his determinist philosophy inevitably assume what has actually occurred – a process 'irreconcilable with any belief in the influence of moral values on the development of civilization', as G. D. H. Cole asserts?[22] Was it any part of Marx's scheme for the emancipation of the people through socialism to set up a ruthless police-state bent on murdering the people into conformity? A violent process it would have to be – but did Marx conceive of the dictatorship of the proletariat as the rule of a terrorizing minority? This was certainly *not* the experience of the Commune. The Commune enacted quite a different kind of rule, which established respect for people as a central principle, and encouraged trust and confidence, an essentially moral responsibility. But Lenin's Russia built its strength on repression, and made the terrorizing weapon of the secret police an essential instrument of state policy. The bureaucratic–military state machine whose destruction Lenin considered a pre-condition for every real people's revolution was even from the start in process of being created in post-revolutionary Russia, and that is the devastating measure of the betrayal of the Revolution. 'If you want to run a state for ever without trouble, says Plato, says Hitler,' Jacob Bronowski comments, 'get rid of those whose make-up is odd, questioning, dissenting. Get rid of truth, get rid of literature, because their common interest is dissent.'[23] But in that case it is better not to think of people at all, let alone respect for people, or their emancipation.

Confronted with such fundamental contradictions, with the evidence of such blinded dogma and its lethal consequences, we are faced with imperative and bewildering questions which we cannot afford to argue away or gloss over, whatever our sympathies. It is not enough to applaud the spirit of the revolution or the nature of its attempt to change the world. We have to understand, in the psychological, the Shakespearian sense, what happened in the process. We have to register the relentless manner in which it was consolidated. We have to match, or to distinguish between, intention and effect. We need to adopt the harshest critical attitude towards, not only the philosophy that lay behind the struggle – that mixture of passionate humanism and rigid planning which was Lenin's massive contribution to the events of 1917 – but also the ways in which that philosophy was changed or failed to adjust itself when applied to the reality. The crucial problem here, as Bronowski points out, writing of Blake's dialectics, 'is that all societies fall short of man's good; but that men cannot be good, because they cannot be themselves, outside society. What is done always distorts what has been imagined. But what has been imagined must be given a shape by doing, and is not fully imagined until it has been done.'[24] The romantic or the worshipper, the absolutist or the cynic, may be able to reconcile the contradictions, because able to ignore the claims of reason; but those who care for people in the basic moral sense in which it is people – people and their diverse legitimate needs – that matter, cannot ignore such claims. After all, the aim of the Revolution was to create a *new kind* of world, a classless world, in which all men could at last begin to work together selflessly towards the common ends and aims of human life. And that world cannot be created on the basis of a murderous repressive system such as Russia instituted for its people almost from the start. The birth of the new society out of the old, accepting that it has to be violent, can only come about by creating a new and unequivocal concept of society that will support the highest aims of man unflinchingly at every turn and that will not in its embodiment betray these aims. 'Man must be set free, to make his good,' as Bronowski again asserts.

But he must still make his good himself. It is not a grace given to him, even by revolutions. They can give him the means to be good. They can free him from the drudgery, the fear, the rigorous forbidding thought, and the hunt of beasts for the mere necessaries of animal life, with which a society cripples and distorts the very will to be good. Revolutions can free him from self-interest: it is the thought which Marx made noble. But they have not then re-made man; they have freed him to re-make himself. The good remains an end to which societies can give means, but which man must know and must make.[25]

But man cannot either know or make this good without the deepest and most rigorous examination of meaning and motive and intention. What we need beyond the dogmas of a Lenin is the kind of searching methods Marx adopted from the very beginning in his approach to his great task.

A merciless criticism of everything that exists – this, if we can sustain it, is the method. And it is certain that without such criticism we shall be incapable of breaking through the conditioning barriers that hold us trapped in subjection to the pre-conceived notions, the dogmatic assumptions, of our particular social environment. Not that it is by any means certain that the adoption of what we *suppose* to be a 'merciless criticism of everything that exists' can give us any *assurance* of breaking through the barriers. But one has to make the attempt, however ill-equipped, because the issues that one faces are too important to be left to chance or to be shrugged away. These issues are as much my business as they were Marx's or Lenin's, and I must deal with them as I can, burdened though I am with all the limitations that make me what I am, even though my aims and interests are not Marx's or Lenin's, and in spite of the fact that I may not have the intellectual equipment to emulate the Marxes of this world. There is too much at stake, for me as well as for others, to leave such questions to the so-called experts. Each of us has his own part to play in the making of the future, and if we are to be able to play a *constructive* part, or to participate in the struggle for a constructive future, we have to do what we can to find out where we stand, and what we can do from where we are and as what we are. It is all very well to be well-meaning vague supporters of a better world and to trust to others to work for that better world, but none of us has any right to expect it to come about of its own accord. It will only come about if we are prepared to think it out and work for it, and to resist the forces that would divert it or corrupt it or destroy it. Lenin himself was unable to prevent the Russia he had struggled for with such ruthless concern from degenerating into the Russia of Stalin. He had visualized the necessary transition from capitalism to communism as a strictly transitional process during which terror and suppression would be unavoidable as a means to bring about the transformation. But he hadn't sufficiently calculated the impact of the psychology of totalitarian force, or the fatal need of the ruling few (including himself) to retain their instruments and, in perfecting them, to outlaw criticism itself. The 'special apparatus' of suppression that he organized and set up to enforce the change he saw not as a permanent weapon of the system, but as temporary. For, as he believed in his utopian wisdom, the suppression of the minority of exploiters by the majority of the wage slaves of yesterday is comparatively *so easy, simple and natural a task that it will entail far less bloodshed than the suppression of the risings of slaves, serfs or wage-labourers, and it will cost mankind far less.*'[26]

This we see in the light of the sixty years of suppression and bloodshed and terror that have succeeded not as a failure of vision but as a miscalculation. For though Lenin did not suggest that the process of transformation would necessarily be immediate, he does here suggest that it would not be difficult to accomplish, whereas the history of Russia – admittedly struggling against the enmity of the West – has proved it to be immensely difficult. Indeed, the prospect of a situation, or a stage of development, being reached in Russia when 'the need for a special machine of suppression will begin to disappear', seems as remote now as it seemed close to Lenin in 1917. 'The exploiters,' he says of the capitalist world, 'are naturally unable to suppress the people without a highly complex machine for performing this task'; and he is correct enough about this; 'but the *people* can suppress the exploiters even with a very simple machine, almost without a machine, without a special apparatus'.[27] The irony is that the Soviet state could not function today without a machine more complex than that of the capitalists, because it has to neutralize or to suppress all political dissent and criticism as traitorous. The terrible spectacle of the thirties, when thousands were hounded down, branded as enemies and liquidated, survives today with the shame of the far-flung labour-camps, demonstrating the cynicism of the claim of the soviets to stand freely for an emancipated communist world in which *all* can play their part.

This is not to suggest that the struggle for socialism in Russia has ceased, however congealed, however vulgarized, however betrayed by its fanatics, its bigots, its careerists. But it cannot claim, for all its material power and success *as* a power, to have achieved even the beginnings of a true socialism. For that there has to be freedom, freedom to think and freedom to criticize, a respect for the truth, trust in the people, and room for all (however critical) who are willing to work for a socialist future. And can we say these things exist? Not on the basis of the record we have of the totalitarian intolerance that has so distorted and deformed the struggle, and broken the spirit of so many splendid socialist men and women, and thus robbed Russia of so much irreplaceable leadership. Or if this is what is meant by socialism in action, this callous indifference to the value of the person, then it is time we turned to some other way of registering respect for people and of encouraging community among them, of creating the conditions that will enable the citizen to recognize the part he has to play in the communal enterprise and in freeing others to participate. Milovan Djilas puts it as one who speaks from knowledge as one of the oppressors, but with the intense awareness of a man alert to the *human* issues that are at stake:

Knowing is also acting. Upon our understanding of people depends our future relationship towards them. Those who accept progress without any reservations are usually people who are driving others and the very tide of life around them towards their own convictions. Tyranny begins with ultimate truths about society and man. And even if every new society in embryo is usually composed of such truths, they become, finally, the hotbeds of that society's putrefaction. There are no ultimate truths about man, any more than there are about the world. The truth about man is boundless and unforeseeable. The truth about man is a continuous but never-the-same expansion of his potentialities in the outside world, a continuous but erratic winning of freedom by man for himself in society.[28]

9

THE NECESSITY OF DISSENT

The questions that confront us with every step we take in the struggle for an equitable world remain as harsh and as grating now as ever. Even for those born in moderate bourgeois Britain the challenge persists, however muffled and cushioned, and will not permit itself to be shrugged away. Whether we like it or not, our lives are governed and conditioned by the abstract materialistic forces, the irrational interests and alien powers of ideology and commerce and technology that define the social systems of our world. We can either passively accept their domination, or assert our right as conscious questioning individuals to challenge it, to pit ourselves against it as agents of change in order to understand the actual dialectical nature of the process we are involved in and to de-mystify it; but we cannot escape it. But how, it might be asked, can *anyone* hope to grapple with such mystifying abstractions and the techniques that operate them? What chance have we against them? Do they even make much sense in the context of the pragmatism and the modest expectation of people's lives as they live them here in Britain?

And, in this particular context, what are we to make of the theories of Lenin or of Marx and the questions *they* deal with? Do they have sufficient bearing upon the concreteness and diversity of the social experience and the history of the people to enrich and to complement their social system? What do they, or the terrible example of Russia, have to offer the mass of the people in human terms that Britain herself – for all her muddled bourgeois democratic opportunist hypocritical social structure – is not capable of offering as a place where justice and community stand a chance, however messily, of being enacted? Is the violence of revolutionary intolerance really preferable to the soft-option, relatively non-violent capitalist tolerance of a liberal democracy such as Britain limps along with? Can a country dedicated to the fumbling evolutionary methods of social transformation defined by parliamentarism, with its cult of moderation and respect for individual rights, ever summon up sufficient strength of purpose to achieve a situation in which the few will have ceased to be able to exploit the many? Or is there going to *have* to be some sort of violent revolutionary process such as Morris had defined for us in *News From Nowhere?* Is this in any sense likely to be a constructive or viable alternative to the inefficiency and injustice of democracy? Are we still confronted with the spectacle of a ruthless capitalism crushing the people beneath its yoke, and a communism representing freedom and emancipation, the establishment of actual democracy? Or have both become so modified or so distorted by their influence upon each other, or so variously transformed, as to make such black and white distinctions inapplicable except for purposes of propaganda? *Can* Russia still be said to be in the preliminary stages of the revolutionary process, as it seems she must be if one is to accept the terms that Lenin (and Marx) have defined for the first, as for the second, phase of communist society? Or does her record offer, even as it stands, yet another melancholy instance of idealist theory (parallel to that of the theory of early Christianity) becoming corrupted by the perversities and depravities of the fallible human world? How can the spirit of justice and confidence and free trust and willing co-operation that are the aims of communism issue from a creed of intolerance and of murderous repression to lay foundations for the observance of 'the simple, fundamental rules of human intercourse' which (as Lenin puts it) 'will leave the door wide open for the transition from the first phase of communist society to its higher phase, and with it to the complete withering away of the state'?[1] It is all very well to have faith in such a future, but how to open the doors of the huge closed institutions that have been built upon the foundations of that future?

The society re-made, as Lenin conceived of Russia as re-made, 'will remain', in Bronowski's reading of Blake's dialectic vision,

a society to be re-made. The society re-made will take on the same rigour of death, unless in turn it submits to progress through its new contrary. The contraries of thesis and antithesis do not end. The progression to synthesis is not made by one revolution, in France or in Russia or in the world. This is the full meaning of the dialectic of contraries in Blake and Marx: *that no revolution is the last*. This is a heavy thought, but it is a living thought, that societies live only as they are re-made. It is the burning thought of Blake's energy, making and re-making, and urgent always with the will to good.[2]

And it has to be the motivating thought of every real people's revolution.

The Russian leaders would tell us that it is not the socialist majority who suffer proscription, but only the dissidents, the revisionists, the reactionaries. But if this is so, are the millions who suffered and died in the thirties, forties and fifties to be branded and dismissed as dissidents, revisionists and reactionaries? Serge had his own comment to make, as one who himself suffered for his convictions, upon the suppressive Stalinist zeal of Soviet authority – that the distinctions between error and true understanding 'are too abstruse for anyone to presume to regulate them by authority'. And this, for him, confronted by the massive and killing presumptions of the Soviet state machine, meant 'that freedom of thought [was] of all values the most essential'.[3] Because without it, true understanding is impossible. And without it, the kind of social future Lenin envisaged, when 'people will become accustomed to observing the elementary conditions of social life without violence and without subordination',[4] must remain the travesty the Soviet state machine has made of it.

And as freedom of thought is essential to the continuity of a genuine dialectic view of reality and the recognition between people of their common interests, so it is indispensable to the creation of any future in which people shall have found sufficient sanity and wisdom and will to overcome the forces that divide them and work together. In this sense, beyond the period of violence that may be initially inevitable to create the right foundations for community, the aim must be to prolong 'mental war and depress corporeal war'[5] in the continuing struggle for social justice and social equity. The fatal mistake is to assert the dogmatic certitude of any (apparently rational) set of abstract principles as an exclusive answer to the problems of society, for that is (once again) to invert the process and to impose upon it the general categories forged *from* the inversion; to put reality (the diverse complex changing reality of the human order) into a straitjacket of abstractions, and thus to falsify and to betray the substance itself. For it is the nature of dogmatic certitude that it cannot, whatever the evidence it is faced with, tolerate criticism.

The fundamental difference between dogmatic certitude, which 'dissolves reality into logic by means of *arbitrary* abstraction', and the 'ordinary consciousness' of real people, lies in the distinction between imposing arbitrary abstractions *upon* reality and refusing all criticism, all adjustment, all the claims made by the real world of human needs, desires, thoughts and actions, and responding to the *actual* conditions by translating logic 'into objective reality'.[6] As Marx has pointed out: 'In democracy the *constitution itself* appears only as *one* determining characteristic of the people, and indeed as its self-determination.' And in any true democracy – by which Marx means a socialist democracy – 'we find the constitution founded on its true ground: *real human beings* and the *real people*'. For 'thus posited, the constitution is the people's own creation. [It] is in appearance what it is in reality: the free creation of man'.[7]

But the Soviet system, as established by Lenin and later consolidated by Stalin, has imposed upon real human beings and the real people an arbitrary concept which permits no deviation from its abstract dogmas. Like Hegel, it 'conceives of man as the subjectivized state', inverting the subject and the predicate. The state is the subject, absolute and all-demanding, and man has become the object. But the concept of a socialist democracy must proceed 'from man and conceives of the state as objectified man';[8] the servant and the object of man's needs.

But this apparently obvious fact requires to be continually fought for against the congealing abstracts, the rigorous enforcements and falsifications of the machinery of the establishment, whatever its politics. For the fact that the state has come into being, like Russia's, by way of revolution, and in order to effect a radical re-shaping of society, is not in itself enough. It has to go on being re-made, adjusting itself, resisting the temptation to institute an absolutist system which in effect betrays what it set out to make. If the new order is to be true to the revolutionary struggle that brought it into being, it must have the courage to expose itself to the process of dialectic dispute, dissent and criticism as an essential pre-condition to growth and change and the fulfilment of its people's changing needs. Otherwise it will remain what it seems the Soviet system has become – an intolerant absolutist power that crushes and frustrates: a mausoleum that seals off the revolution created to overthrow such power; a tyranny that serves

> To turn man from his path,
> To restrain the child from the womb,
> To cut off the bread from the city,
> That the remnant may learn to obey,
> That the pride of the heart may fail,
> That the lust of the eyes may be quenched,
> That the delicate ear in its infancy
> May be dulled, and the nostrils closed up,
> To teach mortal worms the path
> That leads from the gates of the Grave.[9]

The history of dissent, in which both Blake and Marx have played so profound and distinguished a part, is vital to the life of man, the living substance of his present, and his freedom in the future. And this history, as Bronowski observes in an eloquent and deeply relevant commentary,

is not yet ended; it does not end. Men die, and societies die. They are not more lasting for being without dissent, they are more brittle; for they are purposeless, because they deny themselves a future. And if at times states are made to work, as all states have wished to work, without dissent, they are the poorer. They may be richer for a time than the pitiful starved societies which men have made hitherto; but they are poorer than they might themselves be. Men who are denied the right to dissent are no longer full men, and do not make a society worthy of men: 'they seem to me,' says Blake, 'to be something else besides Human Life.' The right to ask and to be answered, truth; the right to judge and to choose, dignity; these, and justice, and pity, and love, and reason, are of the shape of man's mind. These drive him to shape as a shadow the societies in which he must try, and will fail, to fulfil himself. Their dissent gives him the hope, their dissent alone gives him the power, to fail by less.[10]

And the suppression of this dissent is a suppression, a stunting, a mutilation, of the living needs of people, and the sources of the creative life in man – that which makes a man a man, 'the sum of his mind, his feelings, his dignity, his knowledge of truth and of love, his reason in the widest meaning: his belief in his own imagination'.[11] It is what, above all, and with all the passion and the power of mind he had at his command, Karl Marx set himself to oppose; for it put his world to shame, even as (in spite of his great effort) it does ours.

For we should not allow ourselves to be deluded into believing that the world of the late twentieth century is so very different in essence from that which Blake and Marx had to fight. Still societies create orthodoxies that suppress and neutralize dissent. Still the contradictions inherent in societies, in the West as in the East, have not been reconciled, and the political state remains separated from what Marx called civil society. Still 'the right of man to freedom is not based on the association of man with man, but rather on the separation of man from man'. And still the principle of the abstract power of class privilege based on economic or political privilege maintains its domination to the detriment of the community.[12]

Perhaps this is inevitable, society being the inadequate abstract framework that it is to the complex non-conformist lives of real people. But if it is so, it is not the less reprehensible and shaming that it should be so. Even the ways in which the world has rejected, misused or wilfully distorted the spirit and the intent of Marx's crucial findings about the intolerance, the injustice, the egoism and the crass materialism of his age demonstrate how little we have learnt from what he had to say, and how far we still have to go. As he made it his task from 1842 onward, so it remains our task, 'to drag the old world into the full light of day and to give positive shape to the new one. The more time history allows thinking mankind to reflect and suffering mankind to collect its strength, the more perfect will be the fruit which the present now bears within its womb.'[13]

And however we may choose to modify Marx's call to thinking mankind and suffering mankind in applying it to the modern world, it still retains its force and validity, because the stifling pressure, the apathetic ill-feeling and narrowness of vision that he denounced persist undiminished in the systems that dominate, in the tyranny of commerce and the market, the deepening stranglehold of technology, the triumph of quantitative values over human needs, and even the relationship of industry and the world of wealth in general to the political world.

The question is, how are we to proceed with the application of this task without foundering on abstractions and confronting the world 'with new doctrinaire principles'? We have to try to look at the world as it is, to show 'why it is struggling'; to unmask illusion, hypocrisy, the mystical consciousness that is obscure even to itself; and, like Marx, to lay the foundations for a new and more rational world born out of the old – a world that would rid itself for good of the kind of tyrannical minority rule that has held mankind enslaved for so long. For Marx had not envisaged his concept of dictatorship as the exchange of one tyranny for another. *His* dictatorship was conceived as the dictatorship of a whole class. *His* aim was to waken the working classes of the world to the terms of the struggle for *emancipation*; to 'make the workmen of different countries not only *feel* but *act* as brethren and as comrades in the *army* of emancipation'[14] – not as a means to the establishment of 'new class privileges and monopolies' or of the dictatorship of a single party, creating new abstractions over the people; 'but for equal rights and duties, and the abolition of all class rule'.[15] But in working for these ends, Marx did not underestimate the nature of the forces and powers that stood in the way of their attainment. He knew that real emancipation could only succeed in terms of international co-operation. For him, 'the emancipation of labour is neither a local nor a national, but a social problem, embracing all countries in which modern society exists, and depending for its solution on the concurrence, practical and theoretical, of the most advanced nations'.[16] And this was a problem not merely of encouraging a connectedness of interests among the oppressed peoples of various nations, but of alerting them to the necessity of an active struggle for their rights as makers, producers and citizens against the tyranny of the abstract alien powers that had enslaved them, and thus re-establishing society as the people's own creation.

To this end it was among the first of his tasks to analyse and to denounce those social structures (so characteristic of nineteenth-century capitalism) founded upon a 'mystical consciousness obscure to itself', and to clear the ground of the misconceptions and confusions, the irrationalities and perversions that lay behind the social and political theory and practice of his time. He knew that it would be futile to try to develop, let alone to establish, any new concept of society except in terms of existing conditions; for society was founded upon complex actualities created by people acting and reacting upon each other in the real world; and these actualities are the consequence of many diverse factors, including the uninspectable psychic energies that govern people's lives, the tortuous fantasies they produce in the attempt to rationalize and to justify their actions, and the alienating abstracts produced from these fantasies.

What was demanded of men (and particularly of the working class) was a dialectic *awareness* of the conditions of the struggle, a grasp of the objective contradictions involved in the struggle and of the forces that would determine its outcome. Hence the necessity of an unwavering application of the weapon of criticism to the phenomenon of theory and practice and its continual confusions. And it was because Marx had grounded his weapon of criticism upon man the individual and the species as the starting-point and the source of all social and political thinking that he was able to expose the underlying irrationality and hypocrisy of a system that claimed as its sacred principle the inalienable rights of the individual. Taking Hegel as the target for his attack upon the operative structures of European societies, as he chose to do, he was attacking not only Hegel but also many of the fundamental preconceptions of nineteenth-century political thought – preconceptions concerning the nature of man's place in society and the right of the few to exploit and control the many, which politicians and philosophers throughout Europe sought to justify. It was the status quo of capitalist licence and oppression that Marx attacked in exposing the inherent inconsistencies of Hegel's Doctrine of the State. The fact that Hegel, as he puts it, 'can treat real public consciousness very marginally because he treats the marginal consciousness as the true public one',[17] is a measure of the extent to which Hegel had separated content and form, implicit and explicit existence, and turned reality itself into a mere consequence of his philosophical Idea, and man into the object, the servant, the lackey of an idealized abstraction. Thus, from the vicious manner in which theory has been allowed to dominate the actual needs of mankind, to the inestimable advantage of the possessing classes, it becomes apparent that between the Idea of society and the diverse requirements of the people whose needs it is supposed to serve, there is a deep and unbridgeable division. Indeed, 'the separation of civil and political society appears *necessarily* as the separation of the *political* citizen, the citizen of the state, from civil society and from his own empirical reality; for as an ideal political entity [*Staatsidealist*] he is a *quite different being*, wholly distinct from and opposed to his actual reality'.[18]

This is the inevitable consequence of a theory which imposes abstract Ideas upon reality and argues as if these Ideas were in effect the sources from which theory springs – whereas in actual fact they serve to obscure the real sources for the purpose of justifying injustices that widen the gap between the possessing classes and the mass of the people. Marx is unequivocal in his condemnation of such a concept. 'At every point,' he says, 'Hegel's political spiritualism' – and in like manner the spiritualism of most nineteenth-century thinking about society – 'can be seen to degenerate into the crassest materialism'.[19] But how is this possible, one might ask? How is it possible for a system of philosophy to be so utterly blind to the fact that all its noble mysticism, when subjected to the ruthless logic of the sceptical intelligence, functions in the service of a debased and dehumanizing materialism? Perhaps the truth is that its very starting-point is that of the apologist. It sets out to justify, to rationalize, or to give a rational framework to, an irrational and inhumane conception of society – to bolster up and give an aura of respectability to a political and social structure that ignores and is contemptuous of the claims and demands of ordinary men and women as men and women, since it is concerned only with the rights and privileges of those who are in control of the resources of power and privilege. According to Hegel's argument, it transpires that 'the political constitution at its highest is . . . the *constitution of private property*. The loftiest political principles are the principles of private property.'[20] This becomes abundantly clear from Hegel's justification of primogeniture, which Marx strips of its pretentious high tone to reveal the unadulterated facts it is the sumptuous clothing for. Whereas in Hegel's view

primogeniture represents the power of the political state over private property, it is in fact the power of abstract private property over the political state. He makes the cause into the effect and the effect into the cause, the determining factor into the determined and vice versa. But what is the content of its political function, of its political purpose? What is its substance? Primogeniture, the superlative form of private property, private property supreme. What power does the political state exercise over private property through primogeniture? It *isolates* it from society and the family by bringing it to a peak of *abstract independence*. What then is the power of the political state over private property? It is the power of private property itself, its essence brought into existence. What remains to the state as opposed to this essence? The *illusion* that it determines where it is in fact determined. No doubt it breaks the *will* of the family and society, but only to make way for the will of a private property purified of family and society, and to acknowledge the existence of this private property as the highest reality of the political state, as the highest *ethical* reality.[21]

Marx here demonstrates what Hegel's rationalization of private property amounts to when all the obscurantist rhetoric has been stripped away. It is little more than an apology for 'private wilfulness in its most abstract form, utterly philistinistic, unethical and barbaric wilfulness'.[22] Hegel attempts to argue that in its highest form, as primogeniture – wealth that is 'inalienable, entailed and burdened' by responsibilities – private property makes man independent of the struggle for wealth and reward, and thus ideally fitted for political service.[23] Which is to say no less and no more than that political independence proceeds not from the nature of the political state as such, but from 'abstract civil law, from abstract private property', and hence that 'the meaning that private property acquires in the political state is its essential, *true* meaning; that the meaning acquired by *class distinctions* in the political state is *their* essential meaning'.[24]

This remains what Marx perceived as one of the principal causes of divisiveness and dislocation in the world. For it offers an irresistible temptation to the instinct of self-interest and personal egotism against the conditions that create community. And *as* private property in the abstract sense, the property of the capitalist, the landlord and the landowner, the domination of the thing itself, the alienating power of money – man transformed into money, or 'money *incarnate* in man'[25] – it encourages and deepens the estrangement of man in society. It is not private property in the sensuous particular meaning, as personal or communal possession – a man's house, his books, his clothes – which he cannot help but share, even as he shares himself in the community of his world, that is at issue. The issue is the alien estranging power of property or of money as 'the highest ethical reality', the motive principle of the political state, by the domination of which 'human individuality, human morality . . . become at once articles of commerce and the material which money inhabits'.[25] For under this domination 'the devaluation of the human world grows in direct proportion to the increase in value of the world of things'.[26]

This tyranny has not been substantially contained or mastered in the hundred years since Marx attacked it, even if the apparent conditions in which it operates have changed, even if new dangers and new challenges have arisen to force us to think out the principles anew. We are still faced with the necessity of grasping 'the essential connection between private property, greed, the separation of labour, capital and landed property, exchange and competition, value and the devaluation of man, monopoly and competition, etc. – the connection between this entire system of estrangement and the money system'.[27] We are faced with the necessity of grasping these connections under the new conditions in which they and their unscrupulous (or unwitting) manipulators persist – conditions of international (and multinational) enterprise by which technology and bureaucracy determine the tyranny of the world of things over the human world.

For the enemies of reason, of community, and the armies of anonymous supporters who maintain (often without knowing they are doing so or understanding why) the world of things, are still in control of the economic forces of society. In other words, in the West the incessant propaganda of materialistic rewards and comforts, the incitements of commerce to privacy and non-connection and political apathy, continue to indoctrinate the mass of the people into a more or less subservient acceptance of the controlling systems. And in the communist states an equally virulent machinery of indoctrination, working by blunter and more openly repressive methods, keeps the people contained against the potential freedoms of emancipated community, which – based upon trust, confidence, dignity, free speech and free thought – cannot be induced by fear or by bureaucratic regimentation.

And it is these potential freedoms and the struggle for them that are (or that ought to be) the major concern of the modern world, whatever the complications, whatever the obstacles, no matter what specious or plausible arguments men put forward as alternatives. If the world is not constructed to give more than a subsidiary place to such a concept of community, then we must work to change the structure of the world to make room for it, for the realization of men's freedoms, the fulfilment that will come for people choosing to work together. And if the comparative minority who have positions of responsibility and control continue to refuse to recognize the necessity of this and persist (against all reason) in their pursuit of self-aggrandizement and the divisive abstracts of power, thus declaring themselves the enemies of community and the agents of repressive force, then they must be *made* to recognize it, exposed to the shame of their role, and drummed out of office, stripped of their power.

How this is to be achieved is another matter. But one thing is certain. It cannot be achieved until the people are awakened to the prospects and the responsibilities of their emancipation, to the knowledge that encourages community and to the 'mental war' that will have to be fought to bring it about. Because it is they who hold the key to the transformation of society – they, not as cyphers living the stunted lives they have been compelled to live, but as concerned and caring human beings. Which means that the problem remains a problem of freeing the consciousness of people, of directing their hopes and desires not 'upon victory over other human beings', as Bertrand Russell puts it,

but upon victory over those forces which have hitherto filled the life of man with suffering and sorrow – I mean, the forces of nature reluctant to yield her fruits, the forces of militant ignorance, the forces of hate, and the deep slavery to fear which is our heritage from the original helplessness of man.[28]

And as long as they are kept divided, split into unconnected groups, distracted from the consciousness of all they have in common, and continue to permit the abstract powers to dominate, their potential community must remain a shadowy possibility, a dream, a mere reflection of the alienating actuality. For as things are man remains a being estranged from himself, and 'his own creation confronts him as an alien power, his wealth appears as poverty, the essential bond joining him to other men appears inessential . . . [and] his power over objects appears as the power of objects over him; in short, he, the lord of his creation, appears as the servant of that creation'.[29]

It is, however, a fact that it is he who has brought into being the inhuman powers that control him; and he will continue to do so as long as he continues to believe that victory over other human beings, triumph by deceit and cunning, are profitable – as long as he continues, that is, to trade in and to sell out his innate humanity, to subjugate his personal flesh and blood existence, his social worth and status, to the service of these alien powers. Of course he may not actually know that he is doing this. Having been conditioned to the prevailing spirit of the social world he lives in, he may simply accept the *values* that govern that world, and the extent to which these values have become inverted or to which he, in his egoistic assertiveness, has perverted them or allowed himself to be perverted *by* them. What he has to learn to recognize, therefore, is the nature of the process that conditions him. For he cannot begin to get things into focus or to see things straight, to grasp the interconnections and distinctions that define his world for what it is capable of, until he has been able to see beyond his conditioning.

It may be that Marx incorrectly predicted the final overthrow of capitalistic society, as brought about by 'an increase in poverty, oppression, slavery, degradation, and exploitation' and a consequent 'increasing resistance by an ever-growing, ever more disciplined working-class, organized and united by the very mechanism of capitalistic production'.[30] For predictions are dependent upon so many unforeseeable factors. But he was not incorrect in his diagnosis of the fundamental nature of the struggle for community or the grounds on which it would have to be fought. Though technology and revolution and war and revolt have radically transformed the elements involved, and have brought about a situation in the world in which the equation 'capitalist/working-class' no longer has the kind of clear-cut pattern of antagonisms it had for Marx, still the alienating powers created by man against himself – powers that have demonstrated such murderous indifference to the actual needs of human beings as to ravage the world – retain control. The essential point is not that the grounds of the struggle have shifted, but that the conditions which permit the few to oppress, enslave, degrade and exploit the many have created new and subtler threats to the future. And thus, in Marxian terms, the struggle for a social structure in which the unity of worker and citizen may be achieved remains as elemental and as challenging as ever. Man still has to pit himself against the power of capital and property and institutionalized dogma and the absolutes it spawns and to answer these powers with his humanizing powers; for if he doesn't, they will have him more completely than ever in their power.

Money, for instance, has not lost its hold upon us; it dominates whole economies, the standards of living of whole societies; and it puts us in its power the moment that we make it a prime purpose of our activities. This hasn't changed in the least. In the midst of the metallic language of exchange-commodities and market values – the price of oil, the price of meat or bread, the cost of roads and transport, the buying and selling of houses over the heads of those who live in them – the specifically *human* voice appealing for sustenance and justice and the values of the community merely emphasizes its peculiarity, its estrangement from, and its ineffectiveness within, the current conventions and procedures of social interchange – such that 'the direct language of man strikes us as an offence against the dignity of man, whereas the estranged language of objective values appears as the justified, self-confident and self-acknowledged dignity of man incarnate'.[31]

Against this concept of reality, in terms of which money is enshrined as 'the universal and self-constituted value of all things',[32] the key to comfort, ease, the good life, the liberty and leisure that lead to fulfilment and emancipation, the Marxian philosophy, above all else that it is or has become, is a supreme attempt to re-establish the *connections* between man and his world, to break the vicious closed circle of estrangement and of class oppression brought into being by the logic of capitalism and its ruthless exploitation of social resources. It was an attempt to forge the links between theory and practice, the world of things and the world of men, society and humanity, politics and culture – a vision of the necessity of class struggle springing from precise awareness of the appalling conditions created for the mass of the people, particularly in England, from the 1840s onward. But Marx knew there was little he or anyone could do at the time to counteract the accelerating drift of European societies away from the rational connectedness that had been the common theme of intellectuals in the early part of the century towards the triumph of divisiveness and dislocation. The struggle seemed increasingly a struggle against the general drift of history, for Marx had to accept not only the frustration of revolutionary action after 1848 (with the extraordinary phenomenon of the 1871 Commune as a lone exception) and the consequent dissipation of humanistic ideals into either the aesthetic *or* the political, but also the ominous and deepening stranglehold of industrial expansion and the rise of imperialism, which were to lay the foundations for the wars of the twentieth century and the astonishing triumphs of technology.

The process by which the energies of the revolutionary Left were gradually frustrated and dissipated and finally neutralized has been well defined by Walter Jens in an article, 'The Classical Tradition in Germany':

> The radicalism of the middle class humanists of the year 1800 was not translated into practice. It remained an aesthetic radicalism and a rebellion of ideas, because the republican imagination lacked the real social force that would have enabled it to make its expectations concrete . . . Heine (for instance) dreamt of synthesis between the political French Revolution and the philosophical German revolution, to be achieved in an uprising of the future which would change the whole social structure fundamentally, but this dream proved to be a mere fantasy. What had long been seen in outline, an expression of the miseries of Germany, now became brute fact: the social debacle of this liberal bourgeoisie which, *intent only on the preservation of its property*, gave up its social objectives. It began to elevate the Prussian element of unity above the jacobinical element of freedom (not to speak of equality) and to raise national above social aims . . . There now began . . . the descent into hell of that classical culture which had at first been in league with the *latent* progressive tendencies of the times and now made its peace with the potent reactionary forces of the period.
>
> Thus . . . the jacobinical tradition broke, the spirit of classical culture no longer created counter-images, ceased to keep the distinctions clear between appearance and illusion, reality and artifice, and . . . became an accomplice of the ruling powers.[33]

This defines a pattern of decline and of triumph which took a strangely similar form (whatever the differences) in France and in England. Everywhere the struggle to maintain a dialogue between possessors and possessed, a dialectic process of interconnected opposites, failed, even as radicalism failed, before the all-pervading forces of divisive and reactionary power, the triumph of the capitalist middle class. And 1848 defines with singular intensity the *moment* of the decisive collision and the moment of *defeat*, the moment of the triumph of irrational, anti-social thinking over that which had sought the community and sanity of an integrated human world. As Jens has put it, in the context of his particular argument:

Not until the second half of the nineteenth century is it possible to speak of classical culture becoming the preserve of the apolitical aesthete . . . It is only now that culture and politics . . . become separate spheres . . . Here was the 'pure' spirit which had renounced all attempts to penetrate and change the world, *the spirit of profundity and inwardness*, the silent spirit purified of 'rhetorical dross', of the 'babble of civilization' and of 'literary' jacobinism, the spirit which Thomas Mann . . . described in his *Meditations of a Non-Political Man* (the same Thomas Mann who a few years later saw in the separation of Marx and Hölderlin a symbol of the German catastrophe) . . .

And as Jens adds trenchantly: 'We have all experienced how deeply his self-consciously sublime spirit made itself compatible with the starkest terror.'[34] For what does this self-consciously sublime spirit, this 'spirit of profundity and inwardness', appeal to if not to the kind of repressive authoritarian values characteristic of Western society by which man himself has been degraded and diminished to the level of an obedient and inhuman machine? And what does it signify if not an irrational abasement or surrender to the domination of ecstatic mystical powers which, in their sublimation of the merely human, pervert the human personality and expose society to the kind of psychic hysteria so recently witnessed in the phenomenal transformation of the mass of the people into fanatical adherents of the Nazi creed?

Marx himself, as one among a small unwavering minority of men and women during a period of unprecedented confusion, was able to resist the onslaught of the forces of reaction that were playing such havoc with the integrating powers of human consciousness, because he understood the nature of the struggle that was taking place, its underlying historical conditions and the issues that were at stake. He continued to stand his ground and to carry on his fight for humanity in the midst of a totally hostile and intolerant world because he had taken the trouble to equip himself, to think things out from the roots, to build firmly and rationally on the foundations laid for him by the heritage of humanist thinking created out of the revolutionary struggles of the late eighteenth century. And having unmasked for himself those forms of mystical authority which claimed to appeal to powers beyond man as powers manipulated by the possessing classes to maintain their domination, he was not to be softened or swayed from his course by the general drift of European thinking. His was a mind and a sensibility nourished on a vision of the creative rationality of man, a profound grasp of the conditions indispensable to the realization of his freedom and of the massive obstacles in the real world that stood in the way of such realization. And he refused to let his vision founder by modifying or relinquishing its rigorous dialectic, for he knew that without it the very concept of wholeness, coherence and integrity could not be sustained against the forces ranged against it.

Marx, looking ahead, defined society at its best as 'the perfected unity in essence of man with nature, the true resurrection of nature, the realized naturalism of man and the realized humanism of nature';[35] and setting this concept against the perverted actuality, the alienating systems of oppression that everywhere prevailed to degrade society and turn man into the dehumanized slave of a destructive process, he affirmed that when such a society is 'fully developed', it will produce 'man in all the richness of his being; the rich man who is profoundly and abundantly endowed with all the senses, as its constant reality'.[36] This vision of a realized and organic relationship of man as individual in creative collaboration with the 'other man',[37] a dual interchange of subject and object, is defined as a context in which man will 'appropriate his integral essence in an integral way, as a total man'. And as such it is of course a vision of emancipated being, which looks beyond the perverted actuality towards what *could* be for man, when 'all his human relations to the world – seeing, hearing, smelling, tasting, feeling, thinking, contemplating, sensing, wanting, acting, loving – in short, all the organs of his individuality, like the organs which are directly communal in form' – have become 'in their *objective* approach . . . to the object, the appropriation of that object'; and thus 'the confirmation of human reality'.[38]

10

BLAKE'S DIALECTIC:
THE PROLONGATION OF MENTAL WAR

A society fully developed and confirmed as the free creation of the people was, as Marx plainly understood, unlikely to find many supporters in the Europe he knew. The opposition was too powerful. An irrational and perverted social philosophy – the philosophy of capitalist expansion – was by the mid-century to be found everywhere vested in the agents and spokesmen of established authority, giving them the energy and will to triumph over their enemies and critics, either by crushing them or by subverting them. The new ruling class had already learnt to utilize and to manipulate to its own ends the deep-seated but inarticulate passions of the masses, their resentments, their despairs, their instinctual yearnings, their stirrings against the abject humiliations of their condition, their awakening consciousness. From 1789 onward, and with increasing confidence and ruthlessness from the moment war was declared between England and France, it began to take command of the European situation; to dominate, to inhibit, to suppress and to re-mould the aspirations that had been invoked with such proud conviction at the outset of the Revolution. And by 1800 the betrayal or the degradation of these aspirations seemed complete – not indeed that it was, because it marked the beginning of a new stage in the historical struggle of the classes; but that many one-time supporters of the Revolution found themselves reduced first to despair, then to acceptance of the status quo, and later on even to enthusiastic support for its reactionary policies. There is no more telling symbol of this degradation than that of the rise to fame and martial supremacy of Napoleon, and no more telling commentary upon the abhorrent fascination of Napoleon's psychology or of the psychology of the 'animal kingdom of politics' that 'centuries of barbarism' had produced and given shape to than Marx's anecdote concerning the man of Destiny:

It is said that he pointed to the mass of drowning men [on the Berezina] and declared to his entourage: 'Voyez ces crapauds!' (Look at those toads!). The story is probably invented, but it is true nevertheless. Despotism's only thought is disdain for mankind, dehumanized mankind; and it is a thought superior to many others in that it is also a fact. In the eyes of the despot men are always debased. They drown before his eyes and on his behalf in the mire of common life from which, like toads, they always rise up again. If even men capable of great vision, like Napoleon before he succumbed to his dynastic madness, are overwhelmed by this insight, how should a quite ordinary king be an idealist in the midst of such a reality?[1]

How indeed? 'Men are rendered selfish and corrupt by the baneful influence of the system under which they live,' as Thomas Holcroft had written in the nineties.[2] They act as they are conditioned to act, and if the system under which they live is corrupt, it is difficult for them to resist the temptation to be rendered so themselves. The process was as rife in the seemingly more ordered and less lethal society of late-eighteenth-century England as in France – in the specious and crippled arguments of a Burke as in the manner in which men like Wordsworth and Coleridge were so easily persuaded to surrender their convictions – to snap their 'squeaking baby-trumpet of sedition', and withdraw from politics to devote themselves to 'such works as encroach not on the anti-social passions'[3] in the haven of poetic purity.

William Blake, however, was one man who refused to surrender his convictions or to allow himself to be diminished. Like Marx, he understood the situation in his own way, and took the trouble to equip himself with the kind of knowledge that would resist corruption and surrender. He cared too much to acquiesce in the ugliness and cruelty of the system under which he lived. His view of the world was founded upon an organic grasp of the interaction of individual and society, subject and object, the particular and the general, the animal–spiritual being of man. And the anger he felt at the derangement and dislocation of his world, rooted as it was in a deep and unwavering sympathy with the dispossessed against the rule of 'the mind-forg'd manacles', sharpened in him that dialectic of the contrary states of human identity which he made the great weapon of his mental war, and of his visionary concept of Jerusalem, of man's ceaseless struggle to create for himself a world in which 'the feet, hands, head, bosom, and parts of love' could 'follow their high breathing joy',[4] and honesty and tenderness would be valued not as attributes of the weak but as the basis of strength and prosperity.

> Must the generous tremble and leave his joy to the idle, to the
>   pestilence,
> That mock him? Who commanded this? What God? What
>   Angel?
> To keep the generous from experience till the ungenerous
> Are unrestrained performers of the energies of nature;
> Till pity become a trade, and generosity a science
> That men get rich by; and the sandy desert is giv'n to the
>   strong?[5]

Blake set himself to master what he had already grasped intuitively: that awareness of the complementary energies and states of being which is the measure of his strength: 'Without contraries is no progression. Attraction and Repulsion, Reason and Energy, Love and Hate, are necessary to Human Existence'; for with him nature and man, delight and duty, sexual energy and reason, the animal and the spiritual are not separate – 'Man has no Body distinct from his Soul, for that call'd Body is a portion of Soul discern'd by the five Senses, the chief inlets of Soul in this age'.[6] And it was this awareness, strengthening the senses, requiring of the mind a pivotal focusing and balancing of such opposites, that enabled him to remain steady under the pressure of events while men like Godwin and Wordsworth yielded and gave up the struggle, unable because perhaps unequipped to cope with its rigorous demands.

Blake saw things deeply but clearly. And with his grasp of the indispensable dualities, the contrary essences of being that provide equilibrium and sanity, nothing – not neglect or failure or his increasing sense of isolation, his disappointment at the defeat and betrayal of the Revolution – could diminish his insight or destroy his happy confidence in himself, his *assurance* that he was fundamentally right. 'The Nature of my Work,' he says in his annotation to *A Vision of the Last Judgement*, 'is Visionary or Imaginative; it is an Endeavour to Restore what the Ancients call'd the Golden Age.'[7] And in this spirit he consistently demonstrates a certainty of conviction which, because it is direct

and generous and caring and quick with delight, is never arrogant
or dogmatic:

> I have Mental Joy & Mental Health
> And Mental Friends & Mental Wealth;
> I've a Wife I love & that loves me;
> I've all But Riches Bodily.[8]

And thus he is sure of the grounds he builds upon. 'Conscience in
those who have it,' as he argues, against what he calls the
'contemptible falsehood and detraction', the 'serpentine dissimu-
lation' of the reactionary Bishop Watson, 'is unequivocal . . . He
who stands doubting of what he intends, whether it is Virtuous or
Vicious, knows not what Virtue means . . . No man can take
darkness for light.'[9] And again, with dazzling simplicity: 'I
question not my Corporeal or Vegetative Eye any more than I
would Question a Window concerning a Sight. I look thro' it and
not with it.'[10]

Thirty-five years of Blake's life were lived in a world disfigured
by the dehumanizing violence and callousness of war, which
culminated in the international, ideological, ruthless wars of the
English and the French, of Napoleon's Decrees and the British
Orders in Council that became *total* war. 'This is the sequence,
step by step more inhuman and more mechanical, which made
Blake identify his two hatreds – hatred of the dehumanized
machine (the "dark Satanic Mills"), and hatred of war.'[11] And, as
Jacob Bronowski further puts it:

> Through all his poems there sound the iron footsteps of the modern
> age: war, oppression, the machine, poverty, and the loss of personality.
> They crowd the pages of his symbolic books as casually as a letter which
> sneers at Pitt or a marginal note which sides with Tom Paine. This is the
> prophetic power of Blake: that he felt the coming disasters of war,
> empire, and industry in his bloodstream, long before politicians and
> economists shivered at their shadows.[12]

As he lays it down in 1793: 'The Giants who formed this world
into its sensual existence, and now seem to live in it in chains, are
in truth the causes of its life and the sources of all activity; but the
chains are the cunning of weak and tame minds which have power
to resist energy.'[13] Because for him, energy is of the essence of all
creative activity – energy together with reason, which is 'the

bound or outward circumference of Energy'.[14] And the particular strength of his work *is* its sensuous rooted energy, its immediacy, its imaginative precision. It bears witness, that is, through the medium of the seeing senses, the 'doors of perception', to the creative attributes of man and his struggle to free himself from the domination of the alienating abstracts of authoritarian power.

Blake did not need to have this pointed out to him. He knew it from the start. 'General knowledge,' he writes in his *Vision*, 'is Remote Knowledge; it is in Particulars that Wisdom consists & Happiness too. Both in Art and in Life, General Masses are as much Art as a Pasteboard Man is Human.'[15] And again, in his Annotations to Reynolds: 'Without Minute Neatness of Execution the Sublime cannot exist! Grandeur of Ideas is founded on Precision of Ideas . . . Singular and Particular Detail is the Foundation of the Sublime.'[16] And if it can be argued that the poet (as artist) was prevented from achieving the sublime in terms of the scope and profundity of his vision, this is a judgement not upon Blake himself but of the world he lived in, that ignored and neglected him, crippled his livelihood, and kept him poor. This world did its best to break him by indifference; but it did not break him. His sympathy with the French Revolution, his sympathy for the poor, his unequivocal sense of justice and of human dignity, his generosity, his capacity for love, his childlike curiosity and zest for life, kept him active and vital to the end. He saw himself as he was and understood his situation as it was. 'A Last Judgement is Necessary,' he wrote, 'because Fools flourish. Nations flourish under Wise Rulers and are depress'd under Foolish Rulers; it is the same with Individuals as Nations; works of Art can only be produced in Perfection where the Man is either in Affluence or is Above the Care of it.' And he adds touchingly: 'Some people and not a few Artists have asserted that the Painter of this Picture would not have done so well if he had been properly encouraged.' Then, with quiet simplicity and indignation: 'Let those who think so reflect on the State of Nations under Poverty and their incapability of Art; tho' Art is above Either, the Argument is better for Affluence than Poverty; and tho' he would not have been a greater Artist, yet he would have produced greater works of Art in proportion to his means.'[17]

Yes, Blake understood his situation; and *because* he understood it, and lived it through, he knew what injustice and neglect and oppression meant to the poor of England under a Tory tyranny of riches, this 'wretched State of Political Science',[18] with its central principle, as defined by Locke: 'the great and chief end of [government] . . . is the preservation of property'.[19] Indeed he was from the first on the side of the dispossessed, robbed of their land and forced away from their cottages into the urban areas which the enclosures and the developments of the Industrial Revolution were bringing into being. He was even among the crowd which burned Newgate Prison on 6 June 1780, though there perhaps only by chance; *he* was not afraid of the crowd, of the poor. Living through a time of callous violence against the masses, with laws of the most barbaric kind newly passed to protect the privileged and their property – the penalty for stealing forty shillings-worth of goods from a house, for instance, or five shillings-worth from a shop, was death – he refused to be intimidated, and is with these propertyless working people in their misery. The indignation, the deep spiritual anger of the poems, leaves us in no doubt of this. It has its clearest embodiment perhaps in the concentrated ironies of the *Songs of Experience* and the poems of the *Pickering Manuscript* – in 'Holy Thursday', 'The Chimney Sweeper', 'The Garden of Love', the devastating indictment of 'London', and with particular ferocity of intent in 'The Human Abstract', where

> Pity would be no more
> If we did not make somebody poor;
> And Mercy no more could be
> If all were as happy as we.
>
> And mutual fear brings peace,
> Till the selfish loves increase:
> Then Cruelty knits a snare,
> And spreads his baits with care.[20]

But again and again this penetrating accusatory voice is to be heard, raised in anger and compassion on behalf of the people against the oppressive powers of Cruelty and Mystery, of Church and State, of Riches and Privilege, of the Cunning and Deceit that are rooted in the human brain. Throughout his work the energy, the passion, the radical conviction, maintain a firm grasp of the contradictory forces of reality and the vision of a freed humanity that is his aim, to make an uncompromising indictment of the inhumanities of his age. And the intensity of the impact of this work as a whole remains as unarguable today as it might have been for his own time had there been anybody prepared to listen. 'Rouse up, O Young Men of the New Age,' he cries in his great call to the just in the Preface to *Milton* in 1804. 'Set your foreheads against the ignorant Hirelings! For we have Hirelings in the Camp, the Court and the University, who would, if they could, for ever depress Mental and prolong Corporeal War.'[21]

In the atmosphere of the time a declaration of this sort would have been considered treasonable if it had ever caught the eye of the authorities. With Joseph Johnson, printer of Paine's *Rights of Man* and Blake's own early work, prosecuted under the 1792 *Proclamation against Divers Wicked Seditious Writings*; with the anti-French fervour deliberately encouraged, with press gangs, workhouses, hangings, enforced prostitution, rising infant mortality, famine, mutiny, the spread of the factory system, and the increase of agricultural prices bringing new suffering to the poor, England was not a country that would have taken kindly to Blake's kind of sanity, however persuasive. This was a fact that he had been forced to accept and to adjust himself to at every level. And by 1804 his situation was such that there was little likelihood of his being even noticed by anyone except a few friends, let alone taken seriously. This was perhaps fortunate for him as a citizen, if not as an artist. But the authorities would not have been able, anyway, to detect the heresies in *Milton*. They would have glanced through the book and dismissed it as the work of an obscure and foolish eccentric printing to satisfy an excess of vanity.

But though as the years passed Blake was to find himself driven back more and more completely upon his own reserves, he never for a moment lost sight of the great struggle for the good society that had engaged him from the start; it was the task of his lifetime. Even with the darkening symbolism of the *Prophetic Books*, their deepening complexity and strangeness, there is no mistaking his intent, the great dialectic issues that are their theme, 'that each shall mutually/Annihilate himself for others' good'[22] in order 'to bathe in the Waters of Life, to wash off the Not Human . . . till Generation is swallow'd up in Regeneration',[23] and

All animals upon the Earth are prepar'd in all their strength
To go forth to the Great Harvest & Vintage of the Nations.[24]

And in passage after passage the voice of the man speaks unequivocally and with passionate commitment of the England of his time, as in these lines from the early *Europe* (1794), where he sees

> Every house a den, every man bound: the shadows are fill'd
> With spectres, & the windows wove over with curses of iron:
> Over the doors 'Thou shalt not', & over the chimneys 'Fear'
>   is written:
> With bands of iron round their necks fastened into the walls
> The citizens, in leaden gyves the inhabitants of suburbs
> Walk heavy; soft and bent are the bones of villagers.[25]

Under such conditions it is not surprising that he should have written on the back of the title-page of his Annotations to Bishop Watson's attack on Paine: 'To defend the Bible in this year 1798 would cost a man his life'; and so he had been 'commanded from Hell not to print'[26] his objections - unlike the scholar Gilbert Wakefield, who was imprisoned for three years for printing his. Blake's caution and the fate of Wakefield graphically demonstrate the intolerable conditions people had to suffer 'because of the Oppressors of Albion in every City and Village'.[27] England was ruled by a class of men who, 'having no Passions of their own because no Intellect, have spent their lives in Curbing and Governing other People's by the Various Arts of Poverty and Cruelty of all kinds'.[28] And for Blake this was not only a source of bitterness and indignation; it must also have made him feel peculiarly powerless. What he saw was inhumanity and injustice triumphing everywhere. 'You smile,' he writes in *Jerusalem*, of the Masters of his world:

> You smile with pomp and rigour, you talk of benevolence
>   & virtue;
> I act with benevolence & virtue and get murder'd time after time.
> You accumulate Particulars & murder by analysing, that you
> May take the aggregate, & you call the aggregate Moral Law.[29]

And it is *this* moral law from which, throughout the French wars, the masters of Europe made huge profits, while the day-labourers became steadily poorer, were forced off the land and turned into the wage-slaves of wealth to work the factories – men, women and children. And how did the owners of industry *argue* their moral law? Since the poor 'will never work any more time than is necessary just to live and support their weekly debauches, we can fairly aver that a reduction in wages in the woollen manufacture would be a national blessing and advantage, and no real injury to the poor'. [30]

Blake has his own biting comment to make upon such inhumanity. The voice of Urizen, cold as ice, reads from his 'book of brass', urging the false imperatives of moral duty:

Compel the poor to live upon a crust of bread, by soft mild
   arts.
Smile when they frown, frown when they smile; & when a
   man looks pale
With labour and abstinence, say he looks healthy and happy;
And when his children sicken, let them die; there are enough
Born, even too many, and our earth will be overrun,
Without these arts. If you would make the poor live with
   temper . . .
Preach temperance: say he is overgorg'd and drowns his wit
In strong drink, tho' you know that bread & water are all
He can afford. Flatter his wife, pity his children, till we can
Reduce all to our will, as spaniels are taught with art. [31]

This, of course, was the kind of advice the masters had no need of; it was the secret of their mastery. But they failed to make a spaniel of Blake. Though their system kept him poor and hemmed him in and almost caught him in its trap – brought to trial in 1804 on a charge of having uttered seditious and treasonable expressions – he could not be corrupted. Though Wordsworth, Coleridge and Southey all shifted their ground at this time to become social reactionaries, Blake stayed firm. We see this right to the end. He kept faith with his highest principles, and refused to turn his back on them. If he came to despair of politics, or of political change, his social conscience did not falter. Against the social and moral hypocrisies of the rich who ruled he was unwavering. Even in the year of his death he makes a scathing parody of Dr Thornton's Tory translation of the Lord's Prayer ('Our Father Augustus Caesar, who art in these thy Substantial Astronomical Telescopic Heavens, Holiness to thy Name or Title, and reverence to thy Shadow. Thy Kingship come upon Earth first and thence in Heaven. Give us day by day our Real Taxed Substantial Money bought Bread . . .'); and makes his own passionate version of it: 'Give us the Bread that is our due & Right, by taking away Money, or a Price, or Tax upon what is Common to all in thy Kingdom'[32] – a strangely moving and shockingly heretical statement that speaks as urgently as ever for the common people and for his own revolutionary concept of the commonwealth of Christian justice.

And then there is his astonishing vision of the growing industrial power of England in *Vala* (1797), *Milton* (1804) and *Jerusalem* (1820) – 'loud with machines, with war, with law; with the cry of men preying on man', as Bronowski puts it;[33] with 'the death-sweat of the dying'[34] and the

> . . . intricate wheels invented, wheel without wheel,
> To perplex youth in their outgoings & to bind to labours in Albion
> Of day & night the myriads of eternity: that they may grind
> And polish brass & iron hour after hour, laborious task,
> Kept ignorant of its use: that they might spend the days of wisdom
> In sorrowful drudgery to obtain a scanty pittance of bread,
> In ignorance to view a small portion & think that All,
> And call it Demonstration, blind to all the simple rules of life.[35]

He recognized the evil, that is. Though he despaired of setting it right, he recognized it for what it was. From the beginning he had understood the terrible contradictions at the heart of his world – 'Heaps of smoking ruins/In the night of prosperity and wantonness'[36] – and all his life he struggled to create a vision of what man is to be beyond how man is to live, in the anger of the spirit that informs all his work. As Jacob Bronowski has written:

> Blake's thought begins at the evil, that society thwarts the fulfilment of man. Thus religion thwarts Christ . . . Thus law thwarts gratified desire . . . Thus, as Blake saw, a man-made famine thwarts the plenty which men make. Blake hated this blight, and fought it his life long . . . And [he] knew that the blight must be fought within society.'[37]

But he also knew that it had to be fought within the self, since – because 'general Forms have their vitality in Particulars, & every/Particular is a Man' – society is rooted there, and is there given shape 'by spiritual gifts,/By the severe contentions of friendship & the burning fire of thought'.[38] It is *this* knowledge, indeed, that gives his anger and his indignation its positive creative strength, and gives *him* the strength to fight his mental war 'with intellectual spears, & long wing'd arrows of thought',[39] for a vision of man as he is to be, of man fulfilled. For this knowledge, developed and systematically explored in the *Prophetic Books*, is forged from a profound awareness of the contradictory forces that are at work in the world, and of the perverted actualities, the alienating conditions, the falsities of abstract Laws and Moralities, that have divided men from themselves and kept them ignorant, locked in singleness of vision. He sees, through the voice of Los in *Jerusalem*, that these divided beings, like those within himself,

> . . . know not why they love nor wherefore they sicken & die,
> Calling that Holy Love which is Envy, Revenge & Cruelty,
> Which separated the stars from the mountains, the mountains
>   from Man
> And left Man, a little grovelling Root outside of Himself.
> Negations are not Contraries: Contraries mutually Exist;
> But Negations Exist Not. Exceptions & Objections &
>   Unbeliefs
> Exist Not, nor shall they ever be Organized for ever & ever.
> If thou separate from me, thou art a Negation, a mere
> Reasoning & Derogation from me, an Objecting and Cruel
>   Spite.

And this Negation, as he adds in a striking anticipation of Marx's attack upon the Hegelian inversion, cannot take any organic form

> But as a distorted and reversed Reflection in the Darkness
> And in the Non Entity: nor shall that which is above
> Ever descend into thee, but thou shalt be a Non Entity for
>   ever.[40]

Such insight (here as elsewhere laying bare the destructive negations of the capitalist system) is of the essence of Blake's strength, which came not from singleness of vision, the divided self, the abstractions of the mind, but from a creative antagonism based upon the nourishment of all the faculties of being in the self – by building out of the self a spiritual power to match the ruthless movements of the outer world (the brutal aggression of the machinery of capitalism in action) with movements and responses that kept him alert and at full stretch as a seeker and a lover of humanity. And the weapons of his mental war against the blinded arrogance and divisiveness of the system are Reason and Energy, Imagination and Intellect working together. The contraries *must*, he stresses, act upon each other; separated, they leave man 'a little grovelling Root outside of Himself', a *false* self, a Spectre. And this false self, this Spectre

> . . . is the Reasoning Power in Man, & when separated
> From Imagination & Closing itself as in steel in a Ratio
> Of the things of Memory, It thence frames Laws & Moralities
> To destroy Imagination, the Divine Body, by Martyrdoms &
>   Wars.[41]

In other words we cannot trust to reason alone, which is merely 'the bound or outward circumference of Energy', any more than we can trust to Energy alone, though 'Energy is Eternal Delight'.[42] We need reason and energy together. And not *only these*. The price of Wisdom and Experience, in the kind of world Blake knew, may have to be, as he says, 'all that a man hath, his house, his wife, his children'. But this too is only part of the struggle, for those (like Blake) to whom the truth is a total experience and a living source of replenishment, because awareness (however bleak) is indispensable. You have to see things as they are, and that has to be faced and absorbed and moved on from. And even if one doesn't literally suffer as the farmer ploughing 'for bread in vain', Blake knew that other people had to, and that other people are extensions of oneself; that you cannot ignore the misfortunes of others without diminishing yourself. Thus, Enion's lament:

> It is an easy thing to talk of patience to the afflicted,
> To speak the laws of prudence to the houseless wanderer,
> To listen to the hungry raven's cry in wintry season
> When the red blood is filled with wine and with the marrow
>   of lambs.
>
> It is an easy thing to laugh at wrathful elements,
> To hear the dog howl at the wintry door, the ox in the
>   slaughterhouse moan;
> To see a god on every wind and a blessing on every blast;
> To hear sounds of love in the thunderstorm that destroys our
>   enemy's house;

To rejoice in the blight that covers his field, & the sickness
   that cuts off his children,
While our olive and vine sing & laugh round our door, & our
   children bring fruits & flowers.

Then the groan and the dolour are quite forgotten, & the
   slave grinding at the mill,
And the captive in chains, & the poor in the prison, & the
   soldier in the field
When the shatter'd bone hath laid him groaning among the
   happier dead.

It is an easy thing to rejoice in the tents of prosperity:
Thus could I sing & thus rejoice: but it is not so with me.[43]

For he knew what the intolerable system of England was doing
to the people, and he cared. 'National wealth,' he would have
affirmed, with Cobbett, 'means, the Commonwealth or Common-
weal, and these mean the general good, or happiness of the people,
and the safety and honour of the state; and these were not to be
secured by robbing those who laboured, in order to support a
large part of the community in idleness.'[44] And for him too,
'where honest and laborious men could be compelled to starve
quietly, with old wheat ricks and fat cattle under their eyes, it was
a mockery to talk of their "liberty" of any sort, for, the sum total
of their state was this, that they had "liberty" to choose between
death by starvation (quick or slow) and death by the halter'.[45]
We are a social world, Blake tells us, and each one of us takes
from or gives to and is affected by those he lives among. And the
wrongs of society are wrongs done to people, by separation and
division, by indifference, by neglect, which men of conscience
have to fight against, whoever they are. And what we have to fight
for, as Blake did continually, is a world re-made, a world modelled
on the innate creative powers of men and women. This is a task
which all systems, all simplifications, all abstract reductions,
falsify, and which the system he himself had to live under seemed
dedicated to stifle and suppress. Hence Blake's sceptical perception
that man in society must always fail to achieve his perfect
framework, his vision of Jerusalem, because there is no society
that can accommodate the multiplicity of men's needs or the
perversity of their passions. And hence the relevance of his

conviction that all men who are truly awake and whole are bound
to be dissenters from, and critics of, the abstract systems of
societies. How can it be otherwise? How can any man who really
cares for people, so he seems to argue, ever bring himself to accept
the values of a world that thrives upon suffering, disorder, fear
and brutal repression; that seeks

> To restrain, to dismay, to thin
> The inhabitants of mountain &
>   plain,
> In the day of full-feeding prosperity
> And the night of delicious songs.[46]

For Blake at least there could be no compromise with such a
world. How could one compromise with the enemies of humanity?
Compromise and forced submission, passivity, surrender of the
will were the means by which they sought to dominate humanity.

> Shall not the Councillor throw his curb
> Of Poverty on the laborious,
> To fix the price of labour,
> To invent allegoric riches?
>
> And the privy admonishers of men
> Call for fires in the City,
> For heaps of smoking ruins
> In the night of prosperity & wantonness?
>
> To turn man from his path,
> To restrain the child from the womb,
> To cut off the bread from the city,
> That the remnant may learn to
>   obey . . .?[46]

The characteristic note of anger, the pity and compassion, are
clear. But Blake has no illusions that the struggle against the
oppressors of humanity can be won finally and for good. It has to
take into account the essential contraries of human existence – the
reason *and* the energy, the passive *and* the active. In his terms
Good, 'the passive that obeys Reason', and Evil, 'the active
springing from Energy',[47] are necessary complements, and
together determine the creative antagonism of the living world, its
continuity. And it is the failure to recognize this or to live up to it

that brings about the destructive imbalance in human society. 'Those who restrain desire,' he points out trenchantly, 'do so because theirs is weak enough to be restrained; and the restrainer or reason usurps its place & governs the unwilling. And being restrain'd, it by degrees becomes passive, till it is only the shadow of desire.'[48] For human freedom is not to be attained by repression, by the dulling down of the active principle, the neutralizing of energy or desire. Such methods, rather, are a formula for enslavement, and Reason then becomes an oppressor, the enchaining power of 'the cunning of weak and tame minds which have power to resist energy'.[49]

No, the struggle is a ceaseless one, and in Blake's terms the conditions of human existence are such as to preclude the establishment of Jerusalem, that great 'Harvest and Vintage of the Nations', in *this* world. Of course it could be argued that such a conclusion merely reflects Blake's own acknowledgement of the triumph of tyrannical power and his defeat; but his challenge is too serious and too fundamental to be dismissed like this. True, he himself seems to stress the unreality of man's claims:

Many persons, such as Paine and Voltaire, with some of the Ancient Greeks, say: 'We will not converse concerning Good and Evil; we will live in Paradise and Liberty.' You may do so in Spirit, but not in the Mortal Body as you pretend, till after the Last Judgement; for in Paradise they have no Corporeal & Mortal Body – that originated with the Fall & was call'd Death & cannot be removed but by a Last Judgement; while we are in the world of Mortality we Must Suffer.[50]

But this does not mean that the struggle for paradise and liberty should cease. Quite the contrary. The mental fight has to be waged as fiercely as ever. For: 'The Whole Creation Groans to be delivered; there will always be as many hypocrites born as Honest Men, & they will always have superior Power in Mortal Things. You cannot have Liberty in this World without what you call Moral Virtue, & you cannot have Moral Virtue without the Slavery of that half of the Human Race who hate what you call Moral Virtue.'[51]

And, for himself at least, if not for others, though he does not speak in selfishness, he was in no doubt 'that to Labour in Knowledge is to Build up Jerusalem, & to Despise Knowledge is to Despise Jerusalem & her builders. And remember: He who despises and mocks a Mental Gift in another, calling it pride and selfishness and sin, mocks Jesus the giver of every Mental Gift, which always appear to the ignorance-loving Hypocrite as Sins; but that which is a Sin in the sight of cruel Man is not so in the sight of our kind God. Let every Christian, as much as in him lies, engage himself openly & publicly before all the World in some Mental pursuit for the Building up of Jerusalem.'[52]

Which was precisely what Blake tried to do. Like Los, the hero of *Jerusalem*, seeking through the chaos of a divided world the four-fold unity of being, the lineaments of Man, 'he kept the Divine Vision in time of trouble'.[53]

11

PROGRESS AND REACTION IN THE AGE OF REVOLUTION:

WORDSWORTH, SHELLEY AND BURKE

By the beginning of the nineteenth century, men like Blake (always rare at the best of times) had been more or less effectively isolated within their world, as Byron, Shelley and Keats – the object on political grounds of active dislike and bitter attack – were to be in their turn. And during the first half of the century the struggle for reason and justice and emancipation was to demand greater strength of mind and greater powers of resistance than could reasonably be expected of any but the exceptional few. For out of the turbulence and confusion of the Revolution and the wars that followed it, in the quickening tempo of the Industrial Revolution, a new and aggressive class of men had emerged to open up the continent and impose its ruthless control upon society in the name of progress. Under the domination of such men and the rapid development of all instruments of production, the capitalist minority thrived upon divisiveness and repression, the power of 'institutes and laws hallowed by time'[1] for the protection of privilege and property and the degradation of the mass of the people in a 'universal exploitation of communal human nature'.[2] And if ever those sources of creative activity which Blake called Giants could be said to be in chains, it was at this time; Europe seemed to have succumbed completely to 'the cunning of the weak and the tame'. For such systematic exploitation could only reduce the idea of civilized society to a brutal mockery, however eloquently the rhetoric of its spokesmen might disguise it.

As early as 1791, it was clear to William Godwin, especially after reading Burke's *Reflections*, that the established powers in England would use every weapon at their command to oppose the principles of reason and of justice so recently defined by the Revolution. 'There is a perpetual struggle,' he writes in his *Political Justice*, 'between the genuine sentiments of understanding . . . and the imperious voice of government, which bids us reverence and obey'[3] the spells and charms of ancient imposture. And now, it seemed to him, 'all the prejudices of the human mind are in arms'.[4] For the point is that Godwin's defence of the principles and conclusions of eighteenth-century rationalism was launched at the very moment of incipient reaction – at a time, that is, when the imperious voice of British government was about to come out into the open as the declared enemy of radicalism and emancipation and seize its opportunity to exploit the hysterical anti-French mood of the English upper classes.

For a while, in Hazlitt's words, Godwin 'blazed as a sun in the firmament of reputation . . . and wherever liberty, truth, justice was the theme, his name was not far off'.[5] But with the mind of England visibly clouding, growing steadily darker and more threatening, his kind of lucid philosophical idealism was soon to suffer eclipse; for such ideas were not to be encouraged in the England of Pitt, Castlereagh and Wellington, the Poor Laws, the Corn Laws, the Factory Laws, the Orders in Council, the war against France, the Luddites and Peterloo – an England explosive with unrest and resentment and misery.

Nor was it surprising in an atmosphere as threatening as this that impressionable men like Wordsworth and Coleridge and Southey should have begun to find the unequivocal support they had given to the principles of liberty and justice and humanitarian politics turning sour on them. From the evidence available it could be argued that the romantic nature of their support for these Godwinian ideals and for the spirit of the Revolution had only the shallowest of roots; that their enthusiasm was no more than the enthusiasm of youth, the 'bigotry of a youthful patriot's mind', as Wordsworth defines it, and formed no part of the deeper convictions of the bounded self; that it was little more than an intoxication of the moment, a spell cast by the excitements of the time; a transitory mood of the soul.

Nevertheless, Wordsworth himself *had* given a great deal of energy and commitment to the issues of the Revolution and its challenge to society; and his sense of indignation and outrage against the injustice and inhumanity of his age seemed passionately convinced, driving him even to the point of considering whether an English revolution might not be necessary to rid the country of a villainous government. It is all the more disconcerting, therefore, to note the completeness with which such ardent and generous political sentiments could collapse before the pressure of events and be rejected as 'an idle dream' associated with 'the meddling intellect'.[6] Even taking into account Wordsworth's own record – the depth of disillusionment he suffered at the way the Revolution had gone wrong, his awareness of the 'terrific reservoir of guilt/And ignorance filled up from age to age',[7] his sense of 'all things tending fast/To depravation'[8] – it is hard to credit. Surely, one asks, rational convictions of the sort the poet held during the five years up to 1795 are not so easily surrendered? The study of human nature may well have suggested the 'awful truth, that, as . . . sin and crime are apt to start from their very opposite qualities, so there are no limits to the hardening of the heart, and the perversion of the understanding to which they may carry their slaves'.[9] But that is not the whole of it; for there are other kinds of truth it may suggest. The study of human nature is not *exhausted* by observing man's capacity for perverting his idealism into sin and crime. What, one might ask, of that perversion of the understanding which had brought *about* the Revolution, defined by the spells and charms of a social order in which 'the man who is of soul/The meanest thrives the most'?[10] What about the capacity of the few to harden their hearts against the needs of a suffering and oppressed mankind? Is this sort of perversion to be accepted as a preferable alternative and the struggle against it to be renounced as invalid?

One can only explain the nature of Wordsworth's retreat from involvement in personal, psychological terms – as a kind of breakdown, a loss of nerve, a form of emotional dissociation (connected even perhaps with the deepening frustrations of his separation from Annette Vallon, the girl he had fallen in love with and left in France) – which left the poet unable to deal either emotionally or intellectually with the onslaught, or to keep the distinctions clear between tyranny and oppression abroad and the proofs of it at home. He was gripped, as he says, by fear – 'the fear that kills;/And the hope that is unwilling to be fed'.[11] How else to explain the two devastating lines in *The Leech-Gatherer*?

We poets in our youth begin in gladness
But thereof come in the end despondency and madness.[12]

Faced with the terror of the abyss, the void, surrounding him,

his mind 'was both let loose,/Let loose and goaded'.[13] So that
when the going became rough, 'the human Reason's naked self'
served only, so it seems, to oppress and to undermine his objective
thinking self, to attack and to impair the findings of the mind and
feelings; to excite 'morbid passions'. The consequence was that,
'endeavouring . . . to probe/The living body of society', he found
himself

> Dragging all passions, shapes of faith,
> Like culprits to the bar, suspiciously
> Calling the mind to establish in plain day
> Her titles and her honours, now believing,
> Now disbelieving, endlessly perplexed
> With impulse, motive, right and wrong, the ground
> Of moral obligation, what the rule
> And what the sanction, till, demanding *proof*,
> And seeking it in everything, I lost
> All feeling of conviction, and, in fine,
> *Sick, wearied out with contrarieties*
> *Yielded up moral questions in despair.*[14]

From the nature of the evidence we have in *The Prelude* and
elsewhere, and the earnestness and honesty of the poet's attempt
to understand his dilemma, it would not be unreasonable to
conclude that Wordsworth found himself unable to sustain the
harshness of that dialectic vision of reality without which the
contrary states of being cannot be reconciled – the tension between
subject and object, self and society, intellect and imagination,
reason and energy, the struggle *for* the self and for man as a social
being, the positive conviction of the necessity of action, which are
the source of creative interchange between man and his world.
Sickened, gripped by fear, wearied out with these 'contrarieties',
having little understanding of the process of history or of historical
change in the wider sense, it seemed he had no choice but to turn
his back on the injustices and wholesale mutilations that were
disfiguring the life of England at large and retire into the country,
to Racedown and Alfoxden and the Lake District, for 'a saving
intercourse', as he phrased it, with his 'true self'.[15]

In confirmation of this interpretation of Wordsworth's change
of heart, it has been suggested that it was not intellectual
conviction at all but only a kind of 'hypochondriacal graft of his

nature' that led him in the first place to take up with Godwin's radical ideas. Not that one should accept such a suggestion as adequate to the conditions, for it does scant justice to the sincerity of Wordsworth's own sense of crisis; for his hypochondria, the sense of contamination from a world 'poisoned at the heart', and of the 'melancholy waste of hopes o'erthrown', was obviously one of the causes of *conflict* between conviction and doubt. More to the point is the observation of Coleridge that 'certain beliefs, at any rate by men of Wordsworth's stamp, are sickness', and 'with the restoration of vitality and the influx of joy they disappear'.[16]

The pity is that such restoration, such influx of joy, and with it much of his best poetry (written in the years immediately succeeding his withdrawal, between 1795 and 1805), should have been gained at such cost in perspective. It is as if, for Wordsworth, sickness had its roots in the stirrings of that conscience which had urged him towards involvement, the pursuit of an objective rational understanding of human society, and health in escape from 'the dreary intercourse of daily life',[17] retreat into the self and a glorification of the 'renovating power' of Nature – which he looks upon with the longing of a sick man for the *sources* of health. This is the illusion that undermined his life. Though at one time, so it seems, the world was too *much* with him – so that 'getting and spending we lay waste our power'[18] – after 1805 he came to settle for too *little* of it, to begin to see people and things as fixed and unchanging and to turn a blind eye to the ugliness and inhumanity, the 'fretful stir' and change, around him, having by then convinced himself (in justification of his retreat) that 'pure intellectualism in morals was more likely to produce or justify crime than virtue', and that the healing power of Nature was an adequate substitute for 'all the ways of men, so vain and melancholy'.[19]

It is a devastating commentary upon the oppressive and illiberal atmosphere of the time and the ways in which its perversions and dichotomies affected men of good faith and goodwill that Wordsworth should have been compelled to make such a choice, and to turn away from the overt antagonisms in the world of urban (and rural) struggle, of social crisis, of political and social challenge. Quite clearly, the pressures were too great for him to sustain the fighting spirit necessary for survival. And, with the forces of reactionary power everywhere triumphant, it was hardly surprising. Thus, from being a confirmed supporter in the 1790s of republican France, a France regenerated in spite of 'lamentable crimes', he was to become by 1803, as his sister writes, 'a determined hater of the French', and to see in what France had to offer nothing but

> Perpetual emptiness! unceasing change!
> No single volume, paramount, no code,
> No master spirit, no determined road;
> But equally a want of books and men.[20]

And from offering such passionate defence of the 'government of equal rights and individual worth', and urging in his 1793 *Letter to the Bishop of Llandaff* the use of violence to overthrow despotism, the claims of manhood suffrage, abolition of the law of inheritance and equality of income, he was to set himself forth sixteen years later in his pamphlet on the *Convention of Cintra* (1809) as a powerful voice for conservatism and nationalism, and in 1818 to contradict every single principle and sentiment so solemnly affirmed in 1793. Such is the manner in which superior force can crush men's hopes and turn them against themselves to diminish and to betray. In one way or another, Wordsworth seemed to find all paths forward blocked; and, appalled by the nature of the obstacles that stood before him, he faltered, and turned back, to try to salvage for himself the parts of the world he knew best and could trust.

'Poet of Nature,' Shelley was to write of him in 1816,

> thou hast wept to know
> That things depart which never may return:
> Childhood and youth, friendship and love's first glow,
> Have fled like sweet dreams, leaving thee to mourn.
> These common woes I feel. One loss is mine
> Which thou too feel'st, yet I alone deplore.
> Thou wert as a lone star, whose light did shine
> On some frail bark in winter's midnight roar:
> Thou hast like to a rock-built refuge stood
> Above the blind and battling multitude:
> In honoured poverty thy voice did weave
> Songs consecrate to truth and liberty –
> Deserting these, thou leavest me to grieve,
> Thus having been, that thou shouldst cease to be.[21]

From this it is clear that Shelley, in his admiration for Wordsworth's genius, felt the older poet's desertion of the field as an impoverishment and a loss. But then Shelley was a radical by conviction rather than (like Wordsworth) by intoxication; and (unlike Wordsworth) he was a man naturally sociable and unselfish, with a sensibility and an intelligence quickened by compassion and by indignation to an objective sense of commitment. Having been brought up in an England at war, and early wakened to a hatred of tyranny, he considered it the poet's place and duty to speak for the people against the injustice, the inhumanity and the intolerance of their oppressors, and to equip himself to resist the tyrannies of his age. Hence his dismay at Wordsworth's retreat. He himself had taken the trouble to think through Godwin's humane concept of political justice for himself, and to build on it, to absorb the lessons it offered – as the notes to *Queen Mab*, very early on, and the prefaces he wrote to a number of the mature poems, and the poems themselves, clearly demonstrate. Because for him the issues at stake were far too important and too serious to be discarded as the passing enthusiasms of youth. Though still young when he died – and therefore not exposed (like Wordsworth) to the disillusionments that often come with middle life – the evidence of his last works, their rigorous defence of the struggles of man towards freedom, suggests that had he lived on he would have continued to stand up to the challenge as positively and as generously as he faced the problems of the life he did live. Indeed, there is a constant interconnection in these works between the imperative concerns of the outer world and his own aesthetic aims as a poet. 'I have sought,' he writes in the Preface to *The Revolt of Islam*,

to enlist the harmony of metrical language, the ethereal combinations of the fancy, the rapid and subtle transitions of human passion, all those elements which essentially compose a Poem, in the cause of liberal and comprehensive morality; and in the view of kindling within the bosoms of my readers a virtuous enthusiasm for those doctrines of liberty and justice, that faith and hope in something good, which neither violence nor misrepresentation nor prejudice can ever totally extinguish among mankind.[22]

And much of his poetry bears compelling witness to this struggle for political and social justice, and to his perception of revolutionary activity in the external world and in the human mind – of 'irrepressible collective energy contained by repressive power'.

This radical vision of reality – at its best in poems like *The Mask of Anarchy, Prometheus Unbound, Hellas* and *The Triumph of Life* – faces up to the difficult necessity of perceiving and grasping the nature of the world in its complexity and contrariety, its energy and vividness, its minuteness and its immensity, as a cosmic phenomenon centred upon the struggles of humanity. And though Shelley did not, or could not, take the logical step of translating his vision into social action, he nevertheless conceived his art as ideological in the most creative sense, as an attempt to give concrete form to the conditions and grounds from which social action springs. He did not, that is, seek ways of escaping or evading the issues that confront those who live in the actual world, as Wordsworth did, unable to sustain the harshness of the conjunction and turning back to 'the calm oblivious tendencies/Of Nature'. For with Shelley politics and culture, society and the individual, the interests of man and the interests of literature, were aspects of a common organic process, an undivided community of interests. Though Arthur Hallam was later to argue that a poet like Tennyson had the advantage over Shelley because 'he came before the public unconnected with any political party or peculiar system of opinions',[23] it is precisely Shelley's passionate sense of commitment, his refusal to separate social and aesthetic issues, his conviction that politics mattered and could not be ignored without ignoring the most crucial issues of the world he lived in, that makes him a more significant, if not a better, poet than Tennyson. But of course for Shelley politics was to be equated not with the paraphernalia as such of political *parties* (and there was no political party in England radical enough for him) but with the clash of ideas and feelings and the sharpening influence of ideas upon the mind and the sensibility. And perhaps most important of all, since Shelley cared, politics meant people and the struggle for a world in which people and their community of interests mattered. It was not enough to be inspired, though Shelley trusted inspiration, and often wrote swiftly and with the spontaneity and directness that is one of the signs of his genius. The challenge was to put that inspiration to use, to feed it with ideas that would be worthy of it, to risk it, to give it *meaning* as a human voice and a voice for humanity.

Such, it is clear, was Shelley's view. His was an astonishingly lucid intelligence working in the service of the imagination. Far from tending to create a 'peculiar system of opinions', it is centrally concerned, even at its most excessive, with the issues and dilemmas of his age, and at its best a delicate impassioned tribute to the potentialities of man, shot through with tenderness, an intuitive generosity, and a poetic insight drawn, as he puts it, 'from the operations of the human mind, or from those external actions by which they are expressed'.[24] And like the Prometheus of his great poem, caught up in the struggle for emancipation from the tyranny of oppression, Shelley himself 'used knowledge as a weapon to defeat evil'. Not that he allowed himself to fall into the trap of believing that the possession of such knowledge could in itself bring about the regeneration of mankind. Though he tended to idealize the real, he knew from the nature of the actual world he lived in – ruled by 'Force and Fraud: Old Custom, legal Crime,/And bloody Faith the foulest birth of Time'[25] – what man was up against. As Demogorgon has it, addressing Prometheus in his sombre declaration at the end of the poem, of what man must be prepared to do to deserve his freedom:

> To suffer woes which Hope thinks infinite;
> To forgive wrongs darker than death or night;
>   To defy Power, which seems omnipotent;
> To love and bear: to hope till Hope creates
> From its own wreck the thing it contemplates;
>   Neither to change, nor falter, nor repent;
> This, like thy glory, Titan, is to be
> Good, great and joyous, beautiful and free;
> This is alone Life, Joy, Empire, and Victory.[26]

There is a harsh and unillusory awareness in these words – an awareness of the contradictory negative powers that block the paths to freedom and fulfilment, and of the need to face up to these powers with courage and conviction, whatever the obstacles. And this is the kind of awareness which, in *The Mask of Anarchy*, calls upon the common people to rise, as at some vast Peterloo, against the Murder, Fraud, Hypocrisy and Anarchy that symbolize the institutionalized powers of England – to

> Rise like lions after slumber
> In unvanquishable number –
> Shake your chains to earth like dew
> Which in sleep had fallen on you –
> Ye are many – they are few.[27]

For such revolutionary implications are fully consistent with Shelley's underlying philosophy of life, and everywhere implicit in his work as an organic expression of his spontaneous affirmation of the creative energies of the life-force. It is a vision naturally incomplete, and often obscured by excess, which is not surprising in a man who died so young. But its great achievement is in the invention and the embodiment of myths which give momentum and focus to the desired, the possible, things as yet unrealized, the 'change beyond the change' – thus provoking a revolutionary attitude towards reality. And there is no doubting the sincerity of the conviction or the intensity and the rightness of the commitment and the expectation. 'Mistake me not!' cries the old Jewish prophet in *Hellas*.

> All is contained in each.
> Dodona's forest to an acorn's cup
> Is that which has been, or will be, to that
> Which is – the absent to the present. Thought
> Alone, and its quick elements, Will, Passion,
> Reason, Imagination, cannot die;
> They are, what that which they regard appears,
> The stuff whence mutability can weave
> All that it hath dominion o'er, worlds, worms,
> Empires, and superstitions.[28]

And out of the awakened consciousness, which sees the future 'shadowed on the Past/As on a glass', will emerge the recognition of the necessity of the struggle for the future and the challenge of the new conditions man can make for himself, the promise of a world in which (perhaps) the tyrants of humanity shall be vanquished and left to 'rule the desert they have made'.[29]

Such a vision of the future, though in itself utopian, is an essential pre-condition to the realization of man's aspirations. For we cannot hope to change the world by turning away from it in disgust or in despair. We must in the first place believe that it can be changed. As Shelley himself puts it: 'Until the mind can love, and admire, and trust, and hope, and endure, reasoned principles of moral conduct are seeds cast upon the highway of life which the unconscious passenger tramples into dust, although they would bear the harvest of his happiness.'[30] In other words, Shelley knew that trust and hope and tenacity were indispensable; and his work honours and respects such an attitude, even in the ways in which it defines the conditions of the struggle. And this passionate conviction is nowhere registered more unequivocally than in the paragraph from the Preface to *Hellas* which all editions till 1892 suppressed as offensive to the tastes of public men:

Should the English people ever become free, they will reflect upon the part which those who presume to represent their will have played in the great drama of the revival of liberty, with feelings which it would become them to anticipate. This is the age of the war of the oppressed against the oppressors, and every one of those ringleaders of the privileged gangs of murderers and swindlers, called Sovereigns, look to each other for aid against the common enemy, and suspend their mutual jealousies in the presence of a mightier fear. Of this holy alliance all the despots of the earth are virtual members. But a new race has arisen throughout Europe, nursed in the abhorrence of the opinions which are its chains, and she will continue to produce fresh generations to accomplish that destiny which tyrants foresee and dread.[31]

Here, Shelley leaves us in no doubt as to where he stands or what he believes must be done. But there is another passage – the prose statement he makes in the Preface to *The Revolt of Islam*, recording his response to the French Revolution, the greatest event of the age – in which the sanity and cogency of the argument give particular weight to the maturity of Shelley's powers of judgement and of perception. It is worth quoting from at length because of the illuminating commentary it provides upon the psychological context that defined the negative position of men like Wordsworth:

The French Revolution may be considered as one of those manifesta-tions of a general state of feeling among civilized mankind produced by a defect of correspondence between the knowledge existing in society and the improvement or gradual abolition of political institutions. The year 1788 may be assumed as the epoch of one of the most important crises produced by this feeling. The sympathies connected with that event extended to every bosom. The most generous and amiable natures were those which participated the most extensively in these sympathies. But such a degree of unmingled good was expected as it was impossible to realize. If the Revolution had been in every respect prosperous, then misrule and superstition would lose half their claim to our abhorrence, as fetters which the captive can unlock with the slightest motion of his fingers, and which do not eat with poisonous rust into the soul. The revulsion occasioned by the atrocities of the demagogues, and the reestablishment of successive tyrannies in France, was terrible, and felt in the remotest corner of the civilized world. Could they listen to the plea of reason who had groaned under the calamities of a social state according to the provisions of which one man riots in luxury whilst another famishes for want of bread? Can he who the day before was a trampled slave suddenly become liberal-minded, forbearing and independent? This is the consequence of the habits of a state of society to be produced by resolute perseverance and indefatigable hope, and long-suffering and long-believing courage, and the systematic efforts of generations of men of intellect and virtue. Such is the lesson which experience teaches now. But, on the first reverses of hope in the progress of French liberty, the sanguine eagerness for good overleaped the solution of these questions, and for a time extinguished itself in the unexpectedness of their results. Thus, many of the most ardent and tender-hearted of the worshippers of public good have been morally ruined by what a partial glimpse of the events they deplored appeared to show as the melancholy desolation of all their cherished hopes. Hence gloom and misanthropy have become the characteristics of the age in which we live, the solace of a disappointment that unconsciously finds relief only in the wilful exaggeration of its own despair.[32]

Such, as Shelley saw it, was the manner in which his age affected the sensibilities of sensitive men and their whole way of looking at the world. That he himself was not tainted by hopelessness is as much due to his objective grasp of the issues involved as to his ability to see beyond the confusions and threats of the time to a concept of community in which the 'loathsome mark of tyranny' will have fallen. But Wordsworth was one of those who were forced to suffer the 'melancholy desolation of all their cherished hopes', and Shelley must surely have had him in mind in the writing of this passage. Reduced to his lowest ebb by the enmities of the tyrant powers of England and France, with 'the lordly attributes/Of will and choice' become a mockery of Being, as 'the dupe of folly, or the slave of crime',[33] Wordsworth could see no way forward, no hope of reconciliation. The Shelleyan assurance of 'a slow, gradual, silent change' for the better, of a 'reflux in the tide of human things' to be brought about by 'the systematic efforts of generations of men of intellect and virtue', was not available to Wordsworth. Shattered and appalled by the record of 'human ignorance and guilt', he could not see beyond it. The world *had* been too much for him; he had felt its oppressive weight upon his spirit, killing, suffocating. What else *could* he have done, faced with such a threat to his own survival, we ask, than what he did? He had, after all, not made that world, or himself. It had shattered all his expectations, and he had not had sufficient resilience to prevent it doing so. Seeing only

> Presumption, folly, madness, in the men
> Who thrust themselves upon this passive world
> As rulers of the world;

seeing in their plans concepts 'bottomed on false thought/And false philosophy', and from this 'the utter hollowness of what we name/The wealth of nations', its betrayal of 'the dignity of individual man',[34] he recoiled in horror and dismay. There was no question, it seemed, of fighting such despair; it had incapacitated him. What he felt he needed above all, and what he sought, was that saving intercourse with 'Nature's self' which would reaffirm his characteristic and fundamental attitudes and beliefs, as 'the anchor of my purest thoughts'.

And of course it is in this anchor that we recognize the peculiar quality of Wordsworth's genius, of what we call the Wordsworthian experience – his deep insight into the transcendental forces which continually operate to transform the world:

> that blessed mood,
> In which the burthen of the mystery,
> In which the heavy and the weary weight
> Of all this unintelligible world
> Is lightened

until a state is attained in which

> With an eye made quiet by the power
> Of harmony, and the deep power of joy,
> We see into the life of things.[35]

This is the sustaining strength and the essence of his genius as a poet. Its peculiarity, the source which gave it life and nourished it, was the extraordinary influence upon Wordsworth's being of the natural world, 'the ghostly language of the ancient earth', from which he drank in 'the visionary power'.[36] As he says in a revealing note: 'I was often unable to think of external things as having external existence, and I communed with all I saw as something not apart from, but inherent in, my own immaterial nature. Many times while going to school have I grasped at a rock or tree to recall myself from this abyss of idealism to the reality.'[37]

The phrasing is significant – that in fact 'idealism' represents an 'abyss', an abyss for the self; that Wordsworth was, in other words, aware of the danger of an imbalance in himself between idealism and reality, and of the difficulty of reconciling the two, of maintaining an organic interconnection between them. This was his dilemma: how to cross or to span the abyss, or to find the means to transform it – for it was, after all, no physical *space* but the recognition of a psychological area in the self, a sense of the void that he feared – the void he recognized even between himself and the world outside him, between the adult and the child, the internal self and the external presence, the actuality of the self and that being rooted in the echoes of a former self. And it may be that in withdrawing from the 'abyss of idealism' which had defined his involvement in the revolutionary events of his time, and attempting to recall himself to what he thought of as the reality, *his* reality, he was actually sharpening the divisions in the self rather than reconciling them.

In one of the most moving and revealing passages from *The Prelude* we find him seeking some kind of resolution to this dilemma which will enable him to create an organic rooted substance out of the estranged parts of being. As he puts it, attempting the connection, reaching across the abyss,

> feeling comes in aid
> Of feeling, and diversity of strength
> Attends us, *if but once we have been strong.*
> Oh! mystery of man, from what a depth
> Proceed thy honours. *I am lost*, but see
> In simple childhood something of the base
> On which thy greatness stands; but this I feel,
> That from thyself it comes, that thou must give,

Else never canst receive. The days gone by
Return upon me almost from the dawn
Of life: the hiding-places of man's power
Open; I would approach them, but they close.
I see by glimpses now; when age comes on,
May scarcely see at all; and I would give,
While yet we may, as far as words would give,
Substance and life to what I feel . . .[38]

There is a sense here that the poet is aware of the nulling effect of the abyss, of the void surrounding him or within him, of his isolation from the world. He is lost, he says, but he is at the same time obscurely conscious of sources of replenishment which, if they could be got at, might give him back his subjective sense of place and of identity, of recognition, of assurance. But the quest has become elusive and shadowy, a groping back into the past, perhaps most of all because it lacks the necessary context of the objective social reality Wordsworth has turned away from. It is a quest for the interconnections of the outer world and the inner, that process of giving and receiving which is the condition of self-knowledge, and Wordsworth makes his supreme attempt in *The Prelude* to maintain the balance between the complementary opposites, but with an increasing sense of the difficulty of standing up to the pressures of the outer world. Drawing, that is, upon the mystery he has felt and the strength he has known, against the fear of dispossession, the intuition of loss, Wordsworth seeks a renewed equilibrium at the roots of his own world. And it could even be said of this, and of Wordsworth's work at the time he was writing (or finishing) the first version of *The Prelude*, that he sensed the very intensity of the need to give substance and life to what he felt as a direct consequence of the intensity of his physical and emotional reaction to the great crisis of spirit he had lived through, the stress and turmoil of revolutionary Europe. Though he had already by this time turned away from involvement and from his own radicalism, the experience still remained as a wakening and motivating charge of energy, in the sense in which the imagination is most likely to develop 'that intensity of application which is the poetic vision'[39] under conditions of stress and conflict. Perhaps this is what Hazlitt meant by hailing Wordsworth's work as 'a pure emanation of the Spirit of the Age'.[40]

But he had a bitter price to pay for his withdrawal, his rejection of the dialectic issues of the historical struggle, his acceptance of a one-sided subjective status quo. For by cutting himself off from the channels through which the antagonistic energies flow and meet, and settling finally for what had given him back his 'settled judgement', he cut himself off from the very sources of replenishment and of creative conflict that had given such a charge of intensity to his work. The gradual decay of his poetic powers was the inevitable consequence, already apparent in the writing of *The Excursion*, which he had planned as the sequel to *The Prelude*. Unable or unwilling to face the ferment of social and historical change, the stress and challenge of the political process in the active spirit of the struggle for the future, feeling himself sapped and threatened by that struggle, he opted for the false quiet and repose, the illusory peace of Nature, and a steady retreat from even such vitality as nature gave him towards 'Duty' and 'Faith'. From 1813 to his death in 1850 he remained but for occasional journeys abroad at Rydal Mount. And increasingly the atmosphere became one of 'domestic tyranny and provincial narrowness; of decaying sensibility and the slow growth of a thick shell of convention – conventional religion, conventional morality, and worst of all, conventional poetry'.[41]

This was indeed a bitter price to have to pay, this decline into a rigid orthodoxy that echoed the hypocrisies of Victorian morality as if they were the precepts of eternal truth; but it was the price that his age and the intolerable pressures it put upon his sensibility had exacted from him. Who borrows pays: on dwindling reserves it is the interest betrays. In return for what he had so eloquently won for his art from the struggle, that 'resolution and independence' which was his choice, he had to pay back at compound interest.

'Sweet Mercy!' he cries out in a late poem, his *Thoughts Suggested near the Residence of Burns*, which seems to reveal something of the anguish of his own bitter sense of defeat:

> Sweet Mercy! to the gates of Heaven
> This Minstrel lead, his sins forgiven;
> The rueful conflict, the heart riven
>   With vain endeavour
> And memory of Earth's bitter leaven,
>   Effaced for ever.

Wordsworth was one among the many who were to come under the spell of Burke's arguments against radicalism and revolutionary principle and to find them persuasive. No doubt he did so because they gave such firm support to his own innate conservatism, his love of nature, his longing for stability, his rejection of the principles of change and progress. But these arguments – forewarning, denouncing, launching forth in keen ridicule 'against all systems built on abstract rights', as he puts it in an 1850 addition to *The Prelude*; proclaiming 'the majesty . . ./Of Institutes and Laws, hallowed by time'; declaring 'the vital power of social ties/Endear'd by Custom; and with high disdain/Exploding upstart Theory' – were the very arguments which the intolerant power of the possessing classes utilized to hold the people of Britain in thrall and to subject them ruthlessly to the cruelties and miseries of war and of economic enslavement, as mere instruments for the production of wealth. 'The times,' as Wordsworth says, 'were big/With ominous change';[42] and Burke was to do much with his eloquent appeal to irrationality and divisiveness – invoking God as the Authoritarian Author and Nature as God's Assistant – to shape the attitudes of these times.

'By a constitutional policy working after the pattern of nature,' the orator states, 'we receive, we hold, we transmit our government and our privileges, in the same manner in which we enjoy and transmit our property and our lives.'[43] The tone of autocratic assumption and superiority, where even the pronoun has the flavour of a Royal plural, is at once apparent; for this is the voice of a governing élite uttering its prescriptive absolutes and dispensations to an awestruck multitude, which in obedience to the laws of the Divine Author, knows that 'our political system is *placed in a just correspondence and symmetry with the order of the world* . . . by the disposition of a stupendous wisdom [that moulds] together the great mysterious incorporation of the human race'. From which it follows, unalterably, that the 'we' that rules enjoys the luxuries of privilege and property as a *natural consequence* of the divinely constituted political system. And this minority of favoured beings, who make up the leadership of order and authority, are no more themselves than humble instruments chosen by natural selection to preserve 'the method of nature in the conduct of the state'.[44] It would be scurrilous of anyone, given such injunctions, to suggest that those who govern with such humility from their appointed place in the scale of things could have *engineered* the laws of nature to preserve their privileged positions, or would have dared to pervert the 'constitutional policies' of nature by drawing up a constitutional policy of their own, so organized as to prevent anyone else from challenging their appointments. To ask whose interests such constitutional policy was intended to serve, if not their own, would be to ask a blasphemous question. Apparently, according to Burke, we adopt 'our fundamental laws into the bosom of our family affections',[45] and it would be invidious to ask which families received the largest share of protection from the laws, for that would be to raise the question of the deprived and mutilated masses, the women and children in the mills, the so-called beneficiaries of the Poor Laws, the Corn Laws and the Factory Laws. But then of course these laws and others relating to the constitutional policy of nature had not been conceived in the bosoms of the poor. As Burke affirms: 'Atheists are not our preachers; madmen are not our lawgivers.' We, in other words, are ruled by wise and humane people who 'fear God . . ., look up with awe to Kings; with affection to parliaments; with duty to magistrates; with reverence to priests; and with respect to nobility. Why? Because when such ideas are brought before our minds, it is *natural* to be so affected.'[46] It is natural, that is, to feel awe, affection, reverence and respect even if we find ourselves confronted, in the words of Shelley's sonnet *England in 1819*, by:

> An old, mad, blind, despised, and dying king –
> Princes, the dregs of their dull race, who flow
> Through public scorn – mud from a muddy
>   spring –
> Rulers who neither see, nor feel, nor know,
> But leech-like to their fainting country cling,
> Till they drop, blind in blood, without a blow . . .[47]

And it is presumably *un*natural to be affected by the cruelties, the miseries, the injustices meted out by kings and parliaments and magistrates; for to notice such aberrations one would have to look down, and it is perhaps unnatural to the awestruck to look down, let alone to care what in the appointed order of things might crawl about beneath one's feet. No, we should not allow ourselves to be distracted by cruelties and injustices when there is so much to be thankful for from the guardians of divinely established truth.

'We know that *we* have made no discoveries,' Burke observes with humility, 'and we think no discoveries are to be made, in morality; nor many in the great principles of government, nor in the ideas of liberty, which were understood long before we were born.'[48] Which is to say that the wisest among us are those who have the magnanimity to leave things as they are – to accept cruelty and injustice, 'a people starved and stabbed in the untilled field',[49] for the sake of the great principles of conservative government, as determined by the laws of nature. Furthermore, since it is by the laws of nature and of God that the wise receive, hold and transmit their government and their privileges, it is apparently quite natural that the laws *they* make (morality having little to teach them) should happen to fall with crushing weight upon the poor. For it is Burke's contention that, since Nature rules benignantly and with a higher wisdom than any man can emulate, we must submit to the conditions she establishes and thus to the authority of her obedient higher servants – who are there to ensure that we remain in our naturally appointed places, rich or poor, great or small, wise or ignorant, for ever.

This is the kind of psychology which – emerging out of the corrupted concept of the Divine Right of Kings, and building irrationality, prejudice and intolerance into a weapon of authoritarian control – had re-established its hold upon, and entered again into the substance of, the social structure of European society to pervert the very nature of man's relationship to man within society. When the superior virtue of prejudice over reason can be argued as a means of organizing society, 'because prejudice, with its reason, has a motive to give action to that reason, and an affection which will give it permanence',[50] we are already in the presence of a consciousness dislocated and crippled by its incapacity to look its abstractions honestly in the face. Why should such a system, if it believed in its own nature, try, as Marx ironically questions, 'to hide that nature under the *appearance* of an alien nature and seek its salvation in hypocrisy and sophism? The Modern *ancien régime*,' he observes, 'is merely the *clown* of a world order whose *real heroes* are dead.'[51] Because what it argues is blind adherence to all established institutions (however inhumane, however bankrupt) as the tried and tested instruments of social intercourse sanctioned by the inviolable laws of nature. It is nature alone, that is – nature above reason – that dictates the structure and the composition of human society. And those who operate the systems of control which hold everything firmly and submissively .in place are merely obeying, so it seems, the superior and superhuman *powers* of nature.

In this way was it possible to justify the system of intolerance and inhumanity that prevailed, by a species of deception under the influence of which many of its functionaries were even convinced that they were supporting the very foundations of tolerant and humane government. Here we see embodied the Hegelian inversion which became the focus for Marx's penetrating criticism. Nature, the universal Abstract, has been placed in the position of man the subject, and man himself turned into an object upon which 'nature' operates as a mystical authority – though it is of course still men who take it upon themselves to act as nature's obedient instruments.

This enthronement of Nature and its inviolable laws as the source of social order represents the manner in which, in the Burkean sense, the separation of man from man and of class from class was determined afresh at the end of the eighteenth century, and the oppression of the many by the few justified and systematically pursued. Defined as God's purposes manifested in society, it was to become the ideology which asserted the ruthless cutthroat principles and the sickening hypocrisies of nineteenth-century capitalism, and, with the expansion of competitive war into an imperialist game of power, the appalling carnage of the First World War.

Marx understood what was happening from the start. He saw that the very tools of thinking had become perverted by abstraction – hence the urgency of his call for a merciless criticism of the existing order, and of all forms of 'mystical consciousness', religious and political. Because the essential task was to make people aware of the real conditions of the struggle for the future, to unmask the deceptions that ruled, and thus to clear the ground for the re-establishment of the links between theory and practice. For him the concept of nature as a mysterious divine law that rules and ordains the contracts of society is in itself a perversion of the order of reality. 'Nature is the immediate object of the science of man,' he writes, and 'man's first object – man – is nature, sense perception'. And even 'the element of thought itself, the element of the vital expression of thought – language – is sensuous nature',[52] since it is rooted in and dependent upon the sensuous animal being of man. Any process, therefore, which separates thought from its proper context – such as that which led Hegel to exalt Nature into an abstract mysterious power – constitutes a threat to the unity of being and thought which defines the integrity of man's existence at all levels.

Quite simply, in the objective and unmystical terms of Marx's argument, 'man is directly a *natural* being. As a natural being and as a living natural being he is on the one hand equipped with natural *powers*, with *vital* powers, he is an *active* natural being; these powers exist in him as dispositions and capacities, as *drives*.' And at the same time he is 'a suffering, conditioned and limited being like animals and plants. That is to say, the *objects* of his drives exist outside him as objects independent of him'; and these objects are 'indispensable to the exercise and confirmation of his essential powers'.[53] But beyond this, and including this, he is also an objective *social* being. And as a social being it is he who in fact creates and organizes the structures and systems of society, which ought to function as the objective complements to his organic human powers. In other words, in the rational and objective sense that is continually being perverted by the imposition of abstract alien powers directed against man: 'I am *socially* active because I am active as a *man* . . . What I create from myself I create for society, conscious of myself as a social being'; and 'my *universal* consciousness is only the theoretical form of that which has its *living* form in the *real* community'.[54]

What then is this mysterious higher power that sanctions everything for us by some pre-ordained plan, according to Burke's philosophy? Should we, as fallible finite beings, each with his own constricted view of things, his small 'private stock of reason',[55] submit unquestioningly to it as to the guiding spirit of God himself and his omniscient, omnipotent authority? Are we to be expected to remain its blind obedient subjects, without even the right to know what its powers *are*? Forbidden forever, as Milton's Satan asks, 'from achieving what might lead/To happier life, knowledge of good and evil?'[56] In Burke's hierarchic view of nature's disposition of powers, 'the fixed compact . . , which holds all physical and all moral natures, each in their appointed place',[57] most men are condemned from the start to servitude, deprived of choice. 'Ah,' we might cry, with Adam, 'why should all Mankind,/For one man's fault, thus guiltless be condemned,/If guiltless?'[58]

Marx deals with the issue in a characteristically convincing manner:

> To the question: 'Who begot the first man, and nature in general?' I can only answer: Your question is itself a product of abstraction. Ask yourself how you arrived at that question. Ask yourself whether your question does not arise from a standpoint to which I cannot reply because it is a perverse one. Ask yourself whether that progression exists as such for rational thought. If you ask about the creation of nature and of man, then you are abstracting from nature and from man. You assume them as *non-existent*, and want me to prove to you that they *exist*. My answer is: Give up your abstraction and you will then give up your question. But if you want to hold on to your abstraction, then do so consistently, and if you assume the non-existence of nature and of man, then assume also your own non-existence, for you are also nature and man . . . You can reply: I do not want to assume the nothingness of nature, etc. I am only asking how it *arose* . . . etc.
>
> But since for socialist man *the whole of what is called world history* is nothing more than the creation of man through human labour, and the development of nature for man, he therefore has palpable and incontrovertible proof of his self-mediated *birth*, of his *process of emergence*. Since the essence of man and of nature . . . has become practically and sensuously perceptible, the question of an *alien* being, a being above nature and man – a question which implies an admission of the unreality of nature and of man – has become impossible in practice.[59]

It is clear that such a rational and defiantly humanistic view of man's place in his world would have been able to do as little to influence the mood or the consciousness of Europe in the 1790s as it was able to in the 1840s. The élitist, violently divisive course had been set, for the men who ruled or were about to rule Europe seemed proof against any sort of social logic that argued for the organic rights of all men as human beings. Intent upon the preservation of privilege and property and the accumulation of power, motivated now by fear, now by greed, now by innate contempt for the squalid pleas of the rioting and beer-swilling poor, they would have heard nothing of the authentic appeal to common human interests in such arguments, only the note of subversion that held out its threat to the mysteries of the sacred framework of the social order that sustained them.

And when the Revolutions of 1848 broke out in city after

European city to offer a seemingly direct challenge to the bastions of inequality, what they achieved in fact was the accession to power of the bourgeois capitalists, who had seized their revolutionary opportunities by linking up with and utilizing the spontaneous passions of the working classes to get them there. The end-result of all these great uprisings of the people was a new confirmation of the sacred framework of the institutionalized status quo, a crushing defeat for radicalism, and renewed oppression for the working classes, as characterized by the two stages of the Paris Revolution, the February triumph of the literary spokesmen, and the June defeat of the workers on the barricades.

The bourgeoisie, having seized power by challenging and thrusting aside, as the Communist Manifesto puts it, 'the motley feudal ties that bound man to his "natural superiors" ', was therefore in a position to utilize the immense resources of society to the demands of the 'naked self-interest' that was the motivating principle of its thirst for power. And in the ruthless embodiment of this policy, what it did was to resolve 'personal worth into exchange value, and in place of the numberless indefeasible chartered freedoms' characteristic of the system it had overthrown, to 'set up that single, unconscionable freedom – free trade'.[60] The process of development thus unleashed exploded in every direction in a feverish quest for new markets, new sources of exploitation; for what distinguishes the bourgeois epoch from all earlier ones is its

constant revolutionizing of production, [its] uninterrupted disturbance of all social conditions, [its] everlasting uncertainty and agitation . . . All fixed, fast-frozen relations, with their train of ancient and venerable prejudices and opinions, are swept away, all new-formed ones become antiquated before they can ossify. All that is solid melts into air, all that is holy is profaned, and man is at last compelled to face, with sober senses, his real conditions of life, and his relations with his kind.[61]

But at the same time 'the need of a constantly expanding market for its products chases the bourgeois over the whole surface of the globe. It must nestle everywhere, settle everywhere, establish connections everywhere.'[62] Hence the inexorable development of those forms of competitive nationalism which were increasingly to dominate the politics of Europe and to take Britain, France and Germany into the obscurest corners of the world in the race for power and influence and territorial acquisition. And all this, it was predicted, could lead in one direction only: from crisis to crisis, an intensification of the class struggle and the sharpening of the contradictions and dichotomies of the system, to its eventual breakdown and the triumph of a revolutionary working class. That, at least, was how it looked to Marx and Engels at the time. Against the apparent logic of such a view, history has added new and unforeseen perspectives of development and change.

Part Four

'*And who are we,*
with Livy's words and Kafka's in our
   heads
and Kaplan dead among the millions
   there,
to break the spell that binds us
to this witches' rationale?
to set dream loose against the spinster fates,
and turn the great machines and
   institutions
into instruments of our subjunctive will?'

                    Christopher Hampton:
                         '*If Only If Only*'

12

THE QUEST FOR A QUALITATIVE
SOCIAL ORDER

Today, in the last quarter of the twentieth century, the world maintains an uneasy balance of social and political alignments, defining the varying stages of political and economic influence from one extreme to another, between the antagonistic ideologies of Russia and America on the one hand and the attitudes of the many developing nations that have begun to assert themselves since the Second World War on the other. This world, dominated by the deterrent of a huge stockpile of atomic weaponry built up and organized by the Great Powers as a mutual strike-force of incalculable destructive power, is rife with unresolved issues and situations of all kinds that threaten the precarious tight-rope balance of power. In the last thirty years, the ideological struggle has continued unabated, with sudden violent confrontations erupting into crisis in an ever-shifting process of transformation, both revolutionary and reactionary. It has been a constant test of nerve and of capacity; and at times the strains and pressures have brought the world very close to disaster. But at the same time nations previously subservient to the Great Powers – notably in China, Cuba, Vietnam, Central Africa and the Middle East – have begun to stand up to them, and to make challenging claims of their own, radically altering the balance. For during this period the unprecedented advance of scientific knowledge has made available to hitherto repressed or quiescent peoples technologies of increasing sophistication which, though they have deepened the risks and problems that face humanity, have made people more sharply aware of their interdependence, their interspatial involvement in a single world. In other words, these revolutionary developments, even as they are the key to the competitive process by which the richer nations have sought to impose their domination over the poorer, have also become the means by which to break the seal of secrecy and of economic ascendance which separates the continents and nations and to open them up to each other. Given the unstable psychology of man himself, however, it cannot be said that the threat to the future defined by his unscrupulous doctrinal abuse of power has been checked or counterbalanced by the scope and promise of scientific inventiveness. For whatever else it is, and however transformed, the world is still as deeply divided in its essential motives and aims, if not in its superficial conditions, as it was for Marx in the nineteenth century.

And in the light of such phenomenal developments, the challenge of Marx's critical terms and methods, if not the dogmas that have issued from them, remains as vital and as indispensable as ever. For it is the essence of these methods that 'all analyses of social life should proceed by seeking the basic divisions that separate societies into antagonistic groups'. And 'even if it turns out that in certain societies these divisions are based on other criteria than the ones Marx formulated for the nineteenth-century bourgeois world, still the very fact of applying this extremely general rule leads the scholar to adopt Marx's characteristic methodology.'[1] For it has forced us to think beyond the divisive assumptions and attitudes by which we are conditioned so that we may begin to build for a world which postulates equilibrium between the realm of necessity and the realm of freedom. Marx used the weapon of criticism as an instrument not only to denounce the hypocrisies of capitalist domination and its nationalistic ambitions, but also to formulate conditions (based upon the terms of the class struggle as he watched it developing) for the emancipation of the people of Europe from that subjugation to the chauvinism of the ruling classes which sought, as he says, 'to perpetuate international struggles' and 'to prevent the international cooperation of the working classes'.[2] As he saw it, for instance, the 1871 Paris Commune represented a great step towards 'the liberation of labour, that is the fundamental and natural condition of individual and social life', from the shackles of state power that held it imprisoned, by offering a 'rational medium to permit the class struggle to run through its various stages in the most rational and humane way'.[3] What it seemed to him to demonstrate was that 'with labour emancipated, every man becomes a working man, and productive labour ceases to be a class attribute'.[4] That is to say, he saw the Commune as aiming 'to abolish that class property which makes the labour of the many the wealth of the few', and 'to make individual property a truth by transforming the means of production, land and capital, now chiefly the means of enslaving and exploiting labour, into mere instruments of free and associated labour'. But, as he exclaims in his address to the General Council on the Civil War in France, two days after the *defeat* of the Commune, 'this is *communism*, "impossible" communism' – that impossibility against the deceptive appeal of which the capitalist leaders would organize all their powers in the defence of 'civilized values'! But at the same time, as Marx points out, 'those members of the ruling classes who are intelligent enough to perceive the impossibility of continuing the present system – and they are many – have become the obtrusive and full-mouthed apostles of *cooperative production*'. And 'if cooperative production is not to remain a sham and a snare; if it is to supersede the capitalist system; if united cooperative societies are to regulate national production upon a common plan, thus taking it under their own control, and putting an end to the constant anarchy and periodical convulsions which are the fatal weakness of capitalist production – what else, gentlemen, would it be but communism, "possible" communism'.[5]

From his analysis of the events in Paris, Marx concluded 'that a new class, including the working class, could only come to power and transform society to its design if it represented, not merely its own particular interest, but a universal interest of historical development, so that only those with a vested interest in the old order would stand in its way'.[6] Of course, he could not have been expected to see far enough into the future to register the dangers of those with vested interests in the *new* order, that 'despotism of the governing minority' which, as Bakunin pointed out, would be the more dangerous in the very fact that it *appeared* to be the 'expression of the so-called people's will'.[7] But Marx clearly recognized the monumental nature of the obstacles that stood in the way of any genuinely constructive transformation of society, and he was not to be deluded into thinking they could be overcome without long years of struggle, 'a series of historic processes, transforming circumstances and men',[8] and involving the risk of failure. The evidence that we now have, a hundred years later, of the progress of this struggle, in China, in Vietnam, in Cuba, in Chile, Portugal, Angola, Libya and elsewhere in the world, demonstrates not only the undiminished relevance of the

Marxian challenge, but also the vigour and tenacity of the opposition. And wherever the revolutionary movements of the post-war world have (as in Russia) seemed to prove Bakunin's point, they have added incalculably to the obstacles, confirming and reinforcing the arguments of liberal capitalism, and underlining how far we are from having achieved even an approximation of the kind of rational social structure Marx envisaged as the basis for emancipation and fulfilment. Now, faced by the confusions and complexities of a world explosive with change, a grasp of the contradictions of progress, in the Marxian spirit, is more than ever indispensable.

It is this dialectic awareness of the terms of the historical struggle that Marx's thinking urges upon us, together with a sense of its qualitative issues, the negative–positive balance of the energies of man to which this struggle is directed. What above all we have to focus *our* thinking upon, wherever we look, is how to bring about this creative equation in face of all that continues to work against it. As much in terms of the new and expanding technological tyrannies of the post-war world as of its politics, the challenge of Marx's concept of the human condition, his belief that man is capable of creating for his race a higher form of civilized co-existence than he has yet known, remains a palpable incentive. For what are our values and principles otherwise worth? What has our vaunted 'freedom of the individual conscience' to offer if we are not prepared to make the attempt to bring about those changes in the social structure that are necessary? To accept the status quo and drift with the current is to leave the action, the re-direction of the current, to others. True, those who are fortunate may well be *content* to accept the status quo for what it offers and not think beyond it. True, since time itself is always at work re-ordering, actively changing, transforming, breaking down and building up, it might be asked whether *any* system can be imposed upon this subtle pattern that would not falsify. But the struggles of men have always been concerned with the necessity of harnessing and re-directing the current, either to obtain power over other men and to exploit their ignorance, or (more rarely) in a spirit of genuine co-operation. And these struggles are an inseparable part of the historical process – the struggle for life, the struggle to create, to recognize, to achieve awareness and mastery, the struggle between the makers and the killers of community.

We have to try to adjust ourselves to change when change is necessary, to make ourselves part of the revolutionary process of a constantly changing universe; to wake to the life around us, the transformational continuity, its potentialities and dangers. For the secret of living – and the endless challenge it confronts us with – lies in the conjunctions of continuity in change, of the constant interaction between being and becoming, the balancing of opposites. We cannot get at reality if we deny this. To deny this is to deny time, to deny life, to accept the conservative principle of arrest (behind the façade of which monopoly controls are strengthened), to cheat ourselves of understanding, to build myths intended to reassure that frustrate and falsify the process. To live fully is to live in terms of the full recognition of the active changing world around us and its contradictory conditions, the transitory balance of things in time – the gain and the loss, the imperfection and the incompleteness, the non-finality of everything that is alive. For that is the condition we belong to. We do not belong to the finished, the finalized, the stilled. Stillness and stability are an approximation to the state of death – and not even that, because even the state of death is a process of change.

Thus the problem of emancipation is the problem of urging people innately insecure or inhibited or governed by fear and anxiety because of their conditioning to expose themselves to the risk of disturbance and disequilibrium. And how can one expect them to respond positively unless they have the equipment to cope with such a risk? This is at once a social and a psychological problem, and one that requires the most delicate handling. It has its roots no doubt in the environmental conditions a person is born into and the attitudes and responses they encourage, the opportunities they offer, that determine his psychology and the scope of his expectations. But this does not help very much. All it does is to indicate the immense complexity of the tasks involved in creating the right conditions for emancipation. Radical changes in the structure of the environment – social, institutional, psychological – are obviously indispensable; but such changes are likely to achieve creative and qualitative results only so long as they continue to respect the dignity and the sensibility of the actual people they affect; and this in itself means caring about them as individuals but treating them as equals and assuming that they have the right and the duty to respond actively and in full awareness of their political and social responsibilities. For up till now the common people have always been treated as instruments of the ruling classes, and kept in a state of ignorance or semi-ignorance, made to feel inferior and confused by the very nature of the divisive process of social systems devised to perpetuate the rule of the minority.

Respect for the people in general must, if it is to mean anything at all, be matched by a complementary respect for the individual, and respect for the individual by respect for the mass of humanity. This may seem obvious, and lip service is always being paid to it, but the balance between the two halves of these equations is always being threatened and perverted – in the one direction by transforming the masses into a superior abstract entity which nullifies the individual, and in the other by deifying egotism and deriding the mass. One might ask what the hand raised in greeting or the appeal to a rational civility can do against the mob, or how the enslaved many are to free themselves from the tyranny of the contemptuous oppressor. Those who bow to the claims of the system that rules can disclaim all responsibility for an answer to such questions, but human beings must accept that they *are* responsible and assert their right to stand up against the acquiescence that sweeps all human answers off the board. This is crucial to the struggle for qualitative change. For acquiescence negates not only the possible community of interests that determines the direction of the struggle but also the contradictions without which it cannot even be conceived. It is one symptom of oppression, which forces conformity upon people, sometimes speaking in the *name* of the people and at others with the arrogant superiority of a Napoleon dismissing the masses as '*crapauds*'. As yet, history has given humanity little chance to attempt the proper balance, let alone to prosper, to develop its powers of responsiveness, its qualitative creative potentialities, because the dominant governing minorities, the makers of systems, the controllers of power have *always* kept the people trapped in a state of dulled subservience.

But now, because more people than ever before are becoming aware of the issues involved, humanity has a greater chance than ever before of breaking out of the trap and working to create a more genuinely humane social order in the world. And if the people do not take this chance, it is either because they do not know how to organize themselves for it against the institutional powers that keep them divided, or because, in spite of their awareness and dissatisfaction, habit and indoctrination keep them passive. But above all what stops us short of committing ourselves to the difficult steps that have to be taken is fear of the risks involved and the daunting obstacles that have to be faced. Better, the fortunate may say, the freedoms we have (however partial and unsatisfactory) than hypothetical concepts of freedom which might crystallize into new forms of repression such as those which have disfigured the establishment of socialism in Soviet Russia, or anywhere else (in the Western liberal view) where any form of revolutionary socialism has been attempted. Better what is, in other words, than what *could* be, they say, looking at the evidence. To dream ahead, envisaging the change beyond the change, is to court disaster, new enslavement, the traps of dogma and totalitarian control. This is an argument the liberal capitalist West comes up with all the time to discourage any sort of Marxian alternative to the so-called democratic process. And there is a mass of evidence to back it up, to confirm the pre-conceived ideas of anti-communists that Marx's plan for the emancipation of humanity was bound to fail, and worse, to bring about a tyranny inimical to freedom. After all, the Soviet Union palpably exists as the ideological enemy and a constant reminder of what can happen. Such violent revolutionary change, far from freeing the people from the alien powers that enslaved them, merely exchanged one kind of tyranny for another, even as Michael Bakunin, confronting Marx himself with yet another challenge to the validity of his theories, prophesied it would. 'The so-called people's state,' Bakunin declared, 'will be nothing else than the despotic guidance of the mass of the people by a new and numerically very small aristocracy of the genuinely or supposedly educated. The people are not scientific, which means that they will be entirely freed from the cares of government, they will be entirely shut up in the stable of the governed. A fine liberation!' This is a cruel point, which has since been cruelly driven home. And Bakunin takes it further. 'The Marxists sense this contradiction and, knowing that the government of the educated will be the most oppressive, most detestable, most despised in the world, a real dictatorship despite all democratic forms, console themselves with the thought that this dictatorship will be only transitional and short.' This is an attack which Marx can counter only with a reiteration of his principle that 'the class rule of the workers . . . can only exist as long as the economic basis of class existence is not destroyed', which in the context of the present economic stranglehold of Soviet power seems to leave Bakunin firmly in possession of the field.[9]

In terms of what they have to offer, however, there can be no comparison between Marx's vision of the struggle for the future and Bakunin's arguments. The crucial difference between the two is in their concept of power, the uses of power and the functions of society. For the one seeks positive answers to the complex problems of the social struggle and the other adopts a dismissive or deprecatory attitude towards these problems. Marx, that is, takes a profoundly affirmative and responsible attitude towards the issues involved and faces them unflinchingly in an incessant effort to provide rational conditions for the reorganization of society; whereas Bakunin refuses to acknowledge even the validity of the existing order, and in his disruptive (and irresponsible) prescriptions for the overthrow of an unjust system, has nothing to offer, beyond the actions needed to destroy it, than a total rejection of *all* government, on the basis that power corrupts, no matter what the principles behind it. Thus, it is only too easy for Bakunin to criticize; he has nothing to lose, since he conveniently disclaims responsibility for answering the most difficult questions. But Marx has everything to lose, because he cares, and makes it his business, in all seriousness, to face up to the necessity of answering these questions and to the inevitable risks involved in the attempt to do so. *What* he had to face up to above all was the question of the transformation of the organs of power and of the rational transference of power, and his answer is defined in terms of a lifetime struggle to formulate the conditions which would enable the working classes of the world to unite to achieve this transformation. It was not, he saw, a merely parochial or national problem. There could be no rational embodiment of such a revolutionary concept unless the working classes were organized to act internationally. Indeed, he stressed the fact again and again throughout his life as a basic *principle* of action, and nowhere more forcibly or more actively than in building on the foundations he had laid for the International Working Men's Association in the sixties and seventies. No one can doubt, therefore, that this is of the very essence of his concept of proletarian power, and the only true safeguard against the *abuse* of power: it was a collective social force to overcome the divisiveness and ignorance upon which the intolerant minority thrived with such arrogance and contempt for the masses. As he puts it in defining the Provisional Rules of the International in October 1864: 'The emancipation of labour is neither a local nor a national, but a social problem, embracing all countries in which modern society exists, and *depending for its solution on the concurrence, practical and theoretical, of the most advanced countries.*' And, further, the great mission of the working classes, to which the International was dedicated, could only be achieved, according to the rules, in the acknowledgement of 'truth, justice and morality, as the basis of their conduct towards each other, and towards all men, without regard to colour, creed, or nationality'.[10] To which he later adds: 'It is the business of the International Working Men's Association to combine and generalize the spontaneous movements of the working classes, but not to dictate or impose any doctrinary system whatever.'[11] In other words, as he reiterates in his speech on the Hague Conference in 1872, international solidarity is the key to the future. For 'we shall only be able to attain the goal we have set ourselves if this life-giving principle acquires a secure foundation among the workers of all countries'.[12]

Is it any wonder, given such a principle, that the 1917 Revolution should have foundered and congealed in the ways it did? That the isolation of Soviet Russia, and her consequent abandonment of the concept of international cooperation, should have led to such a perversion of Marxism? That the term 'proletarian dictatorship' should have come to seem synonymous with what Bakunin predicted for it – a 'despotism of the minority', a new tyranny, a new and monolithic obstacle to the establishment of the kinds of freedom and of social order envisaged by Marx? What has to be taken into account is the extraordinary capacity of the capitalist world to survive successive crises – even the catastrophe of the First World War – and to frustrate the international spread of communism, thus further deepening the isolation of Russia. Indeed, the obstacles have been so great as to make one wonder how it was ever possible for the spirit of Marxism to survive at all. That it has done so in face of the monstrous perversions of justice and morality that are embodied in so many of the states that profess to uphold its principles is tribute enough to the resilience and power of the Marxian philosophy. It survives as an aim, as a concept of social achievement that has still to be fought for; that challenges, and stands in critical opposition to, the status quo, wherever it exists, in the people's democracies as in the West. It urges upon us a critical questioning attitude to events. It asks us to take risks and to make determined efforts to move forward out of the rigid systems of control that hold people trapped and divided from each other. This is particularly important as far as Soviet Russia is concerned, because it is Russia above all that gives authority and credence to Marxism, for good or ill. Can the Soviet Union free herself of the stifling weight of her bureaucratic intolerance with its network of repressive controls and lead the world forward, or will she continue to deserve to be condemned for having betrayed the Revolution and become a new and intolerable conservatism?

Marx's vision of civilization remains inseparably linked to the concept of international co-operation, the idea of an objective universal order, a community of common interests based upon truth, justice and morality. It is a vision of a healed world, offered in the conviction that man has it in him – given the establishment of economic equality and a firm enough set of rational procedures on which to build for sanity – to overcome his deadly temptation towards irrational self-interest and the thirst for power, and actually to respond to his instinct for the civilizing process. And as such it is, of course, for all its profession not to be so, a utopian vision that has 'brought /To human consciousness a thought /It thought unthinkable'[13] – a vision of unity like that which quickened Christian Europe in the ninth century and which for a couple of centuries the Church itself attempted to embody in its institutions. Or rather we should say that it is a vision of reality that has certain utopian elements difficult to reconcile with the actualities of the world as we know it, though it has its *roots* in that world.

13

THE DERANGEMENT OF EUROPEAN
CIVILIZATION

Marx's vision of the civilizing process, in its revolutionary challenge of the hypocrisies upon which the standards and values of European capitalism have been built, strikes at the very foundations of that civilization. What, it has asked, can *any* civilization be worth that bases itself upon repressed majorities that serve, in economic terms, as the mere instruments of a privileged minority? How, it has asked, can a system that has prospered upon such profound injustices as those which defined the attitudes of the possessors in the nineteenth century to the mass of the people be anything but miserably deficient in the primary attributes of social health without which 'civilization' is a mere façade, a deceit, a sham? What connotations are we to give to such a term as applied to a social system that, for as long as it was able to carry on doing so, has denied its citizens all but the most elementary rights? How is it to be reconciled, for instance, with acquisition of wealth for the few at the expense of the squalid poverty of the many? Or with the rabid nationalism of the modern age, involving the Great Powers of Europe in a competitive expansion that took no account of the freedoms of other peoples? It is useless to talk of the improvements that have been brought about as a consequence of the struggles of the deprived, for these have only been brought about in the face of the bitterest opposition. Of course there are the great achievements of Europe to cite as evidence of the civilizing energies of European culture – achievements in science, in art, in thought, in architecture, in the development of industrial and technological resources, in the creation (or the maintenance) of such institutions as the churches, the schools, the universities. But these have to be judged as civilizing social assets not only on the evidence of those they have benefited, but also in terms of cost to the community. And in sober judgement of that cost – the enormous price paid by millions of people for riches they had no share in and no direct experience of – it is a matter for doubt whether we can even begin to talk of civilization as a humanizing process without perverting the meaning of the word. On these terms, taking the evidence of the past hundred years, what may be called civilization has been little more than a glittering façade for the protection of minority interests and the pursuit of policies of unscrupulous exploitation by the few against the lives and livelihoods of millions.

'It is not a chance,' as Tawney observes of this phenomenon,

that the last two centuries, which saw the growth of a new system of industry, saw also the growth of the system of international politics which came to a climax in the period from 1870 to 1914. Both the one and the other are the expression of the same spirit and move in obedience to similar laws. The essence of the former was the repudiation of any authority superior to the individual reason. It left men free to follow their own interests or ambitions or appetites, untrammelled by subordination to any common centre of allegiance. The essence of the latter was the repudiation of any authority superior to the sovereign state, which again was conceived as a compact self-contained unit . . . Just as the one emancipated economic activity from a mesh of antiquated traditions, so the other emancipated nations from arbitrary subordination to alien races or governments, and turned them into nationalities with a right to work out their own destiny.

Nationalism is, in fact, the counterpart among nations of what individualism is within them. It has similar origins and tendencies, similar triumphs and defects. For . . . like individualism it appeals to the self-assertive instincts, to which it promises opportunities of unlimited expansion. Like individualism it is a force of immense explosive power [which] if pushed to its logical conclusion . . . is self-destructive.[1]

Thus, according to this logic, nationalism becomes imperialism. Nations are launched (as Germany, France and Britain were at the end of the nineteenth century) upon a process of territorial expansion

in which they devour continents and oceans, law, morality and religion, and last of all their own souls, in an attempt to attain infinity by the addition to themselves of all that is finite. In the meantime their rivals, and their subjects, and they themselves, are conscious of the danger of opposing forces, and seek to purchase security and to avoid collision by organizing a balance of power. But the balance, whether in international politics or in industry, is unstable, because it reposes . . . on an attempt to find an equipoise which may avoid a conflict *without abjuring the assertion of unlimited claims*. No such equipoise can be found, because, in a world where the possibilities of increasing military or industrial power are illimitable, no such equipoise can exist.[2]

Under these hazardous conditions, it was inevitable that the reassertion of the aggressive and unregenerate spirit of European capitalism after the First World War should have led to an intensification of the conflict of interests that divided the nations; and that this conflict should have swept away the newly established concept of international co-operation defined by the League of Nations, to culminate in the brutalizing perversions of fascism. Thus, when we talk of the barbarism from which the nations of Europe have in this century suffered so grievously, and of that barbarism as linked to the breakdown of rational consensus, the triumph of tribal emotion, the myth of racial superiority and the mystical entity of the state, we must I think talk not only of Germany and Italy and Japan and Spain, but of the whole of what we are accustomed to think of as civilized Europe. The barbaric outbreak of fascism is not a phenomenon to be blamed upon those countries directly exposed to its evils. Its roots are embedded in the very foundations upon which European capitalism had developed throughout the nineteenth century – the divisive double standards it had long functioned in terms of as an economic, political and social process. How could it be otherwise, with wealth and property the province of the few and the foundation of public esteem, at the expense of the mass of the people? How could such an irrational and insensitive concept of society, with its grudging response to the well-being of the mass of its citizens, make itself secure against the fascist principle of contempt or the brutality of its methods? The civilized few who lived their affluent and cultured lives off the depressed many in England, France and Germany between the wars – the industrialists, financiers, businessmen, diplomats, politicians – liberal, conservative or apolitical – helped to create the *ground* for fascism, even if they did not literally offer it their moral or financial support, which many of them did.

What they would have argued in doing so was not that they had any truck with fascism but that they were trying to make Europe safe against communism – because of course the 1917 Revolution and the short-lived threat of communism in Central Europe had profoundly shocked the Western powers, calling forth economic and military blockade against the risings of a starving continent and applied with particular ruthlessness against Germany, Austria, Hungary and Russia. It was this determined attempt of the ruling forces of the West to strangle communism at birth which (from 1918 onward) encouraged the forces of reaction to organize against the Left and even to cripple the growth of democratic socialism, thus fertilizing the dormant seeds of fascism.[3] And Germany in particular became a breeding-ground for the irrational hatreds aroused by the Nazi party. The humiliating treatment meted out by the Allies in the immediate aftermath of the war created conditions leading to the collapse of the mark in 1923 and the consequent resentment and deprivation, the disorder and insecurity created among the middle and lower-middle classes, upon whose fears Hitler was to feed with such deadly success, after the partial recovery of the Weimar Republic between 1924 and 1929.

In the larger view, Germany's degradation – by the mid-twenties she had become the explosive nerve-centre of Europe's diseased and predatory system – can be seen as the end-result of a historical process that had started as far back as 1848 with the failure of the bourgeois revolution and the abortion of democratic principles that followed. And as we are now able to judge, this failure was symptomatic, in the most extreme sense, of the general condition of Europe and its failure to act in any spirit but that dictated by an insatiable demand, both nationalist and individual, for wealth and property and territorial expansion. It was the sequence of events leading from 1870 to the First World War, dominated by the ambitions of the Great Powers, and above all the war itself, that laid the foundations for Germany's breakdown.

As a federation of backward-looking states forcibly welded or dragooned into unity by Bismarck's ruthless promotion of war, and his pursuit, after the defeat of France in 1870, of a balance of power that would favour the industrial and military development of Germany against her greatest rivals, the pressures must have been extreme. Under the harsh regimentation of Prussian fanaticism, all the machinery of aggressive nationalism was assembled for the creation of a Pan-German *Weltpolitik* which, in the post-Bismarck Empire of the Kaiser, came into direct competition with Britain in a bid for economic, military and naval supremacy, and thus brought about the steadily worsening relationships between the ruling minorities that governed Europe which led to the war. It was inevitable – the massive build-up of arms and the war-psychology of the Prussian Officer-Corps, clashing with the imperialist market-policies of Britain and the deepening mistrust of both France and Russia over the crises in the Balkans, could hardly have ended otherwise, given the aggressive demands that prevailed. But the arrogant power of the warlords who had engineered the war brought Germany only the shame and insult of an inconclusive defeat. And thus – the superstructure of empire swept away, launched upon an experiment with democracy for which there had been little or no preparation, cheated, stripped of all the insignia of its pride, and smouldering with resentment – Germany the victim of Versailles was softened up, made ripe for exploitation. The National Socialist party, bred out of the chaos, took ruthless advantage of the innate instability and derangement of the social structure and the degradation of the people. Its triumph, based upon Hitler's uncanny grasp of the shifting moods of the mass psyche and his fervid vision of a nation regenerated by military discipline and racial hatred, was made secure by the backing it received from leading industrialists and anti-communist businessmen. And it was achieved by a violent irrational appeal to the spirit of nationalistic pride and a hypnotic assertion of the will to power that transformed an apathetic humiliated people into a new and lethal instrument of Teutonic rule. This, on the face of it, must have seemed to all who witnessed the phenomenon of 1933 an astonishing achievement. Within three years, on the basis of a massive reconstruction programme, Hitler had virtually solved the problem of unemployment, had stabilized prices, and welded Germany into an aggressive and dominating military power. But, engineered as it was by the most brutal and unscrupulous methods, this would not have been possible but for the support of the leaders of finance, business and industry, building upon the unstable economic and social conditions that had so deeply undermined the morale of the people. Such total submission to an enflamed cause, such mass euphoria as that displayed by the organized crowds at the great public rallies, can only be explained as a surrender of the will, a resignation of rational social conscience to the concept of force. It was a moral resignation in the face of absolute confidence – particularly among the middle classes, governed by fear and insecurity; a resignation even of the power to resist, a blind submission to the will of the strong, to the intoxication of the unknown, to the wild ecstasies of the mystical, to the irrational spirit of ritual sacrifice, to the Valhalla-call of the dark.

It may be, as Auden puts it in his poem *September 1, 1939*, standing at the very edge of the abyss into which Europe was about to plunge, that

> Accurate scholarship can
> Unearth the whole offence
> From Luther until now
> That has driven a culture mad,
> Find what occurred at Linz,
> What huge imago made
> A psychopathic god.[4]

But if such scholarship is capable of tracing the roots of this madness, it can do so only in the aftermath, and not then even without some extraordinary act of insight or of psychological penetration, a sort of descent into hell – that hell which is 'the being of the lie /That we become if we deny /The laws of consciousness and claim /Becoming and Being are the same'.[5] For it is in this denial – in the liberal cult of the inner life, the pursuit of metaphysical pure spirit in the dark of the self, its withdrawal from the 'crudities' of the external world – that the betrayal begins. Having retreated to an apolitical defence of 'culture', the liberal idealist invokes the unseen, the invisible spiritual essence, undefinable and thus irrational – what, in Marcuse's words, 'must be acknowledged absolutely, against all that is first to be known critically; as the essentially dark against all that derives its substance from the clarity of light; as the indestructible, against everything subject to historical change'.[6]

The laws of consciousness enlighten and define. And light, the Apollonian principle, is essentially their element, an attribute of reason. In the light we see, we know where we are, we can grasp the nature of the structure of the world that surrounds us and assert our interdependent reasonable place in that world. It lends itself to the observable scientific process of life, of developing growing changing things; to the constructive procedures of rationality, the unspectacular piecemeal rule of reason and common sense. People tend to behave temperately in the light, because in the light they are not afraid. And in the light even death takes its place in the natural order of things, as an aspect of life. Set in such a context, night itself is the natural complement and obverse of the day.

But when darkness (the inner darkness of subjectivity) becomes the governing principle of things, people change. They become afraid, they feel insecure, they lose their bearings, they are denied (or they deny themselves) the reassuring logic and order of the Appollonian universe, and seek the dionysiac rituals of togetherness for comfort and security. And then it is that the fantasies, the dreams, the nightmares, the changing contortions of the unknown and the suppressed begin to operate and to act upon the will, and fear takes over; so that anyone who is unscrupulous enough to seek to exploit them will find the people malleable material in their hands.

But how is it, one might ask, that the dark is ever allowed to become the governing principle of things? After all, we live our lives daily in the light, and the light of reason is always available. How is it possible then? For as the thirties have demonstrated,

> even the best,
> Les hommes de bon volonté, feel
> Their politics perhaps unreal
> And all they have believed untrue,
> Are tempted to surrender to
> The grand apocalyptic dream
> In which the persecutors scream
> As on the evil Aryan lives
> Descends the night of the long knives,
> The bleeding tyrant dragged through all
> The ashes of his capitol.[7]

There can be no straightforward answer to this. But one fact is clear: that such collective surrender of the will is bred out of the peculiar conditions on which such a society as that of post-1848 Germany was nourished, and the manner in which the ruthless and intolerant policies of its leaders inhibited and stunted the free development of the political and social process. When irrational and arrogant powers begin to exert their pull upon and to sap the body of the social organism, exaggerating certain extremist aspects of its physiognomy at the expense of others, such as the fanatical cult of militarism in Prussia or the unchecked exploitation of industrial potentiality Bismarck initiated after the Franco-Prussian war in a ruthless bid for supremacy, the stability of the state is endangered, strained to breaking-point, and its equilibrium undermined. And though Lewis Namier can write of Hitler and the Third Reich being 'the gruesome and incongruous consummation of an age which, as none other, believed in progress and felt assured that it was being achieved'; and of 'the 150 years 1789–1939' as 'an era of confident hope and strenuous endeavour, of trust in the human mind and in the power of reason', what he omits to point out is that all this was based upon a superior indifference to the rights and needs of millions of subject peoples. According to Namier, 'nationalism became a disruptive force intertwining with social radicalism';[8] but in fact it would be truer to say that nationalism became a disruptive force blatantly *opposed* to social radicalism, a divisive and destructive force issuing as a logical consequence from the irrational anti-democratic principles of capitalistic enterprise. It was so because too many of the rational leaders of mankind belonged to that hypocritical class which, regarding all radicals as anarchic and subversive, gave its support to specious and inhumane social values – values that paid little more than lip-service to the needs of the labouring and oppressed masses. It was not the 'strenuous endeavours' of the socialists that released the demonic forces of fascism into the arena, but the arrogant contempt of the anti-democratic ruling classes for the aspirations of the common people everywhere and the repressive inequalities enshrined in their institutions.

Marx had perceived that the very concept of the state had been perverted to embody those organs and institutions of repression which the possessing classes used against the people to keep them submissive and obedient – organs and institutions 'separate from and antagonistic to civil society',[9] as a 'parasite feeding upon, and clogging the free movement of, society'.[10] He regarded the Paris Commune of 1871 (that transitory attempt to resist the European psychosis) as 'a revolution against the *state* itself, this supernaturalist abortion of society', and 'a resumption by the people for the people of its own social life'.[11] For him, the state the Commune superseded was an inseparable part of the psychosis, a derangement of the social process, which the ruling classes made a weapon for the suppression of utopia. Indeed, the institutions of the state, as organized in Europe in the nineteenth century, had become the *essential* weapons for the enforcement of submission and the stamping out of all revolt. And in the Germany of the Kaiser and his Prussian visionaries, these institutions achieved the building of that deadly weapon of aggrandizement which, cumbersome and rigid though it was, in challenging the dominance of England and the claims of France, made war its logical aim. And out of the collapse of this monstrous superstructure, building on foundations rooted deep in the psychology of the people, came the Nazi creed, a perverted re-incarnation of the concept of the state, with Hitler its embodied god. The Thousand-Year Reich, the absolute infallible instrument of German supremacy: this was the nightmare outcome of German absolutism and of European nationalism, warped beyond imagination. And the German people, crushed beneath the weight of that machinery, surrendered their birthright to it as in ritual worship to a god – a dionysiac god reborn beyond death to lead them through the ritual dance of mass hysteria into the ring of fire from which they were then to emerge deathless and purified, like some new unkillable Siegfried.

Of course, it might all have worked out differently if the radical and democratic opposition had been given just a little more encouragement. But that is mere conjecture; for the people of Europe remained obedient under the vice-like grip of the institutions that imprisoned them, despite the existence of radical parties and the activities of people like Keir Hardie, Karl Liebknecht and Rosa Luxemburg. How was it, for instance, that the revolutionary Social Democrats in Germany, dedicated to the overthrow of the capitalist order, 'failed to pass the test at the outbreak of the First World War[?] On 28 July 1914, the day Austria declared war on Serbia, hundreds of thousands of German workers were still demonstrating against the war in all major cities; on 2 August 1914 British workers were still taking to the streets for the same reason. But in the meantime, the patriotic hysteria of national and European suicide had gripped the German masses.' And the S.P.D., in spite of its clear recognition of the nature of the existing order of power, failed to 'foresee that it would be possible to exploit pseudo-national emotion with such explosive force against any vestige of reason. They could not believe that all rational thought would be extinguished among the masses once they had been brainwashed into believing that the "nation" was threat-ened . . . It had been the hope of revolutionary Social Democrats that the proletariat would, in a revolutionary upsurge, prevent the war, regarded as inevitable in the late capitalist order, and thus avoid mass slaughter.' But 'the manipulation of public opinion by the government, and by the vested interests of imperialism, extended its grip to the proletariat, and the working class bureaucracy became its instrument'.[12]

Nothing, apparently, could stop Europe from committing this act of madness, for it was the consequence of psychic disorders rooted in the very substance of the so-called civilizing process. But no greater damage could have been done to the stability and sanity of European society than by the ruthless development of industrial and commercial capitalism after 1848 and the imperialist policies of Germany, Britain and France at the end of the century. The Great Powers became locked in a deadly battle for economic and political supremacy, which by predatory enterprise in com-bination with the machinery of institutional force and the servitude of the masses, sought to dominate the markets of the world. This relentless game of power, played for the highest stakes according to a set of shifting rules, often in contemptuous indifference to the rights of its subject peoples – at home, in Africa, in India, in the Far East – could only have led the nations down the narrowing paths they trod towards confrontation and disaster. William Morris prophesied as much as early as 1885, when he spoke out against the 'wars of exploitation [engineered] amongst European nations these last few years' against defenceless countries, and declared that in the long run we 'will even risk wars which . . . must . . . embroil us with nations who . . . no more lack the resources of civilization than ourselves'.[13] The war of 1914 that was the culmination of this competitive nationalism – unleashed upon the acquiescent masses in an inconceivable degradation of the civiliz-ing process – cannot be regarded as anything other than insane. Not that it was seen as such by those who brought it about; it was simply one more move in a familiar game, planned in terms of a 'quick victory'. Deadlock having been reached over the Balkan crises, the crucial test had come, and so the people were manoeuvred into a state of patriotic fervour, and the game of war had begun.

It was such a game as only the lunatics of the Absolute could have ordered – acted out with a fury of destructiveness that was itself a proof of the incubus-like power of the state and its leaders; battening upon the people, sapping them of all will to resist and inspiring in them the zeal of a sleepwalking mob to kill and be killed. Naturally, this was not the way its leaders *looked* upon it. For them, from their remote positions of command, it had the flavour of heroic adventure – or so it would seem from Churchill's comment in *The Gathering Storm*. 'Apart from the excesses of the Russian Revolution,' he declares, 'the main fabric of European civilization remained erect at the close of the struggle.' He, as one of the architects of the British effort, persuades himself, in the rhetoric of eighteenth-century militarism, that 'when the storm and dust of the cannonade passed suddenly away, the nations, despite their enmities, could still recognize each other as historic racial personalities'. But this is to say no more than that afterwards, in spite of Russia, the ruling classes still retained control, and unwittingly it demonstrates how totally the war had failed to solve any of the basic problems, even if it did destroy the German empire. As for the fighting itself – the unspeakable carnage of Ypres, the Somme, Arras, Passchendaele, where millions died in futile obedience to the inefficiency, bankruptcy and blind obstinacy of their generals – in Churchill's view, 'the laws of war had on the whole been respected'. And apparently the upshot of all this gentlemanly experience between the rival generals (for it didn't seem to matter what had happened to the ordinary soldiers) was that 'there was a common professional meeting-ground between military men who had fought one another'! In other words, it was *they* – the generals, the statesmen, the diplomats, the makers of the war, 'vanquished and victors alike' – who, stepping out of their offices or their comfortable HQs and ignoring the bewildered disillusionment and the stunned silence of the millions, 'preserved the semblance of civilized states'. And it was they too who made their 'solemn peace', in conformity, as Churchill observes innocently, with 'the principles which in the nineteenth century had increasingly regulated the relations of enlightened peoples'.[14]

With this solemn peace proclaiming 'the reign of law', and the 'indifference', as Herbert Read puts it, 'which people in power felt for the opinions of the men who had fought',[15] the nations settled bitterly and exhaustedly back behind the 'erect' façades and frontiers of their fractured worlds, battered and constrained, and thus left in a state of torpid exposure to those insecurities and fears and crises which lead people to surrender their rights and destinies to the mercy and protection of the so-called strong. And so the institutions of state power and the men of blinded conscience who had driven the people into war or manipulated those who governed them were again confirmed. 'The past has deceived us,' Yeats was to write of the disillusionment of 1918; 'let us accept the worthless present.'[16] And that present was to continue to deceive not only writers but whole societies into acquiescence and appeasement. The prediction of Wilfred Owen in the very last poem he wrote seems almost literally applicable to the depressing submissiveness of the times. 'None will break ranks,' he says, 'though nations trek from progress.'[17] The thirties defined the direction of that backward march, by the combination of weakness and aggression with which the disciplined strength of the Third Reich was conjured into being, and the coming war determined.

This was the direction Europe had been moving in, as we see it with the useless clarity of hindsight, for a hundred years or more. In the 1930s, the Western democracies, with their continual attempt to placate and to accommodate the forces of reaction they had done so much to strengthen in their fear of communism, seemed intent upon destroying the foundations of the rational framework of order they believed they were protecting. Blindly, obtusely, it would seem, by 'imbecility of will and weakness of intellect, . . . a defective sense of responsibility, and a feeble and sometimes inoperative regard for the truth', as R. G. Collingwood wrote in 1939,[18] the leaders of Britain and France gave way before the violence of fascist power in a sequence of shaming defeats which, culminating in the betrayal of Czechoslovakia and the fall of Spain, led directly to war. And no one was to define this treachery with more trenchancy or with more of a sense of moral outrage than the exiled Thomas Mann, writing in the immediate aftermath of Munich:

The events of the past few weeks have plunged a large part of the world . . . into profound disillusionment, discouragement, and even despair. We have been shocked and cruelly bewildered spectators at proceedings of far-reaching significance; proceedings too positive, rooted too deep in the collective will of Europe, employing as its instrument the classic hypocrisy of English statesmanship, not to be regarded as decisive for many decades to come.[19]

And the peace which meant life to uncountable millions? In Brecht's words:

> The chiefs of state
> Have gathered in a room.
> Man in the street:
> Give up all hope.
>
> The governments
> Write non-aggression pacts.
> Little man:
> Write your testament.[20]

Brecht was among those who were forced to watch the noose of barbarism gradually tightening. And though his constant appeal is to the hope and the belief that refuses to give in, he and others like him knew that by the mid-thirties it was already too late to do anything to hold the fascists back. For by then the Left, as the only genuine alternative, was everywhere having to fight for survival against the institutionalized powers and interests of the capitalist world, and even against Russia, where the Stalinist purge-trials came like a series of death-blows to further strengthen the argument of the pro-fascist Right. In England, the most crucial defeat for the socialists had come earlier, with the 1926 General Strike, which left the working class stunned and betrayed and led directly to the disarray of Labour, followed by the depression and the mass unemployment which successive National Governments failed to solve. Thus the Conservatives re-asserted their control over the country; and thus, on the Continent as in England, socialism was effectively prevented from organizing any sort of coherent policy to combat fascism. The Spanish Civil War was a last desperate bid to stem the tide. For in essence this, as Orwell pointed out, 'was a class war. If it had been won, the cause of the common people everywhere would have been strengthened.'[21] But Britain and France (perhaps for this very reason) refused Spain all support; and so it was lost.

Against such a background as this, it is hardly surprising that so many radical intellectuals in England and France should have been driven into disillusioned retreat – resigned by 1938 to the degradation and the nightmare of the coming war.

International betrayals, public murder,
    The devil quoting scripture, the traitor, the coward, the
      thug,
Eating dinner in the name of peace and progress,
    The doped public sucking a dry dug;
Official recognition of rape, revival of the ghetto,
    And free speech gagged and free
Energy scrapped and dropped like surplus herring
    Back into the barren sea;
Brains and beauty festering in exile,
    The shadow of bars
Falling across each page, each field, each raddled sunset.[22]

For Louis MacNeice and for most of his contemporaries among the radical middle class, fighting their rearguard action against the killers, 1938 (Vienna and Munich) was the last squalid straw. The clever hopes of 'a low dishonest decade' were expiring.

How different it all might have been! But the governing classes of Europe, and of England in particular, had made their choice. The pusillanimous spirit of compromise which had dictated the attitudes of the Western democracies towards fascism led inexorably, step by step, from Manchuria to Munich, from the fall of Czechoslovakia and the victory of Franco in Spain, to total war. Europe was in the grip of a nightmare, and no one seemed capable of standing out against the forces of irrationality and barbarism that had conjured it up. By early 1939, the so-called democracies had lost the battle against fascism. Their failure was a failure of conviction, of moral integrity, of rational belief in the principles of real democracy; a failure of the democratic will to act in defence of those values which uphold the rights and interests of the people as a whole. Above all it was a failure of responsibility. For whether through ineptitude or sheer reactionary obtuseness, the political leaders of European democracy chose to appease the fascists rather than to act resolutely against them, proceeding in the undemocratic divisive spirit characteristic of the economic class system they were protecting, which had itself determined the conditions on which fascism prospered. And so, once again, Europe was dragged to the precipice and over, into the horrors of global carnage that followed, which were to expose humanity to such evils as the thousand bomber raids and Auschwitz and Hiroshima.

And has Auschwitz or the development of the hydrogen bomb and the neutron bomb now shocked us into rationality? Has Europe emerged from its condition of genocidal madness cured? Has the world at last begun to see the writing on the wall? There are many *signs* of health, and today it could be said the privileged élites no longer have the power to bargain people's rights away at will, or to dictate the course of events. From the struggles of the Cold War, and in the aftermath of Stalin, Korea, the Berlin Wall, Hungary, Suez, Czechoslovakia, has emerged a stronger and more deeply determined will to peace involving millions, even against the atrocities of Vietnam. But there has been no cure. Though Europe has been muted, Russia still stands rigidly opposed to the basic freedoms essential to human society, and the Western world still proclaims the rights of individual self-interest, however disguised, in terms of property and capital, as defined by its institutions, dedicating vast resources to the predatory exploitation for profit of the common wealth of the various nations. But above all, as Andrei Sakharov has declared in the bluntest and simplest terms:

The division of mankind threatens it with destruction. Civilization is imperiled by: a universal thermonuclear war, catastrophic hunger for most of mankind, stupefaction from the narcotic of 'mass culture', and bureaucratized dogmatism, a spreading of mass myths that put entire peoples and continents under the power of cruel and treacherous demagogues, and destruction or degeneration from the unforeseeable consequences of swift changes in the conditions of life on our planet. In face of these perils, any action increasing the division of mankind, any preaching of the incompatibility of world ideologies and nations is madness and a crime. Only universal cooperation under conditions of intellectual freedom and the lofty moral ideals of socialism and labour, accompanied by the elimination of dogmatism and pressures of the concealed interests of ruling classes, will preserve civilization.[23]

14

DEMOCRATIC FREEDOM:
RHETORIC AND ACTUALITY

The conditions that determine the limits of freedom in an advanced capitalist democracy such as that of modern Britain are echoed in the puzzling questions that confronted Hans Castorp (the hero of Thomas Mann's novel *The Magic Mountain*) in the very different world of pre-1914 Germany. Thus:

A man lives not only his personal life as an individual, but also, consciously or unconsciously, the life of his epoch and his contemporaries. He may regard the general, impersonal foundations of his existence as definitely settled and taken for granted, and be as far from assuming a critical attitude towards them as Hans Castorp was; yet it is quite conceivable that he may none the less be vaguely conscious of the deficiencies of his epoch and find them prejudicial to his own moral well-being. All sorts of personal aims, ends, hopes, prospects, hover before the eyes of the individual, and out of them he derives the impulse to ambition and achievement. But what if the life about him, however outwardly stimulating, seem to be at bottom empty of such food for his aspiration? What if he privately recognize it to be hopeless, viewless, helpless, opposing only a hollow silence to all the questions man puts as to the final absolute and abstract meaning of reality . . .? Then, in such a case, a certain laming of the personality is bound to occur, the more inevitably the more upright the character in question – a sort of palsy, as it were, which may even spread from his spiritual and moral into his physical and organic being. In an age that affords no satisfying answer to the eternal questions 'Why?' 'To what end?', a man who is capable of achievement . . . must be equipped either with a moral remoteness and singlemindedness which is rare indeed and of heroic mould or else with an exceptionally robust vitality . . .[1]

Castorp's vague awareness of the deficiencies, the disabling conditions, of his world defines the crippling effects of the world of European capitalism upon the psychology of the middle classes at the beginning of the century as a kind of sickness. In terms, that is, of the metaphors Mann employs in his novel, the individual is sick because society itself is sick. And society is sick because of the economic laws that characterized the general impersonal foundations of European civilization – creating an irrational and oppressive ethic of liberty which, based upon the rights of property and capital, had deprived millions of their rights, dividing class from class, dislocating particular (subjective) interests from general (objective, social) interests, subjective demands from objective responsibilities, and bringing about the alienation (or the laming) of the citizen at all levels within society.

It was impossible, under such conditions, to maintain anything more than a semblance of formal respect for the principles of liberty, rationality and justice, which are the nourishing roots of social health and social continuity. And it was inevitable that this hypocritical assertion of the rights and liberties of certain classes of citizens should, in its callous indifference to the degradation of others, have led to a deepening of the divisions and dislocations in the basic structure of society and an alienating divergence of interests between the classes, and thus have brought into sharper and sharper definition the innate violence and injustice of the capitalist system, not only internally but in the conduct of the nations towards each other and towards the territories they competed for control of. The persistent refusal of the ruling classes of Europe to connect their theories of liberty and justice to the actual miseries that confronted them led in turn to a progressive breakdown of those primary links which bind men together in common recognition of their mutual rights and needs, and from this inexorably to the insanities of 1914 and the psychotic violence bred from the disorders of the twenties that produced the Nazi state.

In the nineteenth century an institutionalized ethic of liberty for the few thrived on the ruthless exploitation of industrial resources and the acquiescence of the common people, who were everywhere deceived into believing it was their ethic too. After 1848, in spite of the steady growth of radicalism, the formation of the International Working Men's Association, the trade unions and the various socialist parties, a stability was encouraged and enforced which could never be satisfied on these irrational terms except in the form of reactionary and hypocritical methods, because it was the product of the same irrational forces that had created the sense of disorder. Hence the appalling consequences of the twentieth century, based upon manipulation of a thoroughly degraded and submissive people. 'What is at issue here is not the objective social reality of our time,' as Georg Lukács has observed, but – 'for those still trapped in the insoluble contradictions of a nineteenth-century *Weltanschauung*; for those who yield or subscribe to the reactionary pseudo-solutions produced by the arbitrary bourgeois thought of the imperialist period'[2] – a rabid contortion of that reality.

In modern Britain, the rational progressive principles of the democratic process in general, and of socialism in particular, have been persistently muted and contained by the pseudo-democratic forces of parliamentary and extra-parliamentary conservatism, of middle-class initiative and enterprise working within a capitalist market economy, and never more disastrously than in the 1930s. So that now, in spite of all the transformations that have taken place since the end of the Second World War, or perhaps because of the ways in which monopoly capitalism has imposed its restrictions upon the social organism, one is conscious of a strange muffled sense of apathy and impotence, of restlessness and uncertainty, as of a world running down, subsiding. This could be defined in terms of dwindling prestige, the gulf created by the break-up of the empire, and the failure to provide new social incentives for the people. A negative dualism divides the subjective sensuous actualities of people's lives on the one hand from the objective deadening abstracts of the institutions that surround them on the other, which separates not only those who control and legislate from those who produce, but also one group of workers from another. It is as if, somewhere at the heart of the social structure, there existed a disabling hollowness, born of the dislocations of the capitalist economy, which has affected the very substance of our lives.

There are no doubt many reasons for this, and no issue has had more impact upon Britain than the general development of the world situation since the war. But one fundamental stumbling block to progress within Britain has been the fact that so many of the underlying attitudes characteristic of late-nineteenth-century liberalism and conservatism remain unchanged. The great majority, whatever their political affiliation, seem still to accept, as an instinctual predilection and almost without question, a social order based upon divided classes in a capitalist economy, with the monarchy as a binding symbol of unity and common wealth, and thus the laws of inequality and privilege on which our system is built. Nothing, whatever the modifications, has occurred to challenge the validity of Mallock's argument that 'men's capacities are practically unequal, simply because they develop their own potential inequalities; and they only develop their potential inequalities because they desire to place themselves in unequal circumstances; and this desire to place themselves in unequal circumstances has its effect upon them only because the condition of society is such that the unequal circumstances are attainable'.[3] Which is to say that inequality is a *natural* law of society, and that you deserve wealth or poverty to the extent to which you desire to rise in the world or develop the ambition to do so. Indeed, the welfare institutions introduced into Britain after 1945 acknowledged this, even in the ways in which they were conceived and have operated since, functioning as a charity shield to protect the underprivileged from the legitimized depredations of those with ambitions.

It was on these principles that the Third Marquis of Salisbury proceeded to consolidate the strengths of conservatism in the last twenty years of the nineteenth century. As A. J. P. Taylor has pointed out, his 'almost imperceptible influence so transformed the Conservative Party that it became *the normal majority government for half a century after his death*. He captured the Liberal Unionists from Gladstone and thus prepared for the dwindling of the Liberal Party. Most of all he invented *the Conservative working man* who has been the standby of the Conservatives ever since.'[4] These were the methods by which the anti-democratic ruling classes were enabled to appropriate and to neutralize the more radical elements implicit in the drive towards democracy. The façades of authoritarian power were adjusted to accommodate the working classes, with just enough of them given the vote to make them feel that the nation was moving by evolutionary means towards democracy, even though in 1911 only 8 million out of 41 million had been enfranchised, all women were excluded, and the wealthiest half million had the right (according to their property) to two or more votes. And even the rise of the Labour Party was to become part of this strategy by which the ruling classes assimilated their enemies; for the acceptance of working-class representatives helped to take the revolutionary momentum out of the socialism that had emerged under Morris and Hyndman in the eighties and nineties, diluting it to conform to the operative parliamentary standards of conservatism that persist today. But it was above all after the 1914 war that the conservative powers found the strongest focus for their ideological war against socialism. The existence of a communist régime in Russia, that 'foul buffoonery of Bolshevism', as Churchill called it, represented everything in statecraft they most abhorred, and was therefore painted in the blackest (or reddest) colours possible, as the destroyer of all civilized values, in a propaganda of abuse and vilification intended to strike fear into the hearts of all true Englishmen. The implications of the active campaign of the Western Powers against 'the Communist Menace' were clearly the stamping out of all such socialist ideologies everywhere, including the 'creeping disease of socialism' in England itself. And it was the success of this insistent campaign among the people that thwarted and diluted the cause of socialism – that is, a qualitative reorganization of society based upon working-class principles and the emancipation of the people from their submissive acceptance of capitalist exploitation. All the machinery of unseen institutional influence and power was used to embarrass and to defeat 'the enemy', and this was as evident in the attitudes of the establishment towards the miners and their supporters during the 1926 General Strike as it was towards the communists. The collapse of the strike was applauded as a vindication of the democratic parliamentary system and of British common sense and 'decency'. But in reality it was a disaster for the progress of socialism, and a triumph for the pseudo-democratic powers of the ruling conservatives. For it confirmed conservative control, even in the guise of what was euphemistically called a National Government, and the depression drove home still further the depth of Labour's defeat, leaving Britain's rulers a free hand to pursue their equivocal, reactionary policy of appeasement, and their own derisory concept of the democratic process.

Of course, the war itself helped to sweep aside many of the more archaic survivals of the ruling-class way of life, for it was a struggle involving the common people as a major force; so that it is now no longer possible to exploit or to repress or to deceive the masses in the blatant ways pursued up till 1939. But the situation was transformed not so much by the actions of those who had the power and the opportunity to change it as by the consequences of their ineptitude and callousness, and the devastating re-orientations forced upon them by the derangements of war. In other words, the basic attitudes may well have hardly changed at all – that is, they may only *seem* to have changed, because the material conditions of society, the economic and social relationships and pressures, initiated by the upheavals of the war and the changed conditions of the peace, have brought about improvements that could not have been withheld from the people anyway. Not that this is to say that no positive political steps have been taken to create the conditions for a more equitable society. In 1945 a profound and half-revolutionary shift of the balance occurred, an extraordinary and unprecedented affirmation from the people of the Labour Party's radical programme of socialism and thus a massive rejection of the old ruling-class ways – which was even acquiesced in for a while and given a momentum of enthusiastic support by large numbers of people other than those that traditionally offered Labour its solid backing. People of *all* classes had come back from the war with the feeling that they wanted to create a different *kind* of future from that which had brought about the war – a future based not upon privilege and exploitation and the selfish ambitions of an élite minority, but upon principles of genuine social equality and a compassionate fraternal concept of citizenship under the terms of which the dispossessed and the deprived would at last be freed from the bonds of insecurity and fear and material denial that had held them shackled to their poverty, to take their place with others 'in the sun'.

But 1945 was a moment of euphoria, of utopian jubilation following stunned relief that the war was over. And for a while, in this illusory period of change and expectation, people might have been excused for believing that they were in on the beginning of a new age – an age of socialism which would see the end of the old divisions and animosities. Inevitably, it did not last long. In the atmosphere of depressive austerity which settled upon the country and lingered for at least three or four years to damp enthusiasm down, it was bound in the end to be succeeded not only by post-natal depression, but by growing disenchantment and deepening opposition from those who had never anyway *wanted* any of the radical social measures that were being enacted. By the early 1950s the characteristic methods of the exploiting classes had again begun to re-assert the claims of inequality; and with increasing confidence and a resurgence of the spirit of free enterprise and self-interest, the financial jugglers and the speculators, the Boardmen, the Bankers and the Brokers, the former supporters of colonialism and empire who had to stand by and watch Britain's possessions, as they saw it, being thrown indifferently away, began to find new roles for themselves and new fields for their ingenious mercenary concepts of the uses of society and of social wealth, at the same time setting back in place the traditional image of the British Way of Life. So that by the late fifties the Conservatives (even in spite of the disastrous adventure of Suez) had persuaded a majority of the people (who had already put them firmly back in the saddle) that *their* philosophy, their free-wheeling manipulation of the laws of the market, their call to individual initiative and the inalienable and sacred liberties of self-interest, was the one which would bring prosperity back to Britain. The rise of the meritocracy? Freedom of movement for the small trader? Carte blanche for the man of enterprise? Encouragement to big business? Capitalism as the beneficent entrepreneur, the Santa Klaus who would hand out 'welfare' gifts to all, from the richest to the poorest? As soon as feasible, the returned Conservatives initiated a policy of buoyant support for self-reliance and self-advancement, and stimulated by their success in three consecutive electoral victories, each with increased majorities, culminating in 1959, started Britain rising on the wave of Macmillan's boom years, the years of 'You've never had it so good'.

The consequence of this thirteen-year period of affluence and expansion was inevitably a slow and at first hardly perceptible degeneration of the community services that 1945 had brought into being, and a strong reaction against the principles of nationalization. For these had been founded on different principles – a philosophy of society that required the rational implementation of a socialist planned economy. And now that Britain had openly reverted to its old-established methods (which had never been surrendered), they were having to fight for survival in the context of a system whose whole structure was diametrically opposed to socialism – the triumphant reassertion of an ethic founded on money and property and free enterprise – a system that encouraged the utilization of vast economic resources to the vagaries of the market for private profit. Little wonder then that the Health

Service and the nationalized industries should have begun to show signs of strain, or that they should be cracking, crumbling and breaking down. For the economic policy of even a Labour government (as the inheritors of the Liberal creed) is committed to maintaining a financial and fiscal system that encourages divisiveness and self-interest against the interests of the community, and a pattern of life dominated by commercial market values and the pressures of economic competition at the expense of social and community values – the largely untapped potentialities of the people themselves. Indeed, the *essence* of this system is the divisive nature of its appeal; and in its emphasis on the acquisitive rights of the individual, its discouragement of the connectedness between one sphere of activity and another, its distrust of ideas, its alienating pressures, the sheer diversity of means that have been invented, developed and put to use to maintain people in the securities and comforts of unfreedom, the overall effect upon the qualitative social process is to frustrate and to undermine those instincts and common interests which would tend to draw people closer together. The implication is that all concepts of community that encourage a communal response from people are bound to fail because unrealistic, utopian and, in their application to society, deadening to initiative and enterprise, turning people into grey nonentities; that it is the individual, in his struggle for place and for self-advancement, who creates the values of society, and that if you take away from him his right to assert himself for his own ends alone you *destroy* incentive and initiative. Against this there is a very different view which holds that 'the totally individuated individual loses his identity, and that it is only when "committed to the cyclic rhythms of community" that a man can be fulfilled and know himself'. In other words, we grow complete not by living aggressively assertive lives at the expense of others, but rather by living our lives in the closest conjunction with the lives of others, because it is in this that our deepest qualitative incentives and satisfactions lie. To point to such distinctions is, however, merely to emphasize how far we are from even beginning to bridge the gaps between the world of the alienated individual and the concept of a genuinely socialist community. In Britain it is compromise, the art of the possible, as they say, that governs – the craft of accommodation: which means, in effect, that in the field of social action, dominated by a capitalist economy, all 'visionary' ideas of community are likely to have to go on fighting a losing battle for accommodation with the propagandists of 'realism'. For the leaders of society, those who have the power, whether publicly or behind the scenes (Conservative or Labour, Macmillanite or Wilsonite), naturally see themselves as the realist protectors of the operative process – the guardians of divided public interest and of the law and order that maintain the status quo against subversion and dissent. And of course these leaders are also the guardians of what, in a capitalist economy, goes *on* behind the scenes. It is their 'decorous equivocation' that continues to safeguard the superstructure for the free play of individual initiative, the struggles for wealth and power, by interposing

a veil between men's minds and the realities, which, though not too opaque to allow the latter to be seen, changes their colour and proportions, and, while revealing their existence, conceals their significance. Thus shielded against too violent an impact of disturbing truths, the rulers of mankind are enabled to maintain side by side two standards of social ethics, without the risk of their colliding. Keeping one set of values for use, and another for display, they combine, without conscious insincerity, the moral satisfaction of idealistic principles with the material advantages of realistic practice.[5]

The economic recession of the early seventies, brought on by a slump in the world market and quickened by the Arab appropriation of oil resources previously governed by Western monopolies, has had violent inflationary effects upon the stability of the capitalist economy. And hitting Britain after an especially virulent dose of Conservative expansionism between 1970 and 1973 in the wake of Labour's attempt to extend the community services, it has in many ways tended to expose the underlying realities and to sharpen the contradictions of the operative system, and thus to expose an imbalance between resources, wages and prices which can only be controlled by some sort of rigid restrictive planning. Suddenly, it had become apparent that no country, however advanced, however powerful, can afford to build its economy without consideration of the interdependent needs of other countries; that in the West it is no longer possible to assume the existence of a market for cheap goods which will be there to exploit for its own advantage. Suddenly, the illogicality and injustice of the distribution of wealth in the world has become an issue even for those who have gained most from it. Suddenly, the claims and moral demands of the developing nations in Asia, Africa and South America, and the anomalies defined by Britain's relationships with such reactionary powers as Rhodesia and South Africa, take on a new and crucial significance in terms of the impact they can have upon other more supposedly advanced nations. Suddenly, the riches of the world are seen to be interdependent, and the issue of their re-distribution becomes an imperative need.

But that is not the logic of the competitive capitalist market. The Western world had built its prosperity upon the exploitation and manipulation of the resources of various parts of the world at a time when Europe and America had almost exclusive control of the means to develop them and thus to set up networks of interest and concession in the territories they commanded. Now, however, in spite of the huge monopolies that continue to operate in countries where it is still possible to operate, the situation is changing, and the Arab take-over of the Middle East oil companies is only the most spectacular symptom of this. And it has already struck hard at the structures of the Western economy, forcing Europe and the United States to make adjustments. In Britain, the immediate effects were rising prices, rising unemployment, the falling value of the pound, and a cut-back on resources for the community services (particularly education and health) as the least profitable aspects of social policy. At the same time, those likely to have gained most from the crisis have been the monetarists, the businessmen, the industrialists, the bankers, the investors and international financiers behind the scenes, as the presumed experts, the indispensable agents of economic recovery; and particularly under conditions of rigid wage-control, with millions of workers agreeing to virtual cuts in the purchasing power of their pay. It is surely symbolic of the ensuing disequilibrium, the inequity and injustice of this complex situation, that a £72 million pound building, now the highest in London, should be dominating the skyline of the city at a time of crisis worse than any that has occurred since the war, and that this building should be the property of the National Westminster Bank.

In a situation of this kind, dominated as it is by the astonishing technological and technocratic developments of the post-war period and their tendency to neutralize the struggle for emancipation and the freeing of consciousness, it is difficult to see how any objective socialist principles can have the power to create a juster distribution of wealth in the qualitative sense, either here or abroad. The strength and resilience of the obstacles that stand in the way of any fundamental change, and the complexity of the problems that have still to be faced, in world terms, are sufficient to daunt even the most convinced among us. Not that this should deter the socialist from his task. Like Morris, he will know that what his socialism gives him is 'the realization that the laws of change may only be grasped by the individual in terms of his alienation – that is, in terms of his reponse to the thwarting of his desires by the world of actuality. The determining role of consciousness begins in the recognition of the nature of its determination by objective contradictions.'[6] And it is from this point that the freed consciousness identifies the antithetical forces by which the struggle for qualitative change must proceed, and defines the conditions for the renewal of the creative dialectic between man-as-individual and man-as-social being.

This is not to simplify the situation. For such identification and such definition will have had to register the fact that the enemies of socialism – and of that creative dialectic without which the struggle cannot be carried on – exist not only in the capitalist world, but also in those countries which have dogmatically asserted the *establishment* of socialism. For there the official creed, with its intolerant systems of control, has perverted the terms of the struggle by pretending it has been won and thus creating a pretext for the suppression of dissent, the indispensable freedom to think forward and to make possible new and necessary changes. 'What sort of government is it,' the heretic Djilas, once a convinced leader of the Yugoslav Communist Party, asks,

that finds its strength, and its justification before its own people, in falsehoods? What is the destination of a society that maintains and restores itself with injustice? What remains of ideas and ideals once they become means of terror and intimidation among their own adherents? What are the real aims and interests of people who have recourse to slander and coercion even towards those most in sympathy with their own views? Why are we Communists, once in power, more exclusive and unapproachable than anyone else? Why am I pilloried when my tormentors themselves know that I only wanted socialism to be closer to the people, in order to make socialism freer and more Yugoslav?[7]

With such questions, the alienated consciousness pits itself against the shut minds that maintain the inhumanities of an intractable order. And so it is that those who seek their concepts of freedom in the attempt to realize a socialism that will embody what it claims find themselves opposed and thwarted as actively in the East as in the West. But ideology is not the only obstacle. A common threat which tends to blur the distinctions between opposing political systems in the struggle for an authentically human world presents itself in terms of the bureaucratic procedures that are rampant everywhere, by which increasingly sophisticated technologies are being applied and manipulated to control and contain people's needs. And this is nowhere more damaging than in the forms these bureaucracies assume in the people's democracies, where the fundamental aims of the struggle for socialism are being deeply undermined by the totalitarian congealments of the system. If, as the Western conservative might put it, there *is* in fact no wholly socialized state which is also free, this is to say no more than that there is no such state that is actually a *socialist* state. What 'wholly socialized' means here, translated into real terms, is 'wholly bureaucratized' – which, to the conservative capitalist, amounts to the same thing, since he is a defender of the privacy of capital, and of the individual as the upright pillar of the state. But modern bureaucracy is not a socialist invention. It is essentially a bourgeois invention, a development from the expansion of the technological and social machinery of industrialized and highly urbanized societies, particularly during the nineteenth century and the period of imperialism. Nor was it a nineteenth-century bourgeois invention – the Rome of Julius Caesar had a huge bureaucratic machine at its disposal, and the history of China is largely a history of a network of bureaucratic organizations formed to run the complex affairs of the provinces of successive Chinese emperors. Bureaucracy as an instrument defines itself as a useful and necessary machinery of the ruling power. What has happened over the last fifty years, and particularly the last thirty, is that it has assumed, in its alliance with the abstract resources of technology, a dominating and dictatorial position in the running of the state, both in the East and in the West. And it has done so with the more ease *because* the revolutionary technologies of the modern world – providing it with increasingly subtle methods of indoctrination, and universally welcomed as the key to progress – have tended to dominate the qualitative human issues and to assume control over them, even though they are essentially no more than a means. In other words, the advanced industrialized nations have been quick to recognize and to exploit its political potentialities, and have indiscriminately transformed the world with methods and procedures at once immensely productive, enriching, vital to survival, and oppressive, threatening, antagonistic to the rhythms of organic life, because increasingly abstract and alienating.

It is difficult for most of us to realize just how deeply and how disastrously we ourselves – living through this revolutionary upheaval – are being transformed by it. For the wizardry of technology has in a fundamental sense *become* our environment. We cannot separate ourselves from the accumulated proofs of it that surround us and intrude upon us, from the psychological impact of the violent changes that are daily taking place around (and within) us. It is a conditioning process, from which we cannot escape, and in its many levels of influence – radio, television, the car, the aeroplane, the computer, the laser beam, the nuclear power station, from the simplest to the most complex – it radically affects the ways people use their senses, the ways they react to things, the ways they think and feel, the whole context of their lives. For in its command of perspective and of space it has fundamentally changed our concepts of perspective, our place in time *and* space, opening us out, extending our capacity to see and to hear and to experience the world beyond us, the physical sensate limitations that define our individual existence. This represents at once a positive enlargement of the scope and power of individual understanding, which can only be an asset to us, and an extension of the machinery of indoctrination. Above all, in the form of the various media of communication developed from electronics, it has the power to dominate and to condition the thinking of whole societies, and with the irresistible prospects of ease and comfort, the short cuts to satisfaction, that it seems to offer us, it tends to divert and to seduce us from all our deepest and most organic needs as human beings, even at the same time as it persuades us that the means it is offering are sufficiently all-embracing to answer these needs.

But what, specifically and concretely, is there, the convinced beneficiary may say, that these astonishing new phenomena of the technological age – so ubiquitous, so democratically available and so convenient – cannot offer? Have we not been immeasurably enriched and our lives greatly enhanced by the invention of all such revolutionary media as the telephone, the car, the aeroplane, the radio, television? It would be useless to answer such questions by pointing out that they *are* no more than means. For they are means which have so transformed our environment and have made themselves so persuasively and insistently present in our lives as to condition us unthinkingly into an acceptance of their demands and to neutralize in us any desire to move beyond them, supposing even that we were able to. Thus they have become means which appear only too successfully to postulate their own *ends*. How can one argue against such deceptive satisfactions in defence of one's organic sensate powers by declaring that genuine recognition and awareness have to be actively sought and fought for, with an essentially critical sense of the distinctions that surround us? How can we be sure that this recognition and this awareness cannot be obtained from contact with the media as an extension of our sensate world? When we talk of truth and of lies what do we mean? When we talk of the illusory, selective and therefore distorted image beamed at us from the television screen are we not deluding ourselves into the assumption that this is any more illusory and selective than what the unaided eye can make of the world it sees? Whose eye does the television image represent? We must make distinctions. We must distinguish ourselves from that which conditions us. Since, as John Goode puts it, 'the determining role of consciousness begins in the recognition of the *nature* of its determination by objective contradictions', it is necessary to *discover* what these contradictions are, and try to face up to them. Because unless we can do so, we cannot even *begin* to distinguish that which alienates from that which frees.

But is it not the function of applied technology, as the question goes, to simplify, to save labour, to provide ever more efficient short cuts to ease and comfort, such as will eventually eliminate all unneccessary effort, all dissatisfaction, all suffering, all unhappiness? In answer, one might cautiously agree, at the same time pointing out that provision of the means to eliminate all obstacles to ease and comfort might, if carried far enough, begin to falsify the complex changing process of reality and the significance of the struggle to reconcile its contradictions. Because for an understanding of this process there are no short cuts. To eliminate *unnecessary* effort is, however, the more important in that it leaves us that much more time to pursue such understanding, and in these terms our own authentic human needs. If we do not use it so, we simply lose what we have saved. If we use it, as we have a perfect right to, on the kind of ready-made and second-hand experience television offers – which asks nothing of us but the passive response of a voyeur – we are not likely to find ourselves much the wiser. For in itself it is little more than a vicarious projection of reality – offering formulas for living which, with all the ingredients thrown in, are superimposed by others upon the actual realities of our lives, thus making it more difficult to keep the distinctions clear between reality and fantasy. Or take another instance. The Botticelli, the Titian or the Picasso that becomes instantly and everywhere available in reproduction may be a useful (and democratic) way of making people familiar with great paintings and giving them adequate cheap substitutes for the originals. But only so long as the two are not confused. For what is reproduced is little more than a diluted, trivialized reflection of the original, contained and absorbed into the all-pervading system of the mass-producing consumer market, fabricated for the art shops and the departmental stores. In this form it loses all its unique subtlety and power to challenge, to arrest, to awaken the sensibility, and exists as a parody, a dulled echo of the uniqueness of the human act that created it. It has been transformed into a commodity, a piece of confectionery, an article made not as the artist makes his work, for the joy of the discoveries he makes, but for profit.

And this, the enemies of the free consciousness and of socialist democracy, the upholders of élitist privilege, the possessors of original paintings, would gleefully point out, is what your misguided advocacy of popular emancipation *does* to art and to all authentic complexities! But then such people would have no interest whatever in tackling the challenge involved in the idea of freeing the consciousness, or in what those who care about the quality of people's lives might be prepared to risk for the sake of genuine communication. One has to answer the apologists for trivialization, the sold consumers, the market manipulators who accumulate sufficient wealth to pay record prices for their Rembrandts, with refusal. One has to turn one's face deliberately against this Disney-land promise and its 'instamatic' culture, as against an enemy, even at the risk of being branded an élitist, because it has nothing to offer people but cheap substitutes for culture that encourage passivity and acquiescence, and would thus prevent them from ever breaking free of their conditioning and seeing straight. And what one turns one's face *towards* – under constant threat from the instruments of the tyranny of the mechanism – is a concept of culture that will reflect and register the dialectic complexities of people's lives, and serve to respect what beauty, in the Hopkins sense, is meant to serve: that which 'keeps warm/Men's wits to the things that are' – and above all to the self that 'flashes off frame and face'.[8]

Take Marcuse's book *One-Dimensional Man*. Its very title concisely defines what this tyranny of methods reduces people to. And the book itself sets out to examine the nature and the impact of the technological transformation of society in order the better to confront an enemy that threatens the basic human freedoms, and threatens them in ways more insidious and more difficult to combat than even the most unequivocal systems of political unfreedom. As such, and in terms of the Marxian argument that Marcuse is an exponent of, it is a scathing denunciation of the kinds of social philosophy that have come to prevail in the modern world and to manipulate, even without their knowing it, the lives of millions of people.

What Marcuse sets out to expose in this book is a universal process of transformation which involves not only 'a sweeping redefinition of thought itself, of its function and content',[9] but also a denial of all those genuinely dialectical forms of thinking that would have the power to resist its imperious dogmas. For it is a process which functions in the quantitative terms of the mass media and of sophisticated techniques that 'appear to be the very embodiment of reason for the benefit of all social groups and interests',[10] while in actual fact manipulating reason to the point at which all contradiction will be made to seem irrational and all counteraction impossible. What he is suggesting indeed is that this is a process which is being utilized by the new bureaucratic ruling classes as a means of controlling and enslaving the mass of the people and imposing upon them new and falsifying ideologies. In other words, 'the more rational, productive, technical and total the repressive administration of society becomes, the more unimaginable the means . . . by which the administered individuals might break their servitude and seize their own liberation'.[11] It is not that an overt intellectual act is at the source of this process of change. What makes it so stultifying and so resistant to the influence of the reasoning mind is its anti-conceptual nature. It is a process grounded upon the totalitarian impact of technology, a mechanistic impulse that forces everything to conform to its own operational and functional terms. That is, by providing for the masses conditions that make life easier, more pleasant, more satisfying, it represses and neutralizes in them all that is not satisfied by these conditions concerning the quality and meaning of life. For those who succumb to this tyranny the needs of life are satisfied, sublimated and absorbed, even by the manner in which its instruments persuade and lull. The changes brought about, that is, by the transformational methods of technology seem in *themselves qualitative* and are insistently *made* to seem so by those who manipulate them, whether for commercial profit or for political domination. The purpose of the manipulators is, of course, to eliminate all opposition that would seek to assert genuine qualitative change – all that serves to make people more aware of themselves and to waken them to the real issues of their lives; because this kind of opposition would (if it were to prevail) break the domination of technology, and hence the domination of those who stand to gain by it.

Marcuse's two-dimensional universe – which defines the struggle for truth as an experience, a struggle between 'Being and Non-Being, essence and fact, generation and corruption, potentiality and actuality'[12] – is of its nature antagonistic to the literalist substitutes of the technological society. It includes, and is enriched by, memory and history, Being and Thought, Logos and Eros; and it encourages the quest for a concept of reality 'not subject to the painful differences between potentiality and actuality, which has mastered its negativity and is complete and independent in itself – free'.[13] It is a 'universe of discourse' that functions to awaken and to extend the mind so that it will have the power to cope with the contradictory nature of the real world of human events and human actions that is its context; and at the same time equip people with the kind of knowledge and awareness that will strengthen them against the forces that have throughout history sought their subjection. Against the one-dimensional universe of technological manipulation, this essentially critical and liberating alternative will need to concentrate all its resource and logic, all its energy and conviction, to have any hope of succeeding. Because the technological process is incessantly and everywhere at work – functioning much in the simplistic and disarming manner of commercial advertisement, by continual repetition breaking down the resistance of those it is aimed at. Deploying the forms of mass communication, the agents of commercial exploitation 'blend together harmoniously and often unnoticeably art, religion, politics and philosophy'[14] by means of highly developed techniques of presentation, thus reducing the distinctions and differences which characterize the life of the mind and the vitality of culture to their lowest common denominator, the commodity. As Marcuse puts it, 'the music of the soul is also the music of salesmanship.'[14] The result is the trivialization, the reduction to absurdity, of all distinctions, all organic forms of thought, all the diversity that enriches the universe of discourse – all that postulates struggle, quest, drama, tragedy, the survival of the human psyche. For it is a process that absorbs and transforms everything into its own package terms, thereby divesting it of all significance, all discomfort, all vividness, all particularity, according to the ambivalent dogma of progress, which is at once 'satisfying in its repressive power, and repressive in its satisfactions'.[15]

This is as much a political process as it is mechanical. For the mechanisms of applied technology (industrial and cultural) have been closely harnessed to the needs of a capitalist economy, and thus utilized and engineered to serve commercial rather than communal ends, the production of 'goods' which the public is persuaded to accept as necessary for the sake of an abstract profit-margin. In terms of the capitalist system, as Marx observed of the way it functioned in the nineteenth century,

each person speculates in creating a *new* need in the other, with the aim of forcing him to make a new sacrifice, placing him in a new dependence and seducing him into a new kind of *enjoyment* and hence into economic ruin. Each attempts to establish over the other an alien power, in the hope of thereby achieving satisfaction of his own selfish needs. With the mass of objects grows the realm of alien powers to which man is subjected, and each new product is a new *potentiality* of mutual fraud and mutual pillage. Man becomes ever poorer as a man, and needs ever more *money* if he is to achieve mastery over the hostile being.[16]

In the modern world this process has been extended, made more abstract. Now, a sophisticated machinery backed by vast capital resources and efficiently organized to exploit the market is continually at work publicizing the diverse wares of a consumer world and persuading people to accept them. It seeks not awareness but domination, and aims therefore to neutralize or to diminish (to alienate) the power of the individual to speak in defence of complexity and diversity, communal social awareness, the primacy of the human process, the qualitative distinctions that reason insists upon making between life as an end and life as a means. Its power lies in the fact that it appears to be the embodiment of reason and the servant of human betterment, to be supplying society with all the things people *need*; for by this means it offers a devastating answer to its critics, making them appear to be the enemies of progress, setting against their dialectic awareness of the essential qualitative issues it diverts attention from, the assets, the benefits, the aids, the goods, the 'indispensable' facilities, the amenities of ease, the miraculous techniques, as qualitative instruments of the 'living standards' (as the propagandists put it) of the human race.

There is no denying the immense potentialities (in the right hands) of the technological developments that have so transformed the pattern of human life in the twentieth century. But it is the alienating uses to which this machinery has been, and is being, put that define the threat to humanity. 'Memory recalls the terror and the hope that have passed,' as Marcuse cryptically remarks; and 'the spectre of man without historical memory'[17] is the spectre of man without historical imagination, man become incapable of recognizing the dialectical nature of the human struggle, because denied the perspectives of historical awareness, of objective social judgement, the power to assert his own critical and creative sensibility; deafened and blinded by indoctrination. In the nineteenth century it was by denying the oppressed working classes the right to think freely and to build perspectives of awareness from the sanity of memory and history, and their own essential dignity, that the ruling classes maintained their supremacy, their privileges, their control of wealth. They treated people as mere machinery to serve their ends, robbing them of their basic rights and freedoms, withholding education, as from creatures who would never have the leisure to benefit from it anyway, and exposing them to the backbreaking exhaustion of their enslaved labour, hence denying them (or so their masters hoped) the time, energy and will to look beyond themselves. For the rulers, in Marx's words, 'nations are merely workshops for production, and man . . . a machine for consuming and producing. Human life is a piece of capital. Economic laws rule the world blindly.'[18] And under these laws the worker 'has the misfortune to be a *living* capital, and hence a capital with *needs*, which forfeits its interest and hence its existence every moment it is not working'.[19] He increases the productive power, the wealth and refinement of society, but is himself impoverished, reduced to a piece of machinery, by his labour.[20]

The tyranny of technology today takes very different *forms*. It dominates by indiscriminate and unselective exposure, by incessant titillation, pouring out its goods and comforts in such quantity and with such seductive appeal as to satiate and to stultify even as they satisfy. But the *motive* – of profit, of commercial exploitation, of economic control – is the same as in the nineteenth century. Because though the methods and the techniques have changed, the process of manipulation by which needs are forced upon people and alien powers established over them has a similar effect, in that it tends to prevent them from looking into and beyond themselves, from thinking about or questioning, from asserting their natural, active powers against, the manipulation, and so from rejecting it. In this spirit all men are diminished, impoverished. 'The man estranged from himself is also the thinker estranged from his *essence*, i.e. from his natural human essence. His thoughts are therefore fixed phantoms existing outside nature and man,' so that nature itself – *his* nature, the nature of his *condition* as a human being – 'taken abstractly, for itself, and fixed in its separation from man, is *nothing* for man.'[21]

Of course, these same methods of persuasion and manipulation can equally be used, and are being used, to waken, to warn, to sensitize, to *develop* awareness, to reveal to people their heritage, their communal responsibilities, their historical position, and to encourage them to think for themselves. But creative integrity, the organic rationalizing vision, the voice that would speak, without cheating or condescending or diluting, for dignity and delight, for emancipation and recovery and fulfilment, has to take its chance in competition with an endless flood of messages that care nothing for integrity or for vision. And because it *cannot* stoop to the use of the cheap but dazzling devices the manipulators use to hold their audiences in thrall without cheapening or falsifying what it has to say, it competes with all the odds against it – cannot, in fact, *afford* to compete unless it can somehow find ways of using the weapons of its enemies that will *not* dilute or cheapen the seriousness and difficulty and scope of its view of reality.

15

MEANS AND ENDS:
THE CLOSING OF THE CIRCLE

'There has been no more mischievous habit of thought,' R. H. Tawney has observed of the manner in which economic and industrial issues are treated,

than the smiling illusion which erected into a philosophy the conception that industry is a mechanism, moving by quasi-mechanical laws and adjusted by the play of non-moral forces, in which methods of organization and social relationships are to be determined solely by consideration of economic convenience and productive efficiency. By erecting an artificial barrier between the economic life of a society and its religion, its art, the moral traditions and kindly feelings of human beings, that doctrine degrades the former and sterilizes the latter.[1]

Fifty years after Tawney wrote the above paragraph, this doctrine of quasi-mechanical laws still operates because it refers in fact to the underlying conditions, the general impersonal structure, by which the superstructure of society is determined. It is mischievous, that is, not in erecting its philosophy of quasi-mechanical laws, but rather in putting up barriers between this concept of the underlying structure and the part that human beings play in shaping and modifying that structure; in denying the interrelation between man and machinery. Man is thwarted in society by the alienating process set in motion as a consequence of the dislocation created by these barriers. He must therefore be given the confidence to recognize, and equipped to understand, that it is not only the underlying structure (the general impersonal process) that determines the shape and direction of the super-structure; but that he *himself* – in grasping the complex nature of the interaction between man and machinery – can modify the structure by his own action upon it. But only if he is *able*, in Gramsci's terms, to 'create his own personality' in an active and conscious involvement in the *struggle* for clarity and understanding; and then only if he is able to see that the nature of his struggle is its commitment to the dialectic which determines it.[2] He who tries to fight in terms of the blacks and whites of what Blake called 'singleness of vision' is (as Blake continually stressed) likely to find himself completely contained and closed in by what he has to contend with – a negative within a negative moving within the closed circle of his conditioning.

The barriers to interaction become alien powers that function to maintain the divisions within society. They are an integral feature of all authoritarian systems; and in the capitalist world they continue to be encouraged by those in control as a powerful means of *retaining* control of the economic structure and of continuing to manipulate the people into submission to its 'iron laws'. For having become abstract powers which separate and enclose, these artificial barriers are imposed upon people as absolutes not to be questioned and therefore not to be overthrown. The aim is to keep things in separate compartments in order to stop people from identifying the *human* interests that control the abstract machinery and thus from being in a position to identify their *own* interests with the machinery and taking steps to play some part in controlling it – that is, in controlling and restricting the movements of those who are actually in control of it.

True, in the period since Tawney made his point, the conditions that determine *who* it is maintains the artificial barriers have changed; for the old governing oligarchies that fifty years ago had control of the economic and cultural life of Britain by 'an appeal to hunger and fear' have been superseded. But can it be said that now men are no longer prepared to 'give their labour and risk their lives for a system which they regard as morally indefensible and professionally incompetent'?[3] If this were so, the system itself would have ceased to exist, and Britain would have achieved its social revolution. But it is palpably *not* so. For the system remains basically intact. Though men are now more conscious of their rights and have made themselves reasonably secure against the barbarous exploitation they suffered in the past, a capitalist economy still controls their labour, still dictates the values of the community and the superstructure. It has simply changed its tactics, adjusted its methods to the new conditions, that is all. Now, people are being attacked from different directions, got at in ways they may not be psychologically equipped to resist. The artificial barriers that define the divided structure of society have been strengthened and extended by the manner in which the abstract techniques of the mass media have been devised to provide sufficient comforts and contentments to stop people asking awkward questions. At this level they are the more insidious and powerful because they seem not to be barriers at all, but rather to encourage access and ease of contact between people and things. By indiscriminate and apparently unqualified exposure, the wakening consciousness is swamped, confused and diverted; and so people are prevented from concentrating upon or thinking seriously about the underlying conditions that determine their lives. They are persuaded to accept as substitutes for these conditions the 'smiling illusions' of reality, which so closely simulate what *is* real as to deceive people into believing that they actually are, and in this way satisfying them by deception.

If it is true to say that 'life as an end is qualitatively different from life as a means',[4] the distinction is being constantly undermined by the irresistible attraction of the means, which we are being conditioned to accept as ends – even to the point that 'many of the most seriously troublesome concepts are being eliminated simply because no adequate account can be made of them in terms of circumstance and behaviour'.[5] This threat to our qualitative human ends, which remain so obstinately obscure and intangible, is likely to become more acute and alarming with every new refinement of technology, every new proof of the superiority of the mechanism. After all, as Marcuse observes, if individuals are pre-conditioned to accept that the 'satisfying goods [they are offered] also include thoughts, feelings, aspirations, why should they need to think, feel and imagine for themselves?'[6]

Under these circumstances, people cannot ever hope to assert their own creative influence upon their world unless they can somehow be alerted to the imperceptible falsifications of the process that is at work upon them, and equipped to recognize these falsifications for what they are, to make the necessary distinctions and keep them clear. The dilemma could perhaps be put in the following terms: 'To the degree to which consciousness is determined by the exigencies and interests of an established society based upon irrational and unjust concepts of rights and duties, it is "unfree"; and the consciousness can therefore *become* free only by opposing the exigencies and interests of the established society.'[7]

But in order to become free, we have to be able to identify the conditions of unfreedom, the restrictions and obstacles that inhibit freedom. In order, that is, to be able to choose between acting upon and *being* acted upon, between 'resisting and doing' rather than passively accepting, between realizing and registering rather than merely reacting to, we have to be able to recognize the terms of our conditioning. And since this process of conditioning – as a social, psychological and technological process – is at the same time a political process, it follows that it is only through political change (and the struggle for political change) that we can transform our conditioning into a qualitative and creative process.

The problem is that the actual conditioning in itself tends to neutralize in us the will to resist it and even to recognize the need for political change. Above all, by persuading us to accept its own standards as terminal and inescapable, it obliterates awareness of the distinctions between means and ends; till, totally conditioned, we cease to be aware that we are *being* conditioned. So it is that the universe of discourse becomes a *closed* universe inside which we are trapped. This is a dilemma not simply for the individual within society, but for society itself as the collective expression of will; because it is after all society and its complex interactions that determine whether or not the individual consciousness shall be free to utilize the available machinery as a means to the achievement of qualitative ends. It is a dilemma for politics and education, and one that demands immediate and urgent attention, against the closing of the circle.

And in Britain it remains unresolved; for the process of manipulation maintained by those who have stood to gain most from keeping people repressed (and conditioned to accept their repression) has continued unabated. We are now in a different situation from that which, in 1952, Tawney was able to comment upon with such confidence and optimism for the future. His tolerant view of British society, and his conviction that socialism in Britain could continue its work of transformation even in the midst of a mixed economy – indeed, with more commitment and ethical purpose because of this – is not so easily upheld in the light of the actual forces arrayed against it. He was writing in the immediate aftermath of a great period of socialist transformation.

But today we are moving through a period of economic uncertainty, of political retrenchment and reaction, in which Labour governments seem obliged to throw aside most of the socialism in their policies against the incessant pressures of the system, thus making the struggle for qualitative change more difficult than ever.

In face of a long experience of such vacillations and collapses, Tawney bases his support for the methods of democratic socialism on a struggle for qualitative change that rejects violence. It is his considered view that the essence of the struggle is the freedom and the right to struggle for it even against the freedom and the right of its enemies to frustrate and to oppose that struggle. He believes that socialism can only prevail by virtue of the superiority of its ethical and moral principles, and can never do so in dogmatic contempt for democracy. He does not share 'Marx's mid-Victorian conviction of the inevitability of progress'; nor does he

regard social development as an automatically ascending spiral with socialism as its climax. On the contrary, I think that, in the absence of sustained and strenuous efforts, the way is as likely to lead downhill as up, and that socialism, if achieved, will be the creation, not of any mystical historical necessities, but of the energies of human minds and wills. The chicanery, discreetly termed relativism, which dismisses ordinary human virtues, from honesty to mercy, as bourgeois morality; falsifies ethical standards; and applauds as triumphs of proletarian heroism on the one side of the frontier episodes denounced by it as Fascist atrocities on the other, appears to me nauseous. I regard it, not as the example of up-to-date realism boasted by its votaries, but as a long-familiar poison.[8]

Tawney is clearly as anxious to avoid hypocrisy and deceit concerning the ethics of socialism and its methods as he is to identify the enemies of socialism. And he is too deeply ingrained with the spirit of his democratic roots to gloss over the dangers of the dogmatic intolerance of Soviet Russia and Eastern Europe or to confuse the systems of these countries with the kind of socialism he wants to see enacted. But in dismissing Marx's monumental contribution to the struggle for human betterment as a system based upon 'mystical historical necessities' he shows little understanding of the nourishing elements of Marx's thinking. Without Marx, indeed, Tawney's own brand of socialism might hardly have developed beyond the forms of radical liberalism it was fed upon.

Marx demonstrated far more deeply than Tawney himself how much socialism owes to the creative 'energies of human minds and wills'. And in his emphasis upon the necessity of historical vindication he was concerned not with any sort of mystical process but with the logic of history. But he was at the same time a prophet, a pioneer, a man fighting immense and seemingly unarguable powers; and to him it appeared impossible that the working classes could achieve any transformation of society without recourse to violence. On the other hand, he did make it clear on more than one occasion that he believed England could achieve socialism without violence, though he never made this a central alternative principle, and considered England (and America) as exceptional cases, contrasting them with what he held to be the general rule that 'in most continental countries the lever of the revolution will have to be force'.[9]

And what has *become* of the possibility that 'the workers can attain their goal by peaceful means'?[9] In the wake of twentieth-century developments it seems remote indeed, in England as in America. Not only do the barriers still exist; in terms of the institutional structures of the country's life the greatest obstacle to revolutionary change is in the psychological attitudes of the people themselves, their acceptance of the parliamentary process. On these grounds alone, the prospect of revolution as such must be discounted. And the form that socialism takes in the eighties is going to continue to be determined by the traditional procedures of the English political system and by the problem of combating the appeal of the Right to the innate conservatism and will to privacy of the British people. Inevitably, by the laws of the democratic process, the wavering electorate (many of whom never vote) will periodically vote a Conservative government in to do what it can to unshackle the system of whatever grossly socialist imprints have been made upon it, as doctors called in to administer their cure for such wounds and bring the ailing nation back to health, according to the logic of its capitalistic body-structure. Tawney insists that there is no rational way of countering this insidious bolstering-up of an unjust system other than by convincing people democratically, in pitched political battle, of the superior logic of socialism. But at the same time as he rejects violence he refuses to accept a concept of socialism 'that consists in socializing everything except political authority, on which', as he says, 'all else depends'. For him, however answered, 'the question for Socialists is not merely whether the state owns and controls the means of production. It is also, and even more important, who owns and controls the state. Democracy, in one form or another, is, in short, not merely one of several alternative methods of establishing a Socialist commonwealth. It is an essential condition of such a commonwealth's existence.'[10]

And this, he would argue, is too valuable and too indispensable a condition to risk. The dogmatists who contend that, since you cannot reason with the enemies of reason, you have no choice but to defeat them by force and *impose* socialism on the people, not only risk the loss of democratic liberties, but must deliberately suppress them, and thus destroy the foundations on which socialism itself is built, becoming indistinguishable from its enemies. How, Tawney asks, is emancipation to be encouraged and assured by means of a rigid totalitarian 'single path'? What can it achieve in the nature of a genuinely socialist ethic by suppressing all opposition? For in the process of suppressing opposition it also creates resentment and suspicion among the people as a whole, and intolerable restrictions of liberty; and to suppress is not to eliminate the problem of the opposition, but merely to drive it underground and to frustrate the dialectic process essential to continuity and renewal – quite apart from exposing the officers of the state to the temptation to act barbarously and inhumanly against all who will not conform. And how, under such conditions, is the reality of socialism, its ethics and its morality, to survive?

Tawney's view is that it cannot, because brute force imposes an arbitrary concept of social justice upon people, which is bound to be inadequate to the true demands and needs of human beings and the requirements of the higher concepts that socialism has as its essential motivating principle. His view affirms the progress of socialism in Britain as 'obstinately and unashamedly ethical'. And as he puts it, unequivocally enough:

The revolt of ordinary men against Capitalism has had its source neither in its obvious deficiences as an economic engine, nor in the conviction that it represents a stage in social evolution now outgrown, but in the straightforward hatred of a system which stunts personality and corrupts human relations by permitting the use of man by man as an instrument of pecuniary gain. The socialist society envisaged by them is not a herd of tame, well-nourished animals, with wise keepers in command. It is a community of responsible men and women working without fear in comradeship for common ends, all of whom can grow to their full stature, develop to the utmost limit the varying capacities with which nature has endowed them.[11]

The difficulty with this view is that it assumes agreement, awareness and willingness on the part of every person associated in the enterprise, a developed consciousness and conscience in respect to the enactment of what is envisaged. It assumes, in a word, *responsibility*. And the problem here is 'not merely the recalcitrance of employers. It is the apathy and torpor of many workers, who in theory desire freedom, but who in practice are too often reluctant to assume the burdens without which freedom cannot be had.' And as Tawney asserts: 'If a Socialist government means business – if it intends to create an economic system socialist all through, and not merely at the top – then it must take the initiative, force the pace, and – I won't say compel – but *persuade* men to be free.'[12]

This is the most basic and the most crucial issue of all, the issue on which everything else turns. How is it possible to take the initiative and force the pace without first changing the economic conditions which are the obstacle to freedom? How can men be persuaded to be free under conditions deeply resistant to socialism? To accept the context of a capitalist economy and at the same time attempt to create within such acceptance an economic system socialist all through is to attempt to storm a fortress from within. And if this can be said to define the strategy of socialism, such a strategy is likely to find itself beset with snares and pitfalls, continual compromises and retreats forced upon it by the operative system. This indeed has been the experience of successive Labour governments since 1945. When socialism has to shelve its most vital principles to suit the mood of the market it is bowing to a more persuasive logic than its own and demonstrating its *inability* to persuade men to be free.

Faced with crippling inflation, the vigorous invisible powers of capitalist action, and a disunited work-force still reluctant to assume the burdens without which freedom cannot be had – a work-force unprepared to commit itself fully to the service of the community because it feels (perhaps rightly) that the system it serves is still a system that works to the advantage of the few and thus *against* the community – socialists face a whole phalanx of negatives which it will demand a sustained and unwavering programme of active encouragement to break. And unless they can waken and persuade the mass of the working class to some form of concentrated response, and a commitment to socialism, in the interests of a freed community, they are going to have to continue to surrender the field to a Conservative government – to the sort of government whose basic aim it is to strengthen and to extend the forces of minority privilege and power and (whenever it can) to reverse the policies and instituted acts which make a socialist community possible.

In a capitalist democracy, the great aims and ends of life – a civilization and a culture that serve to sensitize and to quicken the potentialities of all citizens in society to the recognition of the interconnected part they have to play in creating the conditions for a genuine commonwealth – are under constant threat not only from the conscienceless and the insensitive, who think of them as the delusive myths of intellectuals and artists, but also (and as often) from the well-intentioned, who put too much faith in the means and are not clear enough in spelling out the distinctions between means and ends. 'Civilization,' as Tawney argues, 'is a matter not of quantity of possessions, but of quality of life. It is to be judged, not by the output of goods and services per head, but by the use which is made of them.'[13] And that is the challenge people must be persuaded to live in terms of and be equipped to fight for against the whole drift of things in the modern world. It is a daunting challenge, and it will demand from people greater courage, greater determination and awareness than many of them think they can command. For the massive barriers, the alienating powers, that stand between people and their freedoms are not to be wished out of the way. They were set up to last, as bastions of law and order created by the ruthless economic powers of the ruling classes, and under the systems of formal Western democracy they were designed to function to the advantage of the comparative few and the subjection of the majority.

So that even all the highest pursuits we can conceive – such as philosophy, science, art, music, literature – are unfortunately stamped (in the minds of the traditionally oppressed) with the signs of privilege and of exploitation that characterize the rule of an oppressive élite. This stigma clearly has to be overcome, and these civilized pursuits made available to, and the common heritage of, all. For it is indeed a disgrace, because of the way society is organized, that they are not. The fact that so many should care so little for the survival of art and literature is not their fault. They have never even been given the opportunity or the confidence or the right to care. It was their place to serve as the economic machines to enable others to benefit from and to enjoy the wealth and the resources of society.

It is obvious that the great aims and ends of life are not to be realized until the many have been freed from this economic and cultural enslavement; which means that the few must be forced to do without their special privileges, for the balance cannot be set right unless some sort of tangible effort is made to *put* it right. Not that this should mean in any sense depriving anyone of the common riches of their world, but that these riches should be opened up to all and shared in common.

With this, no doubt, the controllers of the capitalist status quo – those who command the material and cultural resources of their societies – would agree. Democracy, they'd say, paying their lip-service to the spirit of modern political ideas and bowing formally and theoretically to the great principles it enshrines, means equality. But the economic system that determines this equality, and the rights that go with it, makes of democracy as it actually functions an admirable means of justifying the right of the few to continue their manipulation of the many. The democracy of capitalist society, in other words, in Lenin's words, remains 'democracy for an insignificant minority, democracy for the rich'.[14] And this holds true even beyond the transformations of the last fifty years. For 'if we look more closely into the machinery of capitalist democracy, we shall see everywhere, in the "petty" supposedly petty – details of the suffrage, in the techniques of the representative institutions, in the actual obstacles to the right of assembly (public buildings are not for "beggars"!), in the purely capitalist organization of the daily press, etc., etc. – we shall see restriction after restriction upon democracy'. And 'in their sum total these restrictions exclude and squeeze out the poor from politics, from active participation in democracy'.[14] In its application as we know it here, that is – not to mention what we gather of its fate in the Soviet Union – democracy means only *formal* democracy. And it is only when 'equality is achieved for all members of society in relation to ownership of the means of production – equality of labour and equality of wages' – that it will become possible for humanity to begin to advance further, 'from formal equality to actual equality'. And as Lenin, putting his finger upon issues that have yet to be resolved anywhere, further states:

By what stages, by means of what practical measures, humanity will proceed to this supreme aim, we do not and cannot know. But it is important to realize how infinitely mendacious is the ordinary bourgeois conception of Socialism as something lifeless, petrified, fixed once and for all, whereas in reality *only* under Socialism will a rapid, genuine, and really mass forward movement, embracing first the *majority* and then the whole of the population, commence in all spheres of public and personal life.[15]

16

SOCIALISM:
THE STRUGGLE FOR THE FUTURE

The future is a nest of unhatched possibilities. We do not know what it will bring into being. But it must be clear to all those who have taken the trouble to think about the problems that confront mankind, and who care what happens to people, that we are going to have to fight as hard for the future as men have ever had to fight for it in the past. Whether or not we are prepared to do so naturally presupposes a structure of values and a historical perspective; we cannot fight for anything with any conviction unless we know both what it is we are fighting for and what we are opposing. Thus, participation in the historical process which creates the shape of the future is a question of awareness; and it is above all a question of vision. For what lies unrealized beyond the conditions that exist, and the immediate objectives these conditions make it possible to achieve, demands the capacity to envisage forms and structures for a pattern of social intercourse which are 'not confined to the world of concrete activity'. 'The change beyond the change'[1] can only be dreamt of, that is, in the sense in which 'dream, the freed consciousness . . . becomes a major, though expendable, register of the antithetical forces invisibly operating against the perceptible reality'.[2]

The perceptible reality, the world that defines itself to us in all its confusions and contradictions, in terms of the struggles of individuals and social groups and nations and ideologies and economic systems, in the fragmentary perceptiveness of the moment and as an accumulation of abstracts or of more or less haphazardly interconnected particulars, remains for most of us so bewilderingly complex and diverse that we may well find ourselves unable to conceive of anything beyond it and be tempted to give up all attempt to do so. And yet it is vital to our continuing development both as individuals and as social beings – people for whom the world we live in is the field of action that makes sense of what we are – that we *do* make the attempt. For there is a future to be won or lost for the human race, however bewilderingly veiled, however difficult to envisage. And the winning or the losing of it is likely to be affected, however minimally, by the integrity and the persistence of the attempt we make against all the obstacles to give it shape. Whether this will be a future that can reconcile the divisive interests and causes of conflict that have kept most men so miserably enslaved and oppressed for most of history depends as much upon the energy and creative integrity we give to the struggle as it does upon the vast abstract forces we seem to be controlled by – which are also, after all, the creation of men and of the human mind.

Many of us recognize the distances between what perceptibly and palpably exists and what as yet remains unrealized – the gaps between the actualities of power and those conditions considered indispensable to the dignity and quality of human life, without which the majority of men and women must remain unfulfilled, unemancipated, inhibited and handicapped from enjoying to the full the communal assets of their world. But before we can even begin to know what can be done to lessen these distances or to move towards the realization of the potential rewards of community, it is necessary to recognize the true nature of the problems and obstacles that confront us. Only when, quickened with conviction, we have freed ourselves from the bondage of the alienating conditions that blind us to the change beyond the change shall we be able to act, and have the confidence to believe that we can join hands across the distances that divide. In order to have the power to enact community, that is, the consciousness of man must somehow be freed from fear and insecurity, the suspicion and mistrust bred in him by those alien forces in the world that have held him so deeply in thrall for so long.

In this context, it is the man who can recognize for what they are the alienating contradictions that determine his existence who puts himself in the position of creating (out of all that thwarts him) grounds from which to build. Not that recognition is in itself any guarantee that he will come to the right conclusions and act creatively. He may be one of those inheritors of the psychology of nineteenth-century liberalism – those victims of a deranged system – whose recognition leads him to proclaim a gospel of despair and disillusionment because he has become incapable of seeing the change beyond the change, or who advocates a policy of disinterested passivity, of essentially abstract contemplation, of privileged uninvolvement. But if he *can* put himself in a position to think forward and to think connectedly, he will know he has to set himself against the derelictions of those who, self-bent, set themselves and all their powers against the closing of the distances between people, who would keep them subjugated, stunted, dulled. And in the quickening spirit of opposition he will seek to *strengthen* and to *sharpen* in himself his recognition of the differences between what for people *is* and what beyond emancipation *could* be. Armed with indignation and delight, a tooled awareness of the kind of justice by which 'the just man justices',[3] he will urge the visionary concept – a concept still visionary because unrealized – that man's self-fulfilment comes not in the assertion of his egotistical rights and liberties but through his participation in the life of the community. It is a difficult concept to act upon precisely *because* it seems so far from what people in the world as it is are capable of realizing. But it is motivated by the stubbornly affirmative conviction that, given the right kind of creative changes in the structure of that world, people would respond creatively because they would then see how much more each has to gain from working together than by continually insisting on their own peculiarly selfish interests. They would know that the self is not denied by living and acting in ways that enrich and enhance the selves of others, but enriched and enhanced in turn.

It may be that this is to dream ahead. But it is not to fantasize so long as it recognizes the actualities for what they are. We *have* to be able to think beyond the actualities even in order to be able to begin to envisage the alternative. What use to anyone or to anything – to the individual or to society, to the survival of love and comradeship and the sanity of art, or the making of community – is the kind of pessimism that stutters into disillusionment and despair because it can see no way beyond the actualities? If a man is pushed as far as this, or permits himself to drift as far as this, he becomes an instrument of negation and surrender, turning his back on all those issues vital to his life and to the lives of others. Granted that knowledge is painful, as Arthur Clough has put it in the pain of knowing it is not enough;[4] but to turn away from the world where action is and love and the possible rewards of community, to let the withering of hope and expectation kill, is to let the principle of death triumph over all that life delights in, leaving a man slumped on the sidelines, neutralized. What we have to understand is that, however cruel the fate that strikes at us, it strikes at us with the *indifferent* cruelty of fate, and it is up to us whether we respond with defiance or go under. In other words, it is *we* (and no one else) who lose, and *our* beliefs that die, if we let them, let ourselves be knocked down, kicked aside and left for dead. We owe it to the life in us to resist this killing process – to find the strength, if we can, to go on fighting back and thinking forward – even in face of the ugliness we see around us, the cheated lives, the stunted beings, the deception, the cunning, the denial of potentiality, the visionless mediocrity we seem to be reduced to by our grey bureaucracies and our materialism; loveless and callous and grasping. Recognizing what it is that shuts people off from each other and that keeps them separate, we have to believe that mankind has a future less constricted than the kind of life most people have had to endure for so much of the history of humanity.

We have to believe, yes. But what can give people, as William Morris asks, 'the day-spring of a new hope? What, save general revolt against the tyranny of Commercial war?' For, as with the situation at the end of the nineteenth century, so today,

the palliatives over which many worthy people are busying themselves now are useless: because they are but unorganized partial revolts against a vast wide-spreading grasping organization which will, with the unconscious instinct of a plant, meet every attempt at bettering the condition of the people with an attack on a fresh side; new machines, new markets, wholesale emigration, the revival of grovelling superstitions, preachments of thrift to lack-alls, of temperance to the wretched; such things as these will baffle at every turn all partial revolts against the monster we of the middle classes have created for our undoing.'[5]

Much has happened since Morris wrote this. The monster he cites – that system of capitalistic enterprise which has governed and determined the kind of lives people are capable of living in the Western democracies – has driven us through the horrors of two world wars, and created other monsters in its wake. And though a great deal of progress has been made on so many fronts, we have still to count the incalculable losses we have suffered to get where we have got. And where, we might ask, *have* we got? How much closer are we now than we were in Morris's time to creating the kind of society Morris envisaged? It seems to me that the issues he raised – of art and commerce, of riches and poverty, of privilege and deprivation, of class and class, of exploitation and freedom, of misery and happiness, of ruin and regeneration, of the struggle for emancipation, for justice and for the principle of human delight – are still as deeply with us today as they were with him. And in spite of all the changes that have come about, we seem to be as far from finding an answer to these issues now as then. Man, he wrote in 1884 – no doubt with the rapid transformations brought about by the industrial and technological developments of his age in mind – 'has almost completely conquered nature, and one would think should now have leisure to turn his thoughts towards higher things than procuring tomorrow's dinner'. But unfortunately he didn't seem able to turn his thoughts towards anything that was not conditioned and determined by the alienating power of property and capital and commerce, the laws of the market and the pursuit of territory and of personal enrichment. And have the ninety years of progress that have followed made much difference? 'Alas!' we might say, with Morris, whose words have lost little of their urgency or relevance,

his progress has been broken and halting; and though he has indeed conquered Nature and has her forces under his control to do what he will with, he still has himself to conquer, he still has to think how he will best use those forces which he has mastered. At present he uses them blindly, foolishly, as one driven by mere fate. It would almost seem as if some phantom of the ceaseless pursuit of food which was once the master of the savage was still hunting the civilized man; who toils in a dream, as it were, haunted by mere dim unreal hopes, born of vague recollections of the days gone by. *Out of that dream he must wake, and face things as they really are.* The conquest of Nature is complete, may we not say? and now our business is and has for long been the organization of man, who wields the forces of Nature. Nor till this is attempted at least shall we ever be free of that terrible phantom of fear of starvation which, with its brother devil, desire of domination, drives us into injustice, cruelty, and dastardliness of all kinds: to cease to fear our fellows and learn to depend on them, to do away with competition and build up cooperation, is our one necessity.[6]

The problem is, how to make this clear; how to create conditions that will diminish fear and encourage inter-dependence; how to overcome selfishness, the desire of domination that drives us to injustice; how to counteract and re-direct blind instinct, to create awareness and a sense of connectedness among people long indoctrinated against the principles of community. This is a problem, of course, of education – not of education as conceived in terms of the ruling establishment, which forms part of the system of indoctrination whose purpose it is to perpetuate the status quo and to neutralize all opposition; but of education for change, education directed to freeing people to think openly and connectedly, in political and social terms. And thus it is first and foremost a problem of political and social awareness – of 'educating people to a sense of their real capacities as men, so that they may be able to use to their own good the political power' which their awareness gives them.[7] Because the larger issues cannot be solved at all unless the problem of the uses (and abuses) of political (and economic) power can be solved, which is the key to the achievement of that equality of condition, that shared and sharing concept of community, men have paid such passionate lip-service to and fallen so disastrously short of when *given* the power to work towards it.

For of course in reality we are, as Morris puts it, 'so hemmed in by wrong and folly, that in one way or another we must always be fighting against them: our own lives may see no end to the struggle, perhaps no obvious hope of the end. It may be that the best we can hope to see is that struggle getting sharper and bitterer day by day, until it breaks out openly at last into the slaughter of men by actual warfare instead of by the slower and crueller methods of "peaceful" commerce,'[8] or peaceful indoctrination by dogma. Which is to say that violent change may be the only solution to the problem of creating a more rational society based upon equality of condition – a solution as necessary and as unavoidable as it is unpalatable, given the stubbornness of those who stand in the way.

Necessary? Have we not, with our astonishing technological advances, made such fundamental changes *un*necessary? Can we not be content to let the liberal bourgeois social order that governs (for instance) the British way of life make its way by evolution to a gradual balancing out of the scales between the imbalanced classes? Has the evolutionary process not demonstrated, over the last two hundred years, a slow and steady progress? Have we not begun at last to see the healing of divisions? The *shaping* of equality? Do we need a revolution?

Morris looked upon his world with open eyes, confronting the filth and squalor, the harshness and the terrifying insensitivity of a system at its brashest height and at its worst. And he looked to socialism as to an untested alternative, the logical outcome of the actual history of capitalism – for, as he saw it, 'while all men, even its declared enemies, will be working to bring Socialism about, the aims of those who have learned to believe in the certainty and beneficence of its advent will become clearer, their methods for realizing it clearer also, and at last ready to hand'. And then, as he saw it, recognizing the unlikelihood that any moral sentiment would induce the proprietary classes to yield up their privileges uncompelled, 'will come that open acknowledgement for the necessity of the change (an acknowledgement coming from the intelligence of civilization) which is commonly called Revolution'.[9]

But what seemed to him a certainty was to find itself up against the most bewildering obstacles, none of which were to prove more dismaying to the expectations of revolutionary socialists or more of an incentive to the enemies of socialism than the evidence of the fruits of revolution in Stalinist Russia, its record of repression and of terror. So that now, though the thrust and the momentum of the tyranny of commerce and its capitalist formulation appear to have been blunted and modified by the devastating pressure of events, even to the point of accommodating itself to the principles of socialism, still the 'decaying system' remains intact and vigorous. Its apologists, in fact, would deny that it *is* decaying. They would claim that it thrives – that Western democracy in its modern forms, based upon a mixed economy and a profit market backed by technological expertise, is a far better answer to the needs of society than the totalitarian repressiveness of communism. Thus, the manipulators continue to exploit the irresistible appeal of private enterprise and private ownership and divisive self-interest (however dressed up) against the spirit of community, and to deceive the people into acquiescence and acceptance, the belief that they are free. Thus, on one side and the other:

> The anti-human forces have instilled the thought
> That knowledge has outrun the individual brain

Till trifling details only can be brought
Within the scope of any man; and so have turned
Humanity's vast achievements against the human mind
Until a sense of general impotence compels
Most men in petty grooves to stay confined.

This is the lie of lies – the High Treason to mankind.
No one but fritters half his time away.
It is the human instinct – the will to use it – that's destroyed
Till only one or two in every million men today
Know that thought is reality – and thought alone! –
And must absorb all the material – their goal
The mastery by the spirit of all the facts that can be known.[10]

Reading the impassioned appeal of a Morris or a MacDiarmid
for renewal beyond change, one registers the nature of the changes
that have occurred, checking them against the situation of the
late-nineteenth-century socialist who looks toward the realization
of a free and unfettered life for man. But in doing so one becomes
more and more deeply aware of all that has remained unresolved,
of all that in a world beset by falsifying ideologies retains its
restrictive hold upon the legitimate needs of people; of the forces
that manipulate and thwart; of the values that dictate – the
principles of a bankrupt materialism that determine the very shape
and scope of the life of societies. So that one begins to see that it
is the constricting circumstances imposed upon them that prevent
the majority of people from enjoying the riches of their world,
and what miserable substitutes they are given in place of that
incentive to the organic pleasure and delight of living which ought
to be the fundamental process of the social community. 'Our
concern is human wholeness,' writes Hugh MacDiarmid –

the child-like spirit
New-born every day – not, indeed, as careless of tradition
Nor of the lessons of the past: these it must needs inherit.

But as capable of such complete assimilation and surrender,
So all-inclusive, unfenced-off, uncategorized, sensitive and
tender,
That growth is unconditioned and unwarped [11]

Against such utopian concern, what has this late-twentieth-century Britain to offer as an incentive to its people but an extension (however modified by social palliatives and economic decline) of the same materialistic principles of progress which were so aggressively fostered at the end of the nineteenth? Are not the majority still being fobbed off with cheap substitutes which deprive them of that 'general cultivation of the powers of the mind [and] of the eye and hand'[12] which would equip them actively to experience the riches of their world? Can we say that we now have a world in which men are generally educated or encouraged to look for excellence and beauty in things? Have we really gone much further towards making a priority of seeking the realization of the human wealth that is the potentiality of man as a *human* being rather than as an instrument for the production of material (that is, non-human) wealth? Has the doctrine changed that everywhere prevailed at the end of the nineteenth century – 'that the essential aim of manufacture is making a profit; that it is frivolous to consider whether the wares when made will be of more or less use to the world so long as anyone can be found to buy them at a price which is profitable to the manufacturer'?[13] Are we in any position, today, to deny that 'all education is directed towards the end of fitting people to take their place in the hierarchy of commerce'?[14] That 'even at the ancient universities learning is but little regarded, unless it can in the long run be made to *pay*'? That it is 'this superstition of commerce being an end in itself, of man made for commerce, not commerce for man, of which art has sickened'[15] and with it the arts of humanity? Can we say that the impoverishment created by the domination of the alien power of money and its priority over people has been checked? That against such domination society itself has now begun to assert the logic of man's place at the centre of things, as the source and the beneficiary of the wealth previously at the disposal of the few? Are those who have worked within the system of capitalist competitiveness to better conditions for the under-privileged now seeing their faith in the potentialities of the system justified by results? Let Morris, writing over ninety years ago, again answer in his own words, for their relevance has its own dialectical and temporal impact.

What have they done? How much nearer are they to the ideal of the bourgeois commonwealth than they were at the time of the Reform Bill, or the time of the repeal of the Corn Laws? Well, thus much nearer to a great change, perhaps, that there is a chink in the armour of self-satisfaction; a suspicion that it is perhaps not the accidents of the system of competitive commerce which have to be abolished, but the system itself; but as to approaching the ideal of that system reformed into humanity and decency, they are about so much nearer to it as a man is nearer to the moon when he stands on a hayrick.[16]

To set such a statement against the present is to provide a strangely focused perspective. For many world-shattering things have happened since those words were written – things that have put the Reform Bill and the repeal of the Corn Laws into the dustiest of neglected corners. Two world wars and many lesser wars, the collapse of the British empire, the Russian and Chinese Revolutions, the rise of the electric age and the mass media, the hydrogen bomb, Stalin and the communist dictatorships, the British welfare state and the British Labour Party, etc., etc. In such revolutionary circumstances, one would think the whole basis of the system of competitive commerce must have been transformed out of all recognition, thus invalidating Morris's statement. Strange to record, therefore, how little it has been. In spite of all that has happened, the system of competitive commerce has remained, and the man on the hayrick is still no closer to the moon than he was, even though technology has actually *taken* man to the moon. How strange, how utterly dismaying! The man and the hayrick have survived, and bourgeois liberal laissez-faire has survived, adjusting itself through all these changes to exploit the newest modes of material wealth, and continuing to function at the expense of the mass of the people. It is difficult to credit; yet it seems that it is so. Still we are left with almost everything to do. And still the system prospers. If Morris's hatred of capitalism was first aroused by the ways in which its ruthless methods had gutted and defiled whole areas of the world, he would not have found much to re-assure him in the twentieth century, with the aggressive exploitation of human and material resources exploding in every direction out of the devastating competitiveness of all-out war.

In other words, we do not seem any closer now than we were in the nineteenth century to eliminating the fundamental obstacles that have so long and so obdurately stood against the making of a social order of the kind that Morris defined in his political writings. Because it cannot be said that we are in any better position to envisage 'a society which does not know the meaning of the words rich and poor, or the rights of property, or law and legality, or nationality: a society which has no consciousness of being governed; in which equality of condition is a matter of course, and in which no man is rewarded for having served the community by having the power given him to injure it'.[17]

Even to outline such terms for society is to underline their remoteness from the divisive conditions of the actual world we know, whatever its ideology, capitalist or communist. It is to enumerate the terms of a society which, for most of us, can be envisaged only as an unattainable and faintly absurd, if not frankly dangerous, utopia. And if this is what Morris calls 'dreaming ahead', we might ask whether, confronted by the evidence of the world as it is, there is any *point* in dreaming ahead.

To which it could be answered that the world is as it is because men have made it what it is, and that without the power to create a blueprint for what remains as yet unrealized, we should be unable to see beyond the alienating conditions that *define* the world as it is, and hence powerless to transform them. Indeed, we cannot hope to bring into being any of the unrealized conditions for a free and full life for man unless we are first of all capable of imagining them, and communicating our vision of them with sufficient intensity to prevail upon others to conceive them as potentialities and to believe that the prospects they offer will be worth the effort and determination and courage required to bring them into existence. Of course there are those who have become so conditioned to an acceptance of the world as it is that they are *incapable* of seeing beyond it; and there are others whose purpose it does not serve to look beyond – who are content to believe that things *should* be as they are because it is more comfortable or more profitable to believe so. But once we have become aware of the dislocations and estrangements we are subjected to by the conditioning process of the world as it is, and the manner in which the operative system encourages a narrow trivializing conception of what man can achieve and be, we shall cease to be content with the status quo, and will begin to *need* the kind of vision that enables us to see beyond it. And then perhaps we shall discover in ourselves the disinterested courage with which to confront the underlying contradictions of progress, and the power to act, to work rationally and positively for the future. This is essentially a question of awareness – the kind of awareness (at once objective, critical, dialectical) that seeks clarity and connection from the multiple references which make up the context of reality, and which in their contradictory influence define the historical perspectives on which to proceed.

This kind of awareness has to take into account the various forms in which the abstracts of power become embodied, both in terms of the halfway compromises of capitalist democracy (with their divisive appeal to the individual) and the rigid extremes of dictatorial socialism, intolerant of (individual) dissent. It has to *create* perspectives from the historical pattern and to encourage at all levels a coming-to-grips with the central problems of a divided world.

In this respect, and as a commentary upon the problems connected with the renewal of socialism in Britain, the value of Morris's work lies in the sharpness of the perspectives, the temporal and historical parallels, it has to offer. For the nature of these perspectives and parallels is determined by the manner in which Morris's vision of the historical and social conditions of his own time comes into conjunction with the present to reflect and illuminate the historical and social conditions of late-twentieth-century Britain. Registering the concept of 'the change beyond the change' that is brought into focus in *A Dream of John Ball*, for instance, one is at once aware of the peculiar resonance of the conjunction. For though the book has its inadequacies, particularly in its use of a pseudo-archaic language intended to reflect the rhythms of medieval speech, it defines in the dialogue between Ball and Morris a very subtle interaction between that crucial period in the history of the Middle Ages (the great Peasant Revolt of 1381), when the peasants were about to break free of the bondage of feudal enslavement, and Morris's own time, when the working class seemed about to assert their own struggle for freedom from the bondage of capitalism. Most interesting of all is the way in which Morris conceives and embodies the interaction. John Ball's vision of the struggle to come, ending in the emancipation of the villeins, is envisaged in terms of the dream of a man from the late nineteenth century who finds himself personally observing the struggle. But at the same time this nineteenth-century man is himself embodied as a projection of the future, a prophetic dream-figure in the mind of John Ball. Thus there is a continual interplay between two ages, two crucial historical periods, and further between these and a third, defined in terms of the reader's grasp of his own world, which at once reveals the parallels between them. In the first place, the twentieth-century reader himself creates a perspective of the past and becomes an extension of the nineteenth-century future in his own present. Then we have the man of the late nineteenth century, conscious of the oppressive rule of capitalism at its height, thinking or imagining himself back into an age before that system had come into being, and implicitly forward to the socialist community of the future. And thirdly we have the fourteenth-century man John Ball, participating in an act of history which would free the peasant of his feudal chains, and thinking forward to a new age of freedom for all men. But out of this threefold interaction emerges the dialectical process by which Ball's concept of the freedom for which he is to fight and to die becomes a pre-condition for the new enslavement of man and thus for the new struggle for freedom, as Morris and his reader see it, each from his particular point in time. Not that, on his own, Ball can conceive of this, of the change beyond the change. For him, the freedom he is fighting to bring into being seems an end, an absolute. It is only through his imaginary dream-encounter with the man from the future that he is able to imagine the historical consequences of the struggle. He has to confess to his visitor that he does not even understand:

'I know a thrall, and he is his master's every hour, and never his own; and a villein I know, and whiles he is his own and whiles his lord's; and I know a free man, and he is his own always; but how shall he be his own if he have nought whereby to make his livelihood? Or shall he be a thief and take from others? Then he is an outlaw. Wonderful is this thou tellest me of a free man with nought whereby to live!'

And his visitor answers: 'He must needs buy leave to labour of them that own all things except himself and such as himself.' Still unable to grasp the significance of this, Ball can only ask: 'Yes, but wherewith shall he buy it? What hath he except himself?' Which receives the devastating answer: 'With himself then shall he buy it; with his body and the power of labour that lieth therein; with the price of his labour shall he buy leave to labour.'

John Ball finds this unbelievable and even absurd. For no man, he says, can be 'so great a fool as willingly to take the name of freeman and the life of a thrall as payment for the very life of a freeman'.[18] He *has* to believe this great rising of the people for which he is willing to sacrifice his life will achieve its aim. And indeed his friend assures him that it *will* do so, in spite of the consequences; that it is a necessary step forward in the struggle for freedom. But this dream voice of the future, answering from beyond the coming change and the scope of John Ball's vision, at the same time has to stress that it is only *one* step among many in a long and contradictory struggle which can only finally be resolved when men, having learned at last to work together against the forces that divide, will have decided to use their freedoms to create another *kind* of world.

It is the essence of Morris's vision of the future that he should have envisaged the struggle for it as rooted in the contradictory patterns of the historical process. He is able to look ahead with confidence beyond the squalid confusions and disorders of his own world because he is able to perceive, out of the links and perspectives of the past, the stages of a living record that reflects and confirms the continuity of the struggle. 'It is not we,' as he says,

who can build up the new social order; the past ages have done the most of that work for us; but we can clear our eyes to the signs of the times, and we shall then see that the attainment of a good condition of life is being made possible for us, and that it is now our business to stretch out our hands to take it.[19]

And though he knew that he himself would never be around to witness the moment of eventual triumph when mastery would at last be changed to fellowship, he did not doubt that this moment would come. It was his task to help to bring it about by working towards it in the practical terms that his vision of the future defined for him as the indispensáble means. Nor did he flinch from the fact that the struggle for it might have to be a violent one. In *News From Nowhere*, set in a world in which the new society has already become an actuality, he had old Hammond recount in detail the terrible period of revolutionary war through which (as he maintains) Britain had to pass before the change could be brought about, and even then at the risk of defeat.

This detailed history of an imagined future conflict is not

invalidated by the fact that in the real world it did not take place at the time Morris specified. In fact, it is in a deep sense authenticated in terms of the nine crucial days of the 1926 General Strike and the ways these reflect and echo the preliminary stages of the struggle delineated in *News From Nowhere*. Though no one in the nineties could have foreseen the actual course of events or would have had the audacity or the courage to face up to such a prospect if they had been given even a *glimpse* of the insane destructiveness of Europe in twentieth century, one cannot help wondering what revolutionary changes might not have occurred if another *kind* of war had not broken out in 1939 to divert and sap the energies of the oppressed millions. But that the revolution Morris depicted in such graphic detail did not take place (as predicted) in the 1950s, and that there seems to be no prospect of it happening in the foreseeable future, simply underlines the resilience and the obstinacy of the barriers that stand in the way of radical change, even as the blunt facts of Morris's revolutionary war underline the intensity of commitment and determination required to break through them.

For of course there can be no illusion, in the struggle against luxury and poverty, privilege and deprivation, that the forces which thrive on deceit, hypocrisy and exploitation will voluntarily yield their ground, or simply melt away. Confronting us on every side, appealing to us to abide by the instituted machinery of law and order set up to protect their interests, often invisibly at work through the medium of technological controls that appear to be the very embodiment of Reason, they remain as unregenerate and as deeply entrenched as ever. And if there is ever to be any hope of *breaking* the power of such forces and of replacing it with a social and political order dedicated at one and the same time to the practice of co-operative and communal principles and the liberation of the individual for the common enrichment of humanity, a great deal is going to have to depend upon our ability to recognize and to mark down those who would frustrate such hopes, and to stand up to them with our own intrinsic human powers. This, the challenge and the task that lies ahead, must be directed towards 'the control and conscious mastery of those powers which, born of the action of men on one another, have till now overawed and governed men as powers completely alien to them'.[20] And it has to be pursued in the full awareness that, since you cannot reason with the enemies of reason, you have to know exactly who these enemies are and what they stand for, clearly and objectively, in terms that lie beyond our own subjective needs and predilections.

If reason can be said to be that conscious ordering process which enables a man to harness his various powers and faculties to an objective realization of the issues and problems of his world, at its highest it is that same process directed towards the liberation of the constructive powers of the human mind, the conquest of fear and insecurity and ignorance, the encouragement of social and communal awareness, and hence the establishment of a free and full life for all men at all levels of their lives. In this sense it is that weapon which, above all others, those who are working to re-shape society must make themselves the masters of and learn to use with honesty and courage, in order that the millions who still live repressed and constricted lives may at last be freed from the bondage that has held them down to become the makers of their world – not 'implicitly and in essence, but in existence and in reality'.[21]

But can such a weapon prevail against the ignorance, confusion and apathy upon which the enemies of reason prosper? Morris believed it could. He believed that, with 'intelligence enough to conceive of a life of equality and co-operation; courage enough to accept it and to bring the necessary skill to bear on working it; and power enough to force its acceptance on the stupid and the interested, the war of the classes would speedily end in the victory of the useful class, which would then become the New Society of Equality'.[22] But unfortunately it is not as simple as that. From where we stand today, it is bluntly apparent that intelligence, courage and power are not in themselves enough, even in their application to a revolutionary situation, to break down the formidable barriers that keep people divided and estranged from each other.

Indeed today it almost seems as though we are still at the beginning. For, in spite of the astonishing technological developments of the last sixty years, and all the transformations that have occurred in that short period of time, the barriers appear to be as immovable as ever, because of the new and lethal abstracts of ideology these developments – and with them the emergence of the so-called super-powers – have brought into being. Still it has to be admitted, as Marx wrote in 1844, that the movement of history has not yet become 'the real history of man as a given subject'; that it is still no more than 'the *process of his creation*, the *history of his emergence*'.[23] In other words, it has yet to become the process of his *emancipation*, the history of his *emancipation* – which must mean, if it is to mean anything at all, the process of his emancipation from *all* the alienating powers that stand against him. For in Marx's dialectic it is only 'through the destruction of the *estranged* character of the objective world, through the supercession of its estranged modes of existence'[24] – in terms of a society fully developed at all levels to provide the economic and social conditions conducive to the development of his highest interests and needs – that man can overcome these alienating powers, and achieve his emancipation, the 'vindication of real human life as his true property, the emergence of practical humanism'.[25]

This is the fundamental problem. It is a problem too intricately bound up with the contradictory process of the humam record to permit us to build for the future with any dogmatic assurance of success. We have to take into account not simply the will and determination of those who are actively working for the socialist transformation of society as against the relative power and scope of those whose aim it is to maintain control of the instruments and divisive conditions of the status quo. The very terms and objectives of this conflict depend upon the general level of awareness among ordinary people of all kinds, and the extent to which they have been conditioned into acceptance or are capable of recognizing the crucial part that they, above all, have to play in the making of their world. And all this in turn depends upon the nature of the general economic, social and historical conditions that determine the structure of a particular society and the directions in which it can develop.

It has been the task of this book to indicate the complex nature of the problems that face us, and the need for an unillusory awareness of what is required of us and what is at stake. But the recognition of all that needs to be done naturally goes far beyond what can be declared and defined within the limits of a book. It demands that we begin from where we are as particular individuals in terms of the conditions that define the actualities of our lives; that we think forward into the future from out of the contradictory grounded proofs of struggle that have made our world what it is, in a ruthless criticism of the existing order of things; and that as we think we create the grounds from which to *build* for the future. We have to concern ourselves, in a divided world, with possibilities and potentialities – keeping the distinctions clear between actuality and dream, desire and despair, holding ourselves open to delight and the challenge of the future, and doing what we can, as new contradictions emerge out of the complex pattern of the historical process, to direct our energies towards the making of a world that will embody that practical humanism Marx envisaged as 'a community of men that can fulfil their highest needs'.[26]

BIBLIOGRAPHY

Acton, Lord, *Essays on Freedom and Power*, Meridian (New York),
     1955.
Arendt, Hannah, *On Revolution*, Penguin Books, 1973.
Arnold, Matthew, *Culture and Anarchy*, C.U.P., 1932.
Aron, Raymond, *Progress and Disillusion*, Penguin Books, 1972.
Barraclough, Geoffrey, *An Introduction to Contemporary History*, Penguin
     Books, 1967.
Benjamin, Walter, *Illuminations*, Fontana, 1973.
Berger, John, *G*, Penguin Books, 1973.
     A Painter of Our Time, Writers and Readers, 1976.
Blake, William, *Complete Writings*, O.U.P., 1974.
Bloch, Ernst, *On Karl Marx*, New York, 1971, selections from *The
     Principle of Hope*.
Brecht, Bertolt, *Plays, Poetry and Prose*, Eyre Methuen.
Burke, Edmund, *Reflections on the Revolution in France*, Penguin Books,
     1969.
Carr, E. H., *What is History?*, Penguin Books, 1978.
Caudwell, Christopher, *Illusion and Reality* (new edition), 1946.
Collingwood, R. G., *An Autobiography*, O.U.P., 1939.
     The Idea of History, O.U.P., 1961.
Craig, David (editor), *Marxists on Literature*, Penguin Books, 1975.
     Includes pieces by Engels, Marx, Lenin, Plekhanov, Trotsky,
     Serge, Kettle, Lukács, Brecht and Fischer.
Debray, Régis, *A Critique of Arms*, Penguin Books, 1977.
Deutscher, Isaac, *Stalin*, Penguin Books, 1966.
     Trotsky, O.U.P., in three volumes – I: *The Prophet Armed;
     1879–1921*; II: *The Prophet Unarmed; 1921–1929*; III: *The Prophet
     Outcast; 1929–1940*.
Engels, Friedrich, *Anti-Dühring*, Foreign Languages Publishing House,
     1959.
     Selected Works of Marx and Engels, Lawrence & Wishart, 1968.
Ewen, Frederic, *Bertolt Brecht*, Calder & Boyars, 1970.
Fischer, Ernst, *The Necessity of Art*, Penguin Books, 1978.
Fromm, Erich, *The Sane Society*, Routledge & Kegan Paul, 1956.
Gramsci, Antonio, *Prison Notebooks*, Lawrence & Wishart, 1971.
     (*See also* Joll.)
Hamburger, Michael, *The Truth of Poetry*, Penguin Books, 1972.
Hauser, Arnold, *The Social History of Art*, Routledge & Kegan Paul,
     1962 – in four volumes – I: *Prehistoric to the Middle Ages*;

II: *Renaissance, Mannerism, Baroque*; III: *Rococo, Classicism and Romanticism*; IV: *Naturalism, Impressionism, the Film Age.*

Hill, Christopher, *The World Turned Upside Down*, Penguin Books, 1975.

God's Englishman, Penguin Books, 1972.

Reformation to Industrial Revolution, Penguin Books, 1976.

Hobsbawm, E. J., *The Age of Revolution: Europe 1789–1848*, Cardinal, 1973.

Huizinga, Johan, *Men and Ideas*, Eyre & Spottiswoode, 1960.

Joll, James, *Antonio Gramsci*, Fontana, 1977.

Kolakowski, Leszek, *Marxism and Beyond*, Paladin, 1971.

Main Currents in Marxism, O.U.P., 1978, in three volumes – I: *The Founders*; II: *The Golden Age*; III: *The Breakdown.*

Lenin, V. I., *Selected Works*, Foreign Languages Press Peking, including: *What is to be Done*; *Materialism and Empirio-Criticism*; *The State and Revolution.*
(*See also* Shub.)

Lucas, John (editor), *Literature and Politics in the Nineteenth Century*, Methuen, 1971.

Lukács, Georg, *History and Class Consciousness*, Merlin, 1971.

The Historical Novel, Penguin Books, 1969.

The Meaning of Contemporary Realism, Merlin, 1970.

Essays on Thomas Mann, Merlin, 1964.

Mann, Thomas, *Selected Letters*, Penguin Books, 1975.

The Magic Mountain, Secker & Warburg, 1954.

Marcuse, Herbert, *One-Dimensional Man*, Abacus, 1972.

Eros and Civilisation, Abacus, 1972.

Reason and Revolution, Routledge & Kegan Paul, 1955.

Negations, Penguin University Books, 1972.

Marx, Karl, *Selected Works*, Lawrence & Wishart, 1968, including *The Communist Manifesto*; *Wages, Price and Profit*; *The Civil War in France*; and Friedrich Engels' *Socialism, Utopian and Scientific*; *The Origin of the Family*; *Ludwig Feuerbach and the End of Classical German Philosophy.*

The Pelican Marx Library, from 1973: *The Early Writings*; *The Revolutions of 1848*; *Surveys from Exile*; *The First International and After*; *Grundrisse.*

Capital, Everyman, 1974; with introduction by G. D. H. Cole.

Capital, Moscow, 1965.

Milliband, Ralph, *The State in Capitalist Society*, Quartet, 1973.

Mitchell, David, *1919: Red Mirage*, Cape, 1970.

Morris, Margaret, *The General Strike 1926*, Penguin Books, 1976.

Morris, William, *Political Writings* (edited by A. L. Morton), Lawrence & Wishart, 1973.

Three Works by William Morris: The Pilgrims of Hope, A Dream of John Ball, News From Nowhere, Lawrence & Wishart, 1973.
(See also Thompson.)

Namier, Sir Lewis, *Vanished Supremacies*, Penguin Books, 1962.

Neruda, Pablo, *Memoirs*, Penguin Books, 1978.

Orwell, George, *Selected Essays*, Mercury, 1961.
Homage to Catalonia, Penguin Books, 1966.
Animal Farm, Penguin Books, 1951.
1984, Penguin Books, 1954.

Paine, Thomas, *The Rights of Man*, Penguin Books, 1969.

Popper, Karl, *The Open Society and its Enemies*, Routledge & Kegan Paul, 1962 – in two volumes – I: *Plato*; II: *Hegel and Marx*.

Reich, Wilhelm, *The Mass Psychology of Fascism*, Penguin Books, 1975.

Rickword, Edgell, *Literature in Society*, Carcanet, 1978.

Rühle, Jurgen, *Literature and Revolution*, Pall Mall, 1969.

Serge, Victor, *Memoirs of a Revolutionary*, O.U.P., 1963.
Birth of Our Power, Writers and Readers, 1977.
Conquered City, Writers and Readers, 1975.

Sholokhov, Mikhail, *The Don Novels*, Penguin Books, from 1967.

Shub, David, *Lenin*, Penguin Books, 1966.

Sinclair, Andrew, *Che Guevara*, Fontana, 1970.

Tawney, R. H., *The Acquisitive Society*, Fontana, 1961.
Religion and the Rise of Capitalism, Penguin Books, 1977.
Equality, Unwin, 1964.
The Radical Tradition, Allen & Unwin, 1964.

Taylor, A. J. P., *The Origins of the Second World War*, Penguin Books, 1964.

Thompson, E. P., *William Morris: Romantic to Revolutionary*, Merlin, 1977.
The Making of the English Working Class, Penguin Books, 1968.
The Poverty of Theory, Merlin, 1978.

Trotsky, Leon, *1905*, Penguin Books, 1973.
My Life, Penguin Books, 1975.
Literature and Revolution, University of Michigan Press, 1971.
The Third International after Lenin, New Park, 1974.
The Struggle against Fascism in Germany, Penguin Books, 1975.
The Revolution Betrayed, New Park, 1973.
(*See also* Deutscher.)

Watt, Richard M., *The Kings Depart: The German Revolution and the Treaty of Versailles 1918–19*, Penguin Books, 1973.

White, George Abbott (editor), *Literature in Revolution*, Holt Rinehart, 1972.

Willey, Basil, *The Eighteenth Century Background*, Penguin Books, 1962.

Williams, Raymond, *Culture and Society*, Penguin Books, 1963.
   Marxism and Literature, O.U.P., 1977.
Wilson, Angus, *The World of Charles Dickens*, Penguin Books, 1972.
Wilson, Edmund, *To the Finland Station*, Fontana, 1974.

NOTES

The following abbreviations are used:

> Blake, *CW*: William Blake, *Complete Writings* (O.U.P., 1974).
> Marx, *EW*: Karl Marx, *Early Writings* (Pelican Marx Library, 1975).
> *FI*: Karl Marx, *The First International and After* (Pelican Marx Library, 1974).
> *R1848*: Karl Marx, *The Revolutions of 1848* (Pelican Marx Library, 1973).
> *SE*: Karl Marx, *Surveys from Exile* (Pelican Marx Library, 1973).
> Morris, *PW*: William Morris, *Political Writings* (Lawrence & Wishart, 1973).

In a few places, minor alterations have been made to the translations of Marx's works.

1. THEORY AND PRACTICE: A DIVIDED WORLD

1. Tom Paine, *The Rights of Man* (Penguin Books, 1969), p. 290.
2. Lucio Colletti, Introduction to Marx, *EW*, p. 50.
3. Marx, *Critique of Hegel's Doctrine of the State*, *EW*, p. 87, and *Excerpts from James Mill's 'Elements of Political Economy'*, *EW*, p. 265.
4. Arthur Bryant, *English Saga* (Collins, 1940).
5. Marx, *Excerpts from James Mill's 'Elements of Political Economy'*, *EW*, pp. 265–6.
6. Marx, *Critique of Hegel's Philosophy of Right*, *EW*, pp. 244–5.
7. Marx, *Economic and Philosophical Manuscripts*, *EW*, p. 349.
8. Marx, *Critique of Hegel's Philosophy of Right*, *EW*, p. 246.
9. Marx, letter to Ruge (Kreuznach, September 1843), *EW*, p. 209.
10. Marx, letter to Ruge (Cologne, May 1843), *EW*, p. 201.
11. Victor Serge, *Memoirs of a Revolutionary* (O.U.P., 1963), pp. 374–5.
12. ibid., p. 373.
13. ibid., p. 374.
14. ibid., p. 372.
15. Bertrand Russell, *Freedom and Organisation* (Allen & Unwin, 1934).
16. William Faulkner, Nobel Prize Declaration.

17. Marx, Letter to Ruge (September 1843), *EW*, p. 208.
18. Marx, *Feuerbach Theses*, II, *EW*, p. 422.
19. Marx, *Theses*, V, *EW*, p. 422.
20. Russell, op. cit., p. 222.
21. Matthew Arnold, 'The Function of Criticism', in *The Essential Matthew Arnold*, edited Lionel Trilling (Chatto & Windus, 1949), p. 247.
22. Arnold, *Culture and Anarchy* (C.U.P., 1932), p. 212.
23. Marx, *Economic and Philosophical Manuscripts*, *EW*, p. 354.
24. Russell, op. cit., p. 222.
25. Edmund Burke, *Reflections on the Revolution in France* (Penguin Books, 1968), p. 195.
26. Paine, op. cit., p. 64.
27. Burke, op. cit., p. 108. The terms of this declaration bind 'us and our heirs, and our posterity, to them, their heirs, and their posterity . . . to the end of time'.
28. ibid., p. 195.
29. Old Testament, Genesis iii: 22.
30. William Blake, *Jerusalem*, *CW*, p. 700.
31. Quoted in Jacob Bronowski's *William Blake and the Age of Revolution* (Routledge, 1972), p. 149.
32. Paine, op. cit., p. 67.
33. Burke, op. cit., pp. 182, 195.
34. Paine, op. cit., p. 79.
35. Lord Acton, 'The History of Freedom in Antiquity', in *Essays on Freedom and Power* (Meridian, 1955), p. 70.
36. Blake, *Jerusalem*, *CW*, p. 714.
37. Tolstoy, *Resurrection*.
38. Fredric Jameson, *Marxism and Form* (Princeton University Press, 1974), p. 41.
39. ibid., Preface, p. xiii.
40. Marx, *Feuerbach Theses*, *II*, *EW*, p. 422.
41. Marx, *Theses*, I, p. 421.
42. Marx, *Theses*, VI, p. 423.
43. W. H. Auden, *New Year Letter* (Faber & Faber), lines 1376–87.
44. Fichte, from the *Wissenschaftslehre* (*Doctrine of Knowledge*) and the later lectures.
45. Fichte, *Addresses to the German People* (1807–8). E. W. F. Tomlin, in *Great Philosophers of the West* (Grey Arrow, 1959), writes: 'Fichte's Addresses to his countrymen, in which he expounded his ideas in words of great patriotic fervour, undoubtedly had a great deal to do with the uprush of German nationalism at a time when the French army, sweeping over Europe, had occupied and dismembered Europe' (pp. 215–6). Bertrand Russell discusses

Fichte in *Freedom and Organisation*. See also the *Encyclopaedia Britannica* (1968), Vol. 9, pp. 234–6.

46. Friedrich Nietzsche, *Also Spracht Zarathustra*: Part One: 'Of the Bestowing Virtue', 2 (Penguin Books, 1961), p. 103.

47. Thomas Mann, *Order of the Day: Culture and Politics* (Knopf, 1942), p. 229.

48. ibid., p. 233.

49. T. S. Eliot, *Gerontion* (1920), from *Selected Poems* (Faber & Faber, 1954), p. 32.

50. Mann, op. cit., p. 233.

2. MARX: THE CRITICAL CHALLENGE AND ITS CONSEQUENCES

1. Leszek Kolakowski, *Marxism and Beyond* (Paladin, 1971), p. 205.

2. Marx, article in the *Neue Rheinische Zeitung*, 31 December 1848, *R1848*, p. 201. One of a series of articles written for the *Neue Rheinische Zeitung* by Marx and Engels between 1 June 1848 and 19 May 1849.

3. Marx, *The Class Struggles in France*, *SE*, p. 58.

4. Marx, article in *N.R.Z.*, 15 December 1848, *R1848*, p. 190.

5. ibid., p. 191.

6. ibid., p. 194.

7. Marx and Engels, Address of the Central Committee to the Communist League, March 1850, *R1848*, p. 323.

8. Frederick Engels, article in *N.R.Z.*, *15 February 1849*, *R1848*, p. 231.

9. Marx and Engels, *N.R.Z. Review*, May–October 1850, *R1848*, p. 316.

10. Giuseppe Mazzini (and others), Manifesto of the Central Committee of European Democracy – To the Peoples, 6 August 1850, *R1848*, p. 317.

11. Marx, letter to Ruge, September 1843, *EW*, p. 208.

12. Marx, *Economic and Philosophical Manuscripts*, *EW*, p. 354.

13. Marx, Address to General Council of the International Working Men's Association on the Franco–Prussian War, 26 July 1870, *FI*, p. 176.

14. Leon Trotsky, *Literature and Revolution* (University of Michigan Press, 1960), p. 98.

15. ibid., p. 98.

16. Marx, *The Communist Manifesto*.

17. Edmund Wilson, *To the Finland Station* (Fontana, 1974), pp. 335–6.

18. ibid., p. 329.

19. Marx, Inaugural Address to the International Working Men's Association, *FI*, p. 78.

20. ibid., p. 82.
21. ibid., p. 83.
22. Marx, *The Communist Manifesto*, II, *R1848*, p. 86.
23. Lenin, *The State and Revolution* (Peking, 1973), p. 107.
24. Isaac Deutscher, *Stalin* (Penguin Books, 1966), p. 253.
25. ibid., p. 255.
26. ibid., p. 275.
27. Trotsky, *My Life* (Penguin Books, 1975), p. 536.
28. Daniel Counihan, Article in *The Listener*.
29. Marx, *Economic and Philosophical Manuscripts*, *EW*, p. 350.
30. ibid., p. 352.
31. Osip Mandelstam, quoted in David Mitchell, *1919: Red Mirage* (Cape, 1970), p. 76.
32. Lenin, *Letter to the Workers of America*, in Mitchell, op. cit., p. 43.
33. Gerard Manley Hopkins, Letter to Robert Bridges, 2 August 1871, in *Poems and Prose*, edited W. H. Gardner (Penguin Books, 1953), p. 171.
34. Arthur Ransome, 'The Truth About Russia', 1919, in Mitchell, op. cit., p. 68.
35. William Morris, *How We Live and How We Might Live* (1884), *PW*, p. 138.
36. ibid., p. 158.
37. Thomas Mann, 'This Peace', in *Order of the Day* (Knopf, 1942), pp. 174–5.
38. William Morris, *Useful Work versus Useless Toil* (1884), *PW*, p. 98.
39. Mitchell, op. cit., pp. 98–9.
40. ibid., p. 324.
41. Lenin, 'The Infantile Disease of Leftism' (1920), in Mitchell, op. cit., pp. 330–31.
42. Lenin, 'At the Tenth Party Congress', in Mitchell, op. cit., p. 332.
43. Lenin, quoted in Mitchell, op. cit., p. 330.
44. Bertrand Russell, *The Practice and Theory of Bolshevism* (Allen & Unwin, 1920), quoted in Mitchell, op. cit., p. 341.
45. Mitchell, op. cit., p. 233.

3 · MASS MANIPULATION AND THE SURVIVAL OF DISSENT

1. Herbert Marcuse, *One-Dimensional Man* (Abacus, 1972), p. 88.
2. ibid., p. 153.
3. ibid., p. 22.
4. ibid., p. 156.
5. ibid., p. 195.
6. Trotsky, *Literature and Revolution* (University of Michigan Press, 1960), p. 101.

7. Leszek Kolakowski, *Marxism and Beyond* (Paladin, 1971), p. 55.
8. ibid., p. 56.
9. ibid., p. 57.
10. ibid., p. 141.
11. ibid., p. 156.
12. ibid., p. 142.
13. ibid., p. 132.
14. ibid., p. 167.
15. ibid., p. 174.
16. ibid., p. 143.
17. ibid., p. 143.
18. ibid., p. 102.
19. ibid., p. 192.
20. Victor Serge, *Memoirs of a Revolutionary* (O.U.P., 1963), pp. 375–6.
21. Bertolt Brecht, *Poems – Part Three 1938–1956* (Eyre Methuen, 1976), pp. 437–8.
22. George Steiner, in *The Listener*.
23. Brecht, op, cit., p. 440.
24. ibid., pp. 450–51.
25. Ernst Bloch, in Jurgen Rühle's *Literature and Revolution* (Pall Mall, 1969), p. 291.
26. Fredrick Ewen, *Bertolt Brecht* (Calder & Boyars, 1970), p. 450.
27. ibid., p. 479.
28. Jurgen Rühle, *Literature and Revolution*, p. 291. This comes from Gropp's *Ernst Blochs Revision des Marxismus* (East Berlin, 1957), p. 10.
29. ibid., p. 290.
30. ibid., details, pp. 287–93. Bloch, regarded, with Karl Korsch and Georg Lukács, as Germany's most outstanding theoretician of revolutionary Marxism (218), left East Germany in 1961 for the University of Tübingen, never to return.
31. Kolakowski, op. cit., p. 178.
32. ibid., p. 189.
33. Marx, *Economic and Philosophical Manuscripts*, *EW*, p. 350.
34. Blake, *Jerusalem*, *CW*, p. 738.
35. Ewen, op. cit., p. 479.
36. Kolakowski, op. cit., p. 109.
37. ibid., p. 203.
38. ibid., p. 157.
39. Isaac Deutscher, *The Prophet Outcast* (O.U.P., 1963), p. 336. See also the account of this period in Deutscher's *Stalin* (Penguin Books, 1966), pp. 366–82.
40. ibid., pp. 323–4.

41. Deutscher, *The Prophet Armed* (O.U.P., 1954), p. 54. From Trotsky's pamphlet; *Our Political Tasks* (Geneva, 1904).
42. Deutscher, *The Prophet Outcast*, p. 259.
43. ibid., pp. 206–7.
44. Serge, op. cit., p. 365.
45. Marx, letter to Ruge, May 1843, *EW*, p. 201.
46. Marx, *The Communist Manifesto*, *R1848*, p. 82.
47. ibid., p. 98.
48. ibid., p. 98.
49. Marx, *Economic and Philosophical Manuscripts*, *EW*, p. 359.
50. Wilhelm Reich, *The Mass Psychology of Fascism* (Penguin Books, 1972), pp. 105–6.
51. ibid., p. 30.
52. ibid., p. 29.
53. Kolakowski, op. cit., p. 52.
54. ibid., p. 99.
55. ibid., p. 96.
56. ibid., p. 58.
57. Marx, Preface to *A Critique of Political Economy*.
58. Kolakowski, op. cit., p. 205.

4. DISLOCATION AND DESPAIR: ELIOT'S VIEW OF HISTORY

1. T. S. Eliot, *Gerontion*, from *Poems 1920*.
2. Cardinal Newman (1801–90), *The Dream of Gerontius* (1865).
3. John Berger, *G* (Penguin Books, 1973), p. 64.
4. R. G. Collingwood, *An Autobiography* (O.U.P., 1939), p. 112.
5. Fredric Jameson, *Marxism and Form* (Princeton University Press, 1974), p. 134.
6. Eliot, *The Idea of a Christian Society*, 1939.
7. These and the following lines are from Eliot's *The Hollow Men* (1925).
8. Joseph Conrad, *Heart of Darkness*, 'Mistah Kurtz – he dead' is the epigraph chosen by Eliot from the Conrad novel, though it seems he had originally chosen Kurtz's own exclamation 'The Horror! The Horror!'
9. Eliot, *Ash-Wednesday*, VI and II.
10. Ezra Pound, *Literary Essays* (Faber and Faber, 1954), p. 420.
11. Eliot, *Four Quartets*, 'Burnt Norton': III.
12. Eliot, Chorus from *The Rock*.
13. Georg Lukács, *The Historical Novel* (Penguin Books, 1969), p. 321.
14. Lewis Namier, *Vanished Supremacies* (Penguin Books, 1962), p. 216.
15. Georg Lukács, *The Meaning of Contemporary Realism* (Merlin, 1963), p. 54.

16. ibid., p. 62.
17. ibid., p. 63.
18. Eliot, *The Love Song of J. Alfred Prufrock*, (1917).
19. Eliot, *The Waste Land*, III: 'The Fire Sermon' (1922).
20. The allusions and literary associations in which *The Waste Land* abounds provide a rich counterpoint, invoking the cultures of the past, the spirit of a lost world, even from the very first line with its ironic echo of the first line of Chaucer's *Canterbury Tales*.
21. Eliot, *Four Quartets*, 'The Dry Salvages': III.
22. ibid., 'Burnt Norton': II.
23. ibid., 'Burnt Norton': III.
24. ibid., 'East Coker': V.
25. Eliot, Introduction to Baudelaire's *Intimate Journals*, 1930 (*Selected Prose*, edited John Hayward, Penguin Books, 1953), p. 193.
26. Eliot, Editorial Commentary in *Criterion* (April 1933).
27. Victor Serge, *Memoirs of a Revolutionary* (O.U.P., 1963), p. 374.
28. Eliot, *After Strange Gods* (1934), p. 12.
29. Eliot, 'The Literature of Fascism', *Criterion* (1928).
30. Eliot, *Criterion* (1929).
31. Eliot, *Criterion* (1928).
32. Eliot, *Thoughts After Lambeth* (1931).
33. Eliot, *The Idea of a Christian Society* (1939).
34. ibid.
35. William Chace, *The Political Identities of Ezra Pound and T. S. Eliot* (Stanford University Press, 1972), p. 205.
36. Eliot, *Four Quartets*, 'The Dry Salvages': V.
37. F. R. Leavis, *The Living Principle* (Chatto & Windus, 1978), p. 228.
38. Eliot, *The Cocktail Party*, Act Two (Faber & Faber, 1953), p. 126.
39. Eliot, *Ash-Wednesday*, the opening lines.
40. Leszek Kolakowski, *Marxism and Beyond* (Paladin, 1971), p. 174.
41. Georg Lukács, *The Meaning of Contemporary Realism*, p. 61.

5. DICKENS: THE INTUITIVE RADICAL

1. Matthew Arnold, *Culture and Anarchy* (C.U.P., 1932; reissued 1960), p. 73.
2. ibid., 69.
3. Arnold Kettle, 'Dickens and the Popular Tradition', in *Marxists on Literature*, edited by David Craig (Penguin Books, 1975), p. 242.
4. ibid., p. 243.
5. Karl Marx, *Economic and Philosophical Manuscripts*, *EW*, p. 379.
6. Shakespeare, Timon of Athens, Act IV, Scene 3.
7. Marx, *Economic and Philosophical Manuscripts*, *EW*, p. 377.
8. It is particularly apt, in the light of Marx's commentary on money

(*EW*, pp. 375–9), to think of the ways in which, in *Our Mutual Friend*, Dickens conceives of money (and property) as an elemental source of corruption, corroding, perverting and undermining the pattern of individual and social relationships. It is a river of filth, a mound of dust, a falsifying standard; it turns people into objects and twists feelings out of all proportion; it creates boredom and disillusionment and voids of class discrimination; it eats away at the personality or distorts it into such crippling and inhibiting forms as to poison the whole being of a man. In one way or another all the characters in this novel are affected – Lizzie and Eugene, Bella and John Harmon, Mr and Mrs Boffin, Bradley Headstone, Wegg and Riderhood, Betty Higden, Jenny, the Wilfers, the Podsnaps, the Veneerings, the Lammles and Twemlow.

 9. Charles Dickens, in *The Examiner*, 1848, from Angus Wilson's *The World of Charles Dickens* (Penguin Books, 1972), p. 73.
10. G. K. Chesterton, Introduction to *A Tale of Two Cities* (Macmillan, The Scholar's Library, 1934), pp. viii–ix.
11. Wilson, op. cit., p. 222.
12. Dickens, a letter of 1844, on *The Christmas Carol*, in Wilson, op. cit., p. 225.
13. Dickens, letter to Miss Coutts, 1856, in Wilson, op. cit., p. 240.
14. Dickens, letter to Layard, April 1855, in Wilson, op. cit., p. 239.
15. Dickens, *Hard Times* (Everyman, 1974), pp. 61–2.
16. Matthew Arnold, op. cit., p. 70.
17. Dickens, *Hard Times*, p. 124.
18. Georg Lukács, *The Meaning of Contemporary Realism* (Merlin, 1963), p. 61.
19. Quoted in G. K. Chesterton's Introduction (1907) to *Hard Times* (Everyman), pp. ix–x.
20. Arnold Kettle, 'Dickens and the Popular Tradition', in op. cit., p. 217.
21. Dickens, *Hard Times*, Part Two, Chapter Five (Everyman), p. 135.
22. ibid., p. 134.
23. John Goode, 'William Morris and the Dream of Revolution', in *Literature and Politics in the Nineteenth Century* (Methuen, 1971), p. 250.
24. ibid., p. 270.
25. William Morris, *A Dream of John Ball* (Lawrence & Wishart, 1973), p. 103.
26. William Morris, *News From Nowhere* – the famous Chapter XVII: 'How the Change Came' (Lawrence & Wishart, 1973), p. 288.
27. John Goode, *William Morris and the Dream of Revolution*, pp. 238–9.
28. William Morris, *News From Nowhere*, Chapter XXII, pp. 337–8.

29. Dickens, *Hard Times*, Part Three, Chapter Six (Everyman),
    pp. 244–5.
30. William Morris, letter, 1882.

6. LITERATURE: THE DIALECTICS OF ACTUALITY

 1. Dickens, *Hard Times*, Part Two, Chapter Six (Everyman), p. 146.
 2. William Morris, *Art and Socialism*, *PW*, pp. 110–11.
 3. ibid., p. 111.
 4. William Morris, *Art under Plutocracy* (1883), *PW*, p. 61.
 5. Blake, *A Vision of the Last Judgement* (1810), *CW*, p. 611.
 6. Marx, *Feuerbach Theses*, I and VI, *EW*, pp. 421 and 423.
 7. Charles Tomlinson, *A Meditation on John Constable* (Penguin Poets
    14), p. 145. '. . . for what he saw /Discovered what he was, and the
    hand – unswayed /By the dictation of a single sense + /Bodied the
    accurate and total knowledge /In a calligraphy of present pleasure.'
8–12. These quotations from Hegel come from an article on Hegel's
    Aesthetics in the *Times Literary Supplement*, 2 January 1976.
13. Bertrand Russell, *Freedom and Organisation* (Allen & Unwin, 1934),
    p. 222.
14. Marx, *Critique of Hegel's Doctrine of the State*, *EW*, p. 65.
15. Lucio Colletti, Introduction to Marx, *EW*, p. 19.
16. Marx, *Economic and Philosophical Manuscripts*, *EW*, pp. 395–6.
17. ibid., p. 396.
18. Lucio Colletti, Introduction to Marx, *EW*, p. 39.
19. ibid., p. 49, quoting from *Capital*, Vol. I (Moscow, 1965), p. 72. As
    translated in the Everyman edition (1974), this passage, taking 'the
    nebulous world of religion' as an analogy, reads: 'The products of
    the human mind become independent shapes, endowed with lives of
    their own, and able to enter into relations with men and women.
    The products of the human mind do the same thing in the world of
    commodities. I speak of this as the *fetishistic character* which
    attaches to the products of labour, so soon as they are produced in
    the form of commodities' (pp. 45–6).
20. Blake, *Annotations to Reynolds*, *CW*, p. 459. Reynolds had said:
    'The whole beauty of the art consists in being able to get above all
    singular forms, local customs, particularities, and details of every
    kind.' He had also advised, in studying the great masters, to 'copy
    only their conceptions . . . labour to invent on their general
    principles and way of thinking.'

7. SHAKESPEARE: THE REVOLUTION OF THE TIMES

1. W. B. Yeats, 'The Trembling of the Veil', in *Autobiographies* (Macmillan, 1955), pp. 273–4.
2. ibid., pp. 291–2.
3. Shakespeare, *The Winter's Tale*, Perdita in Act IV, Scene 3, celebrating the 'art that nature makes'.
4. Shakespeare, *Troilus and Cressida*, Ulysses in Act I, Scene 3.
5. ibid., Hector in Act II, Scene 1.
6. ibid., Ulysses in Act I, Scene 3.
7. Shakespeare, *King Lear*, the King in Act I, Scene 1.
8. ibid., Edmund's soliloquy in Act I, Scene 2.
9. ibid., Cordelia in Act I, Scene 1.
10. ibid., Gloucester in Act I, Scene 2.
11. ibid., Lear's opening speech.
12. ibid., the Fool in Act I, Scene 4.
13. ibid., Lear in Act I, Scene 1.
14. ibid., Lear in his madness, Act IV, Scene 6.
15. ibid., Edgar in Act II, Scene 2, resolving 'to take the basest and most poorest shape / That ever penury in contempt of man / Brought near to beast'.
16. ibid., Lear in Act III, Scene 4.
17. ibid., Lear, Act IV, Scene 6.
18. ibid., Lear in Act IV, Scene 7.
19. ibid., Kent in the last scene of the play.
20. Christopher Caudwell, *Illusion and Reality* (1946), in *Marxists on Literature* (Penguin Books, 1975), p. 99.
21. Shakespeare, *Timon of Athens*, Act IV, Scene 3.
22. Kenneth Burke, Commentary on *Timon of Athens* (The Laurel Shakespeare, Dell, 1963), pp. 25–6.
23. Shakespeare, *Timon of Athens*, Act III, Scene 2.
24. Shakespeare, *Coriolanus*, Act V, Scene 3.
25. Shakespeare, *Timon*, Act I, Scene 2.
26. ibid., Act IV, Scene 3.
27. ibid., Act I, Scene 2.
28. ibid., Act III, Scene 1.
29. ibid., Timon's Third Servant, Act III, Scene 3.
30. ibid., Act IV, Scene 2, lines 13–15.
31. ibid., lines 31–6.
32. ibid., lines 11–12.
33. ibid., Act V, Scene 1.

34. G. R. Hibbard, Introduction to *Coriolanus* (New Penguin Shakespeare, 1967), pp. 13–14.
35. Shakespeare, *Timon*, Act II, Scene 2.
36. ibid., Act IV, Scene 3, lines 383–90.
37. ibid., lines 28–9.
38. Marx, *Economic and Philosophical Manuscripts*, *EW*, pp. 378–9.
39. Shakespeare, *Timon*, Act III, Scene 6.
40. ibid., Act IV, Scene 1.
41. Paul Celan, *Atemwende* (Frankfurt, 1967), quoted in Michael Hamburger's *The Truth of Poetry* (Penguin Books, 1972), pp. 320–25.
42. Georg Lukács, *Essays on Thomas Mann* (Merlin, 1964), p. 99.
43. T. S. Eliot, 'John Ford' (1932), in *Selected Prose* (Penguin Books, 1953), p. 103.
44. Shakespeare, *The Winter's Tale*, Act V, Scene 3.
45. G. Wilson Knight on *The Winter's Tale*, in *The Crown of Life* (Methuen, 1958), p. 126.
46. Shakespeare, *The Winter's Tale*, Act V, Scene 2.
47. ibid., Camillo in Act IV, Scene 3.
48. ibid., Leontes in Act II, Scene 1.
49. ibid., Act V, Scene 2.
50. L. C. Knights, 'Shakespeare's Sonnets', in *Explorations* (Penguin Books, 1964), p. 71.
51. Shakespeare, *The Tempest*, Act IV, Scene 1.
52. Shakespeare, Sonnets 63 and 64.
53. Shakespeare, *The Tempest*, Act III, Scene 2.
54. Wallace Stevens: *The Poems of Our Climate*, in *Collected Poems* (Faber & Faber, 1955), p. 193.
55. Shakespeare, *The Tempest*, Act I, Scene 2.
56. ibid., the same.
57. ibid., Act IV, Scene 1.
58. ibid., Act I, Scene 2.
59. ibid., Act III, Scene 2.
60. ibid., Act V.
61. ibid., Act V.
62. ibid., Prospero's Epilogue. In this context, see my own poem 'Prospero's Third Thoughts', in *A Cornered Freedom* (Harry Chambers: Peterloo Poets, 1980), pp. 61–2.
63. ibid., Act V.
64. ibid., Act III, Scene 1.
65. ibid., Act V.
66. ibid., first Alonso, then Gonzalo, in Act V.

8. ACTUALITY AND THE ABSTRACT: THE ALIENATING PROCESS

1. Milovan Djilas, *The Unperfect Society* (Methuen, 1969).
2. These lines have been adapted from my poem 'Prospero's Third Thoughts', in *A Cornered Freedom* (Peterloo Poets, 1980), pp. 61–2.
3. Marx, *Critique of Hegel's Doctrine of the State*, *EW*, p. 90.
4. Lucio Colletti, Introduction to Marx, *EW*, p. 33.
5. Marx, *Critique of Hegel's Doctrine of the State*, *EW*, p. 137.
6. ibid., p. 146.
7. Fredric Jameson, *Marxism and Form* (Princeton University Press, 1974), pp. xvii, xviii.
8. Marx, *Critique of Hegel's Doctrine of the State*, *EW*, p. 62. See also pp. 58–65.
9. Shakespeare, Sonnet 29: 'When in disgrace with Fortune and men's eyes /I all alone beweep my outcast state . . .'
10. Marx, *Economic and Philosophical Manuscripts*, *EW*, p. 377.
11. George Abbott White, 'Ideology and Literature', in *Literature in Revolution*, edited G. A. White and Charles Newman (*Triquarterly*, 1972), p. 441.
12. Conor Cruise O'Brien, 'Passion and Cunning: The Politics of W. B. Yeats', in *Literature in Revolution* (op. cit.), p. 197.
13. White, op. cit., pp. 441–2.
14. Lenin, *The State and Revolution* (Peking, 1973), p. 17.
15. ibid., pp. 45–6.
16. ibid., p. 45.
17. ibid., p. 34.
18. Marx, *Critique of Hegel's Doctrine of the State*, *EW*, pp. 63 and 65–70.
19. Karl Mannheim, *Ideology and Utopia* (1929).
20. Lenin, op. cit., p. 57.
21. Djilas, op. cit., p. 126.
22. G. D. H. Cole, Introduction (1957) to *Capital* (Everyman), p. xxxiii.
23. Jacob Bronowski, *William Blake and the Age of Revolution* (Routledge, 1972), p. 188.
24. ibid., p. 183.
25. ibid., p. 180.
26. Lenin, op. cit., pp. 107–8.
27. ibid., p. 108.
28. Djilas, op. cit., p. 105.

9. THE NECESSITY OF DISSENT

1. Lenin, *The State and Revolution*, (Peking, 1973), p. 122.
2. J. Bronowski, *William Blake and the Age of Revolution*, (Routledge, 1972), p. 181.
3. Victor Serge, *Memoirs of a Revolutionary* (O.U.P. 1963), pp. 375–6.
4. Lenin, op. cit., pp. 97–8.
5. Blake, Preface to *Milton*, *CW*, p. 480.
6. Marx, *Critique of Hegel's Doctrine of the State*, *EW*, p. 128.
7. ibid., p. 87.
8. ibid., p. 87.
9. Blake, *The Song of Los*, *CW*, p. 247.
10. Bronowski, op. cit., p. 189.
11. ibid., p. 184.
12. Marx, *On the Jewish Question*, *EW*, p. 229.
13. Marx, letter to Ruge, May 1843, in *EW*, p. 206.
14. Marx, Instructions for delegates to the Geneva Congress, 1866, *FI*, p. 86.
15. Marx, Provisional Rules of the International, in *FI*, p. 82.
16. ibid., p. 82.
17. Marx, *Critique of Hegel's Doctrine of the State*, *EW*, p. 124.
18. ibid., pp. 143–4.
19. ibid., p. 174.
20. ibid., p. 166.
21. ibid., pp. 167–8.
22. ibid., p. 169.
23. ibid., p. 164.
24. ibid., p. 176.
25. Marx, *Excerpts from James Mill's 'Elements of Political Economy'*, *EW*, p. 264.
26. Marx, *Economic and Philosophical Manuscripts*, *EW*, pp. 323–4.
27. ibid., p. 323.
28. Bertrand Russell, *Fact and Fiction* (Allen & Unwin).
29. Marx, *Excerpts from James Mill's 'Elements of Political Economy'*, *EW*, p. 266.
30. Marx, *Capital*, Book I, Chapter 32 (Moscow, 1965).
31. Marx, *Excerpts from James Mill's 'Elements of Political Economy'*, *EW*, pp. 276–7.
32. Marx, *On the Jewish Question*, *EW*, p. 239.
33. Walter Jens, 'The Classical Tradition in Germany', from *Upheaval and Continuity* (Wolff, 1977), p. 73.
34. ibid., p. 74.

35. Marx, *Economic and Philosophical Manuscripts*, *EW*, pp. 349–50.
36. ibid., p. 354.
37. ibid., p. 355.
38. ibid., p. 351.

10. BLAKE'S DIALECTIC: THE PROLONGATION OF MENTAL WAR

1. Marx, letter to Ruge, May 1843, *EW*, pp. 201–2.
2. Thomas Holcroft, quoted in Basil Willey's *The Eighteenth Century Background* (Penguin Books, 1962), p. 229.
3. Coleridge, Letters, quoted in Willey, op. cit., p. 242.
4. Blake, *The French Revolution* (1791), *CW*, p. 142.
5. Blake, *America* (1793), *CW*, p. 200.
6. Blake, *The Marriage of Heaven and Hell* (1790–93), *CW*, p. 149.
7. Blake, *A Vision of the Last Judgement* (1810), *CW*, p. 605.
8. Blake, MS Notebook (1808–11), *CW*, p. 558.
9. Blake, *Annotations to 'An Apology for the Bible in a Series of Letters Addressed to Thomas Paine by Bishop Watson'* (1798), *CW*, pp. 385–6.
10. Blake, *A Vision of the Last Judgement*, *CW*, p. 617.
11. J. Bronowski, *William Blake and the Age of Revolution* (Routledge, 1972), p. 14.
12. ibid., p. 16.
13. Blake, *The Marriage of Heaven and Hell*, *CW*, p. 155.
14. ibid., p. 149.
15. Blake, *A Vision of the Last Judgement*, *CW*, p. 611.
16. Blake, *Annotations to Sir Joshua Reynolds' Discourses* (1808), *CW*, pp. 457, 459.
17. Blake, *A Vision of the Last Judgement*, *CW*, p. 612.
18. Blake, Notebook (1810), *CW*, p. 600.
19. John Locke, quoted in Bronowski, op. cit., p. 49.
20. Blake, *Songs of Experience* (1789–94), *CW*, p. 217.
21. Blake, Preface to *Milton* (1804), *CW*, p. 480.
22. Blake, *Milton – Book the Second*, *CW*, p. 530.
23. ibid., p. 533.
24. ibid., p. 535.
25. Blake, *Europe* (1794), *CW*, p. 243.
26. Blake, *Annotations to Bishop Watson*, *CW*, p. 383.
27. Blake, *Jerusalem* (1804–20), Chapter 2, *CW*, p. 656.
28. Blake, *A Vision of the Last Judgement*, *CW*, p. 615.
29. Blake, *Jerusalem*, Chapter 4, *CW*, p. 738.
30. Unknown, quoted by Bronowski, op. cit., p. 99.
31. Blake, *Vala or the Four Zoas* (1795–1804), *CW*, p. 323.

32. Blake, *Annotations to Dr Thornton's New Translation of the Lord's Prayer* (1827), *CW*, p. 786.
33. Bronowski, op. cit., p. 121.
34. Blake, *Vala or the Four Zoas*, *CW*, p. 281.
35. Blake, *Jerusalem*, Chapter 3 (*CW*, p. 700); and *Vala*, Night the Seventh (*CW*, p. 337). In Vala, Blake has 'file' for 'grind' and 'workmanship' for 'task', and the second line is shortened, omitting 'in Albion' at the end.
36. Blake, *The Song of Los* (1795), *CW*, p. 247.
37. Bronowski, op. cit., p. 180.
38. Blake, *Jerusalem*, Chapter 4, *CW*, p. 738.
39. ibid., see pp. 742, 744–5.
40. ibid., Chapter 1, *CW*, p. 639.
41. ibid., Chapter 3, *CW*, p. 714.
42. Blake, *The Marriage of Heaven and Hell*, *CW*, p. 149.
43. Blake, *Vala or the Four Zoas*, *CW*, p. 290.
44. William Cobbett, *Autobiography* (Faber & Faber, 1933), p. 184.
45. ibid., p. 182.
46. Blake, *The Song of Los*, *CW*, p. 247.
47. Blake, *The Marriage of Heaven and Hell*, *CW*, 149.
48. ibid., pp. 149–50.
49. ibid., p. 155.
50. Blake, *A Vision of the Last Judgement*, *CW*, pp. 615–16.
51. ibid., p. 616.
52. Blake, *Jerusalem*, *CW*, p. 717.
53. ibid., p. 742.

11. PROGRESS AND REACTION IN THE AGE OF REVOLUTION: WORDSWORTH, SHELLEY AND BURKE

1. William Wordsworth, *The Prelude* (1850 version), Book VII (Penguin Books, 1971), line 526.
2. Marx, *Economic and Philosophical Manuscripts*, *EW*, p. 359.
3. William Godwin, *Political Justice*, Book 5, Chapter 5, quoted by Basil Willey in *The Eighteenth Century Background*, p. 209.
4. Godwin, Preface to *Political Justice*, quoted in Willey, op. cit., 207.
5. William Hazlitt, *The Spirit of the Age*, quoted in Willey, op. cit., p. 223.
6. Wordsworth, *The Tables Turned*, from the *Lyrical Ballads*.
7. Wordsworth, *The Prelude* (both versions), Book X, lines 437–8 (477–8).
8. ibid., 1805–6 version, lines 806–7. In 1850 version, Book XI, lines 223–4.

9. Wordsworth, Prefatory note to *The Borderers*, quoted in Introduction to *Lyrical Ballads* (O.U.P., 1969), p. xxxii.
10. Wordsworth, *The Prelude* (both versions), Book IX, lines 353–4 (346–7).
11. Wordsworth, *The Leech-gatherer*, Stanza 17.
12. ibid., Stanza 7.
13. Wordsworth, *The Prelude*, Book X (Book XI), lines 863–4 (272–3).
14. ibid., lines 890–901 (294–305).
15. ibid., lines 915–16 (341–2).
16. Coleridge, quoted in Willey, op. cit., p. 256.
17. Wordsworth, *Tintern Abbey*, line 132.
18. Wordsworth, Sonnet, *The World is Too Much With Us*.
19. Wordsworth, *The Leech-Gatherer*, Stanza 3.
20. Wordsworth, Sonnet, 1803.
21. Shelley, *Poetical Works* (O.U.P., 1947), 'Sonnet, *To Wordsworth*', p. 526.
22. ibid., Preface to *The Revolt of Islam*, p. 32.
23. Arthur Hallam, in *Modern Poetry*.
24. Shelley, *Poetical Works*, Preface to *Prometheus Unbound*, p. 205.
25. ibid., Sonnet, *Feelings of a Republican on the Fall of Napoleon*, p. 527.
26. ibid., *Prometheus Unbound*, p. 268.
27. ibid., *The Mask of Anarchy*, Stanzas 38 and 91, pp. 341, 344.
28. ibid., *Hellas*, p. 471.
29. ibid., *Hellas*, p. 476.
30. ibid., Preface to *Prometheus Unbound*, p. 207.
31. ibid., Preface to *Hellas*, p. 448.
32. ibid., Preface to *The Revolt of Islam*, p. 33.
33. Wordsworth, *The Prelude* (1850 version), Book XI, lines 309–10, 320.
34. ibid., Book XIII (1850), lines 66–81.
35. Wordsworth, *Tintern Abbey*, lines 38–50.
36. Wordsworth, *The Prelude*, Book II, lines 328–30.
37. Wordsworth, *Note on the Ode: Intimations of Immortality made in 1843*.
38. Wordsworth, *The Prelude*, Book XII (1850), lines 269–84.
39. Herbert Read, *Wordsworth* (Faber & Faber, 1938), p. 172.
40. William Hazlitt, *The Spirit of the Age*.
41. Herbert Read, op. cit., p. 152.
42. Wordsworth, *The Prelude*, Book VII (1850), lines 523, 524–9 and 534–5.
43. Edmund Burke, *Reflections on the Revolution in France* (Penguin Books, 1968), p. 120.
44. ibid., p. 120.

45. ibid., p. 120.
46. ibid., p. 182.
47. Shelley, Sonnet, *England in 1819 (Poetical Works)*, pp. 574–5.
48. Burke, op. cit., p. 182.
49. Shelley, op. cit.
50. Burke, op. cit., p. 183.
51. Marx, *Critique of Hegel's Philosophy of Right*, *EW*, p. 247.
52. Marx, *Economic and Philosophical Manuscripts*, EW, pp. 355–6.
53. ibid., pp. 389–90.
54. ibid., p. 350.
55. Burke, op. cit., 183.
56. John Milton, *Paradise Lost*, Book IX, 696–7.
57. Burke, op. cit., p. 195.
58. Milton, *Paradise Lost*, Book X, 822–4.
59. Marx, *Economic and Philosophical Manuscripts*, *EW*, p. 357.
60. Marx, *The Communist Manifesto*, *R1848*, p. 70.
61. ibid., pp. 70–71.
62. ibid., p. 71.

12. THE QUEST FOR A QUALITATIVE SOCIAL ORDER

1. Leszek Kolakowski, *Marxism and Beyond* (Paladin, 1971), p. 195.
2. Marx, first draft of *The Civil War in France*, *FI*, p. 263.
3. ibid., p. 253.
4. ibid., *The Civil War in France* – read to the General Council of the International Working Men's Association on 30 May 1871, two days after the defeat of the Commune; later published as a pamphlet. *FI*, p. 212.
5. ibid., p. 213.
6. David Fernbach, Introduction to Marx, *FI*, p. 37.
7. Bakunin, quoted by Marx in *Conspectus of Bakunin's Statism and Anarchy*, *FI*, p. 336.
8. Marx, *The Civil War in France*, *FI*, p. 213.
9. Marx, *Conspectus*, *FI*, p. 337.
10. Marx, Provisional Rules of the International, as ratified by the Geneva Congress, September 1866, *FI*, pp. 82–3.
11. Marx, Instructions for delegates to the Geneva Congress, *FI*, p. 90.
12. Marx, Speech on the Hague Conference of the International, 8 September 1872, *FI*, p. 325.
13. W. H. Auden, *New Year Letter* (Faber & Faber), lines 681–3. These lines refer specifically to Marx. 'Some dream,' Auden writes, that the Russian Revolution

    > realized the potential Man . . .
    > While others settled down to read

The theory that forecast the deed,
And found their humanistic view
In questions from the German, who,
Obscure in gaslit London, brought
To human consciousness a thought
It thought unthinkable, and made
Another consciousness afraid. (lines 673–83)

13. THE DERANGEMENT OF EUROPEAN CIVILIZATION

1. R. H. Tawney, *The Acquisitive Society* (Fontana, 1961), pp. 45–6.
2. ibid., p. 47.
3. Of course, the ruling-class view was exactly the opposite. As Churchill puts it in *The Gathering Storm* (Cassell, 1964, p. 11): 'Fascism was the shadow or ugly child of Communism . . .' And, for him, 'as Fascism sprang from Communism, so Nazism developed from Fascism'.
4. W. H. Auden, *September 1, 1939*, Stanza 2.
5. W. H. Auden, *New Year Letter*, lines 898–901.
6. Herbert Marcuse, *Negations* (Penguin Books, 1972), p. 6.
7. W. H. Auden, *New Year Letter*, lines 284–94.
8. Sir Lewis Namier, *Vanished Supremacies* (Penguin Books, 1962), p. 216.
9. David Fernbach, Introduction to Marx, *FI*, p. 38.
10. Marx, *The Civil War in France*, *FI*, p. 211.
11. ibid., first draft of *The Civil War in France*, *FI*, p. 249.
12. Wolfgang Abendroth, 'The Absolutism of the Hohenzollern State and the Rise of the Social Democratic Party', from *Upheaval and Continuity* (Wolff, 1977), p. 64.
13. William Morris, Lecture on Commercial War, in E. P. Thompson's *William Morris: Romantic to Revolutionary* (Merlin, 1977), p. 385.
14. Sir Winston Churchill, *The Gathering Storm* (Cassell, 1964), p. 13.
15. Herbert Read, *Poetry and Anarchism* (Faber & Faber, 1938).
16. W. B. Yeats, *Letters*.
17. Wilfred Owen, *Strange Meeting*. 'Now men will go content with what we spoiled. /Or, discontent, boil bloody, and be spilled . . .'
18. R. G. Collingwood, *An Autobiography* (O.U.P., 1939), p. 164.
19. Thomas Mann, 'This Peace', from *Order of the Day* (Knopf, 1942), p. 167.
20. Bertolt Brecht, 'Svendborg Poem': Gedichte IV, 12, in Frederic Ewen's *Bertolt Brecht* (Calder & Boyars, 1970), pp. 314–15.
21. George Orwell, 'Looking Back on the Spanish Civil War' (1943), in *Collected Essays* (Mercury, 1961), p. 201. 'The hatred which the Spanish Republic excited in millionaires, dukes, cardinals,

playboys, Blimps and what-not would in itself be enough to show one how the land lay. In essence it was a class war.'
22. Louis MacNeice, *Autumn Journal* (Faber & Faber, 1939), Canto XVIII, p. 73.
23. Andrei Sakharov, *Sakharov Speaks* (Collins, Harvill, 1974), p. 58.

14. DEMOCRATIC FREEDOM: RHETORIC AND ACTUALITY

1. Thomas Mann, *The Magic Mountain* (Secker & Warburg, 1954), p. 32.
2. Georg Lukács, *Essays on Thomas Mann* (Merlin, 1964), pp. 81–2.
3. W. H. Mallock, *Social Equality*, pp. 96–7.
4. A. J. P. Taylor, Review in *The Observer*, 24 December 1978.
5. R. H. Tawney, *Equality* (Unwin, 1964), p. 190.
6. John Goode, 'William Morris and the Dream of Revolution', in *Literature and Politics in the Nineteenth Century* (Methuen, 1971), p. 246.
7. Milovan Djilas, *The Unperfect Society* (Methuen, 1969), pp. 126–7.
8. Gerard Manley Hopkins, *To What Serves Mortal Beauty?*, lines 3–4 and 11 (Penguin Poets, 1953), p. 58.
9. Herbert Marcuse, *One-Dimensional Man* (Abacus, 1972), p. 92.
10. ibid., p. 22.
11. ibid., p. 20.
12. ibid., pp. 109–10.
13. ibid., p. 107.
14. ibid., p. 58.
15. ibid., p. 99.
16. Marx, *Economic and Philosophical Manuscripts*, *EW*, p. 358.
17. Marcuse, op. cit., pp. 88, 89.
18. Marx, *Economic and Philosophical Manuscripts*, *EW*, p. 306.
19. ibid., p. 335.
20. ibid., p. 287. 'While the division of labour increases the productive power of labour and the wealth and refinement of society, it impoverishes the worker and reduces him to a machine.'
21. ibid., p. 398.

15. MEANS AND ENDS: THE CLOSING OF THE CIRCLE

1. R. H. Tawney, *The Radical Tradition* (Allen & Unwin, 1964), p. 101.
2. Antonio Gramsci, *Prison Notebooks* (Lawrence & Wishart, 1971), p. 360. 'Men create their own personality, 1. by giving a specific and concrete ('rational') direction to their own vital impulse or will;

2. by indentifying the means which will make this will concrete and specific and not arbitrary; 3. by contributing to modifying the *ensemble* of the concrete conditions for realizing this will to the extent of one's own limits and capacities and in the most fruitful form.'

3. Tawney, op. cit., p. 137.

4. Herbert Marcuse, *One-Dimensional Man* (Abacus, 1972), p. 28.

5. ibid., p. 25 (modified).

6. ibid., p. 53.

7. ibid., p. 175.

8. Tawney, op. cit., p. 170.

9. Marx, Speech on the Hague Conference, 1872, *FI*, p. 324.

10. Tawney, op. cit., p. 170.

11. ibid., p. 168.

12. ibid., p. 177.

13. ibid., p. 167.

14. Lenin, *The State and Revolution* (Peking, 1973), pp. 104–5.

15. ibid., pp. 118, 119.

16. SOCIALISM: THE STRUGGLE FOR THE FUTURE

1. William Morris, *A Dream of John Ball*, from the title to Chapter XII, where this issue is dealt with. See A. L. Morton in his Introduction to *Three Works by William Morris* (Lawrence & Wishart, 1973), p. 23.

2. John Goode, 'William Morris and the Dream of Revolution', in *Literature and Politics in the Nineteenth Century* (Methuen, 1971), p. 246.

3. Gerard Manley Hopkins, Sonnet, 'As kingfishers catch fire' (Penguin Poets, 1953), p. 51.

4. John Goode, 'The Strange Disease of Modern Love', in op. cit., p. 57. For Clough, 'finally there is no pseudo-Hegelian "idea" to act as refuge. Multitudinousness, the immediacy of experience, is therefore precisely what his poetry seeks to confront.'

5. Morris, *Art and Socialism* (1884), *PW*, pp. 126–7.

6. Morris, *How We Live and How We Might Live* (1884), *PW*, pp. 146–7.

7. ibid., p. 101.

8. Morris, *Useful Work versus Useless Toil* (1884), *PW*, p. 108.

9. Morris, *The Hopes of Civilisation* (1885), *PW*, p. 181.

10. Hugh MacDiarmid, *Third Hymn to Lenin* (Penguin Poets, 1970), p. 108. 'Let us take our stand,' he writes later in the poem 'with Richard Carlile: "The enemy with whom we have to grapple / Is one with whom no peace can be made. Idolatry will not parley,

/Supersition will not treat or covenant. They must be uprooted
/Completely for public and individual safety" ' (p. 110).

11. ibid., p. 111.
12. Morris, *Useful Work versus Useless Toil*, *PW*, pp. 104–5. See also pp. 128, 194–204.
13. Morris, *Art under Plutocracy* (1883), *PW*, p. 74.
14. Morris, *Useful Work versus Useless Toil*, *PW*, p. 101.
15. Morris, *Art and Socialism*, *PW*, p. 123. See also pp. 116, 118.
16. Morris, *Art under Plutocracy*, *PW*, pp. 76–7.
17. Morris, *The Society of the Future* (1887), *PW*, p. 201.
18. Morris, *A Dream of John Ball*, in *Three Works* (Lawrence & Wishart), Chapters VIII and IX, pp. 96–7.
19. Morris, *How We Live and How We Might Live*, *PW*, p. 154.
20. Marx, *The German Ideology*.
21. Marx, *Critique of Hegel's Doctrine of the State*, *EW*, p. 87.
22. Morris, *Communism*, *PW*, p. 229.
23. Marx, *Economic and Philosophical Manuscripts*, *EW*, p. 382.
24. ibid., p. 395.
25. ibid.
26. Marx, letter to Ruge, May 1843, *EW*, p. 201.

INDEX

Abyssinia, 61, 111
Acton, Lord, 30–31
Adam, 11, 12, 27
Aeschylus, 135
Africa, 12, 37, 247, 266, 281
Allied Blockade (1918–19), 63–4, 260
American War of Independence, 11
Amin, Idi, 57
Ancien régime, 11
Angola, 249
Arab world, 280, 281
Aristotle, 30
Arnold, Matthew, 23, 24–5, 117–18,
    120, 121–2, 126
Asia, 37, 266, 281
Athens, 118–19, 151–8
Auden, W. H., 33, 256, 262, 263,
    342–3
Auschwitz, 270, 271
Austria, 41, 61, 111, 265

Bakunin, Mikhail, 249, 253–4, 255
Baldwin, Stanley, 106
Balkans, 261, 266
Ball, John, 315–17
Balzac, 124, 127, 135
Barcelona, 19
Barnaby Rudge (Dickens), 120
Basle (IWMA Congress 1869), 49
Batista, 57
Baudelaire, 109
Beethoven, 127, 135
Belli, Gioacchino, 127, 135
Berger, John, 101
Berlin, 39, 40, 84; the Berlin Wall, 84,
    271
Bismarck, 16, 36, 260, 264
Blake, William, 27, 31, 86, 110, 136,
    141, 142, 173, 189–90, 192–3,
    205–20, 221, 294; *Songs of
    Experience* (1789–94), 210; *The
    French Revolution* (1791), 206–7;
    Marriage of Heaven and Hell
    (1790–93), 142, 207, 208–9, 216,

218, 219; *America* (1793), 207;
    Europe (1794), 212; *Song of Los*
    (1795), 192, 214, 218; *Vala*
    (1795–1804), 213, 214, 216–17;
    Milton (1804), 173, 190, 211, 214;
    A Vision of the Last Judgement
    (1810), 207, 208, 209, 219;
    Jerusalem (1820), 86, 212, 214, 215,
    216, 219, 220
Bleak House (Dickens), 119–20, 127,
    131
Bloch, Ernst, 79, 80, 82–5, 269
Bolsheviks, 50–56, 59, 62–5, 70, 89,
    180, 182, 276. *See also* Lenin,
    Revolution, Russian, Soviet Russia,
    Stalin, Trotsky, 1917
Bornemann, Ernst, 81
Botticelli, 286
Brecht, Bertolt, 77–82, 83, 86
British Empire, 47, 313
Bronowski, Jacob, 183, 184, 189–90,
    192, 208, 214
Bruno, Giordano, 169
Brussels (IWMA Congress 1868), 49
Burke, Edmund, 26–30, 221, 237–40,
    241
Burke, Kenneth, 151
Burns, Robert, 236
Byron, 221

Camphausen, Ludolf, 39, 40
Carlyle, Thomas, 23
Castlereagh, 222
Castro, Fidel, 58, 88
Caudwell, Christopher, 151
Célan, Paul, 158
Chace, William, 112
Chamberlain, Neville, 62, 106, 268
Chartism, 120, 125
Chesterton, G. K., 121
Chile, 249
China, 12, 93, 247, 249, 283, 313
Christianity, 23, 29, 30, 103, 104, 107,

Christianity – *cont.*
108–12, 124, 189, 213–14, 219–20, 256
Churchill, Winston, 59, 66, 267, 276
Clough, Arthur Hugh, 306
Cobbett, William, 217
Cold War, 56, 107, 176, 271
Cole, G. D. H., 183
Collingwood, R. G., 268
Commune (Paris 1871), 44, 92, 182, 183, 201, 248–9, 264
Communism, 25, 50, 57, 77–85, 93, 109–10, 129, 175, 249, 259–60, 276, 282–3; and passim
Communist Manifesto (1847), 38, 47, 50, 51, 92, 243
Congo, 103
Conrad, Joseph, 103
Conservative Party, 275, 276, 278, 280, 301
Copernicus, 169
Coriolanus (Shakespeare), 152, 155–6, 158, 177
Counihan, Daniel, 55
Cuba, 247, 249
Culture and Anarchy (Matthew Arnold), 117–18
Cymbeline (Shakespeare), 160
Czechoslovakia, 61, 268, 270, 271

Daladier, Édouard, 106
Daniel, Arnaut, 108
Dante, 108, 135
Davies Giddy, 28
Delacroix, Eugène, 135
Democracy, 12, 43, 48, 49, 64, 111, 191, 250–52, 272–92, 299, 301
Dessau, Paul, 81
Deutsche, Isaac, 53
Dickens, Charles, 115, 117–32, 133, 134, 332–3. *See also Barnaby Rudge, Bleak House, Hard Times, Little Dorrit, Our Mutual Friend*
Disraeli, 23
Djilas, Milovan, 175, 182, 187, 282–3
Dr Zhivago (Pasternak), 73
Dream of John Ball, A (William Morris), 304, 315

Eastern Europe, 45, 63, 76, 77–85, 282–3
East Germany, 77–85
Eden, 12, 13, 27
1848, revolutions, 11, 20, 36, 38–42, 120, 201, 202, 242–3, 260, 263, 266, 273
1832, the Reform Bill, 28, 312, 313
Einstein, Albert, 159
Eliot, George, 127
Eliot, T. S., 37, 99–116, 159, 179
Engels, Friedrich, 42, 244. *See also Communist Manifesto*
England, 17, 36–7, 50, 93, 118–32, 146, 147, 180, 202, 205, 206–12, 216–17, 221–32 passim, 265, 268, 269, 270, 276, 298. *See also* Great Britain

Fascism, 29, 62, 64, 66, 92, 106, 107, 112, 179, 259, 260, 264, 269, 297
Faulkner, William, 21
Feudalism, 146–50, 152, 176, 177, 315
Feuerbach, Ludwig, 22, 32, 33, 136
Fichte, Johann Gottlieb, 34–5, 36
First World War, 17, 60, 63, 100, 242, 255, 259, 260, 265–7, 276, 307
France, 17, 36, 39, 40, 61, 106, 189, 202, 205, 208, 226, 232, 243, 258, 259, 260, 264, 265, 266, 269. *See also* Revolution, French
Franco, General, 61, 270
French Revolution, *see* Revolution, French

General Strike (1926), 60, 269, 276, 318
Genesis, 27
Geneva, 55; I W M A Congress 1866, 49
Georgia (Russia), 52, 53
Germany, 17, 33–7, 38–41, 50, 62, 63, 64, 77–85, 92, 93, 112, 202–3, 243, 258, 259, 260–66, 267
Gerontion (T. S. Eliot), 99–101
Giotto, 135
Godwin, William, 207, 221, 222, 225, 227

Goethe, 127, 159
Goode, John, 285
Gordon Riots (1780), 120, 210
Goya, 135
Gramsci, Antonio, 293–4, 344–5
Great Britain, 59, 60, 61, 106, 147,
    188–9, 222, 237, 243, 258, 260,
    261, 265–81 passim, 294–9,
    309–10, 312, 315. *See also* England
Gropp, Otto, 82
Grotewohl, Otto, 77

Hager, Kurt, 84
Hague (IWMA Congress 1872), 255
Hallam, Arthur, 228
Hamlet (Shakespeare), 177
'Hands off Russia', 60
Hansemann, David, 39, 40
Hardie, Keir, 60, 265
Hard Times (Dickens), 119–20, 122–7,
    131, 133
Harich, Wolfgang, 84
Harmsworth, Cecil, 64
Hazlitt, William, 222, 235
Hegel, Freidrich, 14, 21, 22, 27, 36,
    38, 42, 138, 139–42, 143, 191,
    195–7, 215, 240
Hiroshima, 270
History, 99–102; and passim
History of Freedom in Antiquity (Lord
    Acton), 30–31
Hitler, 16, 35, 57, 62, 63, 66, 78, 85,
    90, 92, 94, 183, 260, 261, 264, 265
Hoare, Sir Samuel, 106
Holcroft, Thomas, 206
Hölderlin, Johann, 203
Hoover, Herbert, 63–4, 66
Hopkins, Gerard Manley, 59, 287, 306
Horthy, Admiral, 63
Hungary, 17, 50, 63, 64, 260, 271

India, 37, 93, 266
Industrial Revolution, 11, 93, 208,
    210, 214, 215, 221
International Working Men's
    Association, 45, 49–50, 254–5, 273
Iron Curtain, 56, 66
Italy, 17, 64, 259

Jacobinism, 89, 202, 203
Jameson, Fredric, 176–7
Japan, 61, 259, 270
Jena, 84
Jens, Walter, 202–3
Jews, 28, 29
Johnson, Joseph, 211
Julius Caesar (Shakespeare), 139, 158
Junker, 36

Kafka, Franz, 107
Kamenev, 88
Kapital, Das (Marx), 15, 75, 91, 141,
    200, 334
Keats, 221
Kerensky, 182
Kettle, Arnold, 118
King Lear (Shakespeare), 146,
    147–50, 177
Knight, G. Wilson, 160
Knights, L. C., 162
Kolakowski, Leszek, 38, 71–6, 79, 84,
    87, 95–6, 116, 248
Korea, 271
Kun, Bela, 63

Labour Party, 275, 276, 277, 278–9,
    280, 297, 300, 313
Lamartine, Alfonse de, 42
Laval, Pierre, 106
League of Nations, 61, 259
Leavis, F. R., 113–14
Ledru-Rollin, Alexandre, 42
Leipzig, 82
Lenin, 9, 45, 46, 50–59, 64–5, 70, 75,
    89–90, 91, 143, 180–82, 183, 184,
    185, 186, 188, 189, 190, 191,
    302–3. *See also* Bolsheviks,
    Revolution, Russian, 1917, Soviet
    Russia, *State and Revolution, The*
Libya, 249
Liebknecht, Karl, 265
Little Dorrit (Dickens), 119, 122, 131
Locke, John, 210
London, 281
Luddites, 222
Lukács, Georg, 106, 107, 116, 124,
    159, 274
Luxemburg, Rosa, 265

Macaulay, Lord, 124
Macbeth (Shakespeare), 177
MacDiarmid, Hugh, 310–11
Macmillan, Harold, 278, 280
MacNeice, Louis, 270
Mallock, W. H., 275
Manchuria, 61, 270
Mandelstam, Osip, 58
Mann, Thomas, 36, 62, 107; 127, 138, 159, 203, 268, 272–3
Mannheim, Karl, 181
Marcuse, Herbert, 68–9, 262, 287–9, 290, 295–6
Marx, Karl, 14–16, 18, 20–26, 32–3, 38–51, 56, 57, 58, 68, 74–5, 76, 82, 85–6, 87, 91–3, 96, 97, 118, 119, 136, 140, 141, 143, 157, 162, 175, 176, 177, 180, 183, 184, 185, 188, 191, 192–202, 203–4, 205–6, 215, 239, 240–44, 248–50, 253, 254–6, 257, 264, 289–90, 291, 297–8, 319–20, 321; *Excerpts from James Mill's 'Elements of Political Economy'*, 14, 197, 199, 201; *Economic and Philosophical Manuscripts*, 16, 25, 44, 57, 85–6, 93, 97, 118, 119, 141, 157, 178, 198, 204, 221, 240–41, 242, 289–90, 291, 320; *Critique of Hegel's Doctrine of the State*, 14, 38, 141, 176, 177, 181, 191, 195–7, 319; *Critique of Hegel's Philosophy of Right*, 15, 16, 239; *Theses on Feuerbach*, 22, 32, 33, 136; *German Ideology*, 38; *The Communist Manifesto*, 38, 47, 51, 92, 93, 243; *The Civil War in France*, 249, 264; *The Class Struggles in France*, 39; *Das Kapital*, 15, 75, 91, 141, 200; *Critique of the Gotha Programme*, 47–8
Marxism, 45, 55–6, 75, 76, 78, 79, 82, 83, 84, 85, 94, 176, 180, 255. *See also* East Germany, Eastern Europe, Kolakowski, Lenin, Marcuse, Revolution, Russian, Soviet Russia, Stalin, Trotsky
Mazzini, Giuseppe, 42
Memoirs of a Revolutionary (Victor Serge), 18–19, 76, 91, 110, 190

Mexico, 90, 93
Michelangelo, 135
Middle East, 247, 271, 280, 281
Mill, J. S., 23
Milton, 241, 242
Mitchell, David, in *Red Mirage*, 58, 59, 64, 65, 66
Money, 14, 37, 61, 118–19, 151–8, 178, 191–2, 200, 201, 210, 212–13, 281, 291, 312, 332–3
Morris, William, 50, 59–60, 129–32, 133–4, 189, 266, 282, 304, 307–10, 311, 312–19. *See also A Dream of John Ball, News From Nowhere*
Moscow, 54, 55, 88; the Moscow Trials, 88, 269
Mozart, 135
Munich, 61, 62, 111, 268, 270

Namier, Sir Lewis, 106, 264
Napoleon Buonoparte, 16, 205–6, 208, 252
Napoleon, Louis, 39
Nationalism, 258–9
Nature (Man and the natural world), 14, 15, 26, 27, 29, 38, 86, 96, 97, 145, 146–7, 149, 152, 159–71 passim, 204, 207, 208, 211, 214–15, 223, 225, 228, 233, 236–41 passim, 275, 291, 308
Nazism, 17, 29, 41, 62, 63, 64, 66, 90, 106, 203, 260, 261, 265, 273
Neue Rheinische Zeitung, 39, 40, 41, 42
Newman, Cardinal J. H., 100
News From Nowhere (William Morris), 50, 129–30, 189, 317–18
Nietzsche, Friedrich, 35
1945, 37, 67, 275, 277, 278, 300
1914, 34, 60, 63, 87, 100, 258, 265, 266, 272, 273, 276
1917, 17, 18, 45, 46, 50, 51, 59, 60, 69–70, 72, 73, 180, 183, 184, 186, 255, 259. *See also* Lenin, Revolution, Russian, Soviet Russia, Stalin, Trotsky
1938 (Munich), 61, 62, 268, 269
1939, 36, 60, 61, 262, 264, 268, 270, 276, 318
1933, 34, 92, 93, 261

1926 (General Strike), 60, 269, 276, 318
Northern Ireland, 17
Novalis, 159
Nuclear Bomb, 270, 271, 313

Orwell, George, 269
Our Mutual Friend (Dickens), 332–3
Owen, Wilfred, 268

Paine, Tom, 11, 208, 211, 212, 219
Palmerston, 16, 122
Papen, Franz von, 62
Paris Commune (1871), *see* Commune (Paris 1871)
Pasternak, Boris, 73
Peasants' Revolt (1381), 315–17
Pericles, 153
Peterloo (1819), 222, 229–30, 239
Picasso, 286
Pitt, William, 16, 208, 222
Plato, 25, 30, 33, 153, 183
Platonism, 23, 169
Plevier, Theodor, 77
Portugal, 249
Pound, Ezra, 105, 179
Pravda, 52, 55
Prelude, The (Wordsworth), 221, 222, 223, 224, 225, 232, 233, 234–5, 236, 237
Prussia, 36, 39, 40, 260, 261, 265. *See also* Berlin, Germany

Radek, Karl, 88
Ransome, Arthur, 59
Raphael Sanzio, 135, 169
Read, Herbert, 236, 267
Realpolitik, 35
Red Army, 88
Red Square, Moscow, 54, 55
Reflections on the Revolution in France (Edmund Burke), 26–30, 221, 237–9
Reich, Wilhelm, 93–4
Rembrandt, 287
Renaissance, 145, 152, 153, 162, 163, 167, 169, 176

Revolution, French, 11, 17, 27, 35, 176, 189, 205, 207, 209, 221, 222, 223, 226, 231–2
Revolution, Russian (1917), 17, 18, 45, 46, 50–55, 58–62, 64–6, 69–70, 181, 183, 189, 255, 267, 313
Revolution Betrayed, The (Trotsky), 88
Revolutions (1848), *see* 1848, revolutions
Reynolds, Sir Joshua, 209
Rhineland, 61, 111
Ricardo, David, 42
Rights of Man (Paine), 11, 211
Rome, 137, 283
Rousseau, Jean-Jacques, 33
Ruhr, 78
Ruskin, John, 23
Russell, Bertrand, 20, 24, 25, 65–6, 199

St Petersburg, 70
Sakharov, Andrei, 271
Sartre, Jean-Paul, 78, 79
Schopenhauer, Arthur, 36, 37
Second World War, 60, 247, 274, 318
Serge, Victor, 17–20, 76, 79, 91, 110, 190
1789, *see* Revolution, French
Shakespeare, William, 28, 115, 118–19, 128, 135, 138, 143–71, 175, 176, 177–78, 183, 307. *See also* Troilus and Cressida, King Lear, Timon of Athens, The Winter's Tale, The Tempest
Shelley, 221, 226–33, 238; *Revolt of Islam*, 227, 231–2; *The Mask of Anarchy*, 228, 229–30; *Hellas*, 228, 230, 231; *Prometheus Unbound*, 228, 229, 231
Shylock, 28
1688, 27
Slavs, 42
'Socialism in One Country', 45, 91
Socrates, 30
Sophocles, 135
South Africa, 281
South America, 12, 281

Southey, Robert, 213, 222
Soviet Russia, 12, 17, 25, 47, 50–55, 58–62, 64–6, 69–71, 72–3, 76, 80, 88–9, 90–91, 94, 180–83, 186, 188–92, 250, 253, 255–6, 260, 269, 271, 276, 302, 310
Spanish Civil War, 61, 92, 111, 259, 268, 269, 270
Stalin, 16, 17, 45, 48, 51–6, 57, 62, 63, 70, 88, 90, 91, 92, 94, 95, 185, 271, 313
Stalinism, 48, 51, 54, 58, 72, 75, 85, 90, 95, 190, 269, 310
State and Revolution, The (Lenin), 51, 180, 182, 186, 302, 303
Steiner, George, 78
Stendhal, 127
Suez, 271

Tawney, R. H., 258–9, 293, 294, 296, 297–300, 301
Taylor, A. J. P., 275
Tempest, The (Shakespeare), 128, 162–71, 175
Tennyson, 228
Thiers, 16
Third Reich, 17, 263, 264, 265, 268. *See also* Hitler, Nazism
Thornton, Dr, 213
Timon of Athens (Shakespeare), 118–19, 151–8, 170, 177, 178
Titian, 286
Tolstoy, Leo, 31–2, 115, 124, 127, 135
Troilus and Cressida (Shakespeare), 146–7
Trollope, Anthony, 23

Trotsky, 17, 46–7, 51–5, 70, 86, 88–92, 94. *See also* Bolsheviks, Revolution, Russian, Soviet Russia
Tukhachevsky, 88

Ulbricht, Walter, 77, 83
Upanishads, 108
United States of America, 59, 63–4, 72, 93, 180, 281, 298

Vallon, Annette, 223
Versailles, 63, 261
Vienna, 270
Vietnam, 17, 247, 249, 271
Voltaire, 219
Vorster, 57

Wakefield, Gilbert, 212
War and Peace (Tolstoy), 31–2
Watergate, 17
Watson, Bishop, 208, 212, 226
Weimar Republic, 260
Wellington, 222
White, George Abbot, 179
White Russia, 55
Wilson, Angus, 121
Wilson, Edmund, 47–9
Wilson, Harold, 280
Winter's Tale, The (Shakespeare), 160–62
Wordsworth, William, 207, 213, 222–7, 228, 231, 232–7

Yeats, W. B., 144, 145, 179, 268
Yugoslavia, 282–3

Zehm, Gunther, 84
Zinoviev, 53, 88
Zweig, Arnold, 77, 79